OPEN OCCUPANCY VS. FORCED HOUSING UNDER THE FOURTEENTH AMENDMENT:

A SYMPOSIUM ON ANTI-DISCRIMINATION LEGISLATION, FREEDOM OF CHOICE, AND PROPERTY RIGHTS IN HOUSING

ALFRED AVINS,

B.A., LL.B., LL.M., M.L., J.S.D.
FORMER ASSOCIATE PROFESSOR OF CONSTITUTIONAL LAW, CHICAGO-KENT COLLEGE OF LAW

GENERAL EDITOR

BOOKMAILER, NEW YORK

Published by
THE BOOKMAILER INC.
New York 16, N. Y.

Distributed by

THE BOOKMAILER, INC.
BOX 101, MURRAY HILL STATION
NEW YORK 16, N. Y.

"The Complete Bookstore-by-Mail Service"
Representing All U.S.
Publishers

CONTENTS

COMMENTS

BOOK REVIEWS

FOREWORD

The Symposium on Anti-Discrimination Legislation, Freedom of Choice, and Property Rights in Housing performs a real service to the American public through presenting this symposium of varied viewpoints and opinions of leaders of thinking who have specialized in evaluating both anti-discrimination legislation in the housing field and the economic and public reactions to this legislation and to the court interpretations of it.

The problems of discrimination in housing are many and complex. There is no one simple solution to these problems. Discriminatory legislation has come about both because of unreasoning prejudices and because of enlightened efforts to give communities attractiveness in the eyes of the public. No one new law, No single executive order, No stroke of the pen, can bring Utopia.

We have come a long way toward working out solutions in the past ten years. We have a long way to go. This symposium, by calmly reviewing the many and varied understandings of men of good will, makes possible better appreciation of existing laws and promotes the sort of discussion which may point the way toward a fuller understanding of this whole area.

NORMAN P. MASON[*]

[*] Administrator, United States Housing and Home Finance Agency, 1959-61; Commissioner, Federal Housing Administration, 1954-9.

INTRODUCTION

This symposium was originally planned and written while I was Associate Professor of Constitutional Law and Faculty Editor of the Chicago-Kent Law Review for use as Volume 40, Number 1, of the Law Review of Chicago-Kent College of Law (April 1963 issue). However, it was never published by the College, and accordingly, this author has decided to publish it. Appreciation is expressed to the College for transferring the material to me.

No prior symposium on this subject had ever before been published in a law review. To obtain the widest possible representation of contributors, numerous knowledgeable persons in every geographic area of the country, of both political parties, and of diverse cultural, social, and occupational backgrounds were solicited by mail to write. This included every retired state supreme court or federal judge whose location could be found. Represented among the outside contributors are judges, public officials, lawyers, law professors, social scientists, real estate brokers, and others with experience in this area. The views of the outside contributors are their own. This author is, however, responsible for certain editorial work, such as proper footnoting of material, editing material copied from other sources, and occasional style revision to conform to law review style.

The signed, but not otherwise identified student comments were written by the student editors and staff of the Chicago-Kent Law Review for the symposium while taking a law review research course under my direction. They were subjected to such editorial supervision and revision of mine as was necessary to meet acceptable law review standards.

The great interest shown in this issue by all who read the manuscript thereof, the considerable labor expended by the numerous outside and student contributors, and the timeliness of the topic, has induced this author to have it published as a book. If it contributes to a better understanding of the field, it will have amply justified the effort expended in its production.

ALFRED AVINS

New York City, August, 1963.

ANTI-DISCRIMINATION LEGISLATION IN HOUSING: A DENIAL OF FREEDOM OF CHOICE

ALFRED AVINS*

I. Introduction *

THE GROWING PROLIFERATION OF LAWS in northern states forbidding discrimination based on race, creed, color or national origin in publicly-assisted or private housing,[1] makes such laws a definite factor in the adjustment of intergroup relations and in the curtailment of traditional private rights. The significance of such legislation is further enhanced by the precedent it sets for similar restrictions imposed by private institutions.[2] It is clear that the cumulative impact of these laws can no longer be viewed as a mere alleviation of the plight of particular depressed minority groups *in vacuo*, but must be considered in terms of the other members of our multi-cultural society who become, willy-nilly, integrated in significant aspects of their lives.

Implicit in anti-discrimination legislation in housing is the "conflict between 'reserved private rights such as freedom of asso-

* B.A. 1954, Hunter College; LL.B. 1956, Columbia Univ.; LL.M. 1957, New York Univ.; M.L. 1961, J.S.D. 1962, Univ. of Chicago. Member of the New York, Illinois, Florida, District of Columbia, and United States Supreme Court Bars. Former Special Deputy Atty.-Gen. of New York. Author: The Law of AWOL. App. Atty., F.P.C. & N.L.R.B., 1958-60; Assistant Professor of Law, John Marshall Law School, 1960-1; Associate Professor of Law, Chicago-Kent College of Law, 1961-3.

1 Alaska Sess. Laws 1962, ch. 49, at 54; Cal. Health & Safety Code §§ 33049-50, 35700-41; Colo. Rev. Stat. Ann. §§ 69-7-1 to -7 (Supp. 1960); Conn. Gen. Stat. Ann. §§ 53-34 to -36 (Supp. 1961); Mass. Gen. Laws Ann. ch. 151B, §§ 1-6, ch. 112, § 87AAA(k) (Supp. 1961); Minn. Stat. Ann. §§ 363.01-.09, .12-.13, 462.481, .525(8), .641, 507.18 (Supp. 1961); N.H. Rev. Stat. Ann. §§ 354:1:2, :4 (Supp. 1961); N.J. Rev. Stat. § 18.25 (Supp. 1961); N.Y. Civ. Rights Law §§ 18(a)-(e); N.Y. Executive Law §§ 290-301; Ore. Rev. Stat. §§ 659.010-.045, 696.300 (1961); Pa. Stat. Ann. tit. 35, §§ 1661-64, 1680.307, 1711, tit. 43, §§ 951-63 (Supp. 1961); Wash. Rev. Code §§ 49.60.010, .217 (1957); V.I. Code Ann. tit. 10, §§ 1-10 (Supp. 1962).

2 For example, landlords seeking to rent living quarters to students at several universities must comply with nondiscrimination regulations or sign such agreements before their properties will be listed by the university housing bureaus. See 106 Cong. Rec. A2145 (1960) (Univ. of California); N.Y. Times, Feb. 1, 1961, Real Estate, Sec. 8, p. R.6, col. 1 (State Univ. of New York, Columbia Univ., Cornell Univ., Ithaca College, all in New York State; Univ. of Colorado and Colorado State College in Colorado; and Yale, Harvard, Radcliffe, the Universities of Washington, California, Minnesota, San Jose State College, Marquette Univ., and Ohio State Univ.); March 15, 1961, p. 9, col. 1 (Stanford). See also N.Y. Times, Oct. 25, 1959, p. 83, col. 3. But "many New Haven landlords are apparently unwilling to sign an anti-discrimination pledge circulated by Yale University's housing bureau." N.Y. Times, Jan. 9, 1960, p. 14, col. 8.

ciation and non-association, and nondiscrimination.' "[3] The traditional rights of freedom of choice and association, long thought so inviolate as not to require formal embodiment in constitutional or statutory guarantees, have now been evaporated by the preemption of laws passed without adequate consideration of the fact that the "rights" they create must necessarily infringe on the freedoms of others, by subjecting them to the exercise of those rights by minority groups. Indeed, the Governor of New York, in stating that he would recommend a state-wide law forbidding discrimination in private housing when the legislature met in 1960 because "I believe every American citizen should be able to live where his heart desires and his means permit"[4] completely ignored the interests of individuals to choose their fellow residents and neighbors and thus live in the kind of neighborhood that they desired.

Adequate reflection on the elimination of rights long deemed basic to our concept of a free society to make way for the creation of new "rights" against individuals heretofore unknown to American law and alien to fundamental constitutional norms is now imperative. This article will deal with the proper identification of those rights, the premises on which they are based, and the persons to whom they properly belong. In so doing, it is hoped that the preservation of these rights may be secured against their prospective demise.

II. *Freedom of Enterprise and Public Utility Regulation*

A. The Right to Choose Customers

The federal and state due process clauses, which protect liberty and property from governmental deprivation, are meaningless gestures without the underlying assumption of an American economic norm by which yardstick governmental intrusion into private business can be measured. It could hardly be contended that the word "property" in constitutional phraseology comprehends only goods intended for personal consumption— that the due process clause goes no farther than prohibiting government from giving one man's toothbrush to his neighbor. If

---

3 Statement, of American Civil Liberties Union as reported in N.Y. Times, June 3, 1959, p. 58, col. 6.
4 See N.Y. Times, July 14, 1959, p. 1, col. 3.

that is all the protection the constitution affords, Americans are no better off than Soviet citizens, who are also protected in personal consumptive property.[5] It is unreasonable to believe that the framers of our fundamental laws provided no protection against legislative adoption of a communist or socialist economy. While it may well be that the framers of our constitution did not intend their drafts to embody all of the footnotes in current economic treatises, it is equally true that Mr. Justice Holmes' famous declaration that "a Constitution is not intended to embody a particular economic theory"[6] cannot be taken literally—and was not taken literally by Holmes himself, whose willingness to overturn economic regulation when it went beyond substantial public need is manifest.[7] Moreover, the abandonment by the United States Supreme Court to the state courts of the task of interpreting and applying substantive due process in the economic sphere[8] has not eliminated the norm any more than it has eliminated the constitutional provision which embodies that norm. It has merely removed the arena where the norm is tested and enforced from Washington to the 50 state capitols. The vitality of substantive economic due process, and the underlying assumptions on which it rests, remain unimpaired, even though enforcement has become more localized.

The American economic norm, ingrained through centuries of legal development, has been a free enterprise system, characterized by private ownership and control over property, a free competitive market, and only such governmental control or regulation as is made necessary by distortions in the free market. The whole philosophy of our anti-trust laws is based on the economic norm of free competition; without such a norm they would be absurd.[9] The concept of a competitive market free from governmental restraints was held at an early date to have been embodied in the

---

5 See Berman, *Soviet Heirs in American Courts,* 62 Colum. L. Rev. 257 (1962).

6 Lochner v. New York, 198 U.S. 45, 76 (1905).

7 See, for example, his attitude in Chastleton Corp. v. Sinclair, 264 U.S. 543 (1924).

8 Carpenter, *Our Constitutional Heritage: Economic Due Process and the State Courts,* 45 A.B.A.J. 1027 (1959); Hetherington, *State Economic Regulation and Substantive Due Process of Law,* 53 Nw. U. L. Rev. 226 (1958).

9 Apex Hosiery Co. v. Leader, 310 U.S. 469 (1940); Standard Oil Co. v. United States, 221 U.S. 1 (1911); United States v. Addyston Pipe & Steel Co., 85 Fed. 271 (6th Cir. 1898), *aff'd* 175 U.S. 211 (1899).

terms "liberty" and "property" in the Fourteenth Amendment,[10] and no doubt state due process clauses have the same fundamental meaning.[11]

A necessary corollary of a free market is the right to choose one's customers free from government dictation. As the Second Circuit recently held:

> [I]t generally has been held that "fundamental assumptions in a free business enterprise," including the belief that "each business enterprise must be free to select its business relations in its own interest," may justify or excuse the act of one who causes harm to another as a collateral consequence of his refusal to continue a business relation terminable at will.[12]

The Fourth Circuit likewise declared: "Absent conspiracy or monopolization, a seller engaged in a private business may normally refuse to deal with a buyer for any reason or with no reason whatever."[13] The United States Supreme Court has consistently upheld the right to refuse to sell when that right has been attacked.[14] And in the landmark *Cream of Wheat* case[15] the court declared:

> We had supposed that it was elementary law that a trader could buy from whom he pleased and sell to whom he pleased, and that his selection of seller and buyer was wholly his own concern. "It is a part of a man's civil rights that he be at liberty to refuse business relations with any person whomsoever, whether the refusal rests upon reason, or is the result of whim, caprice, prejudice, or malice." Cooley on Torts, p. 278.
>
>   . . . .
>
> Before the Sherman Act it was the law that a trader might reject the offer of a proposing buyer, for any reason that appealed to him; it might be because he did not like the other's business methods, or because he had some personal difference with him, political,

10 Allgeyer v. Louisiana, 165 U.S. 578 (1897).
11 *Supra*, n.8.
12 House of Materials, Inc. v. Simplicity Pattern Co., 298 F.2d 867, 872 (2d Cir. 1962).
13 McElhenney Co. v. Western Auto Supply Co., 269 F.2d 332, 337 (4th Cir. 1959). See also Handler, *Trade Regulation* 272-3, n.2 (3d ed. 1960), and the cases cited therein.
14 United States v. Colgate & Co., 250 U.S. 300 (1919); Times-Picayune Publishing Co. v. United States, 345 U.S. 594 (1953). In Barber, *Refusals to Deal Under the Federal Antitrust Laws*, 103 U. Pa. L. Rev. 847, 885 (1955), the author says: "The Supreme Court has steadfastly protected the entrepreneur's freedom to deal and not to deal when that freedom has been attacked as such. Unilateral refusals to deal where considerations of monopoly are not involved are normal incidents of the enjoyment of that trade freedom which has been a unique characteristic of our economic system. Refusals to deal are not evil in themselves; suggestions that they are and that it would be in the public interest to impose on ordinary private business standards of conduct not unlike those imposed on public utilities stem from political considerations. . . ."
15 Great Atlantic and Pacific Tea Co. v. Cream of Wheat Co., 227 Fed. 46 (2d Cir. 1915).

racial, or social. That was purely his own affair, with which nobody else had any concern. . . . We have not yet reached the stage where the selection of a trader's customers is made for him by the government.[16]

The rule of the *Cream of Wheat* case has been so often cited and approved by the courts as to become axiomatic.[17] Indeed, no other result could be reached in a free economy or a free society.[18]

[16] *Id.* at 48.

[17] By 'ie United States Supreme Court: Federal Trade Commission v. Raymond Co., 263 U.S. 565 (1924).

By lower federal courts: Naifeh v. Ronson Art Metal Works, 218 F.2d 202 (10th Cir. 1954); Paramount Film Distributing Corp. v. Applebaum, 217 F.2d 101 (5th Cir. 1954); Brosious v. Pepsi-Cola Co., 155 F.2d 99 (3d Cir. 1946); Johnson v. J. H. Yost Lumber Co., 117 F.2d 53 (8th Cir. 1941); Lukens Steel Co. v. Perkins, 107 F.2d 627 (D.C. Cir. 1939), *rev. on other grounds*, 310 U.S. 113 (1940); Federal Trade Commission v. Paramount Famous Lasky Corp., 57 F.2d 152 (2d Cir. 1932); Green v. Victor Talking Machine, 24 F.2d 378 (2d Cir. 1928); Mennen Co. v. Federal Trade Commission, 288 Fed. 774 (2d Cir. 1923); Reliable Volkswagen S. & S. Co. v. World-Wide Auto Corp., 182 F. Supp. 412 (D.N.J. 1960); McElhenney Co. v. Western Tire and Auto Supply Co., 167 F. Supp. 949 (W.D.S.C. 1958); Miller Motors v. Ford Motor Co., 149 F. Supp. 790 (M.D.N.C. 1957); Schwing Motor Co. v. Hudson Sales Corp., 138 F. Supp. 899 (D. Md. 1956); Klein v. Lionel Corp., 138 F. Supp. 560 (D. Del. 1956); Dipson Theatres v. Buffalo Theatres, 86 F. Supp. 716 (W.D.N.Y. 1949); Sorrentino v. Glen-Gery Shale Brick Corp., 46 F. Supp. 709 (E.D. Pa. 1942); Mid-West Theatres Co. v. Co-operative Theatres, 43 F. Supp. 216 (E.D. Mich. 1941); Westway Theatres v. Twentieth-Century-Fox Film Corp., 30 F. Supp. 830 (D. Md. 1940); Arthur v. Kraft-Phenix Cheese Corp., 26 F. Supp. 824 (D. Md. 1937); Baran v. Goodyear Tire and Rubber Co., 256 Fed. 571 (S.D.N.Y. 1919) per Augustus Hand, J.; United States v. Colgate & Co., 253 Fed. 522 (E.D. Va. 1918), *aff'd*, 250 U.S. 300 (1919).

By state courts: A.B.C. Distributing Co. v. Distillers Distributing Corp., 154 Cal. 2d 189, 316 P.2d 71 (1957); Burroughs Wellcome & Co. v. Johnson Wholesale Perfume Co., 128 Conn. 596, 24 A.2d 841 (1942); Ploog v. Roberts Dairy Co., 122 Neb. 542, 240 N.W. 764 (1932); Thorp v. General News Bureau, 242 App. Div. 330, 275 N.Y. Supp. 41 (1934); Biber Bros. News Co. v. New York Evening Post, 144 Misc. 405, 258 N.Y. Supp. 31 (1932); Nissen v. Andres, 178 Okla. 470, 63 P.2d 47 (1936); State v. Standard Oil Co. of California, 190 Wash. 496, 498, 68 P.2d 1031, 1032 (1937); "It is established that a trader may buy from whom he pleases and sell to whom he pleases and, if he refuses to sell, his reason for doing so is not material."

In Brown, *The Right to Refuse to Sell*, 25 Yale L.J. 194 (1916), the author says: "This decision [the Cream of Wheat case], and the decision of the U.S. District Court, of which it is an affirmance, establish the right of a private trader to refuse to sell, as a constitutional property right, which cannot be taken away by legislative interference, either state or national."

[18] In Barber, *supra* n.14, at 848 the author says: "In a free economy, the seller's freedom to sell and the buyer's freedom not to buy are both essential elements in the price-determining process. In this context, the seller's right to refuse to sell is unqualified. Deprived of this freedom, some other form of regulation would have to be provided to protect the seller's right in his property." The author further declares at page 857: "Absent conspiracy or monopoly, the cases indicate that an individual has full freedom to refuse to sell to or buy from any person for any reason." And a student note in 29 Harv. L. Rev. 446 (1916) stated: "If a farmer covets his neighbor's horse, and the neighbor declines to part with it, no sane system of jurisprudence would think of furnishing the farmer with any legal means of compelling the neighbor to sell against his will. The farmer's only interest in the horse is his desire for it, and this is not of sufficient social importance to warrant legal protection at the expense of the neighbor's equally significant desire to keep it."

The entire assumption in our economic structure, that economic needs can best be fulfilled by sellers and buyers free to deal with each other, is set at naught when government dictates a choice to either. Such regulation is at war with basic economic norms embodied in our due process clauses, state and federal, and cannot stand because it denies the essential concepts which these constitutions affirm, that a free market is the best guarantee of prosperity, abundance, and the satisfaction of material needs of all.

B. Public Utility Regulation

The main characteristic of a public utility is that the public may demand the service as of right.[19] An industry may be closely regulated and yet not be a public utility if it can choose its customers.[20] Of course, not every member of the public has an absolute right to the utility's services at all times; there may be an insufficient supply as of a given time for all who desire to obtain it. Rather, the true hallmark of a public utility is that everyone is entitled to the service without arbitrary discrimination. It is this duty to serve any applicant on equal terms without unreasonable discriminations which constitutes the main difference between public utilities and all other businesses.[21] Accordingly, assuming

19 73 C.J.S., *Public Utilities*, § 1 (1951). In Junction Water Co. v. Riddle, 108 N.J. Eq. 523, 526, 155 Atl. 887, 889 (1931) it was held: "A true criterion by which to judge the character of the use of any plant or system alleged to be a public utility is whether or not the public may enjoy it of right or by permission only." In the *Restatement, Torts* § 191a, it is stated: "The phrase public utility is used in the Restatement of this Subject to describe a person, corporation or other association carrying on an enterprise for the accommodation of the public, the members of which as such are entitled as of right to use its facilities." And the court in Chronicle & Gazette Pub. Co. v. Attorney General, 94 N.H. 148, 48 A.2d 478 (1946) said that since a newspaper is not a public utility it cannot be compelled to accept political advertising.

20 See, e.g., Allaman v. Pennsylvania Public Utility Comm., 149 Pa. Super. 353, 27 A.2d 516 (1942). In Pulitzer Pub. Co. v. Federal Communications Comm., 94 F.2d 249, 251 (D.C. Cir. 1937), it was held: "But we have never said that a radio broadcasting company is a public utility in the sense in which a railroad is a public utility. . . . The use and enjoyment of such facilities the public has the legal right to demand. . . . The licensee of a radio station chooses its own advertisers and its own program, and generally speaking the only requirement for the renewal of its license is that it has not failed to function and will not fail to function in the public interest."

21 73 C.J.S., *Public Utilities* § 7b (1951). In Claremont Gas Light Co. v. Monadnock Mills, 92 N.H. 468, 32 A.2d 823, 824 (1943), the court said: "Service to the public without discrimination is one of the distinguishing characteristics of a public utility." Likewise, in Highland Dairy Farms Co. v. Helvetia Milk Condensing Co., 308 Ill. 294, 139 N.E. 418, 420 (1923), the court declared: "A public utility implies . . . the duty of the producer . . . to serve the public and treat all persons alike, without discrimination." In Springfield Gas and Electric Co. v. City of Springfield, 292 Ill. 236, 126 N.E. 739, 746 (1920), the court observed: "The term 'public utility' implies a public use carrying with it the duty

that discrimination in tenant or vendee selection based on race, creed, color or national origin is arbitrary, it nevertheless follows that an anti-discrimination law converts private dwellings in particular, and the housing industry as a whole, into public utilities.

It may be argued that not all discrimination is banned by those statutes which refer to race, creed, color, and national origin, and hence only partial public utility duties are imposed on real property owners. But of what value is it if the legislature takes away those aspects of a right which people would like to exercise and leaves only those which they would not want to exercise. As one New York case pointed out:

> Lastly, there is plaintiff's argument that he may limit his tenancies to ladies with red hair if he so elects. As an argument, this is not quite as bizarre as it seems, because, if he can exclude all men and the great majority of women, why can he not exclude Negroes? The answer is a practical one. While there may be an occasional landlord who would allow such a vagary to control his rental policy, the situation, if it exists at all, is so rare that legislation in regard to it has not been occasioned. Landlords, like others in business, are actuated by a profit motive. Any such policy would no doubt soon see a landlord out of business, so instances do not occur.[22]

Moreover, New York, at least, imposes additional regulations of a public utility nature on the housing industry, such as the requirement that families with children not be discriminated against,[23] and "emergency" rent control growing out of the "war."[24] Even absent these regulations, however, if the legislature with-

---

to serve the public and treat all persons alike. . . ." In Trans·World Airlines v. City and County of San Francisco, 119 F. Supp. 516, 518 (N.D. Calif. 1954), the court said: "The factor which . . . determines whether an agency is a public utility, is whether all persons . . . who from the nature of the service rendered are in a position to require it, have a right to be supplied the service on equal terms. The limitations of place, requirements, ability to pay, and other facts determine the customers that will use a particular service." And in Buder v. First Nat. Bank, 16 F.2d 990, 992 (8th Cir. 1927), the court declared: "We cannot find that [the term 'public utility'] has ever been applied to corporations performing a public function or affected by a public interest, which may arbitrarily select their customers, such as banks, insurance companies, and the like." See, generally, the discussion in Avins, *Trade Regulations (Compulsory Housing Integration Law)*, 12 Rutgers, L. Rev. 149, 150-2 (1957).

22 Martin v. City of New York, 22 Misc. 2d 389, 391, 201 N.Y.S.2d 111, 112-3 (1960).

23 N.Y. Penal Law § 2041.

24 N.Y. Unconsolidated Laws § 8581 et seq. In view of the fact that rent control has been in existence since 1946, for seventeen years, it would seem that the legislature should at least identify just exactly which war has created the emergency, e.g., World War II, the Korean War, the Cold War with Russia, or perhaps the war against real property owners.

draws the only grounds on which people might really want to discriminate, and leaves other grounds on which nobody would ever dream of relying, it cannot be said that the right to discriminate in fact remains. A right does not remain when the legislature removes the substance and leaves only the shadow.

The production of housing, like the production of food, has never traditionally been considered a public utility. "An ordinary producer, manufacturer, or shopkeeper may sell or not sell, as he likes, . . . [and this feature] usually distinguishes private from quasi-public occupations."[25] A public utility exists where business has a complete or substantial monopoly, and "where fear of monopoly prompted, and was held to justify, regulation of rates. There is no monopoly in the preparation of foods,"[26] and even less of one in the construction or rental of housing. Accordingly, there is no basis in fact for classifying housing as a public utility.

The United States Supreme Court has repeatedly held that "the state could not, by mere legislative fiat . . . convert [private business] into a public utility . . . for that would be taking private property for public use without just compensation, which no state can do consistently with the due process of law clause of the 14th Amendment."[27] A public utility "must serve all . . . without discrimination," and these "onerous duties" may not be imposed on private businesses by "legislative fiat," for "that would be taking private property for public use without just compensation."[28] Since anti-discrimination legislation in housing attempts to impose the obligations of public utilities on private businesses, it is unconstitutional.

[25] Wolff Packing Co. v. Court of Industrial Relations, 262 U.S. 522, 537-8 (1923).

[26] *Id.* at 538. Compare the thousands of entrepreneurs building or renting housing with the handful of grain elevator companies involved in Munn v. Illinois, 94 U.S. 113 (1877).

[27] Producers Transportation Co. v. Railroad Comm., 251 U.S. 228, 230-1 (1920). See also Frost v. Railroad Comm., 271 U.S. 583, 592 (1926) ("consistently with the due process clause of the 14th Amendment, a private carrier cannot be converted against his will into a common carrier by mere legislative command"); Film Transport Co. v. Michigan Pub. Utilities Comm., 17 F.2d 857, 858 (E.D. Mich. 1927) ("an attempted exercise of the power of the state by legislative fiat to convert property used exclusively in the business of a private carrier into a public utility would be taking private property for public use without just compensation, in violation of the due process clause of the Fourteenth Amendment"); Allen v. Railroad Comm., 179 Cal. 68, 175 Pac. 466, 474 (1918) ("even a constitutional declaration cannot transform a private enterprise, or a part thereof, into a public utility and thus take property for public use without condemnation and payment").

[28] Michigan Pub. Utilities Comm. v. Duke, 266 U.S. 570, 577-8 (1925).

III. *Police Power and Property Rights*

A. Police Power and Market Distortions

As has already been pointed out, a free competitive market with the corollary of the right to choose customers, is ingrained in American constitutional concepts of "liberty" and freedom of enterprise. Such concepts are likewise basic to property rights. However arbitrary or capricious a private property owner's refusal to deal with a prospective tenant or purchaser may be, the state may not interefere, for this is the very essence of private property.[29]

Moreover, there is no question that people have the legally protected right to purchase or decline to purchase property on the basis of their passions, prejudices, or arbitrary whims.[30] Significantly, in the trade regulation area the United States Supreme Court has not only recognized this right but has gone so far as to impose a duty on prospective sellers to disclose facts which have no scientific or other relevance to the product to be sold and are useful solely in the making of arbitrary decisions.[31] It is obvious that if purchasers have a legally protected right to make whimsical decisions from whom to buy, sellers should have, by a parity of reasoning, the right to make equally whimsical decisions as to whom to sell.

Those few decisions which uphold anti-discrimination legis-

[29] Globerman v. Grand Central Parkway Gardens, 115 N.Y.S.2d 757, 760 (1952), *aff'd*, 281 App. Div. 820, 118 N.Y.S.2d 917 (1952) ("The landlords have the absolute right, under the law, to choose their tenants"); Novick v. Levitt & Sons, Inc., 200 Misc. 694, 108 N.Y.S.2d 615 (1951), *aff'd*, 279 App. Div. 617, 107 N.Y.S.2d 1016 (1951). See also Johnson v. Levitt & Sons, Inc., 131 F. Supp. 114 (E.D. Pa. 1955); Dorsey v. Stuyvesant Town Corp., 150 Misc. 187, 74 N.Y.S.2d 220 (1947), *aff'd*, 274 App. Div. 992, 85 N.Y.S.2d 313, *aff'd*, 299 N.Y. 512, 87 N.E.2d 541 (1948); Kemp v. Rubin, 188 Misc. 310, 69 N.Y.S.2d 680, *aff'd* 273 App. Div. 789, 75 N.Y.S.2d 768 (1947), *rev'd on other grounds*, 298 N.Y. 590, 81 N.E.2d 325 (1949). In Alsberg v. Lucerne Hotel Co., 46 Misc. 617, 92 N.Y. Supp. 851 (1905), in an action under the Civil Rights Law for refusing to lease an apartment to plaintiff because she was Jewish, the court, in holding for the defendant, said: ". . . when the defendants refused to lease apartments to the plaintiff, they exercised only the right which every landlord undoubtedly has to make his own selection of tenants."

[30] In Federal Trade Comm. v. Royal Milling Co., 288 U.S. 212, 216 (1933), the court held: "If consumers or dealers prefer to purchase a given article because it was made by a particular manufacturer or class of manufacturers, they have a right to do so, and this right cannot be satisfied by imposing upon them an exactly similar article, or one equally as good, but having a different origin. . . ."

[31] In Federal Trade Comm. v. Algoma Lumber Co., 291 U.S. 67, 78 (1934), a unanimous court, speaking through Mr. Justice Cardozo, said: "In such matters [buying goods], the public is entitled to get what it chooses, though the choice may be dictated by caprice or by fashion or perhaps by ignorance."

lation as against due process arguments rely on a series of generalized clichés about the use of the police power, as "one of the least limitable of government powers."[32] The insertion of a legislative declaration that a statute is designed to protect public health, safety, welfare or morals adds nothing to the constitutionality of the law, since if adding a shibboleth to a statute immunized it from constitutional limitations, "the legislatures of the states would have unbounded power, and it would be enough to say that any piece of legislation was enacted to conserve the morals, the health, or the safety of the people; such legislation would be valid, no matter how absolutely without foundation the claim might be. The claim of the police power would be a mere pretext,—become another and delusive name for the supreme sovereignty of the state to be exercised free from constitutional restraint."[33]

Traditional exercises of the police power fall into two major categories. The first consists of regulating property so that its use does not injure the health or safety of others, or destroy their use of their own property. Examples of this abound, and include the destruction of diseased trees[34] or cattle,[35] regulation of explosives,[36] fire and sanitation regulation,[37] and zoning.[38] The necessity of preventing the spread of fire or disease to one's neighbor's property, or preventing disease or injury generally, is obvious. Zoning is needed so that property will not be subjected to a use which lessens the ability of owners of neighboring property to use their property. The concept that no person can use his property in such

32 Jones v. Haridor Realty Co., 37 N.J. 384, 181 A.2d 481, 485 (1962).

33 Lochner v. New York, 198 U.S. 45, 56 (1905). As previously noted, the abandonment of this line of cases by the United States Supreme Court as an undue infringement on states' rights in recent years does not absolve state courts of the duty of applying their own due process clauses in state constitutions. As the Supreme Court of Minnesota pointed out in National Tea Co. v. State, 208 Minn. 607, 608, 294 N.W. 230, 231 (1940), on remand from the United States Supreme Court in Minnesota v. National Tea Co., 309 U.S. 551 (1940): "Judicial duty does not permit us to shift or avoid the responsibility resting upon us to exercise our own honest judgments in the 'interpretation of our own Constitution' with finality." Cf. Van Cott v. State Tax Comm., 98 Utah 264, 96 P.2d 740, 741 (1939) ("such interpretation [by us] is still correct regardless of any change in decision of the United States Supreme Court").

34 Miller v. Schoene, 276 U.S. 272 (1928).

35 Smith v. St. Louis & Sw. Ry. Co., 181 U.S. 248 (1901).

36 Pierce Oil Corp. v. City of Hope, 248 U.S. 498 (1919).

37 Queenside Hills Realty Co. v. Saxl, 328 U.S. 80, 82-3 (1946): Thomas Cusack Co. v. Chicago, 242 U.S. 526, 529 (1916); Hadacheck v. Los Angeles, 239 U.S. 394, 408-9 (1915); Welch v. Swasey, 214 U.S. 91, 107-8 (1909). Cf. American Print Works v. Lawrence, 23 N.J.L. 9 (1850); Conwell v. Emrie, 2 Ind. 35 (1850).

38 Village of Euclid v. Amber Realty Co., 272 U.S. 365, 387-8, 394 (1926).

a way as to diminish the health, safety, or use of property of others is basic to any orderly society. Anti-discrimination legislation has no relevance to such enactments since it is not the *use* but the failure to convey the property which is restricted. No attempt has ever been made to support such legislation on this ground; any such attempt would be frivolous.

The other class of cases involves state legislation which was passed to correct deleterious social or economic conditions arising from a distortion in the normal free competitive market, resulting in an inequality in bargaining power and hence the inability of individuals to obtain the benefits of a free competitive market. In such instances, government intrusion is not designed to supplant the market, but simply to protect against undue distortions produced by deviations from the competitive market norm.

The earliest examples of such laws were public utility regulations. Since utilities are by nature monopolies, they represent a permanent distortion of a competitive market norm, and hence justify permanent economic regulation.[39] However, other inequalities in bargaining position were soon recognized, such as that between employee and employer, and even in the heyday of *laissez-faire* thinking in the United States Supreme Court, it permitted states to regulate the number of working hours as a health measure,[40] the right to be compensated for industrial accidents via workmen's compensation,[41] and eventually minimum wages.[42] Finally, where a temporary economic condition, such as war or depression, distorts the normal economic market, the police power permits the state to correct dislocations produced by this condition through temporary legislation which goes no further than the minimum needed to correct the condition, and lasts no longer than the temporary emergency.[43] In all of these cases, regulation is justified by an abnormal economic market.[44]

[39] Munn v. Illinois, 94 U.S. 113, 127-8, 131 (1877).
[40] Holden v. Hardy, 169 U.S. 366 (1898); Mueller v. Oregon, 208 U.S. 412 (1908).
[41] New York Central R.R. Co. v. White, 243 U.S. 188 (1917).
[42] West Coast Hotel Co. v. Parrish, 300 U.S. 379 (1937).
[43] Nebbia v. New York, 291 U.S. 502 (1934).
[44] There are, of course, numerous businesses which are regulated in one particular or another because of a lack of a normal competitive market, such as insurance, securities, employment agencies, etc., and which justifiably require state interference because the bargaining position of the consumer is inadequate and unequal. Cases are collected in

In this connection, rent control is of particular significance because several of the cases which uphold anti-discrimination legislation in housing rely strongly on this precedent.[45] However, rent control is emergency legislation designed to deal with a temporary market imbalance. As Mr. Justice Holmes put it:

> The regulation is put and justified only as a temporary measure . . . . A limit in time, to tide over a passing trouble, well may justify a law that could not be upheld as a permanent change.[46]

Moreover, since this exercise of the police power is invoked by, and may only last for, a genuine emergency, the courts may continuously review the existence of the emergency as the constitutional fact on which the legislation may be sustained.[47] "Rent controls, all will agree, ought not achieve a status of permanence in our economy. They have no justification except in periods of emergency."[48] When the emergency ceases, the controls become unconstitutional.[49]

Anti-discrimination legislation is, of course, nowhere predicated on, or drafted to last for, any purported emergency. Aside from Negro housing, no one has seriously contended that any shortage of housing exists for other groups who are just as much

---

Kauper, *Constitutional Law* 1027-9 (2d ed. 1960). These represent merely specific illustrations of the general rule.

It might be noted that this was not merely the philosophy of the pre-Roosevelt majority on the Supreme Court, but likewise represented a generally-agreed-on legal principle, however much the justices might differ in respect to particular application. Thus, Mr. Justice Stone, dissenting in Tyson & Bros. v. Banton, 273 U.S. 418, 451-2 (1927), said: "An examination of the decisions of this court in which price regulation has been upheld will disclose that the element common to all is the existence of a situation or a combination of circumstances materially restricting the regulative force of competition, so that buyers or sellers are placed at such a disadvantage in the bargaining struggle that serious economic consequences result to a very large number of members of the community. Whether this situation arises from the monopoly conferred upon public service companies or from the circumstances that the strategical position of a group is such as to enable it to impose its will in matters of price upon those who sell, buy or consume, . . . or from the predetermination of prices in the councils of those who sell, promulgated in schedules of practically controlling constancy . . . or from a housing shortage growing out of a public emergency . . . the result is the same." Any laxer standard would atrophy the due process clause, as the United States Supreme Court at present, but fortunately not the state courts, has done. *Supra* n.8.

45 Massachusetts Comm. Against Discrimination v. Colangelo, 182 N.E.2d 595, 601 (Mass. 1962) ("Perhaps the most persuasive analogy is in the field of rent control"); New York Comm. Against Discrimination v. Pelham Hall Apts., Inc., 10 Misc. 2d 334, 341, 170 N.Y.S.2d 750, 758 (1958).

46 Block v. Hirsh, 256 U.S. 135, 157 (1921).

47 Chastleton Corp. v. Sinclair, 264 U.S. 543 (1924).

48 Lincoln Bldg. Associates v. Barr, 1 N.Y.2d 413, 135 N.E.2d 801, 806 (1956).

49 Warren v. City of Philadelphia, 387 Pa. 362, 127 A.2d 703 (1956).

entitled to use the law as Negroes. A look at the New York experience, where the first anti-discrimination law in private housing was passed,[50] shows how utterly baseless is the claim that this legislation is needed to assure good housing to any other segment of the population. Yet the law covers them also.

For example, in the first ten months of the operation of New York City's anti-discrimination ordinance, while most of the complaints came from Negroes, ten came from Jews, two from persons of Italian descent, one from a Roman Catholic, and one from a member of the Greek Orthodox faith.[51] After four years of operation, three precent of the complaints are still based on religious discrimination.[52]

Moreover, some of the more publicized cases are of such a nature. Discrimination in an estimated third of Manhattan's 175 highest-priced luxury cooperative apartment houses against Jews[53] led to a complaint by the president of New York's wealthiest Reform Jewish temple, the head of a major public accounting firm, that he had been denied an apartment in a luxury cooperative apartment house because of his religion. This complaint, upheld by the City Commission on Human Rights, received publicity on the front page of the New York Times, and involved a Park Avenue apartment with a down payment of $5000, into which the complainant sought to move from his luxury Fifth Avenue apartment.[54] Likewise, the New York State Commission Against Discrimination compelled a suburban luxury Bronxville apartment house to cease discriminating against Jews[55] in what the Commission's Vice-Chairman called a "historic breakthrough."[56]

Nor were these examples unforeseen by the legislators. When

50 New York City Local Law 80 of 1957, New York City Administrative Code, c. 41, tit. X, secs. X 41-1.0 (1957).

51 N.Y. Times, Feb. 8, 1959, Sec. 4, p. 7, col. 3.

52 N.Y. Times, July 1, 1962, Real Estate, Sec. 8, p. R. 1, col. 8.

53 N.Y. Times, Jan. 18, 1962, p. 13, col. 2; June 10, 1961, p. 29, col. 1.

54 N.Y. Times, Oct. 4, 1962, p. 1, col. 2. See also N.Y. Times, April 5, 1963, p. 17, col. 1; April 6, 1963, p. 14, col. 2, involving an investigation of discrimination against "Jews, diplomats and 'theatrical people'" by the New York City Commission on Human Rights in a luxury cooperative apartment house which had apartments ranging in price from $165,000 to $200,000 and which also discriminated against Democrats and foreigners.

55 N.Y. Times, Nov. 14, 1962, p. 35, col. 8.

56 N.Y. Times, Nov. 18, 1962, Real Estate, Sec. 8, p. R. 1, col. 8.

the New York City ordinance was being considered by the City Council, an amendment was proposed exempting luxury cooperative apartment houses from the law on the grounds that anyone who could afford that rental could afford to rent or build elsewhere. The amendment was opposed by city officials concerned with enforcement of the law on the grounds "that luxury cooperative apartments were 'the hard core of residential anti-Semitism in New York City' "[57] and the amendment was defeated.[58]

No one has ever contended that the above complainants lack an equality of bargaining power with landlords, or suffer from any deprivation of housing through a normal competitive market. No one would dream of asserting that they cannot obtain housing elsewhere, or need the particular apartment applied for. No one would seriously argue that, as a group, persons of the Jewish, Roman Catholic, or Greek Orthodox faith, or of Italian, German, or Anglo-Saxon descent (who are equally entitled to use the law) cannot get adequate housing in a normal market. Jewish tenants as a group are not doomed to poor housing; the "gilded ghettoes" of Long Island and Westchester, excoriated by SCAD officials, contain homes in the $100,000 class.[59]

A legislative fiat that, in a normal competitive market, a seller must not refuse a buyer's offer because his reasons are unsatisfactory to the legislature is no different from a requirement that a buyer must not refuse a seller's offer because the legislature finds his reasons unsatisfactory. It is a mere naked assertion of power which cannot exist so long as written constitutions guarantee fundamental property rights. As Mr. Justice Brandeis once declared for a unanimous United States Supreme Court:

> The use of the pipe line owner's wells and reserves is curtailed solely for the benefit of other private well owners. . . . Our law reports present no more glaring instance of the taking of one man's property and giving it to another. . . . And this Court has many

[57] N.Y. Times, July 31, 1957, p. 1, col. 2. See also a similar statement by Charles Abrams, former Chairman of the New York State Commission Against Discrimination, reported in the New York Post, July 9, 1957, p. 5, col. 2. And see the recent statement of Edward Rutledge, Housing Director of the State Commission Against Discrimination, attacking exclusive Jewish suburban areas as "gilded ghettos." N.Y. Times, Oct. 15, 1959, p. 35, col. 1.

[58] N.Y. Times, Dec. 6, 1957, p. 1, col. 4.

[59] *Supra* n.57. And see the statement of Mr. Abrams critical of exclusive Jewish suburbs in N.Y. Times, April 29, 1958, p. 31, col. 8.

times warned that one person's property may not be taken for the benefit of another private person without a justifying public purpose, even though compensation be paid.[60]

B. Negro Housing Needs

Those courts which have done any more than enthuse on how un-American racial or religious discrimination is[61] have totally ignored the alleged need to ban such discrimination against anyone else but Negroes. Instead, they have justified this sweeping legislation on asserted Negro housing needs.[62] We can therefore assume that this constitutes a concession, *sub silento*, that the statute is unconstitutional as applied to anyone else, and turn to the law as if it singled out Negroes for protection.

As has been noted above, statutes correcting inequalities in bargaining position and thus restoring a normal competitive market have been upheld as appropriate exercises of the police power. However, the mere fact that the state may have a limited interest at some period in time in the correction of a distortion caused by an absence of a normal market does not give it the power to regulate the whole area indefinitely as to both time and people.[63] Such a regulation would infringe on the constitutionally protected right to be free from unjustified legislation, and make the need a mere pretext for the sweeping statute.

[60] Thompson v. Consolidated Gas Utilities Corp., 300 U.S. 55, 78-80 (1937). That this type of legislation constituted the taking of private property for private use was noted by Mallery, J., in O'Meara v. Washington State Board Against Discrimination, 58 Wash. 2d 793, 801, 365 P.2d 1, 5 (1961), and by Hall, J. in Colorado Anti-Discrimination Comm. v. Case, —— P.2d ——, —— (1962). The answer given by the majority, that there was no taking because the seller has indicated a willingness to sell, evades the issue, because the seller has not offered to sell to the particular complainant. As for the fact that he will get his price, the short answer is that, as Mr. Justice Brandeis pointed out, private property may not, consistently with the 14th Amendment, be taken for private use even with just compensation.

[61] See Colorado Anti-Discrimination Comm. v. Case, *supra* n.60; N.Y. State Comm. Against Discrimination v. Pelham Hall Apts., Inc., *supra* n.45.

[62] Burks v. Poppy Construction Co., 57 Cal. 2d 463, 20 Cal. Reptr. 609, 370 P.2d 313, 317 (1962); Massachusetts Comm. Against Discrimination v. Colangelo, 182 N.E.2d 595, 600 (Mass. 1962); Jones v. Haridor Realty Corp., 37 N.J. 384, 181 A.2d 481, 485 (1962).

[63] Weaver v. Palmer Bros. Co., 270 U.S. 402 (1926); Adams v. Tanner, 244 U.S. 590 (1917); State v. Gateway Mortuaries, Inc., 87 Mont. 225, 287 Pac. 156 (1930). In Tyson & Bros. v. Banton, 273 U.S. 418, 443 (1927), it was held: "It is not permissible to enact a law which, in effect, spreads an all-inclusive net for the feet of everybody upon the chance that, while the innocent will surely be entangled in its meshes, some wrongdoers also may be caught." And in Massie v. Cessna, 239 Ill. 352, 359, 88 N.E. 152, 154 (1909), it was held: "While we think this evil exists, it is yet apparent, upon a careful examination of this statute, that it is too broad in its terms to be justified as an exercise of the police power for the purpose of mitigating or remedying the wrong at which it is aimed."

Applying these principles to Negro housing, one would expect to find the following limitations to make the statute valid: (1) The Negro who sought to use the law in fact needed housing. (2) At the time and place the law was in effect, a shortage of Negro housing did in fact exist, similar to the shortage producing rent control, and that this shortage did in fact distort a normal competitive market. (3) Government could find no way consistent with the constitution other than regulation to alleviate the shortage and restore normal market conditions. (4) The regulation was reasonably calculated to restore normal market conditions. An examination of the typical anti-discrimination law in housing shows that it lacks all four of the above attributes.

First, such legislation does not require that the Negro complainant need the housing. Quite the contrary, the natural tendency of anti-discrimination legislation in housing, as a practical matter, is to benefit those least in need of housing, a sharp contrast from such legislation in employment. For example, suppose an employer intent on discriminating advertised a job as vice-president of his corporation at a salary of $25,000 a year. This employer would be so flooded with applicants that he could select one before he saw a Negro, or, if he had a Negro applicant, he could select someone else, and the discriminatory intent would be almost impossible to prove.[64] On the other hand, the dearth of applicants for, let us say, a position as messenger boy at $50 a week would be such that a refusal to employ a Negro and continued advertising would lend considerable credence to a claim of racial discrimination. Thus, anti-discrimination legislation in

64 Substantial evidence must support a finding of racial discrimination. A mere suspicion is insufficient. McKinley Park Homes, Inc. v. Commission on Civil Rights, 20 Conn. Supp. 167, 129 A.2d 235, 237-8 (1956). And the Commission Against Discrimination has the burden of proof of showing such discrimination. Cf. N.L.R.B. v. Swinerton, 202 F.2d. 511, 514 (9th Cir. 1953); Local 3 v. N.L.R.B., 210 F.2d 325, 328-9 (8th Cir. 1954), cert. den. 348 U.S. 822 (1954); N.L.R.B. v. Hunter Engineering, 215 F.2d 916, 918 (8th Cir. 1954); N.L.R.B. v. National Die Cast Co., 207 F.2d 344, 349 (7th Cir 1953); N.L.R.B. v. MacSmith Garment Co., 203 F.2d 868, 871 (5th Cir. 1953). Even where there are few applicants, in a high salary job personal qualifications become significant. Thus, applicants for legal, executive, or other professional positions could seldom trace refusal to prohibited discrimination because of the vague standards for selection and the ever-present possibility that they could not meet such unknown criteria. Indeed, as any lawyer knows, the question of whether a particular lawyer-applicant is better than other applicants for a particular job even absent any element of discrimination is so open to conflicting opinions that reference to any fixed standards is a virtual impossibility. Cf. Jeanpierre v. Arbury, 4 N.Y.2d 238, 173 N.Y.S.2d 597 (1958).

employment is unenforceable in high salary jobs, but is effective in low-level jobs where most Negroes in economic need seek work. Hence, this type of legislation may be argued to benefit the mass of Negroes in need of it.

However, in lower-rent housing, into which Negroes who need housing fall, the shortage of apartments prevents anti-discrimination legislation from being effective because there are enough white applicants to fill all vacancies, while in luxury housing, the small number of Negroes who can afford such accommodations can also afford to have new living quarters built for them.

An extreme hypothetical example will illustrate this point. Suppose a landlord builds two identical apartment houses, and, after completion, advertises one for $5 per room a month and the other for $100 per room a month. He will certainly be flooded with applicants for the first house and can pick tenants who are white, although he may have Negro applicants, without any evidence of discrimination. But since renting in the high-priced house will be slow, if a Negro applies and is refused, and advertising for tenants continues, discrimination is easily demonstrated. In fact, this example is borne out by the cases involving housing discrimination, all of which concern more expensive housing.[65]

[65] Jones v. Haridor Realty Corp., *supra* n.62, involved a $20,000 house. N.Y. Times, July 8, 1962, Real Estate, Sec. 8, p. 6, col. 8; May 23, 1962, p. 18, col. 7. Redd v. Zier, 229 N.Y.S.2d 582 (1962) involved a $175 a month apartment. N.Y. Times, July 14, 1962, p. 8, col. 8. A recent Massachusetts case involved homes priced from $14,900 to $22,000. N.Y. Times, Aug. 3, 1960, p. 30, col. 1. Massachusetts Comm. Against Discrimination v. Colangelo, *supra* n.62, involved apartments renting for $145 a month, and in which the complainant had obtained other accommodations for $175 a month. Burks v. Poppy Const. Co., *supra* n.62, involved houses selling for $27,950. O'Meara v. Washington St. Bd. Against Disc., *supra* n. 60, involved a $18,000 house. And N.Y. State Comm. Against Disc. v. Pelham Hall Apts., *supra* n.45, involved an apartment renting for $158 a month. N.Y. Times, June 28, 1957, p. 23, col. 2, In fact, the executive director of New York's Urban League stated of the New York City anti-discrimination ordinance: "the main impact has been felt in middle and high rent buildings. . . The Negroes' greatest housing need is in the low income field." N.Y. Times, March 13, 1962, p. 24, col. 1.

Moreover, the Commission's brief in the Pelham Hall case declared at p. 44: "Finally, it should not be forgotten that we are concerned with more than broad principles. We are dealing with the rights of a man and his family: Norris G. Shervington, a Negro, who needed an apartment. . . . The need for the legislation here in issue is illumined by his individual house-hunting frustrations. . . . The evil of housing discrimination is limited in New York by the Metcalf-Baker Laws. To the Shervingtons and many others there will be significant relief upon judicial affirmance of the action so taken by the Legislature."

In sharp contrast to these crocodile tears is the statement in a front page article reporting the court's decision that the complainant was then living in the Morningside Gardens Housing Project, a relatively new and highly desirable modern middle-income

Since anti-discrimination laws in private housing operate in actuality only in higher rent apartments where there are more vacancies than applicants, only a relatively small percentage of Negroes who are in the upper income brackets and can afford to apply[66] are benefited by them. It is these very people, moreover, who can afford to build new Negro housing. Hence, the small Negro minority which these laws benefit is precisely the group not in need of them to secure good housing. In short, this legislation is *pro bono* social climbers and nothing more. Invoking such laws for their benefit is like enforcing minimum wage legislation for Elizabeth Taylor.

Secondly, anti-discrimination legislation is nowhere limited to places where Negro housing is in short supply, nor is it limited to periods of time during which such shortage exists. The cases simply assume the existence of a shortage,[67] and commentators on both sides have followed suit.[68]

However, the shortage of Negro housing which developed as a result of World War II has now been eliminated in many areas. In a recent survey of ten midwestern cities, it was found that doubled-up households among Negroes had virtually been eliminated between 1950 and 1960, and that "the present housing supply of both races in this region is the best on record."[69] Moreover, the survey found that in seven of these cities, Detroit, Cincinnati, Pittsburgh, Indianapolis, Columbus, Dayton, and Grand Rapids, no Negro housing shortage existed at all and only in Chicago,

---

project in Manhattan much closer to his place of work in midtown Manhattan than New Rochelle was, "according to S.C.A.D. representatives who believe he still wants to settle . . . at the Rochelle Arms." N.Y. Herald Tribune, Jan. 17, 1958, p. 1, col. 2, p. 9, col. 6. When the suit was settled, the complainant then informed the landlord that he wasn't even interested in the apartment any more. Cf. N.Y. Times, editorial, Oct. 4, 1958, p. 20, col. 2.

In a late case, involving a 12-room Park Avenue apartment in New York City, allegedly refused to a Jewish couple, sale price was $157,500 and monthly maintenance was $1,100. N.Y. Times, April 5, 1963, p. 17, col. 1; April 6, 1963, p. 14, col. 2.

66 See Report of the United States Commission on Civil Rights (1959), Part 4 (Housing), p. 375: "In New York City a few years ago it was found that only 13,000 Negro families, or less than 7 percent of the Negro population, had incomes high enough to purchase new homes in the suburbs even if such were available."

67 *Supra* n. 62.

68 Van Alstyne & Karst, *State Action*, 14 Stan. L. Rev. 3, 47 (1961); Note, 107 U. Pa. L. Rev. 515, 525 (1959). This author made the same assumption in Avins, *Anti-Discrimination Legislation as an Infringement on Freedom of Choice*, 6 N.Y.L.F. 13, 21 (1960).

69 Midwestern Minority Housing Markets 25 (Special Report by Advance Mortgage Corp., Dec. 1, 1962).

Cleveland, and Milwaukee was there any asserted backlog of demand for non-white housing, produced primarily by continued migration.[70] As for the quality of housing, the survey concluded:

> The physical housing gains of non-whites in this period were extremely impressive. . . . Starting from a very low base (more than half the Negro-occupied units in 1950 were substandard,) the quality of the non-white housing supply ten years later was at the level of the white supply in 1950.[71]

The midwest was not alone in this trend. In 1950, there was one unit of housing for every five non-whites in New York City, but by 1960, there was a unit for every three non-whites. By comparison, whites had a ratio of 3.2 persons a unit in 1950, and 2.88 persons a unit by 1960.[72] Thus, Negro housing supply almost equals white housing supply in New York.

The result of Negro housing gains in the last decade is to make the claim of a Negro housing shortage a myth in many areas and a fading problem elsewhere. If these gains continue at their present rate, the alleged shortage will become fiction in a relatively short time. Like emergency rent control, anti-discrimination legislation in housing is invalid because the emergency is over, and a normal market has been established in many areas.

Thirdly, regulation is not the only way to alleviate what shortage exists. In fact, it is the least efficient. The average Negro needs a house, not a lawsuit.

States can supply housing by building public housing projects for low income Negroes who cannot afford other dwellings, by encouraging private builders to build non-white housing through tax abatement, mortgage reinsurance, and other assistance, and probably most important, by creating a business climate which encourages private building for Negroes.[73] Elimination of restric-

---

70 *Id.* at 7.

71 *Id.* at 4.

72 N.Y. Times, Dec. 31, 1961, p. 35 col. 1.

73 As proof of this, it is a real eye-opener to read the Report of the United States Commission on Civil Rights (1959), Part 4 (Housing), on Negro housing in Atlanta. The following is taken from that report, pp. 421-2:

"But even the most critical Negro spokesman, the president of the Negro real estate board, agreed that . . . it was correct to say that 'the Negro population of Atlanta is housed in more modern, decent, safe and sanitary housing in proportion to the population than are the Negroes in any city of the United States.'

. . . .

tions designed to promote integration, such as the ban on newspaper advertisements that indicate that housing is for Negroes,[74] would help, by permitting builders for Negroes to reach their market more directly.

Nevertheless, where a demand for new Negro housing exists, building for Negroes is going on.[75] A state may lend its assistance and thereby aid in actually putting up needed Negro housing instead of just adding useless laws to overcrowded statute books whose enforcement is resented when and if they can be enforced at all. These alternatives make anti-discrimination laws palpably unnecessary.

"But also in Atlanta a corridor has been opened for Negro expansion into the outlying areas and middle and upper-income Negro suburbs in the country. Mayor Hartsfield drove us through this growing area of beautiful homes, including some in the $50,000 to $100,000 class. Even more significantly, perhaps, a procedure has been devised by which the problems connected with Negro expansion can be handled through biracial negotiation.

"In 1952, the Mayor established the biracial West Side Mutual Development Committee. Its purpose was to plan an orderly development of the city's West Side, to bring about better public understanding of the problems of Negro expansion, to stabilize some of the white neighborhoods to promote a peaceable transition from white to Negro occupancy that would permit a Negro corridor to undeveloped suburban land.

"(p. 426:) there is probably more new land available for Negro housing and more construction of new houses for Negroes in Atlanta than in any other major American city. Of the units added to the Negro housing supply in the last 2 years, half are in outlying residential areas, an unusually high proportion. And of the 17,000 units added to the Negro housing supply since 1950, some 72 percent were added by construction and first occupied by Negroes. A nationally respected city planner testified that he knew 'of no other city in America of whatever size, large or small, North or South, East or West, in which a higher percentage . . . had been new construction.'

"The fact is, as the president of the Atlanta Real Estate Board stated with some pride, that the white suburban ring around Atlanta 'has been broken and large areas of land in the West Side have been opened for new Negro housing.' . . . the fact that the work of the West Side Committee has won for this development the support and approval of the organized white community, and that the expansion and improvement of Negro housing is increasingly viewed 'as a matter of pride and profit rather than as a threat,' stands as an important and perhaps a unique achievement."

74 See, e.g., N.Y. Herald Tribune, July 3, 1960 (Connecticut). The New York City Commission on Intergroup Relations, which administers the city's anti-discrimination law in housing, refuses to permit a builder to advertise new housing for Negroes, although builders "complained that Negroes were being deprived of an opportunity to find better housing because racial identification was eliminated," in order to prevent "Negroes and other minority groups (from seeking) housing in segregated areas." N.Y. Times, Aug. 30, 1959, Real Estate, Sec. 8, p. R. 1, col. 8.

75 See N.Y. Times, Oct. 17, 1958, p. 16, col. 1, which related the opening of Lenox Terrace, a 1,716 unit luxury apartment house in Harlem with units renting for about $50 a room. This "$20,000,000 apartment development, with gold braided doormen, oversized living rooms, private balconies, high rents and other luxury features" belies the assertion that anti-discrimination legislation is needed to open decent housing accommodations to Negroes who can afford to pay the market price. And see N.Y. Times, July 1, 1962, Real Estate, Sec. 8, p. R.11, col. 1, relating a $10,000,000 development of 800 Negro homes being built near Washington, D.C.

Fourthly, anti-discrimination legislation in housing is not only not calculated to restore normal bargaining conditions, but as a whole further distorts them. This is because it is both ineffectual in adding to the total Negro housing supply, and creates a number of grave, built-in administrative abuses in being enforced. To demonstrate the problem, we may once again refer to the New York experience, which has the oldest anti-discrimination commissions and laws in housing in the country.

Three years ago, this author pointed out the following facts:

> When the law [New York City anti-discrimination ordinance] first went into effect . . . the City Commission on Intergroup Relations, the administrative body charged with administration of this ordinance, received an annual appropriation of $358,050. A year later, only 27 complaints were adjusted to the satisfaction of the complainant or the Commission, for a total cost per dwelling unit obtained via the anti-discrimination law of over $13,000. With this money, the city could virtually have built each of the complainants his own apartment or house.[76]

Four years of experience has simply reinforced the above observation. During this period, the city commission's budget rose to almost a half million dollars.[77] It had 1,167 cases, but only 101 complainants eventually got apartments through the agency's efforts.[78] This averages almost $20,000 per apartment.

As can be expected in the case of a law which is highly unpopular with a large proportion of the white community,[79] all the

---

[76] Avins, *op. cit. supra* note 68, at 18, citing N.Y. Times, April 2, 1958, p. 35, col. 1; April 5, 1959, Real Estate, Sec. 8, p. R.1, col. 8. See also 1959 U.S. Civil Rights Comm. Report 403: "Chairman Abrams did not try to give a rosy picture of what had so far been accomplished. 'We're not making many gains in housing itself,' he stated candidly." Moreover, during the first 14 months of the New York City law, C.O.I.R. closed 196 complaints, of which only 49 were settled satisfactorily. Probably a significant fraction of this figure involved religious discrimination, which is easier to settle. In addition, the only relief in some cases was to put the applicant on a waiting list. The opening of a few dozen units of housing for a million Negroes hardly rises to the level of a drop in the bucket. *Id.* at 402; N.Y. Times, July 19, 1959, p. E. 7, col. 1.

[77] It was $483,215 in fiscal year 1960-1. N.Y. Times, Sept. 9, 1960, p. 1. col. 1. In fact, even its ex-chairman thought the budget should be reduced by $100,000. N.Y. Times, Sept. 12, 1960, p. 12, col. 6. This year it is $600,000. Id., May 11, 1963, p. 10, col. 7.

[78] N.Y. Times, July 1, 1962, Real Estate, Sec. 8, p. R.1, col. 8.

[79] See N.Y. Times, April 14, 1961, p. 21, col. 5, reporting that 37% of white residents surveyed in Connecticut by the State Commission on Civil Rights, three years after an anti-discrimination law in housing had gone into effect, opposed residential integration, while only 29% favored it. It might be noted further that it is likely that anti-discrimination legislation in housing is opposed by an actual majority of the population. When the New York City ordinance, the first in the country, was under consideration in the New York City Council, the mayor's office received 3,300 letters opposing

faculties of human ingenuity are brought to bear to devise ways
of evading it in a manner sufficiently subtle to leave no provable
evidence of racial discrimination.[80] Some of the techniques have
touches of humor, such as real estate salesmen fleeing from a project at the approach of a Negro family, and not returning until they
have left.[81] These techniques of evasion have brought forth more
stringent enforcement measures,[82] so that enforcement leads to
evasion, which leads to more stringent enforcement, which results
in more subtle evasion, in a never-ending cycle.

In such a situation, built-in administrative abuses are inevitable and grave. It is impossible to enforce an intensely unpopular
law without them. Such enforcement cannot be left to juries, who
may refuse to convict, or to judges, who will insist on legal standards of proof which cannot be forthcoming because of refined evasive techniques. Hence, it must be entrusted to dedicated zealots
in administrative commissions, not because the issue of whether a
person refused to sell a house to another because of race is so
complicated that a jury cannot understand it[83] or a judge would
be lost[84] and hence expertise is needed, but because only such

---

the measure and only 1,000 letters in favor of it. The mail of city councilmen ran four
to one against the measure. N.Y. Times, June 19, 1957, p. 1, col. 1. More recently, the
City of Berkeley, California, having a 20% Negro population, and in which the largest
campus of the University of California is located, voted 22,720 to 20,323 to repeal an
ordinance adopted by the city council forbidding discrimination in housing, notwithstanding the urging of the governor and speaker of the Assembly to support the law.
N.Y. Times, April 4, 1963, p. 25, col. 1.

80 N.Y. Times, March 13, 1962, p. 24, col. 1. See also N.Y. Times, June 2, 1960,
p. 27, col. 4, where the chairman of the New York City commission "conceded that . . .
the anti-bias law had not had a material effect on racial dwelling patterns." And see
N.Y. Times, Sept. 13, 1962, p. 37, col. 7: " 'Subtle and sophisticated' discrimination
against minorities has developed in New Jersey despite state laws that forbid it, the
United States Commission on Civil Rights reported here today. The observation was
made by Spottswood W. Robinson 3d, dean of the Howard University Law School, at
the closing session of a two-day public hearing by the commission. . . . Dr. Robinson
said, 'the laws have also made denials of equal protection more subtle and sophisticated
—hence, more difficult to pinpoint and correct.' "

81 Wall St. Journal, March 11, 1960, p. 17, col. 2.

82 N.Y. Times, April 5, 1962, p. 33, col. 1; Feb. 7, 1962, p. 29, col. 3; Dec. 31, 1961,
p. 1, col. 1.

83 If a jury can understand the complex financial transactions involved in many
fraud or income tax evasion cases, such as United States v. Guterma, 281 F.2d 742 (2d Cir.
1960), cert. denied, 364 U.S. 871 (1960), they can certainly understand whether a person
refused to sell a house to another because he was a Negro.

84 Courts handle many complex patent cases. See, e.g., W. M. Welch Mfg. Co. v.
Coe, 149 F.2d 12 (D.C. Cir. 1945) ("fused quartz articles"); Kistler v. Coe, 142 F.2d 94 (D.C.
Cir. 1944) ("inorganic aerogel"); Minnesota Min. & Mfg. Co. v. Coe, 33 F. Supp. 602
(D.D.C. 1940) ("isomeric rubber composition"). They could surely understand the issues
here.

commissions would be sufficiently dedicated to depart from norms of legality to accomplish their missions.

Several examples will suffice. Thus, because the New York State Commission Against Discrimination, like other commissions, practically places the burden of proof on the defendant to exculpate himself,[85] in plain violation of its statute which requires the Commission's staff or complainant to sustain this burden,[86] the complainant and staff have never lost a case for the last 18 years in a hearing before the Commission, an experience duplicated by most such commissions around the country.[87] Likewise, in *Banks v. Capitol Airlines*,[88] where complainant filed her complaint more than 90 days after the refusal to hire occurred, allegedly based on racial considerations, the Commission Against Discrimination avoided the bar of the statute of limitations by holding: "The unlawful discriminatory practices alleged and proved here are of a continuing nature."[89] However, the procedural provisions of the New York Law Against Discrimination[90] were taken from the Labor Law[91] which in turn was copied from the National Labor Relations Act,[92] a point recognized by both the Court of Appeals and the Commission's staff itself in citing N.L.R.B. cases.[93] Hence, "decisions on the National Act . . . are apposite here."[94] The timely filing of a charge is jurisdictional,[95] and all the federal cases which have passed upon almost identical contentions of a "continuing wrong" theory have rejected them.[96] Nevertheless, without

85 Note, *The Right to Equal Treatment: Administrative Enforcement of Antidiscrimination Legislation*, 74 Harv. L. Rev. 526, 553 (1961).

86 *Supra* n.64; N.Y. Executive Law, § 297.

87 *Supra* n.85 at 556.

88 5 R.R.L.R. 263 (1960).

89 *Id.* at 277.

90 N.Y. Executive Law, §§ 297, 298.

91 N.Y. Labor Law, § 707; Jeanpierre v. Arbury, 3 A.D.2d 514, 162 N.Y.S.2d 506, 513-4 (1957).

92 29 U.S.C.A. § 141 et seq. Metropolitan Life Co. v. N.Y. State Labor Relations Bd., 280 N.Y. 194, 20 N.E.2d 390, 391-2 (1959).

93 Holland v. Edwards, 307 N.Y. 38, 45, 119 N.E.2d 581, 583-4 (1954); Memorandum of Law of N.Y.S. Commission Against Discrimination, filed Nov. 26, 1957, in opposition to motion for intervention, p. 4, in N.Y.S. Comm. Against Discrimination v. Pelham Hall Apts., 10 Misc. 2d 346, 171 N.Y.S.2d 558 (1958).

94 N.Y.S. Labor Relations Bd. v. Interborough News Co., 170 Misc. 347, 10 N.Y.S.2d 396, 399 (1939).

95 N.L.R.B. v. National Licorice Co., 104 F.2d 655 (2d Cir. 1939), *aff'd*, 309 U.S. 350 (1940); N.L.R.B. v. Hopwood Retinning Co., 98 F.2d 97 (2d Cir. 1938).

96 N.L.R.B. v. Textile Machine Works, 214 F.2d 929 (3d Cir. 1954); American Federation of Grain Millers, A.F.L. v. N.L.R.B., 197 F.2d 451, 454 (5th Cir. 1952);

even bothering to mention these cases, the Commission simply evaded its own statute to achieve a desired result.

Another example of glaring administrative abuse is found in the New York City ordinance, which now permits the city's commission to obtain an injunction against the rental or sale of any housing which a complainant wants merely upon the filing of his complaint and without giving the property owner a hearing on the alleged discrimination. This was designed to prevent the owner from disposing of the property during investigation.[97] Under this power, the commission has sought an injunction in at least one case of alleged discrimination against a Negro couple although the building already had other Negro families living in it.[98] In another case, the commission sought an injunction because a landlord desired to evict a colored superintendent living rent-free in the apartment who refused to perform his duties, and refused to rent him another apartment.[99] In still a third case, after the commission obtained an injunction, the apartment was offered to the Negro complainant, who refused the lease and said that he could not afford the rent. No compensation for loss of rent was paid to the landlord.[100]

The short of the matter is that anti-discrimination legislation in practice is a grave infringement on property rights, subject in administration to incurable abuses, and most important, helps only the Negroes who do not need it. The fallacy that these laws have something to do with good housing, carefully nurtured by their proponents, is but a mask behind which parades compulsory integration. It is clear that the cry of good housing for Negroes urged in justification of anti-discrimination legislation in housing is a fraudulent sham paraded before the public and a tragic deception of the many Negroes whose need for good housing is real

---

N.L.R.B. v. Childs Co., 195 F.2d 617, 621 (2d Cir. 1952); N.L.R.B. v. Pennwoven, 194 F.2d 521, 524-5 (3d Cir. 1952). See also N.L.R.B. v. Newton, 214 F.2d 472, 473-5 (5th Cir. 1954); N.L.R.B. v. Vare, 206 F.2d 543 (3d Cir. 1953); Joanna Cotton Mills v. N.L.R.B., 176 F.2d 749, 754 (4th Cir. 1949).

97 N.Y. Times, April 5, 1962, p. 33, col. 1.

98 N.Y. Times, Aug. 28, 1962, p. 10, col. 4. And see N.Y. Times, Nov. 19, 1962, p. 29, col. 6, where the commission sustained a charge of discrimination against a Negro couple although several Negro families were living in the building.

99 N.Y. Daily News, Oct. 16, 1962, p. B3, col. 1.

100 N.Y. Times, June 21, 1962, p. 27, col. 2.

and present and for whom such legislation raises but a mirage which vanishes as they approach it. Were a fraction of the energy, money, and effort now devoted to battling with unwilling landlords and hostile tenants turned to a solution of the Negro's housing problem in terms of real need, viz., good housing at a price he can afford, the problem of festering colored slums in such cities as New York City would be well on the way to solution. As it is, New York City vainly struggles to keep an ever-widening portion of its dwellings from falling into slum conditions[101] because of the reluctance of landlords in Negro or fringe areas to put money into their houses[102] while devoting prime attention to miniscule integration which hardly makes a dent in the Negro housing problem. The enactment of ever more stringent anti-discrimination legislation in housing is unquestionably the great panacea, and the most widespread delusion of this century. Compared to this, Prohibition of liquor was the quintessence of far-sighted statesmanship.

IV. *Compulsory Integration and Freedom of Choice*

A. Integration as the Motivation for Anti-Discrimination Laws

Notwithstanding the dubious effect which anti-discrimination laws have on the Negro housing market, proponents of such legislation have hoisted the "property rights versus human rights" banner to their masthead to push such legislation,[103] and have depicted this problem in terms of the dry legal insistence of the

---

101 Between 1950 and 1960, according to census figures, Chicago reduced the number of its substandard units of housing from 246,251 to 169,664. Thus, in 1950, 22% of the housing was substandard; by 1960, only 14% was so classified. Research Section, Chicago Dept. of Urban Renewal, *Housing Quality; Condition and Plumbing Facilities, City of Chicago, by Community Area,* 1950-1960 (mimeograph, May 1962). In New York City, by contrast, in 1950 there were only 335,295 substandard units of housing; in 1960 there were 553,527 such units, according to census figures. In 1950, less than 15% of all the units fell into this category; by 1960, more than 20% did, although the total number of units in the city rose by about 300,000. N.Y. Times, Jan. 1, 1962, p. 23, col. 1.

102 It might be noted that some of the worst slum landlords in Negro sections are wealthy Negroes who are the very people crying the loudest for anti-discrimination laws to cure the Negro slum problem. Thus, not long ago, Sugar Ray Robinson, the Negro boxer, was fined for nine building code violations on a tenement in Harlem which he owned. N.Y. Times, Nov. 21, 1957, p. 28, col. 8. And recently, Roy Campanella, the former Negro baseball player, received a summons when he failed to answer charges of twenty-one violations on a tenement he owned in Harlem. N.Y. Times, Dec. 4, 1959, p. 26, col. 6. See also N.Y. Times, April 9, 1960, p. 34, col. 2 (N.Y.C. Negro Welfare Investigator owns tenement with 60 violations.)

103 See, e.g., Scanlan, *Racial Restrictions in Real Estate—Property Values Versus Human Values,* 24 Notre Dame Law. 157 (1949).

mythical landlord in clutching to the last ounce of his legal rights by whimsically, so we are told, refusing to rent an apartment to a deserving colored couple.[104] Indeed, Russian caricatures of American capitalists, relabeled "landlord," would approximate the representations drawn of property owners on the defensive.

But the asserted justification for these laws as good housing laws cannot stand close scrutiny because it is not in fact their true motivating reason, but only their ostensible excuse. It is well settled that the courts may examine the true legislative purpose behind a statute, and declare it unconstitutional based on its true purpose, regardless of its ostensible purpose.[105] The evidence is overwhelming that anti-discrimination laws in housing are motivated by the desire to promote compulsory integration.

The attitude of leading Negro proponents of anti-discrimination legislation[106] and of Negro organizations against proposals for

104 Kozol, *The Massachusetts Fair Housing Practices Law*, 47 Mass. L.Q. 295, 304 (1962). See also Note, 107 U. Pa. L. Rev. 515, 527 (1959).

105 Coulter v. Pool, 187 Cal. 181, 183, 201 Pac. 120, 122 (1921): "a legislative declaration, whether contained in the title or in the body of a statute, that the statute was intended to promote a certain purpose, is not conclusive on the courts, and they may and must inquire into the real as distinguished from the ostensible, purpose of the statute, and determine the fact whether, after all has been said and done by the Legislature, the statute, in its scope and effect, departs from the declared legislative design and contravenes the fundamental and supreme law of the state." Accord: Mugler v. Kansas, 123 U.S. 623, 661 (1887); Matter of Jacobs, 98 N.Y. 98, 110 (1885); State v. Redmond, 134 Wis. 89, 108, 114 N.W. 137, 141 (1907). Moreover, "in construing a statute which is alleged to be unconstitutional, it should be scrutinized very carefully, and no matter what its form, if its true purpose and probable effect is to violate a constitutional provision, it will be held void." Caldwell v. Board of Regents, 54 Ariz. 404, 406, 96 P.2d 401, 403 (1939). Thus, "constitutional provisions . . . cannot be evaded by any legislation which, though not in terms trespassing on the letter, yet in substance and effect destroy the grant or limitation." Fairbank v. United States, 181 U.S. 283, 300 (1901); Macallen Co. v. Massachusetts, 279 U.S. 620, 629 (1929).

106 Indicative of this is the attitude of Robert Weaver, U.S. Housing and Home Administrator and former Rent Administrator in New York, whose writing is often cited to show that anti-discrimination legislation is needed to assure good housing to Negroes. See, e.g., Note, *Race Discrimination in Housing*, 57 Yale L.J. 426 (1958), n.4, 6, 23, 24, 25, 29, 67; *Special Issue on Integration in Housing*, 18 Law. Guild Rev., No. 1, at 5, 20, n. 1, p. 21, n. 17, p. 22, n. 27, 29, 32 (1958); Note, *Is There a Civil Right to Housing Accommodations?* 33 Notre Dame Law. 463, 486, n.108 (1958); Comment, *Application of the Sherman Act to Housing Segregation*, 63 Yale L.J. 1124, n.1, p. 1126, n.11, p. 1127, n.26, p. 1129, n.33, p. 1130, n.39, p. 1138, n.77, 79, p. 1141, n.93, 97, 98, 99, p. 1142, n.107, p. 1143, n.111 (1954). Speaking before the NAACP's fiftieth annual convention, Weaver rejected the suggestion of cooperation with persons seeking improved Negro housing on a non-integrated basis. N.Y. Times, July 15, 1959, p. 13, col. 1. So too, the Urban League has opposed low-rent slum clearance housing projects in Harlem unless white tenants can be persuaded to come. N.Y. Times, Feb. 23, 1958, p. R.1, col. 8, commented on Note, 33 Notre Dame Law. 463, 481, n.83 (1958). See also N.Y. Times, June 8, 1962, p. 33, col. 8 (Harlem Negro leaders don't want more low-rent housing).

good Negro housing unless it was integrated[107] is well known. Their willingness to sacrifice housing for integration is a matter of record.[108] However, probably the most significant evidence that anti-discrimination legislation is really designed to promote integration comes from New York, which had instituted integration policies in housing at the time such legislation was passed, and pursues them with a single-minded purpose. The evidence of such policies is so strong that it would be worthwhile to review it in detail.

Early in 1958, right after the city's anti-discrimination ordinance had been passed, a 1,940-unit housing project was built in Harlem. "Every effort was made to persuade eligible white families to apply . . . but . . . only 142 (a scant 7.3 per cent) have white

[107] See, from the 1959 U.S. Civil Rights Commission's Report, pp. 508-9:

"In 1954 the National Association of Home Builders announced a program to build 150,000 dwelling units annually for minority groups. Each local builders' association throughout the country was urged to adopt a community goal and 'start an aggressive campaign and effective production program to improve the housing conditions of minority groups in their own community.'

"Negro spokesmen generally opposed this program for 'minority housing.' 'We do not want jim-crow dwellings whether they are new or old,' the annual conference of the NAACP resolved, adding specifically: 'We condemn and oppose the policy advocated by the National Association of Home Builders for planned housing developments directed toward any specific minority group on the basis of race, color, national origin, or religion.' The National Urban League also announced that it was 'opposed to and unwilling to support or assist in the construction of segregated privately financed housing.'

. . . .

"Most private construction of new housing for Negroes has taken place in the South, where many Negro leaders have gone along with the concept of 'minority housing.'"

See also N.Y. Times, June 20, 1961, p. 35, col. 8, where Negro residents of Lakeview, Long Island, discouraged other Negroes from buying homes in a mixed area by putting up signs saying: "Negroes: your purchase of a home in this neighborhood is your contribution to segregation." For similar signs in Teaneck, N.J., see N.Y. Times, Nov. 26, 1961, p. 148, col. 3; Aug. 10, 1962, p. 6, col. 5; Long Island, March 19, 1962, p. 42, col. 3.

[108] In Chicago, as of Jan. 1, 1959, 85% of the tenants of public low rent housing were Negro, 13% were white, and 2% were Puerto Rican, largely because a very high proportion of the projects were located in Negro areas, and "low income white families . . . could not be expected to flock to projects in all-Negro neighborhoods." The Chicago Housing Authority selected these sites "reluctantly, because of the opposition and delays that might occur if sites were selected in white areas . . . . locating the projects in the Negro slums was 'expeditious right now to get the thing done.' There were 20,000 families with children in substandard conditions waiting for public housing [the Executive Director] said. 'Our prime consideration is better housing for these kids,' he said. The Authority had to get a project in 'where we can get it in the fastest,' rather than get into any long-drawn-out controversy about where sites shall be or shall not be.

"Not all Negroes appreciate this discrimination in their favor, at the price of accentuating the pattern of segregation. Rev. A. Lincoln James of the Greater Bethesda Baptist Church, a member of the Civil Rights Commission's Illinois State Advisory Committee, suggested to Mr. Rose that because of this policy of site selection 'the Council of Chicago is guilty of practicing to a certain degree segregated housing.'" 1959 U.S. Civil Rts. Comm. Rept. 438-9.

tenants."[109] In addition the New York City Housing Authority is "making a special effort to inform white families and solicit their applications" because of their refusals to apply for integrated public housing.[110]

Moreover, the New York City Housing Authority admitted keeping an average of at least 65 apartments in public housing in Negro areas vacant rather than rent them to waiting Negroes in order to obtain whites to better integrate them. This resulted in a rental loss, in one reported project alone, of $115,000 in less than a year.[111] Refusal to rent to needy Negro tenants to promote integration in Negro areas became so widespread that the New York State Commission Against Discrimination was provoked by the complaints of a number of Negro families to investigate the situation.[112] The Commission described one such situation as follows:

> A Negro woman lives with her two children in a Staten Island project. She travels each day to her job in upper Manhattan [a two hour ride each way]. To save money and spend more time with her children—reasons the authority would ordinarily accept—she asks to be transferred to a project near her job. She is turned down because she is a Negro and the available units are being held for whites to improve integration at the project.[113]

It was further reported:

> Housing authority officials have conceded that advantages might be given to members of one racial group over those of another in renting a particular apartment in a particular project. But, they have argued, without this policy, projects in certain areas would be tenanted predominately by members of one racial group. . . . "Our program . . ." William Reid, chairman of the Authority, said . . . ". . . is a positive program designed to . . . bring about true integration."[114]

---

109 N.Y. Times, Feb. 23, 1958, Real Estate, Sec. 8, p. R.1, col. 8.

110 N.Y. Times, Nov. 19, 1959, p. 24, col. 5. In an area "cleared for luxury housing in Manhattan, sixteen families eligible for three-bedroom apartments in public housing declined to apply . . . . They had eviction papers in their hands, but not one would take public housing." *Ibid.*

111 N.Y. Times, Aug. 29, 1960, p. 39, col. 1. New York City is not alone in this policy. Greenberg, *Race Relations and American Law* 292 (1959) states: "New Haven and other cities have to some extent followed an affirmative integration policy, based on a quota system, sometimes withholding vacant apartments from Negroes while waiting for white applicants." See N.Y. Times, April 21, 1963, p. 80, col. 3.

112 N.Y. Times, Sept. 28, 1960, p. 31, col. 2; Sept. 24, 1960, p. 22, col. 2; Sept. 21, 1960, p. 24, col. 1, p. 30, col. 5; Sept. 18, 1960, p. 1, col. 2.

113 N.Y. Times, Jan. 7, 1961, p. 1, col. 1, p. 8, col. 6.

114 N.Y. Times, Sept. 18, 1960, p. 1, col. 2, p. 40, col. 1. Other similar examples occur. Negroes were moved out of a low-income, all-Negro housing project in Buffalo, New

Another technique used by the Housing Authority is the selection of sites in white areas for projects so as to promote integration.[115] This is in accord with a New York State Housing Division requirement that all urban renewal projects be located so as to promote integration.[116] Of course, site selection to promote integration has resulted in vigorous white opposition on the part of residents in the area of the proposed project and consequent delays in building the projects.[117] Indeed, the United States Commissioner of Public Housing told a Senate subcommittee that "many communities are reluctant to begin new public housing projects because of requirements that they be racially integrated" and "integration is the cause of a wide gap between the nation's need for public housing and the requests for projects by cities."[118]

With all of this effort, 2,000 units in the New York City Housing Authority's middle-income cooperatives remained unsold because many whites who could afford them "do not want to live

York, to convert it into a middle-income, cooperative apartment house. N.Y. Times, Jan. 8, 1960, p. 11, col. 3. And a Negro engineer was forced to sue recently in Connecticut to get into an integrated housing development because of a refusal to sell to him based on the belief that the project would lose its racial "balance." N.Y. Times, Dec. 24, 1961, p. 39, col. 5; Nov. 5, 1961, p. 9, col. 5; Nov. 2, 1961, p. 33, col. 3.

115 N.Y. Times, July 5, 1959, p. 1, col. 4. And see the statement of Authority member Ira S. Robbins that "the Housing Authority was seeking to promote integration by situating new public housing in openland areas or in racially mixed neighborhoods." N.Y. Times, Feb. 19, 1959, p. 18, col. 1. Likewise, 1959 U.S. Civil Rights Comm. Rept. 406 observes: "The public housing projects operated by the New York City Housing Authority have been a major testing ground for the city's policy of integration." The Report adds at pp. 407-8: ". . . one of the first acts of the . . . Housing Authority after [its creation] . . . was to . . . [appoint] a consultant on race relations in order to help restore integrated occupancy. . . . In addition, the members of the New York Authority intend to promote integrated housing projects by the selection of sites in areas conducive to integration. . . . Moreover, to win public understanding and support of this program for true housing integration, the authority has started a community relations program under the direction of its new race relations consultant." See also the statements of Manhattan's Borough President urging such site selection. N.Y. Times, April 23, 1962, p. 3, col. 8; April 13, 1962, p. 31, col. 1.

116 N.Y. Times, Aug. 30, 1962, p. 17, col. 6; June 2, 1962, p. 21, col. 8.

117 N.Y. Times, Aug. 24, 1962, p. 1, col. 2. See also N.Y. Times, Sept. 9, 1962, p. 73, col. 2: "The new state regulation [requiring public housing site selection to promote integration] caused wide dismay among local urban renewal directors. . . . One of them . . . said: '. . . it's tough enough just to find relocation housing. But now, when you've got to prove integration too, it's hopeless. Most communities just aren't ready for open occupancy.' "

118 N.Y. Times, May 10, 1960, p. 1, col. 5. The same report is found in 1961 U.S. Civil Rights Comm. Report 113 (Book 4, Housing). It is ironic to find U.S. Housing and Home Finance Agency Administrator Robert C. Weaver deploring the drop in housing construction, N.Y. Times, March 3, 1961, p. 41, col. 3, and yet insisting on integration, the prime cause of this decline. *Supra* n.106; N.Y. Times, Oct. 18, 1961, p. 35, col. 1.

in integrated buildings," and banks therefore will not finance them.[119] Moreover, in 1961 the Authority "discontinued its practice of giving applicants the opportunity to specify which development they wanted to live in," so that it could dictate where the tenant shall live to promote integration.[120]

The decent housing for Negroes sacrificed on the altar of integration by the New York City Housing Authority represents many times the 101 apartments obtained in the last four years through the coercive processes of the city's anti-discrimination law. Yet the Commission on Intergroup Relations, which administers the law, praised the Authority for "its efforts to reduce concentrations of Negro and Puerto Rican families"[121] and called for still more "integrated" neighborhoods.[122] Thus, between 1950 and 1960, Chicago, which has no anti-discrimination law in housing or affirmative public housing integration policy,[123] reduced its inventory of substandard housing by about one third.[124] Many midwestern cities made similar strides.[125] However, New York City, with its integration policy, increased, not reduced, its supply of substandard housing by about two-thirds in the same period.[126] While some of this can be traced to rent control, no doubt a substantial share of the credit for slum formation must go to integration. And since a disproportionately large share of low income Negroes live in slums in New York City,[127] as they do elsewhere in the country,[128] the burden of slum formation falls most heavily

119 N.Y. Times, Sept. 26, 1961, p. 48, col. 3.

120 N.Y. Times, March 24, 1962, p. 24, col. 2. In spite of integration in the houses, tenants still segregate themselves. The Authority chairman declared: "We would like to break down the tendency of those in each [ethnic] group to associate only with their own kind." N.Y. Times, Dec. 26, 1961, p. 27, col. 4.

121 N.Y. Times, April 30, 1961, p. 62, col. 6.

122 N.Y. Times, April 16, 1961, p. 74, col. 5. See also the statement of the Philadelphia Commission on Human Relations urging Negroes to move into white neighborhoods. N.Y. Times, March 6, 1960, p. 49, col. 1.

123 *Supra* n.108.

124 *Supra* n.101.

125 *Midwest Minority Housing Markets*, 2-3, 25 (Special Report by Advance Mortgage Corp., Dec. 1, 1962). In addition to Chicago, Cincinnati, Cleveland, Columbus, Dayton, Detroit, Grand Rapids, Indianapolis, Milwaukee, and Pittsburgh all reduced the percentage of substandard housing for both whites and Negroes, both owner and renter-occupied, between 1950 and 1960. However, Pittsburgh, which has an anti-discrimination ordinance, had the smallest reduction.

126 *Supra* n.101.

127 N.Y. Times, Dec. 31, 1961, p. 35, col. 1.

128 N.Y. Times, March 23, 1961, p. 26, col. 6.

on them. Thus, the price of miniscule integration in New York City has been to condemn a progressively larger proportion of low income Negroes to slum habitation. Those courts which have assumed that anti-discrimination legislation will promote better housing for most Negroes, or is designed to do so,[129] are simply living in a dream world.

A lower court New York judge who upheld the constitutionality of the New York City law was at least more candid and realistic about its purpose. He stated: "It is now believed that many of our problems arising from the diverse nature of our population will be brought nearer solution by integration."[130] Accordingly, we may ignore the question of Negro housing and turn to the constitutionality of compulsory integration *per se*.

B. Compulsory Integration as a Negation of Freedom of Choice

The notion that government can subject people to experiences such as integration to vaccinate them with ideas like it can vaccinate them with medicine[131] must seem a little raw even to the most devoted adherents of an all-powerful state. True, mass brainwashing is not unknown in modern times. In varying degrees, it has been used, and sometimes with remarkable success, in Nazi Germany, Fascist Italy, Communist Russia, and Communist China. But such seeds seem unable to flourish in the soil of non-totalitarian states, where many people are of the view that government has no business meddling with what is in the minds of people.

In a democracy, people make up their own minds. It is a basic premise that "freedom of the individual in and under a democracy has implicit in it, as an absolute, the freedom of association."[132] The right to individual and uncoerced freedom of choice and association, including the right of the individual to decline to associate with another, is an individual right, a natural right, a human right, and a civil right, and such right to choose to asso-

129 *Supra* n.62.
130 Martin v. City of New York, *supra* n.22. As 1959 U.S. Civil Rts. Comm. Rept. 365 pointed out: "In New York . . . there is an established city and state policy to promote integration."
131 Cf. Jacobson v. Massachusetts, 197 U.S. 11 (1905).
132 Re Noble & Wolfe, [1949] 4 D.L.R. 375, 391. Even in the army, with its strict discipline and relative lack of privacy, this right has attained at least implicit recognition. CM 307107, Hart, 60 BR 247 (1946).

ciate or decline to associate extends to ethnic grounds. This un-coerced individual right to choose to associate or decline to asso-ciate based on ethnic grounds is basic to a free society, and its denial threatens not only the rights and proper privileges of the individual, but menaces the institutions and foundations of a free society, and tends to the creation of a totalitarian society devoid of the right of the individual to freely choose with whom he shall associate.[133] This right is not only compatible and consistent with the basic equality of all persons before the law in a democratic state, but as an expression of the right of the individual to freedom of choice in a free society, it is a facet of the dignity of the indi-vidual and thus an indispensible prerequisite to full equality in such society. As a Canadian court declared:

> I do know that in thousands of ways there exist restrictions which have always existed, and always will continue to exist, by which people are enabled to exercise a choice with respect to their friends and neighbours.[134]

When faced with the fact that anti-discrimination legislation collides head-on with freedom of choice, advocates of compulsory integration lose their glib self-assurance and begin to equivocate by trying to find excuses as to why such rights should not be con-sidered. These excuses, examined seriatim, are hardly convincing.

---

133 Cf. Black, *They Cannot Choose But Hear*, 53 Col. L. Rev. 960 (1953). Several recent decisions have recognized this right. See, e.g., City of Montgomery v. Gilmore, 277 F.2d 364, 369 (5th Cir. 1960), where the court referred to the "right of each person to select his own associates," and declared: "In their private affairs, in the conduct of their private businesses, it is clear that the people themselves have the liberty to select their own associates and the persons with whom they will do business, unimpaired by the Fourteenth Amendment. . . . Indeed, we think that such liberty is guaranteed by the due process clause of that Amendment." In Pettit v. Board of Education, 184 F. Supp. 452, 457 (D. Md. 1960), the court observed: "The people of Maryland believe in such freedom of choice." See too, State v. Board of Trustees, 126 Ohio St. 290, 185 N.E. 196 (1933). Even commentators favoring such legislation admit the existence of the right. Van Alstyne & Karst, *State Action*, 14 Stan. L. Rev. 3, 48 (1961) say: "Of course, the interest in non-association is legitimate; of course, it is relevant, and it cannot be ignored." They add: "But when the state action issue is raised in the case of a single homeowner who wishes to exclude Negroes from his property, the balance of constitutionally protected interests may properly be found to have shifted to the side of privacy, and the private control of property." Likewise, Henkin, Shelley v. Kraemer: *Notes for a Revised Opinion*, 110 U. Pa. L. Rev. 473, 498 (1962) says: "For the state, then, to decree that one may not bar Catholics, or redheaded persons, or even Negroes from his home would, I believe, be a violation of rights of privacy—of free association and nonassociation—under the four-teenth amendment." This author thinks that the right is much broader than they do.

134 Re Noble & Wolf, *supra* n.132, at 389. See this author's previous remarks in Avins, *Trade Regulations (Compulsory Housing Integration Law)*, 12 Rutgers L. Rev. 149, 157 (1957).

The first such argument is moral preachment. A recent case declared:

> The private ownership of private property free of unreasonable restriction upon the control thereof, is truly a part of our way of life, but, on the other hand, we, as a people do hold firmly to the philosophy that all men are created equal. Indeed, discrimination against any individual here on account of race, color, or religion is antagonistic to fundamental tenets of our form of government and of the God in who we place our trust.[135]

It is clear that the only antidote to such a visceral reaction is a theological brief. Research of old cases is only a fruitless road to unnecessary eyestrain. The possibility that government could enact through penal sanctions whom one shall associate with or talk to is just as absurd as the notion that it could enforce through positive law good table manners or the Boy Scout Code. The intrusion of particular sectarian religious doctrines into the statute books which the above case would sanction is an alarming innovation for a nation of such diverse customs, ideas, and ideals.

The second theory, advanced in the same case, is equally unsatisfactory. Faced with the unquestioned fact that a majority of tenants in the house did not want a Negro co-tenant,[136] the court simply held that tenants were not interested in the matter at all.[137] This is pure fantasy.[138] The new tenant is there in the house; other tenants must see him in the elevator and listen to him when tenants' meetings are called to discuss common problems. Ten-

[135] N.Y. State Comm. Against Disc. v. Pelham Hall Apts., Inc., 10 Misc. 2d 334, 341, 170 N.Y.S.2d 750, 757 (1958).

[136] See New Rochelle Standard Star, Nov. 26, 1957, p. 1, col. 1. The existence of this majority was confirmed by the General Counsel of the State Commission Against Discrimination in open court.

[137] *Supra* n. 135, 10 Misc. 2d 346, 171 N.Y.S.2d 558. The procedural aspects of this problem are interesting. In this case, the court held that tenants were not "aggrieved" or legally interested in the order issued to the landlord to rent to a Negro. Moreover, in Mass. Comm. Against Disc. v. Colangelo, *supra* n.62 at 598, the court held that "whatever may be said of the right of a home owner freely to choose his neighbors or to rent only to persons of his choice," the landlord "lacks standing to raise" these rights because "he is not being compelled to live near anyone by the commission's order." However, in American Jewish Congress v. Carter, 19 Misc. 2d 205, 23 Misc. 2d 446, 190 N.Y.S.2d 218 (1959) mod. 10 A.D.2d 833, 199 N.Y.S.2d 157 (1960) *aff'd*, 9 N.Y.2d 223, 173 N.E.2d 788, 213 N.Y.S.2d 60 (1961), the court held that outside non-profit organizations were aggrieved by the order of the Commission. Thus, while neither tenants nor landlords can raise the infringement on freedom of choice, outside groups having no personal interest in the matter can. This is simply another example of the Alice-in-Wonderland quality of anti-discrimination legislation enforcement.

[138] See Lustgarten v. 36 C.P.S., Inc., 101 N.Y.S.2d 709 (1950). Cf. Wyatt v. Adair, 215 Ala. 363, 110 So. 801 (1927); Hannan v. Harper, 189 Wis. 588, 208 N.W. 255 (1926).

ants' wives will see his wife. Other tenants will hear him entertain friends, argue with his wife, scold his children, and play television or the radio. Perhaps most significant of all, it is almost impossible to stop one's own children from playing with his children. In short, while he may not be physically in one's apartment, his voice, habits, manners, ideas, mode of life, and whole cultural matrix come with him and do in fact affect his fellow residents.[139]

Of course, when an unwelcome neighbor moves in close proximity, other residents who cannot leave can and do try to isolate themselves from the intruder.[140] But in light of the use of common neighborhood facilities, such as churches, schools, recreational facilities, and the like, success is sometimes problematical. At any rate, his presence means that someone of the same ethnic group cannot occupy that space, and the resident is thus deprived of a family he would like to associate with.

The actions of residents themselves are frequently what motivates a landlord to discriminate,[141] by threatening not to lease as tenants or purchase as buyers. That their motive is primarily personal, rather than financial, is shown by their reactions when being forced to integrate. It cannot be seriously contended that they care whether property values go up, down, or sideways that much when Negroes move in. If people who lost their whole life savings during the 1929 crash and subsequent depression did not riot in

---

139 See generally, Conn. Comm. on Civil Rights, *Racial Integration in Public Housing Projects in Connecticut* (1955). See also the statement of Ira S. Robbins, Member of the New York City Housing Authority, urging tenants to tell landlords not to discriminate. "Mr. Robbins said that such 'landlord education' would probably open more private housing to members of minority groups than would a sudden and wholesale enforcement campaign." N.Y. Times, Feb. 19, 1959, p. 18, col. 1. See also N.Y. Times, June 8, 1958, Real Estate, Sec. 8, p. R. 1, col. 2 (effect of habits of one tenant on others).

140 See Conn. Comm. on Civil Rights, *Private Interracial Neighborhoods in Connecticut* 22-7 (1957).

141 In happy contrast to the New York City Housing Authority's coercive policy is that of the Atlantic City, New Jersey, Housing Authority in rejecting a local branch N.A.A.C.P. demand that the authority integrate three low-income projects because "the occupants wanted the projects as they were. 'The authority cannot force integration against the rights and will of the people to live where they choose,' it said . . . . The authority acknowledged that two of the projects are occupied entirely by whites and the other entirely by Negroes. The statement said that this was 'entirely as a result of the will of the applicant.' The authority said the N.A.A.C.P. 'had asked that the authority arbitrarily place tenants without regard to the express choice of the tenant.' Such action 'would be most undemocratic and expressly opposite of what N.A.A.C.P. contended for, which is the right of each family to live in the neighborhood of their own choosing.' . . ." N.Y. Times, Oct. 2, 1962, p. 38, col. 6.

the streets, how can it be contended that the Levittown, Pennsylvania, or Cicero, Illinois riots[142] were caused by the problematical and infinitesimal decline of real estate values because one Negro moved into a city of 15,000 people? Indeed, Chicago's Trumbull Park rioting,[143] and the rent strike recently called by British tenants of a public housing project to protest the moving in of a Pakistani family,[144] hardly stemmed from any concern by tenants, traditionally at odds with landlords over financial matters, that the public housing property would decline in value. Indeed, a recognition of the personal relationships created by integrated housing is the only possible motive for many Negroes themselves to refuse to move into integrated neighborhoods.[145]

Another line of attack is the assertion that the exercise of freedom of choice so as to discriminate based on ethnic grounds

142 N.Y. Times, Aug. 15, 1957, p. 15, col. 2; Aug. 16, 1957, p. 10, col. 5; Aug. 18, 1957, p. 73, col. 5 (Levittown, Pa.); Abrams, *Forbidden Neighbors* 103-119 (1955) (Cicero and Trumbull Park).

143 *Ibid.*

144 N.Y. Times, July 29, 1961, p. 6, col. 2; July 25, 1961, p. 7, col. 3.

145 See N.Y. Times, Dec. 5, 1961, p. 39, col. 1 (despite a listing of over 100 homes for sale in white neighborhoods in Long Island, New York, by an integrationist group, "few Negroes have shown interest in them"); Oct. 15, 1959, p. 35, col. 1 ("reluctance of Negroes to move into communities recently 'opened' to them by antidiscrimination legislation"). And see 1959 U.S. Civil Rights Comm. Rept:

p. 365: "Thus, the pattern of racial concentration is in part voluntary. As the executive secretary of the National Association for the Advancement of Colored People testified, there are 'colored people in Harlem who wouldn't move out of Harlem if you gave them a gold-plated apartment.' Jewish enclaves remain on the lower East Side, and there is a German concentration in Yorkville, even though others of these groups have dispersed throughout New York City."

p. 381 (California Advisory Committee Report): "Perhaps one important reason [for the concentration of minority groups] is the existence of cultural ties which create a preference on their part for living with persons of their own racial or national origins."

p. 382 (Colorado Advisory Committee Report): "Minority group members must be educated against the gregarious tendency which permits the finger to be pointed, indicating that they like to live together and are unhappy elsewhere."

p. 382 (Massachusetts Advisory Committee Report): "A survey by the Boston Urban League found only two out of 400 nonwhite families willing to move into white areas."

p. 382. (Oregon Advisory Committee Report): ". . . . an apparent reluctance on the part of many Negroes to break away from the Negro neighborhoods where their friends are and where they feel more secure."

p. 383 (Washington Advisory Committee Report): "Choice is a factor in the nonwhite's continuing to live in his present situation. Some are reluctant to live among persons of differing ethnic background."

p. 385 (Summary by the Governor of Oregon): "Partly, this concentration [of minority groups] is due to the desire for fellowship among people of their own group."

For those Negroes who desire homogeneous neighborhoods, compulsory integration violates their rights also. See the protest of a group of 82 Negro residents who opposed having a white family move into their neighborhood. N.Y. Times, Sept. 5, 1959, p. 17, col. 7.

lacks a rational basis. To begin with, this contention is irrelevant. It is no more persuasive than would be the contention that freedom of religion should be abolished unless the worshiper could scientifically demonstrate that his mode of worship had a rational foundation, or that freedom of speech should be eliminated unless the speaker could first prove that his thoughts should be heard, or that the right to listen to the radio station which one wants should not be permitted unless the hearer can demonstrate that he has good taste, or the right to choose one's friends should be curtailed unless the person can show that his choice is rational as a matter of social science. The transferring of choice from the individual to government in the realm of personality is the essence of a totalitarian police state.

However, ethnic distinctions are not always irrational.[146] American society today is a multi-cultural society, composed of numerous racial, religious, cultural, and ethnic groups. Not only has the immigration of such groups contributed to American culture, but the continuation of such subcultural patterns and groups makes a continuing contribution both to the development of the individual members of the groups and to the society as a whole, and the very diversity of these groups is a substantial benefit to American society.[147] Hence, the maintenance of the above groups

146 1959 U.S. Commission on Civil Rights Report 376: "This does not mean that Negroes are barred only because of race prejudice. Many people in established residential areas no doubt fear and resist the arrival of low-income migrants because of what they regard as the low cultural and social standards of the newcomers. In the Back-of-the-Yards area of Chicago, for instance, the predominantly Central European Roman Catholic residents are said to view not only the intrusion of Negroes but of white Protestants or even Irish Catholics as a threat to the homogeneity of the community.
"It may be that the presence of a small number of such outsiders would be acceptable, but what is feared is inundation. The first newcomers might be upper-class members of their group, otherwise acceptable in terms of cultural and social standards, but their arrival would be viewed as the opening of the dike to the lower class majority, walled in the central city areas."
147 As Justice Frankfurter observed in Hughes v. Superior Court, 339 U.S. 460, 464 (1950), "The differences in cultural traditions . . . [add] flavor and variety to our common citizenry." Compare this with Myrdal's theory of abandonment of subcultural patterns which runs like a dominant thread throughout his writing. Myrdal, *The American Dilemma*, 927 et seq. (1944). See also N.Y. Times, Sept. 9, 1962, p. 123, col. 1 ("San Francisco Negroes Press Pride of Race in Its Heritage"); May 29, 1962, p. 20, col. 2 ("2 visitors decry U.S. 'melting pot'—Special effort should be made to preserve the culture and language of Puerto Rican children living in the United States, two visiting educators from the island urged yesterday"); May 15, 1962, p. 48, col. 1 ("immigrants [to Canada] urged to retain culture"); Jan. 21, 1962, p. 15, col. 1 (world Jewish assembly to combat "assimilation"); June 11, 1961, p. 78, col. 1 ("The head of the Zionist Organization of America said . . . that assimilation was 'the greatest peril to Jewish survival,'

and their continuing development is a value which both the individual members thereof and a democratic society as a whole has an interest in preserving.

Since ethnic differences are beneficial, their perpetuation is likewise a rational value. But subcultural groups cannot perpetuate those differences in the face of the general tendency to amalgamate and lose them unless these different heritages are institutionalized and instilled into both children and adults alike through numerous reinforcing techniques. And a most powerful technique for instilling feeling for subcultural values is to reverse the cause of the loss of such values, viz., by the association of group members with persons in other groups, and to reinforce that learning process through association with members of one's own group.

This process of horizontal learning and continued reinforcement through association with other members of the same subcultural group is particularly important in the case of children whose values are still in the formative stage.[148] Because of the tendency of children to play with others in the immediate vicinity of their home regardless of their parents' associations,[149] to subject them to a horizontal learning process through their playmates requires that some degree of residential homogeneity be maintained; otherwise, they are likely not only to learn about other group mores, but to adopt them. The widespread use of parochial schools in-

---

and called on American Jews to strengthen the Jewish day school system"); Nov. 26, 1961, p. 84, col. 3 (same); June 11, 1960, p. 21, col. 4 (nationality day); Feb. 8, 1960, p. 28, col. 1 (Negro history week); Feb. 7, 1960, p. 35, col. 1 (same); June 28, 1959, p. 68 col. 6 ("Negro should return to his African cultural roots"); June 27, 1959, p. 3, col. 8 (same); May 15, 1959, p. 15, col. 1 (assimilation threatens Jews).

148 See the testimony of Dr. Bettie Belk, expert witness for the NAACP, in Brown v. Board of Education, 98 F. Supp. 797 (D.C. Kans. 1951), rev. 349 U.S. 294 (1955). Her statements, contained in the record before the United States Supreme Court, p. 183, are as follows:

"A. Well, I think our recent studies have shown that children, adolescents particularly, take most of their social pattern from their peers rather than their parents; in fact, it's one of the real problems in our American society today that this is true.

"Q. Who are the children, what do your mean by that, that the Negro children they would look upon as their peers and therefore would follow them; what do you mean?

"A. I mean that all adolescent children take most of their social patterns from people their own age; they tend to see each other as authorities. It's an age at which they break away completely from parental authority, in fact to the extent that it becomes a difficult problem in homelife, so it is not always the patterns of the parents that they are repeating; in fact, during this time they are forming their own values."

149 Private Interracial Neighborhoods in Connecticut, *supra*, n.140 at 27-8.

stead of merely religious instruction after school hours is a clear indication that the value of this horizontal learning process is widely recognized. The United States Supreme Court has upheld the constitutional right of parents to send children to such schools instead of public schools as against the state's contention that mingling with children of other groups is necessary to promote intergroup contact and harmony in the community.[150] And a lower federal court recently declared in the race relations area:

> People of any race, religion, or political faith may assemble and associate for the advancement of their interests. No sound public policy would destroy the interesting diversity of life. If the aim and end of democracy should be to reduce all men to the same shape and shade and common opinion, then it could and should not survive. It would counter one of the fundamental principles of evolution.[151]

Another common argument adduced to avoid the effect of the violation of freedom of choice by anti-discrimination legislation is that dissatisfied tenants or residents can move to a homogeneous area.[152] The short answer to this contention is that it may not be possible to move. As one note declares:

> The shortage of inexpensive non-government-aided dwellings where segregation could be continued reduces the possibility of wholesale vacating by established residents. Since FHA assistance is becoming the prevalent financing device of the private developers, mass vacating will become increasingly futile unless vacators move into luxury apartments. Therefore, developers are not likely to find their tenants departing in droves.[153]

In addition, if an anti-discrimination law is really effective, there will be no place to hide.[154] Hence, the argument about moving is unreal.

Moreover, this contention begs the very question at issue. Proponents of anti-discrimination laws would hardly be satisfied with the assertion that applicants who are discriminated against can look elsewhere; indeed, they would contend that this require-

---

150 Pierce v. Society of Sisters, 268 U.S. 510, 525, 534 (1925). See also Meyer v. Nebraska, 262 U.S. 390, 394, 401-2 (1923).
    151 Goshen v. Bar Assn. of the District of Columbia, 152 F. Supp. 300, 306 (D.D.C. 1957).
    152 Note, 12 Rutgers L. Rev. 557, 562 (1958).
    153 *Id.* at 563.
    154 See the statement of the Deputy City Administrator of New York: "I say to those who would try to run away . . . that there is no place to run. There is no place to hide." N.Y. Times, March 19, 1962, p. 42, col. 3.

ment is part and parcel of the very discrimination they seek to eliminate. By the same token, the fact that established tenants or residents would have to be constantly on the move to retain their freedom of association is a major facet of the violation here at issue.

The short of the matter is that, for all of its fancy trimmings and wrappings, a law banning discrimination in housing is, and is intended to be, a law compelling people to integrate who do not desire to do so. To thus treat human beings as chess pieces, to be moved at the will or whim of others who would like to plan their lives for them, is as flagrant a violation of basic human rights and dignity as can be found in the worst totalitarian system ever devised. Moreover, such integration for the sake of integration over the obvious objections of the people being integrated is patently violative of their constitutional rights.[155] To hold otherwise is to reduce fundamental human rights to the level of norms which can be changed at each passing fad or fancy in social engineering by self-appointed planners for the lives of others.

V. *Conclusion*

The 1959 United States Civil Rights Commission report found that "the need is not for a pattern of integrated housing. It is for equal opportunity to secure decent housing. . . . The Negro's need for . . . securing housing must be met just as the legitimate interests of white neighborhoods . . . must be protected."[156] Likewise, this report also declared that "what is at issue is not the imposition of any residential pattern of racial integration. . . . There may be many Americans who prefer to live in neighborhoods with people of their own race, color, religion, or

---

155 Cf. Note, 56 Mich. L. Rev. 1223, 1225 (1958): "A further possibility is that anti-discrimination legislation will expand into the area of purely social regulation, and prohibit private discrimination in such matters as membership in private clubs. This would seem to be an infringement of liberty under the due process clause, and would also seem to be beyond the present scope of the police power. . . . Anti-discrimination legislation aimed at purely social relationships, however, would probably violate the due process clause for two reasons. First, while anti-discrimination legislation which deals with economic relationships can be justified by the modern concept of the police power, legislation which deals with purely social relationships is not normally within the scope of the police power. Secondly, social anti-discrimination legislation would tend to infringe individual liberty rather than property rights, and the court has shown a tendency to give liberty greater protection from state regulation than property."

156 1959 U.S. Civil Rights Comm. Rept. 535.

national origin. The right of voluntary association is also important."[157]

Freedom of association is a value which must be protected.
Laws forbidding discrimination in housing are compulsory integration devices, and are designed to eliminate freedom of choice.
As such, the issue is not merely to what extent freedom of association should be balanced against other values and objectives
which the state may properly seek to promote, but rather whether
this freedom itself should be eliminated in favor of social compulsion manipulated according to the plans of self-appointed social
engineers. Such a proposal carries its own inherent refutation.

The labels of "bigot," "bias," "reactionary," "prejudice,"
"ignorant," and so forth, so freely bantered about in the race relations area as semantic substitutes for thinking cannot obscure
the simple fact that compulsory integration is a program by which
some people presume to dictate to others in which type of environment they shall live. In so doing, they arrogate to themselves the
right of choice of others which constitutes a fundamental human
right inseparable from the dignity of each person as an individual.
All the fancy phrases of "democratic living," "fair housing," "open
occupancy," and "equality" cannot substitute for the denial of
the right of freedom of association. Infringement of this right
makes anti-discrimination legislation in housing violative of fundamental liberties.[158]

157 *Id.* at 332.
158 Cf. Douglas, J. concurring in Gibson v. Florida Legislative Investigation Comm.,
83 S. Ct. 889, 905 (1963) ("the need for a pervasive right of privacy against government
intrusion has been recognized, though not always given the recognition it deserves");
Weisner v. 791 Park Avenue Corp., 6 N.Y.2d 426, 190 N.Y.S.2d 70, 160 N.E.2d 720, 724
(1959) ("there is no reason why the owners of the co-operative apartment house could
not decide for themselves with whom they wish to share their elevators, their common
halls and facilities, their stockholders' meetings, their management problems and
responsibilities and their homes"); Penthouse Properties, Inc. v. 1158 Fifth Avenue, Inc.,
256 App. Div. 685, 11 N.Y.S.2d 417, 422 (1939) ("the residential nature of the enterprise,
the privilege of selecting neighbors and the needs of the community are not to be
ignored").

DISCRIMINATION AND THE STRUGGLE FOR SHELTER

CHARLES ABRAMS*

IN THE TWENTY-FIVE YEARS preceding the end of World War II, no less than 75% of new developments for owner occupancy were built in peripheral sections of cities. Nearly one-half the recent national population rise has been in the city outskirts. These suburbs were the answer to a number of thorny problems and disaffections flowing out of industrialization, the machine, and the rise of big cities. The suburb met the demand for space, privacy, and the nostalgia for country life. Here was the place to find a home, and to acquire the bundle of rights, dreams, satisfactions and illusions that came wrapped up with the deed.

These houses in the suburbs were bought largely by "little people"—skilled and semiskilled workers, clerks, small merchants, young professionals, people comprising America's great middle class. Their contact with the city, its culture and civilization, was now more ephemeral than before. Some had come straight from the cities with the conscious or subconscious wish to escape from neighborhoods where they once had brief contacts with Negroes or other migrants in shops and schools. Most had invested their life's savings in homes, and they became peculiarly sensitive to fears and rumors of events which might threaten either their equities or their status.

* LL.B. 1922, St. Lawrence Univ. Chairman, New York State Commission Against Discrimination, 1955-9; State Rent Administrator and Commissioner, New York State Housing Rent Commission, 1955; Special Counsel to the New York Joint Legislative Comm. on Housing and Multiple Dwellings, 1946; Counsel, American Federation of Housing Authorities, 1937-9; Counsel, New York Housing Shortage Investigation, 1936; Counsel, New York City Housing Authority, 1934-7. Former Consultant, U.S. Housing Authority and Federal Public Housing Authority. Chief of the United Nations Housing Mission to Gold Coast (Ghana), 1954, Turkey, 1954, Pakistan, 1957, Philippines, 1958, Bolivia, 1959. Lecturer in Economics and Housing, Professor, Graduate Faculty, New School for Social Research, 1936 to date; Visiting Professor, Massachusetts Institute of Technology, 1957 to date; Visiting Professor, Housing and City Planning, University of Pennsylvania, 1951 to 1956. Author, Revolution in Land (1939); The Future of Housing (1946); Race Bias in Housing (1947); A Housing Program For America (1947); Current Information On Urban Land Policies (U.N. Rept. 1952); Urban Land Policies and Problems (U.N. 1953); Forbidden Neighbors (1955). Director: National Housing Conference; N.Y.C. Slum Clearance Comm.; N.Y. State Comm. on Discrimination in Housing; Nat'l Comm. Against Discrimination in Housing. Member of the New York Bar. This article is an abridgement of the one first printed in 6 New York Law Forum 3 (Jan. 1960) and is reprinted by permission.

The common thread that bound the suburbanites together was not culture or tradition, or civic pride, but neighborhood dignity. The home magazines told them so repeatedly, and so did the realtors, the neighborhood associations, and even officials of the FHA.

While these social developments were occurring in the suburbs, a housing famine now confronted the newly in-migrating minorities in the cities. It was affecting their opportunities in life, their educational patterns, their aspirations, and their children's prospects. However firmly the courts might strike at segregation in schools, such segregation would continue as long as there was segregation in neighborhoods—in fact, the latter might now become the very vehicle for achieving the school segregation indirectly, which the courts had outlawed directly.

The blocks to an economic and social advance by minority groups have been challenged in some states, but they continue in most—deficiencies in environment and home life; hostile community attitudes; resistance to hiring by management; educational lag; lack of apprenticeship and on-the-job training opportunities; deficiencies in the counseling services; discriminatory practices by private employment agencies; failure by minorities to train or apply for jobs; opposition by some unions; transience, which prevents the sinking of roots into the community and its available opportunities; lack of leadership, contacts, know-how, unrealistic aspirations or opportunities for emulation; the language and communication difficulties of some groups.

Whether these obstacles will disappear with time will depend largely upon whether existing patterns are altered—patterns of housing and environment; of attitudes; of jobs and competition for jobs; of education; of training and guidance; and of the official programs designed to eliminate the barriers that frustrate equal access to opportunity in life.

Yet if economic and social advance is to continue as a fact in the American scene, not only is equal access to housing and to employment imperative, but there must be equal access as well to the essential educational equipment with which to compete for opportunities. But this is far from the fact today. In a recent study by the New York State Commission Against Discrimination, it was found that Negroes must have higher qualifications than whites to compete for jobs; that lack of formal schooling is more of a handicap for the Negro than for the white; that there is a considerably higher drop-out among nonwhites than among whites at the high school level; that while one of five white high school graduates completes college, only one out of nine Negro high school graduates does so; that stability of the home affects the school record of youth. The better records are of those born in the North of parents in stable homes.

In a city like Elmira, however, where there is a relatively small and stable Negro population, when Negroes were compared to whites from the same class background, "the Negroes show a more positive and constructive attitude toward school than the corresponding white youth. . . . The Negro expects more of himself and maintains more of a direction in his academic pursuits. . . . The Negroes do as well as, if not better than, the whites . . . according to traditional educational standards . . . fewer Negroes drop out of school before graduation . . . of those who have graduated, more Negroes have actually gone on to college."

It should be clear that the educational system of the South is reaping its price in the North; that it is having and will continue to have lasting repercussions upon the minority youth; that one of its effects is the perpetuation of the Negro at a lower cultural level and that this will continue to hamper Negro youngsters in the generation to come and to depress their opportunities, hopes and ambitions.

With the Negro migration from the South continuing and with the Puerto Rican migration only in its first stages, it must be manifest that the low educational level of migrants and their lack of housing are no longer a Southern or a Puerto Rican problem alone but one of national concern and responsibility. Yet, with a few sporadic exceptions, the problems of the migrating groups and minorities continue to be ignored.

The situation demands the emergence of a more realistic and more constructive leadership than ever before at the national executive level—one that will mobilize public opinion to an awareness of the issues; that will make better use of the devices existing at the executive level for insuring compliance by Southern communities with their constitutional obligations. Such leadership need not rely entirely on statute or on the compulsive processes. It can also embrace the wise use of all the prestige inherent in the executive power to reach and build up the more enlightened elements of the South. The power to earmark funds for improvements, the use of the patronage powers and other devices which lie within the domain of the executive, are all tools in this process which have remained unutilized and which, properly utilized, could help build up the more progressive Southern leadership which has recently been subordinated and submerged in influence.

So, too, must we in the North be more alert to our own responsibilities. The basic approach of official and unofficial agencies should be to treat disadvantaged groups not as a special kind of human being but rather as human beings with a special kind of problem. Among the proposals deserving support are more full-time school counselors; more clinical services in the schools to counteract the pressures of poor environment; extended use of group guidance in the schools to identify and encourage talented youth; guidance workshops for parents; special guidance programs in neighborhood houses; closer cooperation between schools and public and private agencies for information on jobs and apprenticeship opportunities; continued research into the field along the lines begun at the State Commission Against Discrimination after 1956.

Yet, while all this would help, it is largely housing that will continue to provide the main barrier to advance. Each time a single family migrates from a depressed area, a capital outlay by some public or private agency is required to supply the housing which that family needs; and since private enterprise does not provide such housing, the obligation must fall on some governmental unit prepared to put up both the capital and the annual subsidy required to bridge the gap between what the family can pay as rent and the annual carrying cost. The level of government with the main obligation for producing such a program is the federal government.

Despite this, most of the federal housing commitments have leaned toward aiding the higher income groups, the builder and the mortgage institution. The programs which once did exist to help the low-income group are either fading from view or are being carried out so that they aggravate as much as help the position of the underprivileged family. The public housing program has been whittled to a shell and is little more than a receptacle for the DPs from urban renewal sites. In most cases, urban renewal has simply displaced minority families from their footholds to make way for new housing they cannot afford. A system which prescribes subsidies for the better-heeled and laissez-faire for the underprivileged can hardly be described as "the American way."

The primary aim of federal housing legislation should be to create decent environments rather than to pay the social costs of poor environment after the fact. The public function should be veered mainly toward benefiting those groups in the economy who are outside the field in which the private housing mechanisms operate. All aspects of existing programs which constrict or diminish the quantity of housing for disadvantaged groups should be modified and a main emphasis placed on increasing the housing supply. Mass clearance of shelter, however it may be justified as "slum clearance" during periods of housing surplus, has little justification when its main impact is to increase overcrowding.

A realistic federal housing program would encompass: (1) A mortgage loan program under which loans would be made for homeownership to poorer families at interest rates they can afford —the range would have to be from 0 to 2%. A $2 billion program would entail a subsidy of not more than $40 million annually. (2) A publicly-aided rental housing program envisioning the creation of neighborhoods in place of the monolithic projects now characteristic of housing programs. This means identifying those neighborhood values that should be preserved and improving rather than uprooting them. It calls for building of smaller projects of a less institutionalized character and for a system of subsidies which can be available for private, cooperative and public projects accessible to those of moderate incomes. In public housing it calls for policies which will remove the uncertainties of tenancy and the fear of dispossession when incomes increase. (3) A policy which will emphasize vacant land operations and the selection of under-occupied sites rather than the wholesale clearance of dense concentrations with their mass upheaval of underprivileged families, as is the present tendency.

It should be clear that only a multilateral attack on the problems of minorities will bring the progress the situation demands. Laws outlawing discrimination in private housing are needed, but they will not afford the Negro or the Puerto Rican the ability to pay the rent. Desegregation is also important but will mean little if white children do not attend the schools. Giving more teeth to a State Commission Against Discrimination is desirable, but it won't help if there are no Negroes qualified for the jobs the agency opens up.

Setting up expertly staffed employment agencies skilled in the finding and placement of specialized minority personnel would be another important step forward. Publicizing opportunities and gains among minority groups through sources that reach them would help break down hesitancy to train and apply for jobs. Talented students should be encouraged to take courses in new fields and become the inspiration for others to follow similar careers. Encouragement of youth to apply for apprenticeships would help overcome the tendency to favor the job with temporarily higher pay but fewer future prospects. The apprenticeship system needs careful attention to widen its benefits—it has escaped scrutiny for all too long.

While the main problem lies in the public apathy, the fact nevertheless is that, in the long run, the impetus for constructive gains must come from such citizens groups and organizations— they are and will continue to be one of the great moving forces in the preservation of American principles against the corrosive influences of prejudice and selfish interests.

As I said in *Forbidden Neighbors* (pp. 279-282, 1955):

> Some homogeneity in neighborhoods may be a good thing. It is doubtless desirable to live in a neighborhood where there is a reasonable number of intelligent and interesting human beings. But this does not mean that a neighborhood is doomed unless all are so or that all must be Catholics, Jews, white Protestants, adver-

tising men, white collar workers, or executives, all of the same age group to boot. If all were drinking men or all devotees of Alcoholics Anonymous, the former would not be on hand to benefit from the latter's ministrations and the latter would have no one to minister to. With the standard living room now able to accommodate only a half-dozen couples at best, and with the increasing need for finding not only five good husbands with a common interest but an equivalent number of wives all tolerable to each other, the element of selectivity would seemingly function better in a neighborhood with variety than in one with unmitigated uniformity.

*   *   *   *

So, too, concentrations of tenants of uniform social status or income in private projects is bringing about a boring uniformity which must ultimately exert a financial and social impact upon the community. Agglomerations of people of a single class and temperament are dull. On the other hand, a sprinkling of poor artists or frustrated writers may be a tonic to a neighborhood of bank clerks or shopkeepers. The presence of a few restaurants with some good Chinese, Italian, or Negro cooks may promote more neighborhood vitality than all the restrictive covenants aimed at these chefs.

DISCRIMINATION, ANTI-DISCRIMINATION LEGISLA-
TION, AND FREEDOM OF CHOICE IN HOUSING:
A DIALOGUE

JOHN HERBERT TOVEY*

I. *Introduction*

Q. Just what do you mean by Freedom of Choice? *A.* Freedom of Choice is the right of the individual to freely choose his
friends, neighbors, and associates without compulsion of government or other institutions, corporations, or persons.

Q. Isn't this another term for segregation? *A.* Certainly not.
Segregation is a compulsory separation of the races by law. Like
compulsory integration, it is a denial of Freedom of Choice.

Q. But Freedom of Choice involves discrimination, and discrimination is segregation. So your distinction is fictitious, isn't it?
A. Not in the least. The distinction is very real.

Q. Perhaps you can explain this distinction for me? *A.*
Gladly. Discrimination means simply to make a choice.[1] Everybody discriminates in many things every day—food, shelter, en-
tertainment, etc. But, in order to discriminate you must be free
to make a choice, or free to prefer one thing or one person to
another.[2] In either segregation or compulsory integration, someone else makes the choice for you.[3] Your freedom is gone. After
all, it's still a compliment to call someone a discriminating person.
It means he has taste.

Q. But it's not a compliment, is it, to say that a person is discriminating to the hurt of another? *A.* I don't understand what
you mean by "the hurt of another"?

* B.S. 1952, LL.B. 1956, Georgetown University; LL.M. 1961, New York University.
Member of the New York Bar. Copyright 1962, John Herbert Tovey.
1 Feng Yeat Chow v. Shaughnessy, 151 F. Supp. 23, 26 (S.D.N.Y. 1957) ("Webster's
New International Dictionary. . . 'discriminate. 1. To make a distinction. . .'"); An-
drews v. Union Savings Bank, 238 Iowa 481, 28 N.W.2d 37, 40 (1947) ("Discriminate
means . . . To separate by discerning differences; to distinguish"); State v. Arkansas Louisiana Gas Co., 227 La. 179, 78 So. 2d 825, 827 (1955) ("The word 'discrimination'. . .
merely means 'The act of treating differently. . .'").
2 Cf. City of Highland Park v. Fair Employment Practices Comm., 364 Mich. 508,
111 N.W.2d 797, 799 (1961).
3 Comment, 38 Chicago-Kent L. Rev. 169, 174 (1961).

II. *Freedom of Choice and the Demand for Housing*

Q. What I mean is not very difficult to understand if you have ever been a Negro and looked for a home. It's very easy to understand how discrimination hurts others. *A.* Let's explore that for a minute. Just how does it hurt others?

Q. Well, when a Negro looks for a place to live, be it a house or an apartment, he has difficulty in finding a decent place. The result is that he is crowded into a narrow ghetto in the central urban areas. This ghetto, because of the limited supply of residential housing available to Negroes, is overcrowded, restricted as to municipal services, has poor sanitation facilities, is plagued with a high crime rate, and costs more in rent than a comparable white area. Negro areas are typically the oldest and most undesirable areas in a community, and if they are not slums when the Negroes move in, they become slums shortly thereafter. When urban renewal programs come along, they are prevented from clearing these slums by the shortage of available housing for Negroes. *A.* While the social conditions you describe may exist, the real question is whether they are caused by racial discrimination. In other words, I'm not arguing with the effect, but rather with the causes you ascribe to that effect.[4]

Q. But isn't the cause obvious? *A.* Quite the contrary, the cause has been obscured.

Q. Perhaps you can tell me wherein the obscurity lies? *A.* I'll do my best. Housing is a commodity like any other. It is bought and sold on the open market like food or clothing. Its only difference is that it is not consumed, and of course it is stationary. Otherwise, like all commodities, it can go up or down in value, depending on supply and demand. It depreciates, or even appreciates. The rental market acts the same way.[5] Thus, a Negro who has the price of the commodity can get it the same as anybody else.

Q. But that is utter nonsense. We all know that Negroes with money can't get housing in many areas, perhaps even in most areas unless they are Negro areas. *A.* Now wait a minute. I didn't say a

[4] See Van Alstyne & Karst, *State Action*, 14 Stan. L. Rev. 3, 47 (1961) for a recent statement of these generalities.
[5] Block v. Hirsh, 256 U.S. 135 (1921).

Negro could get housing in any area. I said he could get housing if he had the market price.

Q. And just how do you get housing if someone won't sell or rent to you? *A.* How would you obtain an auto if the man next door refused to sell you his car? *Q.* I probably wouldn't approach the fellow next door. I'd go to an auto dealer.

A. And why doesn't the same procedure apply to Negroes seeking housing? *Q.* That's easy. Dealers in the business—brokers —are as discriminating, if not more so, than anyone else.

A. Suppose no one would sell you a used car? What would you do if you wanted a car? *Q.* I'd contribute to Detroit's prosperity and buy a new one.

A. Then, as a Negro, you could contribute to the prosperity of the building trades and buy a new house, or combine with others and build a co-operative apartment.

Q. But suppose I can't afford a new house? *A.* If you can't afford a new house, in all probability you can't afford an old one.

Q. That doesn't make sense. *A.* Of course it does. A new house is worth more than an old, isn't it? *Q.* I'll buy that. *A.* And it has a longer useful life, doesn't it. *Q.* Yes. *A.* So, with a new house you can get a larger mortgage. True, a person may not be able to afford a new house which is comparable in all respects to an old house, but dollar for dollar what you get in a new house is the same as what you get in an old one.

Q. But forcing a man to buy a new house limits his freedom of choice in housing, doesn't it. *A.* True, but no more so than I would limit your freedom if I refuse to sell you my car. In fact, if I refuse to sell you my car and I have the only car of this type, your recourse would be to do without or to manufacture a new car of the kind I have. The cost of manufacturing a car is prohibitive for most of us. Not so with the building of a new house.

Q. Let's go back a moment. If I can afford an old house, it doesn't necessarily mean I can afford a new house with the same number of rooms. After all, new houses cost more, room-for-room. *A.* That's true, but, room-for-room, you get more in a new house.

The wood is new, and better, the paint is fresh, the house is modern, the plumbing is newer, and so forth.

Q. But suppose I need eight rooms, and not modern plumbing? *A.* You can get it in a new house also. Just tell the builder not to install that new kitchen or brand-new bathroom fixtures. Get second-hand fixtures. Or, you can tell him to install old pipes, use second-hand lumber, or otherwise obtain lower cost by giving up another item of value.

Q. But a custom built new house is still more expensive than an old house of equivalent value. *A.* True, but houses of equivalent value built under equivalent conditions cost the same. It is inevitable. Housing is a commodity with a market value. An old house which has a desirable location or other desirable features will rise in value to become equivalent to a new house of the same quality and desirability. A free housing market will inevitably do this.[6]

Q. But what about all those cases which declare that discrimination against Negroes in the sale and rental of housing results in inadequate housing for them, thus compelling them to live in circumscribed areas under substandard, unhealthy, unsanitary and crowded living conditions? If you look in my footnote, you will see three such recent cases.[7] *A.* I've looked at the cases in your footnote and I remain unmoved. No real scientific study has ever been made which has proved any connection between discrimination in housing and inadequate housing. As I have pointed out, any inadequacy in housing could be, and would have been, allieviated by building new Negro housing, if there was a will to do so. If you will look at my footnote in return, you will see this clearly.[8]

Q. But if the Negro housing market could be satisfied by new

---

[6] See generally, Newcomb and Kyle, *The Housing Crisis in a Free Economy*, 12 Law & Cont. Prob. 186 (1947).

[7] Burks v. Poppy Const. Co., 57 A.C. 503, 515-6, 20 Cal. Reptr. 609, 370 P.2d 313, 317 (1962); Massachusetts Commission Against Discrimination v. Colangelo, 182 N.E.2d 595 (Mass. 1962); Jones v. Haridor Realty Co., 37 N.J. 384, 181 A.2d 481 (1962).

[8] Avins, *Anti-Discrimination Legislation as an Infringement on Freedom of Choice*, 6 N.Y.L.F. 13, 34-5, n.86 (1960).

housing, why isn't it being done. *A.* It is. Try looking at another footnote of mine. [9]

Q. But wouldn't discrimination in housing impede the relocation of families affected by urban redevelopment programs, as one recent case pointed out?[10] *A.* No more so than it otherwise restricts the housing market generally. And, as I have shown above, the restriction is illusory.

Q. Why, then, is it so difficult for Negroes to get housing, and why do they get so little and pay so much? *A.* While nobody has ever made a really scientific study of the problem that I know of which is based on unbiased empirical data—although there are lots of propaganda pieces floating around—I suspect that this is a problem of economics,[11] credit,[12] and, as I have already hinted at, the unalterable opposition of Negro leaders to good housing unless it is integrated.[13]

Q. Why is economics and credit such a factor? *A.* Well, look at it this way. The cost of money consists of two factors, the market price of capital, and the risk. If the risk is low, the cost of capital is lower. Negroes generally are at the bottom level of the economic scale.[14] Hence, builders or sellers fear that payments will not be made and that the house will have to be resold. This increases the risk and correspondingly dries up mortgage money or increases its cost beyond the ability of the Negro buyer to conveniently pay. The problem of good Negro housing is primarily a problem of financing. Antidiscrimination legislation is typically valueless in this area.[15]

---

[9] For example, see *id.* at 18, 22, n.24, 38. See also N.Y. Times, July 1, 1962, Real Estate, sec. 8, p. R. 11, col. 1; Dec. 31, 1961, p. 35, col. 1; Dec. 5, 1961, p. 35, col. 1.

[10] Massachusetts Comm. Against Disc. v. Colangelo, *supra*, n.7 at 600.

[11] According to 1960 census figures, the median nation-wide white family income was $6,433, and the median nonwhite family income was $3,711. In Chicago, the difference was $7,680 to $4,786; in Detroit it was $7,175 to $4,385, and in Cleveland it was $7,350 to $4,768. See *Midwest Minority Housing Markets* 23 (Special Report by Advance Mortgage Corp., Dec. 1, 1962).

[12] *Id.* at 26.

[13] *Id.* at 8: "Resistance to any form of segregated housing—a position stated with increasing frequency by Negro spokesmen—may tend to limit the market for minority housing developments among those who can best afford to buy."

[14] *Supra*, n.11.

[15] Even tax laws can materially affect housing investment. See Sporn, *Some Contributions of the Income Tax Law to the Growth and Prevalence of Slums*, 59 Colum. L. Rev. 1026 (1959).

Q. What did you mean when you said that Negro leaders were often opposed to good housing for Negroes? That seems to be a ridiculous statement. *A.* It's not the statement which is ridiculous, it's the situation which is absurd. Negroes need good housing, but as much Negro building as could be done is not being done because efforts are concentrated on integration in housing.

III. *Freedom of Choice and Integration in Housing*

Q. I don't understand what you mean. *A.* It's very simple. Negro leaders would prefer to see the mass of Negroes living in substandard housing rather than building new housing for them unless that new housing was integrated.[16]

Q. And what's wrong with that? Recent decisions have repeatedly favored integration in housing. In fact a New York judge stated as justification for antidiscrimination legislation in housing as follows: "It is now believed that many of our problems arising from the diverse nature of our population will be brought nearer solution by integration."[17] And the Supreme Court of New Jersey declared: "Segregated housing seriously complicates the problem of public school integration."[18] *A.* But this doesn't affect the ability of Negroes to get good housing, and manifestly doesn't bolster the argument that antidiscrimination laws are needed to secure good housing.

Q. All right, let's concede for a minute the inapplicability of that argument and go on to the promotion of integration. Surely you'll concede that antidiscrimination legislation in housing promotes integration, won't you? *A.* Not only will I concede it, but I affirm it. In fact, that's the principal object of this legislation.

Q. So we've agreed then that antidiscrimination legislation has a valid purpose, the promotion of integration. *A.* We are indeed agreed that it has the purpose of promoting integration, but I don't agree the purpose is valid.

Q. Well, why not? People who get to know each other by be-

16 Avins, *op. cit. supra*, n.8 at 20-22; N.Y. Times, June 8, 1962, p. 33, col. 8; June 20, 1961, p. 35, col. 8.

17 Martin v. City of New York, 22 Misc. 2d 389, 391, 201 N.Y.S.2d 111 (1960).

18 Jones v. Haridor Realty Co., *supra*, n.7 at 485.

ing together will be able to get along better together. They will develop fewer prejudices and stereotypes. Their children will play with each other. Irrational biases will steadily be eliminated. If that is not a public good, I cannot imagine what is. *A*. You have a bushelfull of assumptions, don't you, a carload of untrue conclusions?

Q. Perhaps you'd like to identify some of these assumptions and conclusions for me. *A*. Certainly. For example, take your most violent assumption, that people who live together don't develop prejudices. According to this assumption, white Mississippians should be the most unprejudiced people in the union against Negroes.

Q. Well, of course, they don't have the right atmosphere there. *A*. I think the air in Mississippi is the same as the air anyplace else.

Q. Obviously, that's not what I mean. They haven't been properly educated to have the right attitudes. *A*. So it's really education and attitude formation, and not merely living together.

Q. I suppose I can concede that. *A*. Well then, conceding that harmonious intergroup relations are a product of education and not of mere physical proximity, we can go on to the assumption that physical proximity will promote intergroup associations. In other words, your assumption is that if the fellow next door is a Negro you will associate with him merely because you live near him.

Q. What could be a more obvious proposition than that? *A*. It's not as obvious as you think. True, a hundred years ago, if you lived on a farm with only old Dobbin to get you anyplace and with the nearest town 30 miles away you would be fairly well compelled to associate with the fellow on the next farm. But the country is a lot more urban than it was 100 years ago, and a lot more mobile than it has ever been before. If you are the average city dweller or suburbanite, by driving an hour there are quite a few people that you can see.

Q. But individual people naturally associate with the fellow next door. *A*. There has been a study which shows rather dramatically that this is not necessarily so.[19] It is true that some contact is coerced, but this can be kept to a minimum. This coerced minimum may increase, rather than decrease, prejudice.[20]

Q. But this surely cannot be true with children. Few five-year-olds are precocious enough to drive the family car across town to see a friend. *A.* Rarely will a selection be that small in a city area. A parent will usually be able to find a child of the same ethnic background for his child to play with if he is bent on segregating the child. Moreover, in suburbs the building of fences for this purpose is not unknown.[21] True, here again, some contact is coerced, but parents may keep it to a minimum, and the strain of so doing is again likely to reinforce prejudice.

Q. But even if there is only a little intergroup contact, that's better than none, isn't it? *A.* Sometimes yes, sometimes no. Sometimes the limited urban intergroup contact produces friction and hostility.

Q. From a theoretical point of view, this hardly seems logical. *A.* The problem is that people are not wholly logical creatures. Some of the worst incidents of intergroup violence have occurred in lower-class neighborhoods containing diverse ethnic groups. Juvenile gangs are a manifestation of this.[22]

Q. That may be true in lower-class neighborhoods, but certainly not in upper-class areas. *A.* Oh no? What about Cicero, Illinois, Levittown, Pennsylvania, and other less publicized incidents? If people don't like each other, they find a way to show it.

Q. That is certainly not a very healthy attitude. We can hardly encourage this, or even give it recognition. *A.* I really don't know what you mean, for once.

---

[19] Connecticut Commission on Civil Rights, *Private Interracial Neighborhoods in Connecticut* 25-6 (1957) reported that in 219 neighborhoods with long established mixed occupancy, a survey showed that 75% of the adults had no contact with Negroes living next door or three doors away in their home, while 83% had no contact with them outside of their home.

[20] See Fishman, *Some Social and Psychological Determinants of Intergroup Relations in Changing Neighborhoods,* 40 Social Forces 42 (1961).

[21] N.Y. Times, June 27, 1962, p. 37, col. 2.

[22] See, for example, N.Y. Times, May 2, 1961, p. 31, col. 1; July 21, 1960, p. 14, col. 2; Sept. 29, 1959, p. 35, col. 1.

Q. I am talking about morals, our Judeo-Christian traditions. *A.* What has that to do with this problem?

IV. *The Morality of Freedom of Choice in Housing*

Q. It seems to me that one can hardly even begin to discuss antidiscrimination legislation without discussing morality. This legislation is anchored in our moral traditions. *A.* Aren't you equating politics with morality?

Q. The problem rises above politics. It is in the domain of the ethical and unethical, the right and the wrong, the good and the evil. In a recent Massachusetts case, a justice of the Supreme Judicial Court of that state declared that "when a person acts so as to create a 'second-class' of citizens, then the injunctive provisions of the law to prevent a recurrence of such a classification should be applied to the fullest extent."[23] Even judges who have voted against the law recognize discrimination in housing as wrong. The dissenting judge in that same case said: "The banishment of discrimination because of race, creed, color or national origin is a wholly desirable moral and social objective."[24] And a Washington State opinion overthrowing such a law said: "This court is fully cognizant of the evils which flow from discrimination because of race, creed, or color in a free, democratic society. The practice of discrimination is utterly inconsistent with the political philosophy upon which our institutions are based and with the moral principles which we inherit from our Judeo-Christian tradition. . . . It may be noted also that elimination of discrimination is necessary for the sake of America's relations with the rest of the world. Our standing with the so-called uncommitted peoples of the world suffers seriously because of the continued discrimination and segregation practiced in America."[25] With everyone in agreement that discrimination is morally wrong, it is obvious that anti-discrimination legislation has a firm moral basis and that freedom of choice is by the same token simply a license to be immoral.

23 Massachusetts Comm. Against Disc. v. Colangelo, *supra,* n.7 at 605.
24 *Ibid.*
25 O'Meara v. Washington State Board Against Discrimination, 58 Wash. 2d 793, 365 P.2d 1, 3 (1961). See also Colorado Antidiscrimination Comm. v. Case, — P.2d — (Colo. 1962).

A. Let's examine this a little bit more closely. *Q.* You'll get the same result no matter how closely you look.

A. I'm not so sure. Have you ever asked a young lady to dinner. *Q.* Obviously.

A. Do you think she would be immoral to refuse you? Would you become a "second-class citizen" if she did? *Q.* Foolish perhaps, but not immoral.

A. Isn't this discrimination—that is to say, a distinction—and hence immoral? *Q.* It's a distinction; and hence discrimination, but it is not immoral.

A. Why wouldn't she be immoral? After all, you wanted to have dinner with her, to be in her company. *Q.* Well, I suppose she is entitled to have dinner with whom she wants.

A. But isn't this a matter of morality? *Q.* I would say it was a matter of taste.

A. How do you distinguish morality from taste? *Q.* Discrimination which hurts another is immoral, but if one is just exercising one's rights, it's simply a matter of taste.

A. Then why would it not be moral for her to have dinner with only those of her own race, if that's what she wants? *Q.* Because discrimination based on race, creed, or color hurts another.

A. Why wouldn't refusing to choose you for a dinner companion hurt you? *Q.* Because such a choice would be based on taste.

A. Why is discrimination on racial grounds not based on "taste"?[26] *Q.* Racial discrimination is arbitrary.

A. Aren't there numerous other discriminations which are just as arbitrary?[27] Some people like blondes, some people like red-

[26] "Taste depends . . . sometimes upon irrational taboo. It varies 'with the period, the place, and the training, environment and characteristics of persons.'" Commonwealth v. Isenstadt, 318 Mass. 543, 62 N.E.2d 840, 844 (1945).

[27] Arbitrary means "Fixed or done capriciously or at pleasure; without adequate determining principle; not founded on the nature of things; nonrational; not done or acting according to reason or judgment; depending on the will alone." King v. Falls County, 42 S.W.2d 481, 482 (Tex. Civ. App. 1931). "Tests which are to apply only to certain particular individuals are necessarily arbitrary." Volpe v. City of New York, 178 Misc. 243, 32 N.Y.S.2d 828, 831 (1941).

heads, and some like brunettes. The color of hair is surely no more related to the objective worth of a person than the color of his skin. And there are numerous other arbitrary distinctions drawn every day in the name of personal preference or taste. Why stigmatize only one as "immoral"?

Q. But a landlord is only interested in the color of one's money, not of his skin. Why should he be entitled to profit from bias? *A.* That assumes the premise. A landlord may be, and frequently is, interested in other personal attributes. If he wasn't, the problem wouldn't exist in the first place. He is interested in keeping out anyone who will be unwelcome to the majority of his tenants. If color of hair were disturbing, he would discriminate on that basis too. He simply is acting as agent, or representative, or use any name you will, for his tenants. Their taste is being protected by him. Thus his choice is not arbitrary unless his tenants' choice is arbitrary. And since all choice based on taste is arbitrary and cannot be justified on purely rational grounds, there is no reason to label only one category of choice as "immoral."

Q. My religion teaches me that discrimination is wrong. *A.* Your religion may also teach you to burn incense at the graves of your ancestors. Would you impose this on the whole country?[28]

Q. Of course, I would not impose religious practices peculiar to a particular sect, but religious obligations universally recognized might be a different question. *A.* This is not a uniformly recognized religious obligation. Some religions are or have been quite discriminatory.[29]

Q. But nondiscrimination is certainly a fundamental religious concept. *A.* How do you know? Do you see it written in the sky? *Q.* It is part of our Judeo-Christian heritage. *A.* What do you mean by "heritage"? *Q.* Our heritage is the traditions and practices of the past which we have inherited.

A. Which traditions and practices are you basing your concept on? The practice of slavery which existed from Biblical times until 1865? The practice of serfdom which was thought not in-

---

[28] Cf. Pfeffer, *Court, Constitution and Prayer*, 16 Rutgers L. Rev. 735 (1962).

[29] The Indian caste system is a prime example of this. 4 Encyclopedia Britannica 973 (1961).

consistent with Christianity? The practice of burning heretics and witches at the stake? Which heritage would you care to rely on? *Q.* Naturally, I am relying on only the progressive traditions in our heritage.

A. How do you know which traditions are progressive? *Q.* We can depend on our inborn moral sense.

A. What about the vast majority of people who discriminate? *Q.* Children don't discriminate. Discrimination must be learned. *A.* Children don't eat with forks or read; that must be learned also.

Q. But we must teach them to have a moral outlook. *A.* Here we go back again to the problem of how you know nondiscrimination is moral.

Q. Well, perhaps I can demonstrate it this way. Negroes have been maltreated for years. They feel that discrimination is wrong when practiced against them. Even if discrimination is generally not harmful, discrimination against Negroes is associated in their minds with past maltreatment and hence cuts them deeply. Isn't it immoral to thus hurt them?

A. If your grandfather had killed a man, would you expect to be hanged? *Q.* I hope not. *A.* Then why should you get special privileges because your grandfather was maltreated?

Q. But supposing I had been maltreated? *A.* If I hit you with my car, should you be entitled to collect from the man next door?

Q. Regardless of our own concepts of morality, we cannot afford to discriminate because in the eyes of the colored two-thirds of the world discrimination based on color is wrong. *A.* This is not universally true. Color discrimination is not unknown in African and Asian countries.[30]

Q. However, it is officially against public pronouncements. Whatever deviations there may be, officially it is wrong. *A.* Why should American policy be dictated by foreign countries? Let us do what is right because it is right for Americans. Should we, although

---

[30] For an outbreak of anti-white and anti-Asian racism in Tanganyika, see N.Y. Times, March 11, 1962, p. 15, col. 2.

believing ourselves in discrimination, practice nondiscrimination solely to please foreigners, we would add the sin of hypocrisy to the vice of regimentation. What kind of morality is that?

Q. If we discriminate and thereby offend foreign countries we will lose our leadership in the free world.[31] *A.* If the price of leadership abroad is regimentation at home, that price is much too high.[32]

Q. If we lose our leadership abroad, underdeveloped countries won't take our aid. *A.* I should live so long! But if that ever happens, we can reduce taxes and people will have more money available to buy or build homes. As you know, the money we give away abroad could clear all the slums in America.[33]

Q. What about the African diplomats who can't get housing in Washington?[34] *A.* With freedom of choice they will have the same rights as everybody else. I know of no reason why they should have privileges greater than those given to Americans.[35]

Q. But you ignore the struggle against communism. As a recent case pointed out, "the entire free world is engulfed in a

[31] See the praise of federal action enforcing integration at the University of Mississippi among African governments in N.Y. Times, Oct. 12, 1962, p. 1, col. 5.

[32] The refusal to subordinate basic domestic legal principles to the dictates of foreign powers or the asserted needs of foreign affairs has a long history in Anglo-American jurisprudence. A striking example is found in Mattueof's Case, 10 Mod. 4, 88 Eng. Rep. 598 (1709). In that case, the Ambassador of Peter the Great, Czar of Russia, was arrested for debt, at the instance of a creditor, contrary to international law. Peter resented this affront very highly, and demanded that the parties concerned in the arrest should be ·punished with instant death. But Queen Anne of England replied "that she could inflict no punishment upon any, the meanest, of her subjects, unless warranted by the law of the land; and therefore was persuaded that he would not insist upon impossibilities." 1 Blackstone, *Commentaries* *255. More recently, in Reid v. Covert, 354 U.S. 1, 14 (1957), Mr. Justice Black declared: "If our foreign commitments become of such nature that the Government can no longer satisfactorily operate within the bounds laid down by the Constitution, that instrument can be amended by the method which it prescribes." And it may be noted that "public ministers are forbidden by international law to interfere, whether by word or deed, with the internal political affairs of the local government." Fenwick, *International Law* 467 (3d ed. 1948). Also, cf. Sipes v. McGhee, 316 Mich. 614, 25 N.W.2d 638, 644 (1947), rev. on oth. gr. 334 U.S. 2 (1948).

[33] During fiscal year 1962, the federal government spent about $2,966,000,000 for foreign aid, but only about $250,000,000 for various housing programs. 1962 Britannica Book of the Year 111, 321.

[34] See N.Y. Times, March 26, 1962, p. 21, col. 4; June 11, 1961, p. 18, col. 3; May 26, 1961, p. 21, col. 5. Cf. U.S. Comm. on Civil Rights, *Civil Rights, U.S.A., Housing in Washington, D.C.* 21-26 (1962).

[35] While ambassadors are not subject to local judicial jurisdiction, they are governed by local law to the same extent as any other person. Dickinson v. Del Solar, [1930] 1 K.B. 376.

struggle . . . [and] tyrannical dictators arrayed against this nation in the struggle proclaim throughout the world . . . that we do not practice what we preach, and that 'equality of opportunity' is a sham and a pretense."[36] Will not discrimination fatally cripple the fight against communism? *A.* To start with, since communism has never won a free election anywhere, I doubt that public opinion in a foreign country about this nation's practices will affect anything. However, more to the point, the world has lots of examples of government regimentation. Instead of apologizing for our lack of it, we should shout from the housetops how this country prizes individual liberty and human privacy. An example of an unregimented nation may be attractive to people of all skin colors.

Q. Equality of opportunity and the ringing phrase of the Declaration of Independence thàt "All men are created equal" would go down the drain. *A.* No, not at all. Equal before the law, all men are. The law knows neither distinctions of race, economic class, taste, intelligence, breeding, creed, or other difference. All vote, all may seek public office, all may speak, work, or do anything the law permits to one. But though all are equal in law, they are not equal in fact, or in the eyes of their fellows. And more important, they are not the same. If a man discriminates against a white person, because he is not worth $20,000, does this deny his equality in law? If it does, then why ban discrimination for race only? If it does not, then why is racial discrimination different from other discriminations? If all have equal freedom of choice, then all have the equality on which American ideals are based.

Q. You ignore the ringing words of Mr. Justice Harlan, who in his dissent in *Plessy v. Ferguson*[37] said: "Our Constitution is color-blind."[38] *A.* But people are not, nor can they be made so if all the statute-books of the land were filled to overflowing.[39]

Q. Mr. Justice Harlan also declared: "In respect of civil rights, all citizens are equal before the law. The humblest is the

---

[36] Colorado Antidiscrimination Comm. v. Case, — P.2d — (Colo. 1962).
[37] 163 U.S. 537 (1896).
[38] *Id.* at 559.
[39] Justice Harlan as much as admitted this when he said: "Every true man has pride of race, and under appropriate circumstances, when the rights of others, his equals before the law, are not to be affected, it is his privilege to express such pride and to take such action based upon it as to him seems proper." *Id.* at 554.

peer of the most powerful. The law regards man as man, and takes no account of his surroundings or of his color when his civil rights as guaranteed by the supreme law of the land are involved."[40]
A. As to *civil rights,* you could not be more correct. But the opportunity to acquire real property is not a civil right.[41] People are entitled to equal protection in the property they have, or in their right to make contracts. But the fundamental distinction is that although "the object of the [Fourteenth] amendment was undoubtedly to enforce the absolute equality of the two races before the law, . . . in the nature of things it could not have been intended to abolish distinctions based upon color, or to enforce social, as distinguished from political equality, or a commingling of the two races upon terms unsatisfactory to either."[42] Otherwise, the amendment, designed to abolish legal discrimination, is itself discriminatory, in failing to abolish any discrimination which is arbitrary other than that of color, such as finances, mode of living, personal traits, or the like, which the state cannot make in "civil rights." Legal discrimination is ended, but personal freedom of choice and the right to make personal distinctions remains as a civil right.[43]

Q. You speak of Freedom of Choice. What about the Freedom of Choice of a Negro to live in the neighborhood he prefers?
A. The Negro has the same rights as anyone else, no more and no less. That means he has no right to live in a particular neighborhood. His rights to purchase property are conditioned on the right and desire of the property owner to sell to him. This doesn't mean the Negro won't get a necessity of life, mind you. He can get housing elsewhere.[44]

Q. But he wants to live in that particular neighborhood.
A. Not because he needs or wants *housing.* If he wants to live in a particular area, it is because he wants to associate with the people there even though they don't want to associate with him. He is not interested in the house as a physical structure. He is

---

40 *Id.* at 559.

41 Dorsey v. Stuyvesant Town Corp., 299 N.Y. 512, 87 N.E.2d 541, 549 (1948).

42 Plessy v. Ferguson, 163 U.S. 537, 544 (1896).

43 "If the two races are to meet on terms of social equality, it must be the result of natural affinities, a mutual appreciation of each other's merits, and a voluntary consent of individuals." *Id.* at 551.

44 Cf. Corrigan v. Buckley, 55 App. D.C. 30, 299 Fed. 899, 901 (1924): "The con-

interested in the people next door, and he hopes the inherent physical proximity will compel them to associate with him.[45] Although he may be right in a few instances, he is attaining his ends at the sacrifice of another's freedom.[46]

Q. What of it? Why should he not have a Freedom of Choice to do so? *A.* Because that is not freedom for him, but subservience for others. If a man whom I chose not to dine with wanted to eat with me, no rational person would claim that I was restricting his Freedom of Choice by refusing to eat with him. My right not to associate with him is clearly superior to his right to force himself on me. Association between people must be based on mutual consent. Mutual consent is the quintessence of true equality.[47]

Q. Are these examples really analogous?[48] Housing is a necessity. *A.* True, but *integrated* housing is not a necessity. After all, the necessary part of housing springs from man's need for shelter from the elements, and comfort. Integration certainly doesn't affect these factors.

V. *The Mechanics of Freedom of Choice*

Q. You couldn't have Freedom of Choice in housing anyway. It's utterly impractical. *A.* I don't see why it's impractical. It seems quite practical to me.

Q. Think of choices that would result. Some people would not want Negroes; some people wouldn't want Jews; some people wouldn't want Irish or Italians or Catholics generally or Orientals, or American Indians or what have you. How would you determine to whom houses would be sold or apartments rented? Would

---

stitutional right of a Negro to acquire, own and occupy property does not carry with it the constitutional power to compel sale and conveyance to him of any particular private property. The individual citizen, whether he be black or white, may refuse to sell or lease his property to any particular individual or class of individuals."

45 *Supra*, n.19 at 34-5.

46 Cf. Keltner v. Harris, 196 S.W. 1 (Mo. 1917).

47 Mays v. Burgess, 79 App. D.C. 343, 147 F.2d 869, 873 (1945): "And it should now be apparent that if ever the two races are to meet on mutually satisfactory ground, it cannot be through legal coercion or through the intimidation of factions, or the violence of partisans, but must be the result of a mutual appreciation of each other's problems, and a voluntary consent of individuals."

48 See Henkin, Shelley v. Kraemer: *Notes for a Revised Opinion*, 110 U. Pa. L. Rev. 473, 498 (1962); Van Alstyne & Karst, *State Action*, 14 Stan. L. Rev. 3, 49-50 (1961).

you hold a house election every time there was an applicant for an apartment? *A*. I hardly see where an election is necessary.

Q. Well, let me give you a specific example. Supposing there was a Negro applicant for an apartment. Some of the people in the house oppose renting to him. Some favor it. Would you have to hold an election every time there was a new tenant? *A*. No, the owner of the house would decide in whatever way he wanted to.

Q. What about those who are dissatisfied by his decision? *A*. They may move to a house which reflects their own preferences.

Q. What if there was no house which reflected their own living preferences? *A*. Same answer as I gave when you asked what if there were no houses for Negroes. They are always free to build. A landlord rents space. If there is a free housing market, and he displeases enough of his tenants, he will go out of business. Thus, the tenants vote, so to speak, with their feet.

Q. That tells me how Freedom of Choice is exercised by tenants, but not what standards can be used to determine Freedom of Choice. *A*. Let me suggest the following: "It is an unfair housing practice, for the owner, lessee, or other person having control of residential premises, to rent or sell such premises, or any apartment, room, or other part thereof, to any person:

"(a) For reasons other than economic, when any existing occupant of the premises, or any other resident of the area in sufficient proximity to the premises to have a substantial interest in the nature of its occupancy, objects.

"(b) For economic reasons, only insofar as such owner, lessee, or other person having control of the premises has failed to exercise reasonable diligence and take appropriate steps to satisfy the objectors specified in part (a) insofar as this may be done consistently with the satisfaction of such economic necessity."

Q. Doesn't this severely limit the property owner's rights? *A*. No. When a property owner brings in people for reasons other than economic, that is to say, for the sake of integration, he should have the consent of the people already there who are being integrated. This is true even though many or most people want integration, because integration for the sake of integration over the objection of people being integrated violates Freedom of Choice. In this, everyone's interest in preserving his right not to associate is paramount to the interest of another in compelling him to associate. Those who want integration for its own sake, a change in the status quo, can move elsewhere instead of subjecting non-assentors to their preference.

Q. But what if a landlord has spaces he must fill? *A.* Then his renting is for economic reasons. In other words, if as a result of the movement of those who want integration, he would have too many vacancies, or if current vacancies cannot be filled except by integration, this simply becomes an inevitable by-product of a legitimate and necessary economic policy. This is no longer integration for the sake of integration over the objections of those being integrated, but is simply an inevitable result of the pursuit of an economic requirement. However, reasonable steps to satisfy objectors should be taken if no economic detriment results. Thus, if a person moves into one side of a building, and an objector living on that side requests transfer to a vacant apartment on the other side of the building, this request should be granted.

Q. When would the property owner be required to consult his neighbors or tenants? *A.* When he had reasonable grounds to believe that the prospective tenant or occupant was objectionable. In most situations, this would not be difficult to discern.

VI. *Conclusion*

Q. Doesn't freedom of choice in housing run contrary to the current trend of America's legal thinking? *A.* To the trend of some thinking, yes, unfortunately. But not to the trend of all thinking by any means.

Q. It does run contrary to the trend of a good deal of thinking, and therefore it hardly seems to be a practical program. Perhaps it might be enacted in Utopia, but not here and now. *A.* Utopia is only as far away as we keep it ourselves. Current thinking is always subject to dramatic reversal.

Q. The idea of Freedom of Choice in housing is visionary. *A.* The visions of today are the policies and laws of tomorrow.

THE FOURTEENTH AMENDMENT AND REAL PROPERTY RIGHTS

CHARLES C. TANSILL,* ALFRED AVINS,** SAM S. CRUTCHFIELD,*** AND KENNETH W. COLEGROVE****

No consideration of anti-discrimination legislation in housing can be complete without an investigation of the original intent of the framers of the Fourteenth Amendment and its companion statute, the Civil Rights Act of 1866.[1] These provisions, and particularly the latter statute, have been used not only in popular writings[2] but even in judicial opinions[3] to support such legislation. The question of whether they do in fact support such legislation in light of the intention of the framers of these enactments has never been investigated. This article will seek to determine the original intent of the Congress which passed the Civil

---

* A.B. 1912, A.M. 1913, Ph.D. 1915, Catholic Univ. of America; Ph.D. 1918, Johns Hopkins Univ.; LL.D. 1949, Boston College. Asst. Prof. of American History, American Univ., 1919-21, Professor, 1921-1939; Albert Shaw Lecturer in Diplomacy, Johns Hopkins Univ., 1930-1; Professor of American History, Fordham Univ., 1939-44; Professor of American History, Georgetown Univ., 1944-1961. Author: Pennsylvania and Maryland Boundary Controversy (1915); Canadian Reciprocity Treaty of 1854 (1921); Robert Smith (Secretary of State) (1927); The Purchase of the Danish West Indies (1931); America Goes to War (1936); United States and Santo Domingo, 1798-1873 (1938); The Domestic Relations Between the U.S. and Hawaii, 1885-89 (1940); The Foreign Policy of Thomas F. Bayard (1940); Major Issues in Canadian-American Relations (1943); The Congressional Career of Thomas F. Bayard (1946); Back Door to War (1952); America and the Fight for Irish Freedom (1958); Documents Illustrative of Formation of Union of American States (Sesquicentennial Memorial Document authorized by the Congress of the U.S. 1927); Proposed Amendments to the Constitution, 1889-1927 (1927). Copyright 1962, by Charles C. Tansill and Sam S. Crutchfield.
** B.A. 1954, Hunter College; LL.B. 1956, Columbia Univ.; LL.M. 1957, New York Univ.; M.L. 1961, J.S.D. 1962, Univ. of Chicago. Member of the New York, Illinois, Florida, District of Columbia, and United States Supreme Court Bars. Former Special Deputy Atty. Gen. of New York. Author: The Law of AWOL. App. Atty., F.P.C. & N.L.R.B., 1958-60; Assistant Professor of Law, John Marshall Law School, 1960-1; Associate Professor of Law, Chicago-Kent College of Law, 1961-3.
*** B.A. 1960, LL.B. 1963, George Washington Univ. Member, D.C. Bar.
**** A.B. 1909, State Univ. of Iowa; Ph.D. 1915, Harvard Univ.; Litt.D. 1945, Columbia Univ. Professor of Political Science, Northwestern Univ., 1919-1952; Professor of Political Science, Queens College, 1953-4; Professor of Political Science, C.W. Post College of Long Island Univ., 1959-date. Member of Bd. of Personnel Examiners, U.S. Dept. of Labor, 1933. Cons. O.S.S., 1943-5, political cons. Gen. MacArthur Hdqrs., Allied Supreme Commander, Tokyo, 1946, with rank of brigadier general. Trustee, Upper Iowa Univ. Author: The American Senate and World Peace (1944); Democracy versus Communism (1957).

1 Act of April 9, 1866, c. 31, § 1, 14 Stat. 27, now 42 U.S.C. § 1982.
2 N.Y. Times, Dec. 8, 1957, Real Estate, Sec. 8, p. 1, col. 8.
3 See Colorado Anti-Discrimination Comm. v. Case, —— P.2d ——, —— (Colo. 1962), concurring opinion of Frantz, J.; Railway Mail Assn. v. Corsi, 326 U.S. 88, 98 (1945), Frankfurter, J., concurring.

Rights Act of 1866 and the Fourteenth Amendment, in order to inquire what was sought to be accomplished by these measures as they affect real property rights.

I. *Black Codes and Other Discrimination in Real Property in 1866*

When the Thirty-Ninth Congress met in December, 1865,[4] it was much preoccupied with the problem of the so-called "Black Codes" enacted by Southern legislatures, which were deemed or depicted in strong language by northerners as returning the newly freed Negro to the status of virtual slaves.[5] Most attention was paid to vagrancy laws, which were depicted as outrageously harsh and unjust.[6] However, restrictions on the right to contract, engage in business, or own real estate also attracted attention.

For example, Congressman M. Russell Thayer of Pennsylvania, a supporter of the Civil Rights Bill, declared that Southern states had enacted laws "which declare, for example, that [freemen] shall not have the privilege of purchasing a home for themselves and their families; laws which impair their ability to make contracts for labor in such manner as virtually to deprive them of the power of making such contracts."[7] Senator Lyman Trumbull of Illinois likewise declared that Southern laws "did not allow him to buy or sell, or to make contracts; that did not allow him to own property."[8] Congressman William Windom of Minnesota

---

[4] A full account of its activities of interest here is contained in Fairman, *Does the Fourteenth Amendment Incorporate the Bill of Rights?*, 2 Stan. L. Rev. 5 (1949); James, *The Framing of the Fourteenth Amendment* (1956).

[5] Bickel, *The Original Understanding and the Segregation Decision*, 69 Harv. L. Rev. 1, 13-14, n.35 (1955). See Cong. Globe, 39th Cong., 1st Sess. 39, 474 (1865) (hereinafter referred to as Globe), wherein Senator Lyman Trumbull (Ill.) said that Southern states discriminate against freemen in their statutes, "deny them certain rights, subject them to severe penalties, and still impose upon them the very restrictions which were imposed upon them in consequence of the existence of slavery, and before it was abolished." See also Globe, 603, 605, 744-5.

[6] Globe 1123 ("Vagrant laws have been passed; laws which, under the pretense of selling these men as vagrants, are calculated and intended to reduce them to slavery again"); 1124, 1151, 1153, 1160 ("In South Carolina and other states there are laws compelling the return of the freedman to his master under the name of employer, and allowing him to be whipped for insolence"); 1621, 1759.

[7] Globe 1151. He also said: "Why should they be deprived of the right to make and enforce contracts . . . of the right to inherit, purchase, lease, hold, and convey real and personal property?" (Globe 1151) "What kind of freedom is that under which a man may . . . be deprived of the ability to make a contract . . . to sell or convey real or personal estate; may be deprived of the liberty to engage in the ordinary pursuits of civilized life . . . ?" (Globe 1152).

[8] Globe 322. He also declared that Congress may "permit the colored man to contract . . . permit him to buy and sell."

told the House that "The State laws of Georgia and South Carolina prohibit any Negro from buying or leasing a home," and set forth in detail the effects of a similar Mississippi statute.[9] And Congressman William Lawrence of Ohio concluded: "If States may deny to any class of our citizens the right to make contracts, to own a homestead [it] may strip men of all that is valuable in life. . . ."[10]

Southern states were not alone in restricting the rights of Negroes to own land or make contracts. The Indiana Constitution of 1851 provided as follows:

> *Sec. 1.* No Negro or mulatto shall come into or settle in the State after the adoption of this Constitution.
> *Sec. 2.* All contracts made with any Negro or mulatto coming into the State contrary to the provisions of the foregoing section shall be void; and every person who shall employ such Negro or mulatto or otherwise encourage him to remain in the State, shall be fined in any sum not less than ten dollars nor more than $500.[11]

This provision was so often referred to during the debates in 1866,[12] that Congressman William E. Niblack was moved to say: "Mr. Speaker, the Constitution and laws of Indiana relating to negroes and mulattoes have been so often referred to in the de-

---

9 Globe 1160. He stated: "Lieutenant Stewart Eldridge writes to Major General Howard from Vicksburg, Mississippi, under date of November 28, 1865: 'I have the honor to include herewith for your consideration the freedmen's bill, which has just become a law in this State, and would respectfully ask your attention to the following points thereon: Section first prohibits the holding, leasing, or renting of real estate by freedmen. . . . Section five authorizes mayors and boards of police by their sole edict to prevent any freedmen from doing any independent business and to compel them to labor as employees, with no appeal from such decision.' . . . Colonel Samuel Thomas, assistant commissioner, writes from Jackson, Mississippi, concerning this same Mississippi freedmen's bill: 'The freedmen bill has become law. It does not allow freedmen to own or lease estate. Thousands of acres have been rented from owners of land by freedmen who expected that they would be allowed to cultivate land in this way. They are notified that they must give up their leases by citizens. What course must I pursue?' " See also Globe 39, 1759. Congressman George Julian of Indiana stated: "Mississippi allows no negro living in any corporate town to lease or rent lands." Globe 3210. See *infra*, n.17.

10 Globe 1837. Cf. Globe 340, 1124, 1680. And Senator John B. Henderson of Missouri declared that the South denied freed Negroes "the right to hold real or personal property." Globe 3034. Testimony before the Joint Committee of Fifteen on Reconstruction tended to reinforce this view. One witness, a loyalist New Orleans attorney, upon being asked "What is the prevailing sentiment among the rebels in regard to allowing negroes to become landholders in the state?" replied: "There is a very general opposition to that." Kendrick, *Journal of the Joint Committee of Fifteen on Reconstruction* 273 (1914). See also 276.

11 Ind. Const., Art. XIII (1851). It is interesting to note that the Supreme Court of Indiana held that the Civil Rights Act of 1866 overruled this provision. Smith v. Moody, 26 Ind. 299 (1866).

12 See, e.g., Globe 318, App. 158.

bates during the present session of Congress, and are so different from those of most, if not all, of the other northern states that I . . . feel called upon . . . to vindicate . . . the policy which our people have seen proper to pursue. . . ."[13] Likewise, the Oregon Constitution of 1857 provided that "No free negro or mulatto, not residing in this state at the time of the adoption of this constitution, shall come, reside, or be within this state, hold any real estate, or make any contracts, or maintain any suit thereon."[14]

Thus, the Thirty-Ninth Congress was faced with state legislation which prohibited Negroes from buying or selling real estate, making contracts, or engaging in business. The problem was not one of forcing private individuals to deal with Negroes, but simply of removing state legislation which prohibited them from leasing or buying land from willing sellers. It was to this that Congress directed its attention.

II. *The Freemen's Bureau Bill*

On January 5, 1866, Senator Trumbull introduced a bill to enlarge the powers of the Freedmen's Bureau.[15] Section 7 provided:

> That whenever, in any State or district in which the ordinary course of judicial proceeding has been interrupted by the rebellion, and wherein, in consequence of any State or local law . . . any of the civil rights or immunities belonging to white persons, including the right to make and enforce contracts, to sue, . . . to inherit, purchase, lease, sell, hold, and convey real and personal property . . . are refused or denied to negroes . . . it shall be the duty of the President . . . to extend military protection. . . .[16]

This bill was in a sense a successor to the one to secure equal rights proposed by Senator Henry Wilson of Massachusetts.[17] That bill was urged by Wilson to "secure to these freemen the right to acquire and hold property, to enjoy the fruits of their own labor. . . . These are among the natural rights of free men."[18]

---

13 Globe 3211-2.
14 Ore. Const., Art. I, § 35 (1857). Illinois had an unrepealed constitutional provision prohibiting Negroes from coming into the state. Ill. Const., Art. 14 (1848). However, legislation effectuating it had been repealed. Globe 3038.
15 Globe 129. The Bureau had been created by the Act of March 3, 1865, c. 90, 13 Stat. 507.
16 Globe 318.
17 S. 9, Globe 39.
18 Globe 42. He also said: "I do not believe the Senator is in favor of that kind of

Trumbull agreed that "it is idle to say that a man is free . . . who cannot buy and sell, who cannot enforce his rights."[19]

The Freemen's Bureau Bill was urged by Trumbull as a temporary expedient, a companion measure to the permanent Civil Rights Bill. He supported it as an enforcement of the Thirteenth Amendment, declaring that Congress had power to "declare null and void all laws which will not permit the colored man to contract . . . which will not permit him to buy and sell."[20] Senator William Stewart of Nevada likewise supported the bill to give Negroes "a chance to hold property."[21]

The Freemen's Bureau Bill never became law. The President vetoed it, and the Senate failed to override the veto.[22] However, the remarks made on its behalf are of significance in an understanding of the Civil Rights Act of 1866.

III. *The Civil Rights Act of 1866*

On January 29, 1866, before the House had acted on the Freemen's Bureau Bill, Senator Trumbull brought up in the Senate his Civil Rights Bill. Section 1 of this bill contained a provision very similar to that of Section 7 of the Freemen's Bureau Bill. It provided:

> That there shall be no discrimination in civil rights or immunities among the inhabitants of any State or Territory of the United States on account of race, color, or previous condition of slavery; but the inhabitants of every race and color, without regard to any previous condition of slavery or involuntary servitude, except as a punishment for crime whereof the party shall have been duly convicted, shall have the same right to make and enforce contracts, to sue, be parties, and give evidence, to inherit, purchase, lease, sell, hold, and convey real and personal property, and to full

---

freedom that turns the emancipated workingman out into the highway, then takes him up as a vagrant and makes a slave of him because he cannot get a home when they do not allow him to lease land or buy a humble home. They have enacted a law in the State of Mississippi that will not allow the black man to lease lands or to buy lands outside of the cities. Where in God's name is he to go? . . . They have enacted a law in the State of Louisiana that he must get a home in twenty days, and they will not sell him land or allow him to lease land. We must annul this; we must see to it that . . . he can . . . work when and for whom he pleases . . . that he can lease and buy and sell and own property, real and personal; . . . who knows that his cabin, however humble, is protected by the just and equal laws of his country." Globe 111.

19 Globe 43.
20 Globe 322. Cf. Globe 209.
21 Globe 298.
22 Globe 915-7, 943.

and equal benefit of all laws and proceedings for the security of person and property, and shall be subject to like punishment, pains, and penalties, and to none other, any law, statute, ordinance, regulation, or custom to the contrary notwithstanding.[23]

The purpose of this bill, according to Trumbull, was to nullify state statutes in Southern states which denied Negroes "fundamental rights as belong to every free person." These rights Trumbull found in court decisions interpreting the "privileges and immunities" clause of the United States Constitution.[24] For example, he quoted one Maryland case interpreting this clause to include "the peculiar advantage of acquiring and holding real as well as personal property, and that such property should be protected and secured by the laws of the state in the same manner as the property of the citizens of the State is protected."[25] From a Massachusetts decision, he again gleaned the right to "take and hold real estate."[26] But his greatest reliance was placed on the enumeration of rights in *Corfield v. Coryell*,[27] including "the right to acquire and possess property of every kind . . . to take, hold, and dispose of property, either real or personal. . . ."[28] He concluded his objects to be to secure:

> The great fundamental rights set forth in this bill: the right to acquire property . . . to make contracts, and to inherit and dispose of property.[29]

Here we may stop for a moment to analyze Trumbull's concept of the clause which gives citizens of one state the privileges and immunities of citizens of the several states. Absent this clause, residents of one state might be considered as mere aliens in another state, and hence disabled from acquiring, under English common law rules, real estate by inheritance, succession, or conveyance, but this clause removes the disability of sister-state residence, and permits residents of other states to hold property they might otherwise acquire.[30] However, it has never been suggested that this clause

---

23 Globe 474. This was previously considered. See Globe 211.

24 U.S. Const., Art. IV, § 2.

25 Globe 474, citing Campbell v. Morris, 3 Har. & McH. 535 (Md. 1797).

26 Globe 474, citing Abbott v. Bayley, 23 Mass. (6 Pick.) 89, 92, (1827).

27 6 Fed. Cas. 546, 551-2 (No. 3,230) (C.C. Pa. 1823). See also Globe App. 135, 293, 1835. This case was also referred to in the debate on the Fourteenth Amendment. See Globe 2765.

28 Globe 475.

29 *Ibid.* He further noted: "A law that does not allow a colored person to hold property . . . is certainly a law in violation of the rights of a freeman. . . ."

30 Magill v. Brown, 16 Fed. Cas. 408, 428 (No. 8952) (C.C.E.D. Pa. 1833). The reference

gives residents of one state the right to compel residents of another to sell them land although the owners are unwilling to do so, even if this unwillingness stemmed from the owner's dislike of non-residents. All the clause does is to sweep away state laws which forbid the sale or devise to non-residents, leaving the latter to obtain land only if the owner is willing to part with it. The use of this clause in urging the passage of the Civil Rights Bill shows that the latter was intended to have the same effect, and nothing in the debates detracts from this view.

The debates in both houses of Congress show that this was the undoubted intent of the proponents of the bill. Senator John Sherman of Ohio said "that these men must be protected in certain rights . . . to acquire and hold property, and other universal incidents of freedom."[31] And after the President's veto of the Civil Rights Bill, Trumbull again asserted "that certain fundamental rights belong to every American citizen as such, and among those are the rights . . . to acquire property."[32]

Statements in the House are to the same effect. Congressman James F. Wilson of Iowa, manager of the Civil Rights Bill from the House Committee on the Judiciary, opened the debate in that body by defining "civil rights." He quoted from Kent, that civil rights were the absolute rights of individuals, including "the right to acquire and enjoy property,"[33] and likewise quoted from the privileges and immunities clause of Article 4 of the Constitution and from *Corfield v. Coryell*.[34] He asserted that "the entire structure of this bill rests on the discrimination . . . made by the States." He emphatically disclaimed any intent to "deprive a white man

---

in Trumbull's quotation of Abbott v. Bayley, *supra* note 26, to the fact that "they shall not be deemed aliens, but may take and hold real estate," supports this view. Likewise, Senator Edgar Cowan of Pennsylvania observed: "but in so far as the right to hold property, particularly the right to acquire title to real estate, was concerned, that was a subject entirely within the control of the States. It has been so considered in the State of Pennsylvania; and aliens and others who acknowledge no allegiance, either to the State or to the General Government, may be limited and circumscribed in that particular." Globe 2890.

31 Globe 744. In opposing the bill, Senator Garrett Davis of Kentucky urged that "Some of the States deny to negroes the right to hold lands," and that the bill would overturn this. Globe 1415.

32 Globe 1781. Senator Edgar Cowan, a moderate Republican from Pennsylvania, agreed "that all men should have the right to contract, and generally to purchase, lease and hold real estate." *Ibid.* Cf. Globe, 1255.

33 Globe 1117.

34 *Supra* note 27. Cf. Globe App. 157-8.

of a single right to which he is entitled."[35] And finally, Wilson returned to Kent as well as Blackstone to drive home his point that property rights were fundamental.[36]

Congressman Cook declared that the Civil Rights Bill would not touch or impair any rights of whites, but only prevent state discriminatory legislation.[37] Congressman Thayer declared that "the sole purpose of the bill is to secure" to freemen "those rights which constitute the essence of freedom, and which are common to the citizens of all civilized States," rights "which are common to the humblest citizen of every free state," the right "to make and enforce contracts" and the right "to inherit, purchase, lease, hold and convey real and personal property."[38] Congressman Lawrence, in urging passage of the bill over the President's veto, reiterated its aim of annulling discriminatory state laws.[39] And even the President, in his veto message, urged as an objection that the bill would "abrogate all state laws of discrimination between the two races in the matter of real estate . . . and of contracts generally."[40]

Nowhere in the extensive debates on the Civil Rights Act of 1866 is it even intimated that the law would do anything more

35 Globe 1118.

36 *Ibid.* He included: "The right of personal property; which he defines to be, 'The free use, enjoyment, and disposal of all his acquisitions, without any control or diminution, save only by the laws of the land.' Sharwood's Blackstone, vol. 1, chap. 1. In his lecture on the absolute rights of persons, Chancellor Kent (Kent's Commentaries, vol. 1, page 599) says: 'The absolute rights of individuals may be resolved into . . . the right to acquire and enjoy property.' "

37 Globe 1123-4. He had previously stated that "every individual citizen of each state in the union has rights in every other state—the right to acquire, possess and dispose of property," and that those rights came from the United States Constitution and not from the States. Globe 899.

38 Globe 1151-2.

39 Globe 1835, declaring that the federal government could intervene "if a State, by her laws, says to a whole class of native or naturalized citizens, 'You shall not buy a house or homestead to shelter your children within our borders;' . . . 'you shall have no right to sue in our courts or make contracts.' " And Congressman Samuel Shellabarger of Ohio stated: "Who will say that Ohio can pass a law enacting that no man of the German race, and whom the United States has made a citizen of the United States, shall ever own any property in Ohio, or shall ever make a contract in Ohio, or ever inherit property in Ohio, or ever come into Ohio to live, or even to work? If Ohio may pass such a law, and exclude a German citizen, not because he is a bad man or has been guilty of crime, but because he is of the German nationality or race, then may every other state do so; and you have the spectacle of an American citizen admitted to all its high privileges, and entitled to the protection of his government in each of these rights, and bound to surrender life and property for its defense, and yet that citizen is not entitled to either contract, inherit, own property, work, or live upon a single spot of the Republic, nor to breathe its air." Globe 1294.

40 Globe 1680.

than eliminate discriminatory state laws. The bill's proponents eagerly asserted that rights of individual whites would remain unimpaired. In light of the fact that laws forbidding private discrimination were completely unknown, it would be absurd to assert that the ability to compel persons to sell, not to mention contract or devise, without their individual right to discriminate, was a right "common to the humblest citizen" or "the essence of freedom." In the tenor of the times, and the prevailing views of rights in property, such anti-discrimination laws might well have been deemed a violation of the civil rights of whites. It certainly could not be argued that it was part of the civil rights of Negroes intended to be advanced by the bill.

IV. *The Initial Version of the Fourteenth Amendment*

The privileges and immunities, due process, and equal protection clauses of the Fourteenth Amendment are a product of Representative John A. Bingham, a Radical Republican from Ohio, who had voted against the Civil Rights Act of 1866 although in agreement with its purposes because he believed that Congress lacked constitutional power to pass it, and because of the potential sweep of the term "civil rights."[41] It was his version of the Joint Committee on Reconstruction's work on a constitutional amendment to secure equal rights which the Committee ultimately accepted and reported out.[42]

The original version of the Fourteenth Amendment, as Fairman correctly points out, was an affirmative grant of legislative power to Congress to secure privileges and immunities and equal protection for life, liberty and property.[43] Bingham and several Radicals defended it on the grounds that it was merely declarative of constitutional rights already granted.[44]

The proposed amendment first came under fire from Representative Andrew Jackson Rogers of New Jersey, a Democratic

---

41 Bickel, *op. cit. supra* note 5, at 22-28.
42 *Id.* at 33.
43 Fairman, *op. cit. supra* note 4, at 24. This was also Hale's view. Globe 1064. The text, at Globe 1034, is: "The Congress shall have power to make all laws which shall be necessary and proper to secure to the citizens of each State all privileges and immunities of citizens in the several States, and to all persons in the several States equal protection in the rights of life, liberty, and property."
44 Globe 1034; Bickel, *op. cit. supra* note 5, at 33-4.

member of the Joint Committee. The main thrust of his attack was that the amendment would overcentralize the government and destroy state powers. While apparently in favor of permitting Negroes to own property,[45] he attacked the proposal on the ground that it would wipe away state discriminatory legislation.[46]

However, the main speaker against Bingham's proposal was Representative Robert S. Hale, a moderate New York Republican, who had formerly been a judge. Hale subjected the amendment to close scrutiny, likewise attacking it as a "provision under which all State legislation, in its codes of civil and criminal jurisprudence and procedure, affecting the individual citizen, may be overridden, may be repealed or abolished, and the law of Congress established instead."[47] To this Congressman Thaddeus Stevens of Pennsylvania, the leader of the Radical Republicans, replied that "Congress could [not] interfere in any case where the legislation of a State was equal, impartial to all" and that the amendment was "simply to provide that, where any state makes a distinction in the same law between different classes of individuals, Congress shall have power to correct such discrimination and inequality."[48]

Hale then turned to the change which the amendment would effect in state legislation over property rights. He pointed to the fact that Congress might require that "married women, in regard to their rights of property, should stand on the same footing with men and unmarried women,"[49] although in all states distinctions still persisted. Brushing aside Stevens' rebuttal that these groups were in different classes, he replied that if that were the distinction,

---

[45] Globe App. 134: "Negroes . . . should be protected in . . . property, and by the States should be allowed all the rights of . . . contracting, and doing every act or thing that a white man is authorized by law to do."

[46] *Ibid.*: "According to the organic law of Indiana a negro is forbidden to come there and hold property. This amendment would abrogate and blot out forever that law, which is valuable in the estimation of the sovereign people of Indiana." See also Globe App. 135: The proposed amendment will "empower the Federal Government to exercise an absolute, despotic, uncontrollable power of entering the domain of the States and saying to them, 'Your state laws must be repealed whenever they do not give to the colored population of the country the same rights and privileges to which your white citizens are entitled. . . . You nowhere find Congress endowed with the right to interfere with the eminent domain and the sovereign power of a State. But each State has sovereign jurisdiction and power over the property, the liberty, the privileges and immunities, and the lives of its citizens.'"

[47] Globe 1063.

[48] *Ibid.*

[49] *Ibid.*

Negroes could be placed in a different class than whites. He objected to the fact that the amendment would overturn the discriminatory provisions of the Oregon Constitution, and probably those of Indiana as well, as an undue interference in state internal affairs.[50]

The next day, Congressman Thomas T. Davis, another New York Republican, echoed Hale's objection about overcentralization. He urged that states were not under federal control "in respect of social arrangement . . . of the rights of property, and control of persons."[51]

Bingham attempted to save his proposal in a long defensive speech. His position was that the amendment would give Congress the power to enforce the bill of rights against the states.[52] In response to a question from Rogers about the meaning of "due process of law," he replied that "the courts have settled that long ago, and the gentlemen can go and read their decisions."[53] He rebutted Hale's argument by declaring that under the proposal, property would still be under state law.[54]

---

50 "*Mr. Bingham.* [The amendment] is to apply to other States also that have in their constitutions and laws today provisions in direct violation of every principle of our Constitution.

"*Mr. Rogers.* I suppose the gentleman refers to the State of Indiana?

"*Mr. Bingham.* I do not know; it may be so. It applies unquestionably to the State of Oregon.

"*Mr. Hale.* . . . And here we come to the very thing for which I denounce this proposition, that it takes away from these States the right to determine for themselves what their institutions shall be. . . . Oregon has not been in rebellion; the gentleman has no charge to bring against her, except that she has incorporated into her constitution and laws provisions that to him are distasteful, and which he thinks unjust. I submit that that should never be a question for us to pass upon here in Congress." Globe 1065.

51 Globe 1083.

52 Globe 1088.

53 Globe 1089.

54 *Ibid.* He said: "But the gentleman's concern is as to the right of property in married women.

"Although this word property has been in your bill of rights from the year 1789 until this hour, who ever heard it intimated that anybody could have property protected in any State until he owned or acquired property there according to its local law or according to the law of some other State which he may have carried thither? I undertake to say no one.

"As to real estate, every one knows that its acquisition and transmission under every interpretation ever given to the word property, as used in the Constitution of the country, are dependent exclusively upon the local law of the States, save under a direct grant of the United States. But suppose any person has acquired property not contrary to the laws of the State, but in accordance with its law, are they not to be equally protected in the enjoyment of it, or are they to be denied all protection? That is the question, and the whole question, so far as that part of the case is concerned."

Bingham then launched into a long discussion of the need to overrule *Barron v. Baltimore*[55] and apply the bill of rights to the states. This case, of course, was one where the state had interfered with real property rights, a point he knew quite well.[56] He asserted that the constitutional guarantees were "disregarded today in Oregon" and in the South, and that the amendment was needed to secure "equal protection to life, liberty or property."[57] In response to a question from Hale, he asserted that the proposal would permit Congress to secure equal protection "to life and liberty and property . . . the right to real estate being dependent on the State law." Hale asked that if Congress could not legislate "in regard to real estate," did Bingham mean "to imply that it extends to personal estate." He answered: "Undoubtedly it is true . . . [because] the personal property of a citizen follows its owner, and is entitled to be protected in the State into which he goes."[58] He concluded that the proposal simply gave Congress power "to see to it that the protection given by the laws of the States shall be equal in respect to life and liberty and property to all persons."

Bingham's remarks did not satisfy his colleagues. Congressman Giles W. Hotchkiss, a New York Republican lawyer, still thought the proposal would give Congress power to establish uniform laws to protect life, liberty, and property, thus overcentralizing the government. Moreover, Congress could repeal or alter such legislation. He suggested an amendment "that no State shall discriminate against any class of its citizens."[59]

The Republican leadership, sensing that the proposal could not pass, moved that it be postponed.[60] The House Republicans,

55 32 U.S. (7 Pet.) 243 (1833).
56 See Cong. Globe, 42d Cong., 1st Sess. App. 83 (1871).
57 Globe 1090.
58 Globe 1094. Bingham stated: "Let the gentleman look to the great Mississippi case, Slaughter and another, which is familiar, doubtless, to all members of the House." No doubt Bingham was referring to Groves v. Slaughter, 40 U.S. (15 Pet.) 449 (1841), where Justice Baldwin declared that if slaves were brought into a free state by the owner, "no law of either State could take away or affect his right of property." *Id.* at 516.
59 Globe 1095. It might be noted that Hale had also pointed out that the proposal differed from the bill of rights in that the latter was a limitation on power. Globe 1064.
60 Kendrick, *op. cit. supra* note 10, at 215. Congressman James A. Garfield, Ohio Republican, who was later to be President, stated: "Now, let it be remembered that the proposed amendment was a plain, unambiguous proposition to empower Congress to legislate directly upon the citizens of all the States in regard to their rights of life, liberty,

including Bingham, followed party leadership,[61] and the proposal
was dropped.

This proposal is significant to show Bingham's thinking. True,
it was hazy, perhaps even confused.[62] The privileges and immunities clause could apply to, and was early held to apply to, real property,[63] as well as personal property, even though only the latter
could be moved from state to state. Certainly, the equal protection
clause could apply to both, and Congress was particularly interested in State laws preventing Negroes from owning real estate.
However, the debate shows clearly that Bingham did not intend
to supplant state law procedures for acquiring property, but merely
wanted to protect property lawfully acquired from confiscation or
undue restriction, as was true in *Barron v. Baltimore.*

V.   *The Final Version of the Fourteenth Amendment*

The final version of the privileges and immunities, due process, and equal protection clauses of the Fourteenth Amendment
likewise was Bingham's product.[64] Stevens introduced it as the
Committee draft in the House. The Radicals considered it a dis-
appointingly mild provision, but congressional Republicans, afraid
of defeat in the fall 1866 elections, rejected any radical proposals
too closely tied with Negroes.[65] Instead, the Fourteenth Amendment was intended as a compromise measure which the majority
of Republican professional politicians in Congress considered a
safe party platform and useful campaign material which would be
valuable in carrying the country. Thus the Chicago Tribune of
May 5, 1866, a Radical newspaper, referred to the first section
as "surplusage," and deemed the measure feeble. However, if
Radicals were unenthusiastic, others could hardly attack it. Op-

---

and property. . . . , After a debate of two weeks . . . it became evident that many leading
Republicans of this House would not consent to so radical a change in the Constitution,
and the bill was recommitted to the joint select committee." Cong. Globe, 42d Cong., 1st
Sess. App. 151 (1871). He also declared: "It will not be denied, as a matter of history,
that this form of amendment received many Republican votes that the first form to
which I have referred could not have received."

   61 Globe 1095.

   62 Bickel, *op. cit., supra* note 5, at 24-25, 39; Fairman, *op. cit. supra* note 4, at 31-36.

   63 Corfield v. Coryell, 6 Fed. Cas. 546, 551-2 (No. 3,230) (C.C. Pa. 1823).

   64 Kendrick, *op. cit. supra* note 10, at 106. The progress of this version is set forth
in Bickel, *op. cit. supra* note 5, at 40-45.

   65 James, *The Framing of the Fourteenth Amendment,* 110-120 (1956).

ponents would have to take an opposite position. "We would like to see them advocate the proposition that local legislatures shall have the authority to abridge the rights of the citizen, or to deprive any person of life, liberty, or property without due process of law."[66]

Stevens, the leading House Radical, did not conceal his disappointment, but confessed it was the best he could get.[67] He stated that the first section was designed to "correct the unjust legislation of the States, so far that the law which operates upon one man shall operate *equally* upon all." He pointed out that the Civil Rights Bill had the same object, but since Congress could repeal it at any time, he desired to secure this beyond the control of a hostile majority.[68] Other Congressmen likewise discussed the first section as a constitutional embodiment of the Civil Rights Act of 1866.[69] A Pennsylvania Democrat opposed it because "the first section proposes to make an equality in every respect between the two races, notwithstanding the policy of discrimination which has heretofore been exclusively exercised by the States."[70] Bingham closed the debate by saying that the first section would protect citizens "from unconstitutional state enactments,"[71] and shortly thereafter the House passed the amendment.[72]

In the Senate, Senator Jacob M. Howard of Michigan opened the debate by tying the privileges and immunities clause to Article IV, § 2 and the Bill of Rights, lamenting that "the restriction contained in the Constitution against the taking of private property for public use without just compensation is not a restriction

[66] *Id.* at 123-4, 134-5, 145.

[67] "This proposition is not all that the Committee desired. It falls far short of my wishes. . . . I believe it is all that can be obtained in the present state of public opinion. . . . Upon a careful survey of the whole ground, we did not believe that nineteen of the loyal States could be induced to ratify any proposition more stringent than this. . . . Believing, then, that this is the best proposition that can be made effectual, I accept it." Globe 2459. Congressman John M. Broomall, a Pennsylvania Radical Republican said: "It is not what I wanted. How far short of it! But the necessity is urgent, and we must take what will obtain the votes of two thirds of both houses of Congress, and the ratification of three fourths of the actual States. . . ." Globe 2498. See also Globe 2511, 2539.

[68] Globe 2459.

[69] See, e.g., Globe 2462 (Garfield); 2465 (Thayer); 2467 (Boyer); 2498 (Broomall); 2502 (Raymond); 2511 (Eliot); 2538 (Rogers). See Bickel, *op. cit. supra* note 5, at 47-8.

[70] Globe 2530 (Congressman Samuel Jackson Randall).

[71] Globe 2543.

[72] Globe 2545.

upon state legislation."[73] He stated that the first section would permit Congress to enforce the bill of rights against the States, and deprive them of power to subject Negroes to different laws than whites. He declared that "section one is a restriction upon the States, and . . . will . . . forever disable every one of them from passing laws trenching upon those fundamental rights and privileges. . . ."[74] When debate resumed after a few days of caucusing by the Republican members,[75] Senator Luke Poland, Vermont Republican and former Chief Justice of that State, referred to the due process and equal protection clauses as an embodiment of the Civil Rights Bill's principles, directed at "partial State legislation," some of "very recent enactment,"[76] a reference to the Black Codes. Senator Timothy O. Howe, a Wisconsin Radical Republican, declared that the first section was necessary because Southern states "denied to a large portion of their respective populations the plainest and most necessary rights of citizenship. The right to hold land when they had bought it and paid for it would have been denied them; the right to collect their wages by the processes of the law when they had earned their wages. . . ."[77]

Senator John B. Henderson, a Missouri Republican, also referred to the Black Codes. He said that the South denied Negroes "the right to hold real or personal property . . . and forced upon him unequal burdens. Though nominally free, so far as discriminating legislation could make him so he was yet a slave." He added that the Civil Rights Bill abolished such laws,[78] but that while women and aliens "are regarded as persons and not dumb brutes;

---

[73] Globe 2765. He also quoted at length from Corfield v. Coryell, *supra* note 63.

[74] Globe 2766.

[75] Globe 2938.

[76] Globe 2961. Senator Garrett Davis, Kentucky Democrat, said the same thing. Globe App. 240.

[77] Globe App. 219. He also attacked the harsh criminal laws and punishments in the South. Globe App. 223.

[78] Globe 3034-5: Congress did "a simple act of justice to the negroes and poorer whites of the South, who had been always loyal to the Government. For that purpose . . . the 'Freemen's Bureau bill,' and . . . 'the civil rights bill,' were . . . adopted . . . their sole object was to break down in the seceded States the system of oppression to which I have alluded. Their only effect was . . . to give the right to hold real and personal estate to the negro, to enable him to sue and be sued in courts, . . . to have the process of the courts for his protection, and to enjoy in the respective States those fundamental rights of person and property which cannot be denied to any person without disgracing the Government itself. It was simply to carry out that provision of the Constitution which confers upon the citizens of each State the privileges and immunities of citizens in the several States."

they enjoy the right to acquire property, to enter the courts for its protection, to follow the professions, to accumulate wealth," if the Civil Rights Bill were declared unconstitutional, Negroes would lose such protection.[79] Finally, Senator Reverdy Johnson, a Maryland Democrat who was a member of the Joint Committee, but who voted against the amendment as a whole, stated that he was "in favor of that part of the first section which denies to a State the right to deprive any person of life, liberty, or property without due process of law,"[80] showing that this provision was intended to be universal and hence commanded even Democratic support.[81] The amendment, with several changes from the House version, was then passed.[82]

On June 13, 1866, when the House concurred in the Senate amendments, there was only brief debate. Rogers said that the first section "simply embodied the gist of the civil rights bill."[83] In the last speech, Stevens, Mr. Radical of the House, expressed his keen disappointment at "so imperfect a proposition," but accepted it "because I live among men and not among angels. . . ."[84] And with but a few brief references,[85] that was all the debate relevant to real property rights.

A few of the subsequent debates collected by Professor Fairman likewise reflect the universality of the first section. The *Cincinnati Commercial* understood it to abolish Black Codes and similar discriminatory legislation. A prominent Illinois Repub-

[79] Globe 3035.

[80] Globe 3041.

[81] Even Senator Garrett Davis of Kentucky, an unreconstructed rebel (Fairman, *op. cit. supra*, n. 4 at 65, Bickel, *op. cit. supra* note 5, at 14, n.36), could find nothing wrong with this provision except that it duplicated the provisions of "every State constitution, and the rights which it is intended to secure are regarded by all as a most important portion of American liberty, and there is no danger of the removal of the defenses which the States have thrown around them." Globe App. 240.

[82] Globe 3042.

[83] Globe App. 229.

[84] Globe 3148.

[85] In another debate Congressman George Julian, an Indiana Republican, stated that the Civil Rights Bill was designed to protect Negroes in their right to "make contracts and to own property." Globe 3209. Congressman John Baker, an Illinois Republican, thought the due process clause "a wholesome and needed check upon the great abuse of liberty which several of the States have practiced," apparently referring to Black Codes. Globe App. 256. And Congressman Samuel Shellabarger, an Ohio Republican, quoted Kent to the effect that "rights of protection of life and liberty, and to acquire and enjoy property" were national privileges which the amendment protected. Globe App. 293.

lican politician said that the rights of citizens it protected included "to sue and be sued, to own property . . . to have protection for life, liberty, and property . . . that the white or black man should collect his debt in court; that either should own and hold property that he pays for." To Congressman Schenck, the amendment removed from Negroes "the weight of inequality in . . . making contracts. . . ," while Congressman Delano viewed it as a protection for northern whites traveling south. Senator Sherman said that it embodied the Civil Rights Bill "to make contracts, to sue and be sued, to contract and be contracted with."[86] State legislatures or governors viewed it as an embodiment of the Civil Rights Bill,[87] or a mere repetition of state bills of rights,[88] designed to eliminate unequal state legislation.[89]

Several points remain to be discussed. The first is that the Fourteenth Amendment was intended to protect white persons as well as Negroes. Bingham repeatedly referred to his desire to protect the "loyal white men . . . against State statutes of confiscation and statutes of banishment."[90] Hotchkiss said that the "white man" as well as the "black man" would derive benefit from a proper constitutional amendment.[91] When Senator Davis argued that the Civil Rights Bill discriminated against whites by creating "partial," special rights for Negroes, Trumbull replied:

> Sir, this bill applies to white men as well as black men. It declares that all persons in the United States shall be entitled to the same civil rights, the right to the fruit of their own labor, the right to make contracts, the right to buy and sell . . . a bill that protects a white man just as much as a black man. . . . [How] can a Senator

---

86 Fairman, *op. cit. supra* note 4, at 70-77.

87 *Id.* at 105-6, 113, 115, 117. See also Flack, *The Adoption of the Fourteenth Amendment*, 143-5, 149-50 (1908).

88 Fairman, *op. cit. supra* note 4, at 109, 114.

89 *Id.* at 114. See also Rowan v. State, 30 Wis. 129, 148 (1872).

90 Globe 1094. In the same remarks he referred to his desire "to protect the loyal white minority" in South Carolina, and declared that unless an amendment were passed, "the loyal minority of white citizens . . . will be utterly powerless." *Ibid.* In a colloquy with Hale, he stated:

"*Mr. Hale:* It is claimed that this constitutional amendment is aimed simply and purely toward the protection of 'American citizens of African descent' in the States lately in rebellion. I understand that to be the whole intended practical effect of the amendment.

"*Mr. Bingham:* It is due to the committee that I should say that it is proposed as well to protect the thousands and tens of thousands and hundreds of thousands of loyal white citizens of the United States whose property, by State legislation, has been wrested from them under confiscation, and protect them also against banishment."

91 Globe 1095. See also Globe 2536 (Eckley), note 78 *supra*.

... say ... that this is a bill for the benefit of black men exclusively when there is no such distinction in it. . . .[92]

And in state debates, the need to protect loyal southern whites, or northern whites traveling south, through the Fourteenth Amendment, was prominently mentioned.[93]

The second point is, as Garfield declared, that the amendment "was throughout the debate, with scarcely an exception, spoken of as a limitation on the power of the States."[94] State legislation primarily, and state action exclusively, was intended to be limited, not only by Bingham,[95] but by the others as well. No restrictions were to be imposed on private individuals or groups.

Finally, the first section, and especially the due process clause, was intended to be a substantive, as well as a procedural, limitation on government.[96] Bingham, as previously noted, had referred

[92] Globe 599. Congressman Samuel W. Moulton of Illinois denounced Alabama "whose aristocratic and anti-republican laws, almost re-enacting slavery, among other harsh inflictions impose an imprisonment of three months and a fine of $100 upon any one owning firearms, and a fine of fifty dollars and six months' imprisonment on any servant or laborer (white or black) who loiters away his time or is stubborn or refractory." Globe 1621.

[93] Fairman, *op. cit. supra* note 4, at 90 ("a minority of whites so small as to be helpless"); 96 ("freedom of discussion . . . was not tolerated in the Southern States"); James, *op. cit. supra* note 65, at 159.

[94] Cong. Globe, 42nd Cong., 1st Sess. App. 151 (1871).

[95] *Id.* at 83-4, where Bingham said: "allow me to say, further, that by the text of the Constitution as you remember it . . . there are negative limitations upon the power of the States; as, for example, that no State shall make an ex post facto law; . . . These are of the negative limitations on the power of the States in the original text of the Constitution. . . . But, says the gentleman to me, why did you change the amendment of February, 1866? Sir, I sat at the feet of . . . that great man, John Marshall, foremost of all the judges, in the hope that by his guidance, the amendment might be so framed that in all the hereafter, it might be accepted by the historian of the American Constitution and her Magna Charta 'as the keystone of American liberty.' . . . I had read—and that is what induced me to attempt to impose by constitutional amendments new limitations upon the power of the States—the great decision of Marshall in Barron vs. . . . Baltimore, where the Chief Justice said . . . 'The amendments [to the Constitution] contain no expression indicating an intention to apply them to the State governments. This court cannot so apply them.' 7 Peters, p. 250. In this case the city had taken private property for public use, without compensation as alleged, and there was no redress for the wrong in the Supreme Court of United States; and only for this reason, the first eight amendments were not limitations on the power of the States.

* * * * *

"In reexamining that case of Barron, . . . I noted and apprehended as I never did before, certain words in that opinion of Marshall. Referring to the first eight articles of amendments to the Constitution of the United States, the Chief Justice said: 'Had the framers of these amendments intended them to be limitations on the powers of the State governments they would have imitated the framers of the original Constitution, and have expressed that intention.' Barron vs. The Mayor, etc., 7 Peters 250. Acting upon this suggestion, I did imitate the framers of the original Constitution."

[96] See the remark of Senator Frelinghuysen of New Jersey that "The fourteenth amendment goes much further than merely establishing 'equality' between whites and blacks." Cong. Globe, 42nd Cong., 1st Sess. 500 (1871).

Rogers to court decisions for the meaning of the due process clause,[97] and these had firmly established the interpretation that the clause limited legislative action impairing vested property rights or interests.[98] Bingham declared that "cruel and unusual punishments have been inflicted under State laws" but the federal constitution did not intervene,[99] that states "took property without compensation, and [citizens] had no remedy,"[100] and that "liberty . . . is the liberty . . . to work in an honest calling and contribute by your toil in some sort to the support of yourself . . . and to be secure in the enjoyment of the fruits of your toil."[101] Bingham not only considered the due process clause substantive, but was "a man who held thoroughly Lockian views concerning the sanctity of property"[102] and "property rights by his view are thus virtually absolute."[103]

Moreover, Bingham intended to secure not only property rights, but freedom of association and freedom of choice as well. He said:

> Sir, before the ratification of the fourteenth amendment, . . . a State, as in the case of the State of Illinois, could make it a crime punishable by fine and imprisonment for any citizen within her limits, in obedience to the injunction of our divine Master, to help a slave who was ready to perish; to give him shelter, or break with

97 *Supra*, n.53.

98 The cases are fully collected in Howe, *The Meaning of "Due Process of Law" Prior to the Adoption of the Fourteenth Amendment*, 18 Calif. L. Rev. 583 (1930). See also Corbin, *The Doctrine of Due Process of Law Before the Civil War*, 24 Harv. L. Rev. 366, 460 (1911). It might also be noted that the adoption of the due process and equal protection clauses was foreshadowed at the 1860 Republican National Convention. Paragraph 8 of the Platform stated: "that as our republican fathers . . . ordained that no person should be deprived of life, liberty, or property without due process of law, it becomes our duty, by legislation, whenever such legislation is necessary, to maintain this provision of the constitution against all attempts to violate it . . . ." Likewise, a special resolution moved by Joshua R. Giddings of Ohio and adopted by the convention stated: "Resolved, That we deeply sympathize with those men who have been driven, some from their native States and others from the States of their adoption, and are now exiled from their homes on account of their opinions; and we hold the Democratic Party responsible for the gross violation of the clause of the Constitution which declares that citizens of each State shall be entitled to all privileges and immunities of the citizens of the several States." 1 Curtis, *The Republican Party* 357, 361 (1904).

99 Globe 2542.

100 Cong. Globe, 42nd Cong., 1st Sess. App. 85 (1871). He also said: "The Government owes high and solemn duties to every citizen of the country. It is bound to protect him in his most important rights. Has he any rights more important than the rights of life, liberty, and property?" *Ibid.*

101 *Id.* at 86.

102 Graham, *The "Conspiracy Theory" of the Fourteenth Amendment*, 47 Yale L.J. 371, 401 (1938).

103 *Id.* at 398.

him his crust of bread. The validity of that State restriction upon the rights of conscience and the duty of life was affirmed, to the shame and disgrace of America, in the Supreme Court of the United States; but nevertheless affirmed in obedience to the requirements of the Constitution. (14 Howard, 19-20, Moore vs. The People.)[104]

This statement is very significant. In *Moore v. Illinois*,[105] the Supreme Court upheld a statute forbidding the assisting of runaway slaves based on "the police power . . . to protect themselves against the influx either of liberated or fugitive slaves, and to repel from their soil a population likely to become burdensome and injurious, either as paupers or criminals . . . . [This conduct tends] to destroy the harmony and kind feelings which should exist between citizens of this Union, to create border feuds and bitter animosities, and to cause breaches of the peace, violent assaults, riots and murder. No one can deny or doubt the right of a state to defend itself against evils of such magnitude. . . ."[106]

Here we see that Bingham has intended to embody in the Fourteenth Amendment the right of individuals to associate or not to associate with each other based on individual decision even as against a great compelling public need satisfied through an exercise of the police power. If the police power cannot restrain freedom of choice even to preserve the public peace and safety, preserve harmony with other states, and prevent a flood of paupers and criminals, it is obvious that the amendment secures it beyond infringement as an absolute right.

VI. *Summary and Conclusions*

Several firm conclusions can be drawn from an analysis of the legislative history of the Fourteenth Amendment. They are:

1. The framers considered property rights to be fundamental, and intended to limit State power to impair them.

2. Congress intended to restrict state legislation primarily, and state action exclusively. Private individuals were not restricted.

3. Congress intended to assure that states would not deprive

---

[104] Cong. Globe, 42nd Cong., 1st Sess. App. 84 (1871).
[105] 55 U.S. (14 How.) 13 (1852).
[106] *Id.* at 18.

Negroes of the capacity to own land or make contracts. The phrase in the debates and the Civil Rights Bill about the "right" to make contracts or own property simply means that state laws shall not prevent a willing seller, testator, or donor from conveying property to a Negro, or a willing person from contracting with him. It does not confer on a Negro power to compel unwilling testators to devise property to them, unwilling owners to give, lease, or sell them property, or anybody to contract with anybody else, nor does it authorize states to do so.

Beyond this, it is impossible to say exactly what the framers of the Fourteenth Amendment intended. No one had ever dreamed at that time of enacting anti-discrimination laws requiring unwilling owners of houses to sell or rent them to Negroes. But the amendment, framed by Bingham, one of the firmest believers in property rights, and not by the equalitarian Stevens, who was disappointed in it, offers little comfort to proponents of such laws. It restricted state laws to enlarge individual rights, and not the converse.

How would Bingham, the conservative Republican corporation lawyer from Ohio, have been struck by a law requiring an unwilling owner to sell to or rent to, or an unwilling resident to live near, people he did not want to do so? Would it have offended his notion of due process? In a recent case, one judge protested that "The Fair Housing Act of 1959 . . . would compel Case to transfer his residential property to the Rhones, not voluntarily, but under compulsion, with sanctions that might lead to imprisonment for failure to comply."[107] This protest seems remarkably like a 1795 case which held that "The legislature . . . had no authority to make an act divesting one citizen of his freehold, and vesting it in another . . . it is contrary to the principles of social alliance in every free government; . . . it is contrary both to the letter and spirit of the constitution."[108] It seems surprisingly like a 1798 United States Supreme Court case holding that a "law that takes property from A and gives it to B; it is against all reason and justice, for a people to entrust a legislature with such powers; and

---

[107] Colorado Anti-Discrimination Comm. v. Case, —— P.2d ——, —— (Colo. 1962), dissenting opinion of Hall, J.

[108] Van Horne's Lessee v. Dorrance, 2 U.S. (2 Dall.) 304, 310 (1795).

therefore, it cannot be presumed that they have done it."[109] Were these concepts part of the notions of Bingham, the conservative man of property, about "due process," as he wrote them into the Fourteenth Amendment? They may very well have been.

[109] Calder v. Bull, 3 U.S. (3 Dall.) 386, 388 (1798).

RACIAL RESTRICTIVE COVENANTS REVISITED

ELMER M. MILLION*

I. *Introduction*

RACIAL RESTRICTIVE COVENANTS, prior to *Shelley v. Kraemer*,[1] were a significant device by which home owners enforced a discriminatory residential policy in their areas. Since that case held racial covenants judicially unenforceable, their value as discriminatory devices has diminished greatly. However, the legal rules concerning covenants are still of interest both because such agreements, according to *Shelley*, are valid if voluntarily observed,[2] and because the *Shelley* doctrine does not yet extend to certain areas, such as the right of reverter.[3]

This article does not deny that *Shelley* changed the law, although Chief Justice Vinson, who wrote the opinion, later protested in his dissent in *Barrows v. Jackson*[4] that the majority was reading into *Shelley* a greater change than he had intended or enunciated. Nor will it discuss the constitutionality, legality, or motivation of the decision, or attempt to predict whether it will at some future time be overruled or modified by the Supreme Court. Instead this article will review the prior learning in the racially restrictive covenant field as if *Shelley* had not been decided.

II. *Reasons For Covenants*

The increasing migration of Negroes to the cities, both North and South, at the turn of the twentieth century and shortly before World War I[5] created tensions due in part to urban integration.

---

* A.B. 1936, Southwestern State Teachers Coll. (Okla.); LL.B. 1935, Univ. of Oklahoma; J.S.D. 1938, Yale Univ. Professor of Law, New York Univ. Co-author, Walsh & Niles, Cases on Property, vol. 1 (1951), vol. 2 (1954), vol. 3 (1957).

1 334 U.S. 1 (1948).

2 *Id.* at 13. See also Gast v. Gorek, 211 N.Y.S.2d 112 (Sup. Ct. 1961).

3 Charlotte Park and Recreation Comm. v. Barringer, 242 N.C. 311, 88 S.E.2d 114 (1955), *cert. denied sub nom.* Leeper v. Charlotte Park and Recreation Comm., 350 U.S. 983 (1956). *Contra*: Capitol Federal Savings and Loan Ass'n v. Smith, 136 Colo. 256, 316 P.2d 252 (1957) (affirming declaratory judgment of unenforceability of an executory interest which recorded agreements containing reciprocal covenants provided should arise in event of violation). Cf. Goldstein, *Rights of Entry and Possibilities of Reverter as Devices to Restrict the Use of Land*, 54 Harv. L. Rev. 248 (1940).

4 346 U.S. 249, 260 (1953).

5 16 Encyclopaedia Britannica 196-8 (1961); 11 Encyclopaedia of the Social Sciences 342-3 (1933).

To alleviate these tensions, and promote interracial peace by separation of racial residential areas,[6] several southern and border cities passed racial zoning ordinances segregating living areas.[7] However, in *Buchanan v. Warley*,[8] the United States Supreme Court held such ordinances invalid as state action unduly restricting property rights (of intending sellers) in violation of the due process clause of the Fourteenth Amendment, and added that the ordinances also violated the rights, privileges, and immunities guaranteed by the Fourteenth Amendment to (in this instance) Negro purchasers. Thus, just as the first major wave of Negro migration flooded into Northern cities during World War I, the Supreme Court shut the door on the use of state police power to prevent residential integration.

An attempt by a state governor to enforce residential racial segregation under the guise of martial law was characterized as void by the Oklahoma court in invalidating a city racial zoning ordinance enacted pursuant to a military order from the Governor.[9] Recently an alleged attempt to exclude Negroes from within the city limits by retracing the city boundaries was also outlawed.[10]

With the avenue of zoning closed to them, city dwellers who desired a homogeneous neighborhood turned increasingly to private racial restrictions contained in covenants running with the land.[11] The reason for these covenants was that "a person who owns a tract of land and divides it into smaller tracts for the purpose of selling one or more may prefer to have as neighbors persons of the white, or Caucasian, race, and may believe that prospective purchasers of the several tracts would entertain a similar preference, and would pay a higher price if the ownership were restricted to persons of that race."[12] Another court declared: "If it was dis-

---

[6] State v. Gurry, 121 Md. 534, 88 Atl. 546 (1913) (Baltimore penal ordinance upheld).
[7] Carey v. Atlanta, 143 Ga. 192, 84 S.E. 456 (1915) (residential segregation ordinance voided).
[8] 245 U.S. 60 (1917).
[9] Allen v. Oklahoma City, 175 Okla. 421, 52 P.2d 1054 (1936).
[10] Gomillion v. Lightfoot, 364 U.S. 339 (1960).
[11] In Meade v. Dennistone, 173 Md. 295, 196 Atl. 330, 333 (1938), it was stated: "The large, almost sudden, emigration of Negroes from the country to the cities, with the consequent congestion in colored centers, has created a situation about which all agree something ought to be done. . . . Since the decisions under the Fourteenth Amendment, *supra*, no public action can be taken to solve what has become a problem, and property owners have undertaken to regulate it by contract."
[12] Chandler v. Ziegler, 88 Colo. 1, 291 Pac. 822, 823 (1930).

tasteful to plaintiff to have a colored man as his adjoining neighbor, he had the legal right to refuse to sell him or his agents the property. . . ."[13]

In *Corrigan v. Buckley*[14] and in numerous other cases[15] prior to *Shelley* the enforcement of racial restrictive covenants was held to violate neither public policy nor the Fourteenth Amendment. Some of the later holdings, since overruled by *Shelley*, were based on the concept that since the restrictions were private, their enforcement did not convert them into "state action."[16] While the discussions of why the enforcement of restrictive covenants did not violate public policy differ from case to case, the underlying nub of many of them seems fairly reflected in the following quotation:

> The foundation stone of a happy, contented, and satisfied people is the home. The building of homes is to be encouraged because of the spiritual contentment a home brings to man. A home owner becomes a solid citizen with a stake in the community and is a supporter and defender of his government. It is the ambition of men and women to have homes in which to seek refuge and peace, and in which to rear families. They are not built or acquired with a view to their monetary value, but, rather, because of their spiritual appeal. Most homes cost the home owner more in dollars and cents than he ever hopes to receive for it; but he receives the monetary difference in "living." People who own a home, or contemplate acquiring one, have a right to protect it against future encroachments of business or other elements distasteful to them. Negroes have the same right in this respect as do those of other races. Home owners and prospective home owners should have confidence in the power and the willingness of the courts to protect their investment in happiness and security. Their solemn undertakings with this object in view will not be lightly set aside by this court, but will be zealously guarded as a gesture of encouragement to our people to become home owners instead of tenants.[17]

---

13 Koehler v. Rowland, 275 Mo. 573, 205 S.W. 217, 220 (1918), quoting Keltner v. Harris, 196 S.W. 1, 2 (Mo. 1917).

14 299 Fed. 899 (D.C. Cir. 1924), aff'd, 271 U.S. 323 (1926).

15 The cases are collected in 9 A.L.R. 120, 66 A.L.R. 531, 114 A.L.R. 1237, and 162 A.L.R. 180. These annotations were later superseded (after *Shelley*) by annotation in 3 A.L.R.2d 466.

16 E.g., Parmalee v. Morris, 218 Mich. 625, 188 N.W. 330 (1922).

17 Porter v. Johnson, 232 Mo. App. 1150, 115 S.W.2d 529, 535 (1938). And in Burkhardt v. Lofton, 63 Cal. App. 2d 230, 146 P.2d 720, 724-5 (1944), the court said: "Racial restrictions have been employed in the development of countless residential communities and have very generally been considered essential to the maintenance and stability of property values. Non-Caucasians are and always have been just as free to restrict the use and occupancy of their property to members of their own races as Caucasians have been. The fact that the members of the Caucasian race have freely availed themselves of this right throughout the nation, even though those of non-Caucasian races have not,

III. *Who May Enforce Covenants*

The general rule is that only a person for whose benefit a covenant is made may enforce it, if he was not a party to the contract or deed.[18] This represents a factual question as to the intentions of the parties to the covenant.[19]

It had been held that where there existed a general plan for the development of a number of lots in the same property by the original owner, each of the lot owners could enforce a racially restrictive covenant against another grantee of their common grantor. Under these circumstances, the covenant was deemed to be made for the benefit of the other lots and their future lot-owners, to make the parcels more salable. Hence, courts construed both the obligation and the benefit of the covenants as running with the respective parcels of land.[20] *A fortiori*, where the subdivider was still in possession of the parcel, he could enforce the covenant too.[21]

In addition, the fact that premises bound by a racial covenant were later purchased at a tax sale did not free the tax deed grantee from enforcement of the racially restrictive use covenant.[22] This accords with the prevailing view that a tax sale of either the dominant or servient estate does not destroy the validity of either ease-

---

is the most satisfactory proof of the public policy of the nation with respect to this phase of the right to contract. No doubt public policy changes and develops with the times, but these changes must have their sources in the citizenry and not in the decisions of courts or the pronouncements of publicists and politicians. The right to contract with reference to their own property is one that is preserved to all citizens and, except where restricted by law, is a right which the peoples of all races may exercise freely. It cannot be denied by the courts to those who make use of it in certain situations because others similarly situated may choose not to avail themselves of it. The responsibility of striking down the validity of racial restrictions with respect to the use and occupancy of real property is one which no court or judge should assume on the strength of individual theories as to what constitutes the 'present' public policy on the subject or of personal belief that the consequences would be for the general good. The desirability of a more understanding and harmonious relationship among the many races of our nation is something no one will deny, but it will come only with time and experience and it is a matter in which public thought and conscience cannot be directed or controlled by the courts through the uprooting of firmly established precedent."

18 14 Am. Jur. Covenants, Conditions and Restrictions § 311 (1938).

19 Herb v. Gerstein, 41 F. Supp. 634 (D.D.C. 1941).

20 Dooley v. Savannah Bank and Trust Co., 199 Ga. 353, 34 S.E.2d 522 (1945); Schulte v. Starks, 238 Mich. 102, 213 N.W. 102 (1927).

21 Janss Inv. Co. v. Walden, 196 Cal. 753, 239 Pac. 34 (1925).

22 Doherty v. Rice, 240 Wis. 389, 3 N.W.2d 734 (1942).

ments *or* restrictive covenants.[23] Similarly, a residuary devisee in whom title to certain premises had vested was held to have power to impose a racial restriction thereon.[24]

However, the mere fact that the plaintiff was a neighboring property owner and would find enforcement of the racial covenant to his benefit did not give him any right to enforce it. Where the neighbor was neither an assignee of the original covenantee (of a merely personal covenant) nor a grantee of land retained by the covenantee at the time the covenant was made and for the benefit of which land the covenant was intended (a covenant running with the land), he may not enforce the restriction.[25]

IV. *Nature of Restriction Enforceable*

The overwhelming majority of racial restrictive covenants found in the cases were directed against non-Caucasians. However, the nature of the restriction which the court was prepared to uphold varied in different jurisdictions.

A number of cases upheld restrictions against the purchase or use of the property by Negroes.[26] Several other cases held valid and enforceable restrictions against the purchase or use of the property by any non-Caucasian, which included Orientals.[27]

However, there is a group of jurisdictions which held that while a restriction on the use of property was valid, no restriction could be placed on the sale of the property since this would constitute an unlawful restraint on alienation.[28] To the argument

23 Annotation, 168 A.L.R. 529.

24 Russell v. Wallace, 30 F.2d 981 (D.C. Cir. 1929), *cert. denied*, 279 U.S. 871 (1929). A devisee could either enforce, or be subject to, a racial use restriction created during the testator's life.

25 Toothaker v. Pleasant, 315 Mo. 1239, 288 S.W. 38 (1926).

26 Mays v. Burgess, 147 F.2d 869 (D.C. Cir. 1945); Torrey v. Wolfes, 6 F.2d 702 (D.C. Cir. 1925); Thornhill v. Herdt, 130 S.W.2d 175 (Mo. App., 1939); Porter v. Johnson, *supra*, n. 17; Pickel v. McCawley, 329 Mo. 166, 44 S.W.2d 857 (1931); Toothaker v. Pleasant, *supra*, n.25; Koehler v. Rowland, *supra*, n.13; Kemp v. Rubin, 188 Misc. 310, 69 N.Y.S.2d 680 (Sup. Ct. 1947), *aff'd without opinion*, 273 App. Div. 789, 75 N.Y.S.2d 768 (2d Dept. 1947) [and, after *Shelley* was decided, *rev'd without opinion*, 298 N.Y. 590, 81 N.E.2d 325 (1948)]; Ridgway v. Cockburn, 163 Misc. 511, 296 N.Y.S. 936 (1937).

27 Russell v. Wallace, *supra*, n.24; Shideler v. Roberts, 69 Cal. App. 2d 549, 160 P.2d 67 (1945); Los Angeles Inv. Co. v. Gary, 181 Cal. 680, 186 Pac. 596 (1920); Chandler v. Ziegler, *supra*, n.12; Doherty v. Rice, *supra*, n.22.

28 Los Angeles Inv. Co. v. Gary, *supra*, n.27; Meade v. Dennistone, *supra*, n.11; Schulte v. Starks, *supra*, n.20.

that it would be anomalous to permit someone to buy property he could not occupy, one court replied:

> The rules against restraints on alienations were only intended to make conveyancing free and unrestrained, and had nothing to do with use and occupancy. It may be an anomalous situation when a colored man may own property which he cannot occupy, but, if he buys on notice of such a restriction, the consequences are the same to him as to any other buyer with notice.[29]

Schulte v. Starks[30] is of some interest in this context. Here, the restrictive covenant vaguely prohibited occupancy by "any person or class of persons whose ownership or occupancy would be injurious to the locality." The court admitted that this description was indefinite, but enforced the covenant against Negro occupancy based on the consistent practice of the parties to the covenant to exclude Negroes, which was conveyed to the defendants prior to purchasing the property.

V. *Nonenforcement of Covenants*

The major reason for refusal of courts to enforce otherwise valid racially restrictive covenants was a change in the neighborhood sufficient to warrant the conclusion that it had lost its previous homogeneous character. In one of the earliest cases, the movement of Negroes into the surrounding area was so great that the burdened property could not be sold to whites for more than 40% to 50% of its sale value to Negroes. This burden induced the court to deny equitable relief to the party seeking enforcement.[31]

A year later, another court refused to enforce a covenant which had been procured in an unsuccessful attempt by a neighborhood property owners' association to stem the influx of Negroes into the neighborhood, the failure of the campaign having resulted in a handful of white-occupied homes in an almost all-colored area.[32] This result was extended to a situation where the subdivider herself permitted the neighborhood to gradually turn.[33] And later still, a court extended the doctrine to a situation where

---

29 Scholtes v. McColgan, 184 Md. 480, 41 A.2d 479, 483 (1945).
30 *Supra*, n.20.
31 Clark v. Vaughan, 131 Kan. 438, 292 Pac. 783 (1930).
32 Pickel v. McCawley, *supra*, n.26.
33 Letteau v. Ellis, 122 Cal. App. 584, 10 P.2d 496 (1932).

the neighborhood had turned through natural population movement.[34]

Numerous cases, however, continued to enforce covenants where the asserted change was insufficient to affect the character of the neighborhood. In a Maryland case, the court held that one Negro on the block was not enough, even though there were all-Negro blocks nearby.[35] In another case, the penetration of four or five Negro families in violation of covenants, then in the process of vigorous enforcement, was held to be insufficient.[36] Likewise, a California court held that the neighborhood had not turned merely because a half-dozen Negro families had moved in.[37]

During World War II, the courts showed a tendency to extend the traditional equitable doctrine that a restrictive covenant would not be enforced where neighborhood changes made it inequitable because of loss of value to the plaintiffs, to include situations where such covenants unduly impeded the acquisition of necessary housing by Negroes. In *Hundley v. Gorewitz*,[38] the United States Court of Appeals for the District of Columbia declared:

> This exception to the rule is applicable in the case of a covenant such as we have here when, in the natural growth of a city, property originally constructed for residential purposes is abandoned for homes of more modern construction in more desirable locations, for a serious decline in values would follow unless the way was open either for use of the property for business purposes or for housing needs of a lower class. And it is also applicable where removals are caused by constant penetration into white neighborhoods of colored persons. For in such cases to enforce the restriction would be to create an unnatural barrier to civic development and thereby to establish a virtually uninhabitable section of the city. Whenever, therefore, it is shown that the purpose of the restriction has been frustrated and that the result of enforcing it is to depreciate rather than to enhance the value of the property concerned, a court of equity ought not to interfere.[39]

34 Gospel Spreading Ass'n v. Bennetts, 147 F.2d 878 (D.C. Cir. 1945).

35 Meade v. Dennistone, *supra*, n.11.

36 Porter v. Pryor, 164 S.W.2d 353 (Mo. 1942). In Kemp v. Rubin, *supra*, n.26, it was held that two Negroes did not create a neighborhood change.

37 Shideler v. Roberts, *supra*, n.27. Three of the six families antedated the filing of the complaint; the other three arose subsequent to the filing and were themselves violations which would presumably be contested.

38 132 F.2d 23 (D.C. Cir. 1942).

39 *Id.* at 24.

In *Fairchild v. Raines*,[40] while the majority of the California Supreme Court refused to enforce the covenant because of substantial Negro penetration into the affected area, Justice Traynor called for an investigation as to whether enforcement would be contrary to the "public interest in the congestion of the limited residential districts for colored people." Pointing out the substantial migration of southern Negroes to northern cities during World War II, and their growing need for housing, he called upon the court "to determine whether the maintenance of this barrier would deprive the colored population of any feasible access to additional housing and compress it within the inflexible boundaries of its present district at the risk of a congestion whose evils would inevitably burst the bounds of that district."[41]

VI. *Miscellaneous*

Space limitations forbid the enumeration of all the niceties of the old learning concerning racial covenants. For example, in addition to the distinctions drawn between "sale to" and "occupancy by" Negroes, the definition of "Negro"[42] or other terms descriptive of race, color, ancestry, or creed,[43] the question of whether a corporation [44] (or partnership, under the Uniform Partnership Act[45]) was itself "Negro" if all or some of its members or stockholders were Negroes, and the application of the general principle of strict construction of restrictive covenants, all invited or required judicial attention.

VII. *Conclusion*

Racial restrictive covenants originated in the desire for homogeneous neighborhoods, and were upheld by the courts as an

---

40 24 Cal. 2d 818, 151 P.2d 260 (1944).

41 *Id.* at 268-9.

42 See Cohen, *Appraisal of the Legal Tests Used In Determining Who Is a Negro*, 34 Cornell L.Q. 246 (1948); Cohen, *Who Is Legally a Negro?*, 3 N.Y.U. Intram. L. Rev. 91 (1948); *Legal Definition of Race*, 3 Race Rel. L. Rep. 571 (1958); Note, 6 Ala. L. Rev. 114 (1953) (burden of proving absence of Negro blood).

43 The United States Department of Justice announced that it construed *Shelley* to apply to covenants based on "creed." N.Y. Daily News, May 5, 1948, p. 30.

44 Perkins v. Trustees of Monroe Ave. Church of Christ, 70 N.E.2d 487 (Ohio Ct. App. 1946) (incorporated church with racially mixed congregation), *appeal dismissed*, 147 Ohio St. 537, 72 N.E.2d 97 (1947), *reversed sub nom.* Trustees v. Perkins, 334 U.S. 813 (1948).

45 Uniform Partnership Act §§ 2, 8(3).

exercise of individual and private freedom of choice and association, including non-association. Equity courts early evolved doctrines against abuse, such as the denial of enforcement where neighborhood change imposed an unnecessary and fruitless hardship. During World War II, as the need for Negro housing became more manifest, incipient steps were taken to consider such needs also in determining whether to enforce the covenants. This development was nipped in the bud by *Shelley*'s hard-and-fast rule.

The NAACP complained in *Shelley* that racial restrictive covenants were confining the exploding Negro metropolitan population into too small an area for healthy growth.[46] Whether this influenced the Supreme Court cannot be known. However, had the judicial trend started during World War II been permitted to continue, it may well be that courts of equity, traditionally sensitive to the public interest, would have developed a doctrine of balancing the rights of the property owner and his freedom of association with local Negro housing needs to achieve the largest possible accommodation between the two, and thus satisfy both competing interests which have a claim to public consideration.

Moreover, in several of the states containing large cities in which the Negro influx had created the most acute conditions of Negro overcrowding and housing shortage, local legislation would have limited or eliminated the enforceability of racial restrictive covenants, had not *Shelley* imposed a constitutional bar to enforceability. In New York, for example, where *Shelley* changed the existing law,[47] it was held that despite *Shelley* a landlord could exclude tenants on the basis of race.[48] In New York City this rental question was more important than that of outright sale of realty to Negroes. Subsequent municipal[49] and state[50] legislation has virtually outlawed racial discrimination in rental or sale of realty.

---

[46] Vose, *NAACP Strategy in the Covenant Cases*, 6 West. Res. L. Rev. 101 (1955).

[47] Kemp v. Rubin, *supra*, n.26.

[48] Dorsey v. Stuyvesant Town Corp., 299 N.Y. 512, 87 N.E.2d 541 (1949) (4-to-3 decision), *cert. denied*, 339 U.S. 981 (1950).

[49] 5 New York City Administrative Code (1957) § W41-1.0 (Local Laws, 1951, No. 41, as am. by Local Laws, 1954, No. 42); 5 *id.* §§ X41-1.0 through X41-4.0 (1962-63 Cum. Suppl.) (Local Laws, 1957, No. 80, as am. by Local Laws, 1961, No. 48 and Local Laws, 1962, Nos. 11, 15). The constitutionality of Local Law No. 80 was upheld in Martin v. City of New York, 22 Misc. 2d 389, 201 N.Y.S.2d 111 (Sup. Ct. 1960).

[50] N.Y. Laws, 1950, c. 287 (barred discrimination in public housing); N.Y. Laws, 1955, ch. 340, 341 (barred discrimination in private housing which received public assistance);

For the time being at least, *Shelley* has eclipsed the interests of established residents in favor of Negro housing gains. Were it not so, however, we might well have seen the former interest substantially restricted by legislation and equity, with possibly a limited balancing of the two interests.

N.Y. Laws, 1961, c. 414 (barred discrimination in sale or rental of commercial space and privately-financed multiple dwellings or private houses where the owner controls the sale or rental of ten or more contiguous houses); N.Y. Laws, 1962, c. 646 (outlaws any racial, etc., discrimination in contracts, deeds, or lease covenants, and forbids any reverter, right of entry, executory interest, or forfeiture to arise by reason of any violation of such discriminatory provision). Cf. N.Y. Laws, 1960, c. 17 (forbidding life insurance company from taking into account the race, color, creed or national origin of the applicant in fixing the premium rate on his life insurance; discrimination because of sex or age is permitted).

THE CONSTITUTIONALITY OF THE PRESIDENT'S ORDER BARRING DISCRIMINATION IN FEDERALLY-ASSISTED HOUSING

CHARLES STERLING HUTCHESON*

ALMOST AS SOON AS THE INK WAS DRY on the recently issued presidential order forbidding discrimination based on race, creed, color, or national origin in housing built or purchased with federal aid,[1] a number of senators attacked it as unconstitutional.[2] No doubt further attacks will be made based on this theory. Hence, it would be well to examine the validity of the order from a constitutional point of view, since it represents an unprecedented governmental intrusion into the housing field.

(a) *Government Aid and Unconstitutional Conditions.* Congressional authorization for federal aid to housing is based on the National Housing Act of 1934, as amended.[3] Under detailed statutory provisions, various federal agencies are permitted to assist the construction, financing, or purchase of housing in the manner set forth by Congress.

It may be argued, in support of the constitutionality of the presidential order, that "like private individuals and businesses, the Government enjoys the unrestricted power . . . to determine those with whom it will deal, and to fix the terms and conditions upon which it will make needed purchases."[4] It may also be argued that government assistance is not a right but a privilege, and that "it is hardly lack of due process for the Government to regulate that which it subsidizes."[5]

However, it has long been recognized that "a constitutional power cannot be used by way of condition to attain an unconstitutional result,"[6] and that government cannot transcend its con-

---

* Chief Judge of the United States District Court for the Eastern District of Virginia (Ret.); Rector of the College of William and Mary; former United States Attorney for the Eastern District of Virginia. The author acknowledges the assistance of Professor Alfred Avins of Chicago-Kent College of Law in preparing the footnotes for this article.

1 The text of the order is contained in N.Y. Times, Nov. 21, 1962, p. 19, cols. 2-4.

2 N.Y. Times, Nov. 22, 1962, p. 1, col. 1.

3 Act of June 27, 1934, c. 847, 48 Stat. 1246, 12 U.S.C. § 1701 et seq. (1952).

4 Perkins v. Lukens Steel Co., 310 U.S. 113, 127 (1940).

5 Wickard v. Filburn, 317 U.S. 111, 131 (1942).

6 Gomillion v. Lightfoot, 364 U.S. 339, 347-8 (1960); Western Union Telegraph Co.

stitutional boundaries by adding the invalid regulation as a condition to the obtaining by the person of a "privilege" or "bounty."[7]

In *United States v. Butler*,[8] the Supreme Court held that Congress could not purchase with federal funds compliance in a matter held to be reserved to the states by the Tenth Amendment.[9] Thus, if the President has no power to issue the regulation unaided by the condition attached to the expenditure of federal funds, he gains no additional power by making the regulation a condition of the expenditure. Accordingly, we may turn to the constitutionality of the order as such.

(b) *Presidential Power Unaided by Congress.* Omitting, for the sake of brevity, the somewhat wordy language of the preamble, we find the assertion of authority of the President in the form of a conclusion, without legal premise, that the grant of federal assistance for housing from which Americans are excluded because of race, color, creed, or national origin is unfair, unjust and inconsistent with the public policy of the United States as manifested by its Constitution and laws, and—that the executive branch in faithfully executing the laws is charged with an obligation and duty to assure that those laws are fairly administered.

There is a passing reference to the Housing Act of 1949[10] in which Congress used some general language concerning the desirability of decent housing by way of explanation of the appropriation of public funds to stimulate or compete with private enterprise.[11] However, the presidential order significantly fails to mention the legislative history of the Act. When that law was upon its passage in Congress, antidiscrimination amendments were introduced in both the House and Senate, but were defeated in

---

v. Foster, 347 U.S. 105, 114 (1918). See also Hanover Fire Ins. Co. v. Harding, 272 U.S. 494 (1926); Frost & Frost Trucking Co. v. R.R. Comm., 271 U.S. 583 (1926); Terral v. Burk Const. Co., 257 U.S. 529 (1922).

[7] Speiser v. Randall, 357 U.S. 513 (1958); Western Union Telegraph Co. v. Kansas, 216 U.S. 1 (1910). See also Willcox, *Invasions of the First Amendment Through Conditioned Public Spending*, 41 Cornell L.Q. 12 (1955); Miller, *Administrative Discretion in the Award of Federal Contracts*, 53 Mich. L. Rev. 781, 802-5 (1955).

[8] 297 U.S. 1 (1936).

[9] See also Stewart Machine Co. v. Davis, 301 U.S. 548, 590-1 (1937).

[10] P.L. 171, 81st Cong., 1st Sess., 63 Stat. 413 (1949).

[11] *Id.* at § 2.

both branches at the urging of 'liberal' Democrats, the law's most ardent supporters, who feared that such an amendment would alienate enough votes to kill the bill.[12] The President, then a 'liberal' Democratic Congressman from Massachusetts, was an ardent supporter of the law,[13] and presumably concurred in this strategy. The President had a chance as Congressman to enact antidiscrimination restrictions on federal housing grants, but failed or refused to do so. Now he wants an encore.

There is no reference to any other Act of Congress. Laws exist forbidding discrimination against families with children[14] and requiring builders to pay prevailing wage rates.[15] In passing it may be observed that the questionable constitutionality of neither of these statutes has been tested, but they indicate that Congress regards such regulations as within the legislative rather than the executive field—if they meet the constitutional test.

Stripped of verbiage, the expressed basis of the order is that "the executive branch . . . in faithfully executing the laws . . . which authorize . . . financial assistance . . . is charged with an obligation and duty to assure that those laws are fairly administered and that benefits thereunder are made available to all Americans. . . ." This is done "by virtue of the authority vested in . . . [the] President . . . by the Constitution and laws. . . ." Again, we have a significant lack of reference to constitutional provision or legislative enactment. In the complete absence of any laws of the United States granting any such authority to the President, we need to take a brief look at just what constitutional provisions are involved.

Article I, Section 1, of the Constitution states: "All legisla-

---

[12] 95 Cong. Rec. 4791-8, 4802, 4813, 4849-61 (Senate), 8554-5, 8656-8 (House) (1949). The question was much agitated at that time. Two years earlier the President's Committee on Civil Rights recommended that Congress condition all federal grants-in-aid and other forms of federal assistance on the absence of racial or religious segregation or discrimination. President's Comm. on Civil Rights, *To Secure These Rights* 166 (1947). However, "adoption of the amendment would have meant rejection of the bill. The NAACP supported the amendment. But Senator Paul Douglas (Dem. Ill.), a friend of civil rights, led the fight against the amendment. It was defeated and the bill was passed." Maslow & Robison, *Civil Rights Legislation and the Fight for Equality, 1862-1952,* 20 U. of Chi. L. Rev. 363, 390 (1953).

[13] 95 Cong. Rec. 8235, A2308, A3548 (1949).

[14] 12 U.S.C. § 1713(b)(2) (1952).

[15] 12 U.S.C. § 1715c(a) (1952).

tive powers herein granted shall be vested in a Congress of the United States. . . ." Section 8, Clause 1, of the same article reads: "The Congress shall have Power to lay and collect Taxes . . . to . . . provide for the . . . general Welfare. . . ." Section 8, Clause 18, gives Congress power "To make all Laws which shall be necessary and Proper for carrying into Execution the foregoing Powers, and all other Powers vested by this Constitution in the Government of the United States, *or in any Department or officer thereof.*" (Emphasis supplied.) Section 9, Clause 7, declares: "No money shall be drawn from the Treasury but in consequence of appropriations made by law. . ." The Constitution is utterly barren of any language which even remotely vests in the President the authority to issue legislative declarations such as the order here involved.

Article II, Section 3, gives the President the right to "recommend" legislation he thinks desirable. Such measures are not laws unless passed by Congress. Congress alone has authority to direct how laws shall be enforced or money spent. The President must "take care that the laws [passed by Congress] be faithfully executed." He cannot make up his own legislative enactments to effectuate his own policies.

While there is an utter lack of legislative authority for this action of the executive, there is controlling judicial prohibition against it.

In 1952, the United Steel Workers of America, C.I.O. gave notice of a nationwide strike. A few hours before the strike was to become effective the President, in reliance upon his previous proclamation of the existence of a national emergency and the assertion of the necessity of a steady supply of steel for use in conducting the military engagements in Korea undertook, without Congressional authority, to take control of the steel industry. He declared this necessary for the success of our armed forces engaged in combat against an external foe. The rationalization of his pronouncement was much more persuasive than the preamble to the housing order we are now considering, for the press dispatches of the day were filled with stories of casualties and suffering of the American troops who were waging the conflict with only token assistance from other members of the United Nations.

The President, without the sanction of Congress, which was then in session, issued the order and on the following day reported his action to Congress.[16] Twelve days later he sent a second report.[17] Congress took no action. Application was made for an injunction against the Secretary of Commerce to prevent him from carrying the order into effect. The District Court granted the injunction, and on certiorari the Supreme Court affirmed.[18]

In the hearing on the application, in its efforts to bolster the executive order, the government filed affidavits, showing dire consequences to be expected from a shortage of steel, executed by the Secretary of Defense, the Chairman of the Atomic Energy Commission, the Secretary of the Interior, the Secretary of Commerce, and the Administrators of the Defense Production Administration, the National Production Authority, the General Services Administration, and the Defense Transport Administration.[19] Surely this is an impressive array of experts!

In stating the issues, Mr. Justice Black, who delivered the opinion said:

> The mill owners argue that the President's order amounts to lawmaking, a legislative function which the Constitution has expressly confided to the Congress and not to the President. The Government's position is that the order was made on findings of the President that his action was necessary to avert a national catastrophe which would inevitably result from a stoppage of steel production, and that in meeting this grave emergency the President was acting within the aggregate of his constitutional powers as the Nation's Chief Executive and the Commander in Chief of the Armed Forces of the United States.[20]

He concluded:

> In the framework of our Constitution, the President's power to see that the laws are faithfully executed refutes the idea that he is to be a lawmaker. . . . The Founders of this nation entrusted the lawmaking power to the Congress alone in both good and bad times. It would do no good to recall the historical events, the fears of power and the hopes for freedom that lay behind their

---

16 98 Cong. Rec. 3962 (1952).

17 *Id.* at 4192.

18 Youngstown Sheet & Tube Co. v. Sawyer, 103 F. Supp. 569 (D.C.D.C. 1952), *aff'd,* 343 U.S. 579 (1952).

19 343 U.S. at 678.

20 *Id.* at 582.

choice. Such a review would but confirm our holding that this seizure order cannot stand.[21]

In his concurring opinion, Mr. Justice Jackson wrote:

When the President takes measures incompatible with the expressed or implied will of Congress, his power is at its lowest ebb, for then he can rely only upon his own constitutional powers minus any Constitutional powers of Congress over the matter. . . . Presidential claim to a power at once so conclusive and preclusive must be scrutinized with caution, for what is at stake is the equilibrium established by our constitutional system.[22]

In the same opinion the following apt statement appears:

I did not suppose, and I am not persuaded, that history leaves it open to question, at least in the courts, that the executive branch, like the Federal Government as a whole, possesses only delegated powers. *The purpose of the Constitution was not only to grant power, but to keep it from getting out of hand.*[23] (Emphasis supplied.)

Pages of apt language might be quoted from the several opinions of the members of the Supreme Court and the able opinion of the District Judge. This would be a mere repetition of the theme that the President then acted without authority, just as the President has now acted without authority. The situations are almost identical with the equities, if any there be, favoring the steel seizure cases.

There we had a state of emergency while engaged in an undeclared but expensive and bloody war. If such legislative power is to ever be exercised by the President, that was a proper time. We are now confronted by no such conditions.

Here we have a proclamation, intended to have the force of legislation, designed to effect a sociological change in the internal affairs of the nation. This was issued while Congress was adjourned, to take effect immediately, and is complete with enforcement procedure, including civil and criminal actions by the Attorney General. It does differ from the usual legislative enact-

21 *Id.* at 587-9.

22 *Id.* at 637-8.

23 *Id.* at 640. In his concurring opinion, Mr. Justice Douglas said: "The legislative nature of the action taken by the President seems to me to be clear." (p. 630.) Even in his dissenting opinion, Chief Justice Vinson conceded that: "The function of making laws is peculiar to Congress, and the Executive cannot exercise that function to any degree." (p. 690.)

ment in that no penalties are prescribed for violations other than forfeiture of contractual rights. In light of the order's purported authority, it will be highly interesting to observe the conduct of lawsuits without supporting legislation. This is particularly the situation where, as here, they would be tried before courts with purely limited and delegated powers.

The order is in every sense of the word new legislation. If it should be argued that it merely effectuates the guarantees of the Fifth and Fourteenth Amendments, nevertheless it is still a legislative effectuation[24] and is unconstitutional as an unwarranted presidential invasion of the province of Congress and violative of the principle of separation of powers.

In the steel seizure cases it was contended that the President was exercising the power of eminent domain. But there, as here, he was confronted with the lack of legislation, which under the Constitution can be enacted only by the Congress. Accordingly, the President's order was beyond his constitutional power.

(c) *Federal Intrusion Into States' Powers.* The United States Constitution gives the federal government no general power to regulate the sale of housing within the states. The making of a contract of sale, a lease, or a deed is not interstate commerce,[25] and it could hardly be contended that a homeowner who sells his house which has a mortgage reinsured by a federal agency thereby becomes a state agency within the meaning of the Fourteenth Amendment's "state action" requirements.[26] Indeed, Representative John A. Bingham of Ohio, a leading framer of the Fourteenth Amendment, specifically disclaimed any impairment of state rights in respect to property by this amendment, and told the House which passed the amendment that "as to real estate, everyone knows that its acquisition and transmission under every interpretation ever given to the word property, as used in the Constitution of the country, are dependent exclusively upon the local law of the States."[27] That this was the rule at the time of the

---

24 The Fifth Section of the Fourteenth Amendment provides: "The Congress shall have power to enforce, by appropriate legislation, the provisions of this article."
25 United States v. South-Eastern Underwriters Assn., 322 U.S. 533, 546-7 (1944).
26 See Civil Rights Cases, 109 U.S. 3 (1883).
27 Cong. Globe, 39th Cong., 1st Sess. 1089 (1865-6). He repeated at p. 1094: "the right to real estate being dependent on the state law."

Fourteenth Amendment, and long before, has never been doubted.[28]

One scholar has asserted that the presidential order which requires government contractors not to discriminate in selecting their employees[29] does not invade the reserved powers of the states,[30] and by analogy it may be argued that the same reasoning would apply to the order governing housing. However, the two cases which might be cited to uphold federal concern with government contractors have no relation to home-building or purchasing.

In *Wickard v. Filburn*,[31] where government regulation of agricultural production was involved, the court specifically found that most wheat moved in interstate commerce and that home-grown wheat affected substantially this national wheat market.[32] *Perkins v. Lukens Steel Co.*[33] involved supplies intended for the federal government, and not government subsidy of private·business supplying private needs. Moreover, by their very nature, government supplies move in interstate commerce, and as such the conditions of their production would, applying more recent cases, be subject to federal control.[34] Indeed, one recent case has held that states may not forbid discrimination in employment by companies doing business in interstate commerce, on the ground that it interferes with Congress' power over interstate commerce,[35] and while the authority of this case has been reversed,[36] at least it provides a legal framework for federal interest. Accordingly, since the federal government may regulate indirectly through its fiscal powers what it may regulate directly,[37] it may at least be argued that Congressional action, were proper

---

[28] McGoon v. Scales, 76 U.S. (9 Wall.) 23, 27 (1869); Clark v. Graham, 19 U.S. (6 Wheat.) 576, 577 (1821); United States v. Crosby, 11 U.S. (7 Cr.) 114 (1812).

[29] Executive Order No. 10557, 3 C.F.R. 69 (Supp., 1954).

[30] Pasley, *The Nondiscrimination Clause in Government Contracts*, 43 Va. L. Rev. 837, 856-862 (1957).

[31] 317 U.S. 111 (1942).

[32] *Id.* at 125-8.

[33] 310 U.S. 113 (1940).

[34] United States v. Darby Lumber Co., 312 U.S. 100 (1941); N.L.R.B. v. Jones & Laughlin Steel Corp., 301 U.S. 1 (1937).

[35] Colorado Antidiscrimination Comm. v. Continental Air Lines, Inc., 368 P.2d 970 (Colo. 1962), cert. granted, 83 Sup. Ct. 26 (1962).

[36] N.Y. Times, April 23, 1963, p. 20, col. 3.

[37] United States v. Kahriger, 345 U.S. 22, 27 (1953).

legislation to be passed, in this area, would not infringe on areas reserved to the states.

It is not, however, necessary to take up this argument further, because it is clear that no activity can be deemed more removed from interstate commerce than residential housing. Mr. Justice Frankfurter has pointed out that "renting office space in a building exclusively set aside for an unrestricted variety of office work spontaneously satisfies the common understanding of what is local business."[38] Moreover, "dwelling houses are not instrumentalities of commerce" and "employees engaged in building or repairing dwelling houses . . . [are] not engaged in interstate commerce."[39]

From the point of view of the consumer, nothing can be considered more local than one's home. There may be a national market in wheat, or in government supplies, or in building materials, or even in some branches of employment, but there is no national market in housing. Wheat may be shipped from areas of surplus to areas of shortage. Labor may be recruited on a nation-wide scale. But a surplus of homes in Chicago cannot satisfy a shortage of housing in Los Angeles, nor can an abundance of land suitable for building residential housing in Atlanta alleviate a dearth of land in New York. If any commodity can be said not to be in interstate commerce, it is residential housing.

The federal government may not regulate indirectly through its fiscal powers that which it may not regulate directly.[40] This constitutes an inadmissible intrusion into the domain of the states. For this reason too, the presidential order is unconstitutional.

(d) *Violation of Due Process.* The order is also contrary to the Due Process clause. It is well-settled that both the due process clauses of the Fifth Amendment and the Fourteenth Amendment protect businessmen against unreasonable restrictions in their business,[41] and individuals against compulsory association.[42] An

---

38 10 East 40th St. Co. v. Callus, 325 U.S. 578, 583 (1945).

39 Coomer v. Durham, 93 F. Supp. 526, 528 (W.D. Va. 1950). See in accord, Morris v. Beaumont Mfg. Co., 84 F. Supp. 909 (W.D.S.C. 1947); Oberdorfer v. Edmund J. Rappoli Co., 207 Misc. 807, 137 N.Y.S.2d 14 (1954).

40 Bailey v. Drexel Furniture Co., 259 U.S. 20 (1922). See Mr. Justice Frankfurter's discussion thereof in United States v. Kahriger, supra, n.37, at 37-9.

41 Goldblatt v. Town of Hempstead, 369 U.S. 590 (1962); Castleton Corp. v. Sinclair, 264 U.S. 543 (1924); Pennsylvania Coal Co. v. Mahon, 260 U.S. 393 (1922); Block v. Hirsh, 256 U.S. 135 (1921); Allgeyer v. Louisiana, 165 U.S. 578 (1897).

42 International Association of Machinists v. Street, 367 U.S. 740 (1961).

executive order cannot, of course, transcend these limitations either.[43] For reasons stated elsewhere, an antidiscrimination order of the kind here involved is an attempt to require compulsory integration in housing, and is therefore a constitutionally invalid regulation of both landlord or builder and tenant or buyer.[44]

It may be argued that the order is merely an attempt to assure that all segments of society benefit equally from programs aided by government moneys. This argument has two answers. First, the order is not nearly so narrowly limited. Such an object could be accomplished by merely requiring that a builder or landlord provide accommodations of equivalent character to the ones sought by the rejected applicant, regardless of where located. This would satisfy a need for housing without infringing on any resident's right to live in the kind of neighborhood he desires or with the neighbors he wants, and the builder's or landlord's right to satisfy that desire.

Secondly, the order is not intended to accomplish this object. The order itself states that one of the objects thereof is to abolish "discriminatory policies and practices [which] result in segregated patterns of housing and necessarily produce other forms of discrimination and segregation."[45] It is settled administrative law that a court "must judge the propriety" of an administrative order "solely by the grounds invoked by the agency," and that "if those grounds are inadequate or improper, the court is powerless to affirm the administrative action by substituting what it considers to be a more adequate or proper basis."[46]

Moreover, although the order lists other purposes as well, it is common knowledge that pressure for the executive order has come from individuals and organizations interested, not in good minority housing, but in integrated housing.[47] A court may look

[43] West v. Lyders, 59 App. D.C. 122, 36 F.2d 108 (1929).
[44] Avins, *Anti-Discrimination Legislation As An Infringement On Freedom of Choice,* 6 N.Y.L.F. 13 (1960); Avins, *Trade Regulations (Compulsory Housing Integration Law),* 12 Rutgers L. Rev. 149, 150 (1957).
[45] N.Y. Times, Nov. 21, 1962, p. 19, col. 2.
[46] S.E.C. v. Chenery Corp., 332 U.S. 194, 196 (1947).
[47] See Avins, *Anti-Discrimination Legislation As An Infringement On Freedom of Choice,* 6 N.Y.L.F. 13 (1960), notes 36, 37, 82, 83, 86, 87. See also N.Y. Times, Nov. 22, 1962, p. 32, col. 5; May 6, 1962, p. 6, col. 1; April 13, 1962, p. 22, col. 1; Nov. 27, 1961, p. 1, col. 5; Oct. 18, 1961, p. 35, col. 1.

behind the ostensible purposes of a legislative enactment to determine its actual purposes,[48] and the constitutional due process requirement "nullifies sophisticated as well as simple-minded modes" of its infringement.[49] A compulsory integration order in housing cannot be validated by casting it in the form of an order requiring that enough housing be made available to all, when in fact its purposes are to compel association by unwilling tenants or homeowners. Constitutional rights do not lend themselves so easily to evasion.

A word may be said on the wisdom of the order. It is true that the Constitution does not protect us against general legislative folly, for which an enlightened electorate is our only guarantee, but on the other hand, legislation which bears no rational connection with any constitutional governmental end transcends our fundamental due process notions.

The order purports to promote the general welfare and preserve internal peace. In the last two decades race relations have become such an agitated and controversial issue as a result of compulsory integration policies, of which this order is one, that it exceeds in emotional impact liquor prohibition, the silver issue, or any of the other great domestic questions which have aroused the country. This storm of steadily mounting racial tensions has caught Americans of both races who desire to make their own quiet personal adjustments in its expanding vortex. The consequent pitting of ethnic groups against each other could result in disastrous internal dissension.

The mutual antagonisms of ethnic groups based on even trivial differences of language, religion, culture, and nationality form an unhappy page throughout the history of mankind.[50] Antipathies based on slight dissimilarities have developed among people living in close contact for centuries, and it is hence not surprising that striking and obvious racial dissimilarities should produce some aversions. Integration is no panacea for these dislikes, nor will it guarantee mutual respect or friendship. Indeed,

---

48 Bush v. New Orleans Parish School Board, 194 F. Supp. 182 (E.D. La. 1961), aff'd sub nom., Gremillion v. United States, 368 U.S. 11 (1961).

49 Cf. Lane v. Wilson, 307 U.S. 268, 275 (1939).

50 Gregor, *On the Nature of Prejudice*, 52 Eugenics Review, No. 4, p. 1 (Jan. 1961).

in our time, it was Germany, which had the most integrated Jewish community in Europe, which turned on and almost exterminated European Jewry.

Societies, ancient and modern, have erected legal prohibitions against racial integration to protect themselves and to reduce friction, but America today witnesses the first time in recorded history where individuals are compelled by the state to mix together. The belief that Caesar may succeed in a decade where the followers of Christ have failed or made only small progress in two milleniums is fatuous. Where individuals want to associate together they will do so without governmental prodding. Compulsion to do so multiplies, rather than alleviates, hostilities, as experiences in Arkansas and Mississippi, *inter alia*, demonstrate. Negro leadership which ignores the experiences of the post-Civil War period risks a terrible price of white antagonism for doubtful gain, for he who ignores history is bound to relive its frustrations. The belief that compelling integration will, in the long run, promote the general welfare or preserve domestic tranquility ignores well settled racial and ethnic preferences of almost inherited vigor, and must be classed, along with the enforceability of prohibition of liquor, as one of the irrational notions which have, from time to time, seized whole nations, to their detriment and regret.

Conclusion. The President's order is clearly unconstitutional on several grounds and appropriate steps should be taken promptly to nullify it. The procedural method of obtaining relief perhaps is beyond the scope of this article. The remedy which immediately suggests itself is action by the Congress to defend the Constitution by legislation repelling this invasion of its province. The definite refusal of Congress to enact the rider previously mentioned would seem an additional reason for such action. Since Congress may act *sua sponte* this would seem the more expeditious method and in conformity with the constitutional concept of the separation of powers. An alternative course of action would be in the form of litigation. However, this would place upon interested individuals the burden of conducting such litigation. In any event, the existing situation calls for speedy remedial action.

THE CONSTITUTIONALITY OF ANTIDISCRIMINATION LEGISLATION IN HOUSING IN ILLINOIS

Donald N. Clausen* and Richard T. Buck**

RECENT PROPOSALS FOR ANTIDISCRIMINATION LEGISLATION in housing in Illinois make consideration of the constitutionality of such legislation timely. In discussing the constitutional aspects of these proposals, consideration will be limited to the Illinois State Constitution. This Constitution is very much like the constitutions of many states in respect to the limitations on the power of government contained therein relevant to the proposed statutes. Consideration will be restricted to these limitations.

(a) *Illinois Due Process Standard.* In common with the United States Constitution's Bill of Rights and most similar state enactments, Article II, § 2 of the Illinois Constitution's Bill of Rights provides: "No person shall be deprived of life, liberty or property, without due process of law." It has long been held that this provision constitutes a substantive limitation on arbitrary or unreasonable government regulation.[1] The general standard that "to sustain an act or ordinance under the police power the court must be able to see that it tends in some degree to the prevention of offenses or the preservation of the public health, morals, safety or welfare,"[2] is illustrated by a variety of cases striking down zoning ordinances as being unrelated to the public welfare.[3]

---

* LL.B. 1923, Chicago-Kent College of Law. Member of the Illinois Bar.

** B.S. 1959, Elmhurst College; J.D. 1962, Chicago-Kent College of Law. Member of the Illinois Bar. Editor-in-Chief, Chicago-Kent Law Review, 1961-2.

1 First National Bank v. County of Lake, 7 Ill. 2d 213, 130 N.E. 2d 267 (1955); Western Theological Seminary v. City of Evanston, 325 Ill. 511, 156 N.E. 778 (1927).

2 Condon v. Village of Forest Park, 278 Ill. 218, 223, 115 N.E. 825 (1917). See also Schroeder v. Binks, 415 Ill. 192, 113 N.E:2d 169 (1953); People v. Brown, 407 Ill. 565, 95 N.E.2d 888 (1950).

3 Trust Co. of Chicago v. City of Chicago, 408 Ill. 91, 96 N.E.2d 499 (1951); People ex rel. Joseph Lumber Co. v. City of Chicago, 402 Ill. 321, 83 N.E.2d 592 (1949); Quilici v. Village of Mt. Prospect, 399 Ill. 418, 78 N.E.2d 240 (1948); 2700 Irving Park Bldg. Corp. v. City of Chicago, 395 Ill. 138, 69 N.E.2d 827 (1946); Anderman v. City of Chicago, 379 Ill. 236, 40 N.E.2d 51 (1942); People ex rel. Kirby v. City of Rockford, 363 Ill. 531, 2 N.E.2d 842 (1936); State Bank & Trust Co. v. Wilmette, 358 Ill. 311, 193 N.E. 131 (1934); Merrill v. City of Wheaton, 356 Ill. 457, 190 N.E. 918 (1934); Forbes v. Hubbard, 348 Ill. 166, 180 N.E. 767 (1932). See also Phipps v. City of Chicago, 339 Ill. 315, 324-5, 171 N.E. 289 (1930): "The legislature may not, under the guise of protecting the people's interests, arbitrarily interfere with private rights. . . . If the means employed have no real, substantial relation to public objects within the State's power or if

In addition to being reasonably related to the public health, safety, morals, or welfare, a legislative regulation must be as narrow as the circumstances will permit, and aim only at the evil to be suppressed.[4] Where a valid legislative purpose appears, a statute will nevertheless be held unconstitutional if all alternatives consistent with elimination of the evil are not allowed. Thus, in one case where a city required certain types of fireproofing materials, and other types were found to be just as fire-resistant, the ordinance was held to be unconstitutional.[5] As the Illinois Supreme Court has held: "While we think this evil exists, it is yet apparent, upon a careful examination of this statute, that it is too broad in its terms to be justified as an exercise of the police power for the purpose of mitigating or remedying the wrong at which it is aimed."[6]

The Illinois due process requirement embodies an equal protection concept.[7] Unreasonable distinctions will invalidate a statute.[8]

In view of the restrictions which would be placed on the right to rent apartments or sell houses, by an antidiscrimination law in housing, it should be noted that the due process clause specifically protects the right to lend property[9] or sell property[10] from unjustified regulation. As one case declared: "It is a necessary incident to the ownership of property that the owner shall have a right to sell or barter it, and this right is protected by the con-

---

those means are arbitrary and unreasonable, courts will disregard mere form and interfere for the protection of rights injuriously affected by such illegal action."

4 Scully v. Hallihan, 365 Ill. 185, 6 N.E.2d 176 (1936); Bailey v. People, 190 Ill. 28, 60 N.E. 98 (1901).

5 McCray v. City of Chicago, 292 Ill. 60, 126 N.E. 557 (1920).

6 Massie v. Cessna, 239 Ill. 352, 359, 88 N.E. 152 (1909).

7 Mathews v. People, 202 Ill. 389, 67 N.E. 28 (1903).

8 City Savings Ass'n v. International Guaranty & Ins. Co., 17 Ill. 2d 609, 162 N.E.2d 345 (1959); People v. Love, 298 Ill. 304, 131 N.E. 809 (1921).

9 Metropolitan Trust Co. v. Jones, 384 Ill. 248, 251-2, 51 N.E.2d 256 (1943): "The privilege of contracting to receive gains and profits for the right to use property granted to another is both a liberty and a property right. The right to make a reasonable contract with reference to the use of an article of property is an attribute of property and a property right. . . . Any restriction upon or abridgement of this right deprives the owner of both liberty and property."

10 Off & Co. v. Morehead, 235 Ill. 40, 85 N.E. 264 (1908); City of Chicago v. Powers, 231 Ill. 560, 83 N.E. 240 (1907); People v. Steele, 231 Ill. 340, 83 N.E. 236 (1907); Noel v. People, 187 Ill. 587, 58 N.E. 618 (1900); Frorer v. People, 141 Ill. 171, 31 N.E. 395 (1892).

stitution as such an incident of ownership. When an owner is deprived of the right to expose for sale and sell his property he is deprived of property, within the meaning of the constitution, by taking away one of the incidents of ownership."[11]

(b) *Eminent Domain and the Public Utility Concept.* Article II, § 13 of the Illinois Constitution's Bill of Rights provides: "Private property shall not be taken or damaged for public use without just compensation." The legislature "cannot transform a private enterprise, or a part thereof, into a public utility and thus take property for public use without condemnation and payment."[12] Likewise, it cannot compel businesses which are not in fact public utilities to serve all without unreasonable discrimination.[13]

It has been held that "a public utility implies a public use of an article, product or service, carrying with it the duty of the producer or manufacturer, or one attempting to furnish the service, to serve the public and treat all persons alike, without discrimination."[14] The very hallmark of a public utility is that "all persons must have an equal right to the use, and it must be in common upon the same terms, however few the number who avail themselves of it."[15] The utility must hold itself out to serve all. The mere fact that a business advertizes for customers does not constitute such a holding out.[16]

The discrimination forbidden to a utility is not any discrimination, but only an unreasonable discrimination. It would be unconstitutional for the legislature to forbid utilities to make reasonable discriminations.[17] Accordingly, the hallmark of a utility is its inability to unreasonably discriminate against customers.

[11] City of Chicago v. Netcher, 183 Ill. 104, 110, 55 N.E. 707 (1899).
[12] Allen v. Railroad Commission, 179 Cal. 68, 175 Pac. 466, 474 (1918).
[13] Chicago Pipeline Co. v. Illinois Commerce Comm., 361 Ill. 296, 300, 197 N.E. 873 (1935): "We have held privately owned business is clothed with a public use only to the extent that it may be formed to deal with a particular class of patrons, or to the extent of the interest created, or held out for that purpose. . . . No unlawful or unreasonable discrimination could therefore result in appellee's failure or refusal to extend its service beyond the scope of its publicly professed obligation."
[14] Highland Dairy Farms Co. v. Helvetia Milk Condensing Co., 308 Ill. 294, 300, 139 N.E. 418 (1923).
[15] State Public Utilities Comm. v. Bethany Mutual Telephone Ass'n, 270 Ill. 183, 185, 110 N.E. 334 (1915).
[16] Meyer v. Rozran, 333 Ill. App. 301, 77 N.E.2d 454 (1948).
[17] Chicago & Alton Ry. Co. v. People ex rel. Koerner, 67 Ill. 11 (1873).

The question of whether a business is a public utility is one of fact, and depends on the inherent nature of the business.. The classic hallmarks of a utility are (1) public need for the service, and (2) the "economic facts of life" have created a virtual monopoly or limited the business to a small number of people, either because the expense makes it impractical for everyone to supply himself, or there are insufficient physical locations for everyone to supply himself, or frequently both.

A good example of the utility created by expense is found in *Inter-Ocean Publ. Co. v. Associated Press.*[18] There the Illinois Supreme Court said:

> The organization of such a method of gathering information and news from so wide an extent of territory as is done by the appellee corporation, and the dissemination of that news, requires the expenditure of vast sums of money. It reaches out to the various parts of the United States where its agents gather news which is wired to it, and through it such news is received by the various important newspapers of the country. Scarcely any newspaper could organize and conduct the means of gathering the information that is centered in an association of the character of the appellee because of the enormous expense, and no paper could be regarded as a newspaper of the day unless it had access to and published the reports from such an association as appellee. For news gathered from all parts of the country the various newspapers are almost solely dependent on such an association, and if they are prohibited from publishing it or its use is refused to them, their character as newspapers is destroyed and they would soon become practically worthless publications.[19]

Munn v. Illinois[20] illustrates a utility created by geography. In that case, there were only a limited number of places in Chicago where grain elevators could be constructed which would be accessible to both the railroads by which grain was brought in and the lake boats by which it was shipped east. In sustaining the regulation, the Court observed:

> In this connection it must also be borne in mind that . . . in 1874 there were in Chicago fourteen warehouses adapted to this particular business . . . . Thus it is apparent that all of the elevating facilities through which these vast productions "of seven or eight great States of the West" must pass on the way "to four or five of the States on the seashore" may be a "virtual" monopoly.[21]

18 184 Ill. 438, 56 N.E. 822 (1900).
19 *Id.* at 449.
20 94 U.S. 113 (1877).
21 *Id.* at 131. In Munn v. People, 69 Ill. 80, 90 (1873), the Illinois Supreme Court

The question of monopoly is the reconciling factor which appears in the two cases decided by the Illinois Supreme Court dealing with antidiscrimination legislation in places of public accommodation. In *Pickett v. Kuchan*,[22] the court held constitutional the Illinois Civil Rights Act as applied to theaters.[23] It did not discuss the reason why the statute was permissible, but merely cited the *Munn* case and *People v. King*,[24] a New York case which in turn also relied on *Munn*.[25] In *People* ex rel. *Gaskill v. Forest Home Cemetery Co.*,[26] the court held that since the company did not have a monopoly, it was not a utility and might discriminate against a Negro.

Private housing is a classic example of a nonmonopoly business. Almost alone among the necessities or luxuries of life, housing is the one commodity which everyone can provide for himself. An urban dweller cannot build his own automobile or raise his own food or make his own clothing or as a practical matter construct most of the other everyday things he uses, but must buy them. He can, and many people do, buy a piece of land and have a house constructed, or combine with others to build a cooperative apartment house.

Even in the rental or purchase of housing from others, no monopoly exists. The number of theaters is very limited,[27] and in

---

declared: "It is idle to talk about the consent of their customers to higher rates of charges than this law allows them to receive. Their customers, before this law was enacted, had no protection against these monopolists. They had no consent to give. They were obliged to have their grain taken to these warehouses, and be subjected to such charges as the organized combination . . . might choose to demand. The producer and shipper had no alternative but submission."

22 323 Ill. 138, 153 N.E. 667 (1926).

23 38 Ill. Ann. Stat. § 125.

24 110 N.Y. 418, 18 N.E. 245 (1888).

25 *Id.* at 249, where the New York court said: "the quasi public use to which the owner of such a place devoted his property gives the legislature a right to interfere."

26 258 Ill. 36, 41-2, 101 N.E. 219 (1913): "Corporations organized to serve the public generally, such as those which furnish water, gas or electric lights in cities, cannot select their patrons but must furnish accommodations to all who apply, on equal terms and at reasonable rates. As to such corporations there is the additional reason that they have exclusive control of the supply and those whom they refuse to serve cannot be served at all, which impresses the property with a public interest. . . . There is no element of monopoly, since it does not control all burial places in the vicinity of Chicago and the community at large is not affected so as to impress its property with a public interest."

27 The classified telephone directory shows that in all of Chicago there were only 204 theaters of all kinds in 1962. In many neighborhoods there are only one or two theaters, and the rising cost of running a theater has been steadily reducing the number.

smaller towns there may be only one, so that exclusion from a theater on racial or religious grounds may deprive the person of theater-going at all, for manifestly it is too expensive to build one's own theater. However, real estate is probably the most widely held commodity, so that every other business would have to be considered a monopoly before housing was so considered.

Housing is thus not a natural public utility. Assuming, *arguendo*, that discrimination on the basis of race, creed, color or national origin is arbitrary, to impose a duty on property owners not to so discriminate results in imposing on them the duties of public utilities and takes away one of the incidents of property without compensation.

Moreover, the taking is not for a public use. As one judge very recently pointed out, the whole effect of such a law would be to divest title or a leasehold interest in one person and transfer it to another. Thus, the "ultimate goal of the act is to enable a private individual to acquire the property of another without the consent of and contrary to the wishes of the owner of the property."[28] It has been repeatedly held that benefit to a single individual is not a public use and that not even payment of fair compensation will authorize exercise of the power of eminent domain.[29] Accordingly, the requirement that a property owner not discriminate, which is enforced by ordering him to sell or rent to a person he does not want to, constitutes the taking of his property for a private use without compensation, and converts his business into that of a public utility pro tanto, all in violation of the constitution.

(c) *Standard of Equality and Inalienable Rights.* Article II, § 1 of the Illinois Constitution Bill of Rights provides that "all

[28] Colorado Anti-Discrimination Comm. v. Case, —— P.2d —— (Colo., 1962).

[29] Illinois Toll Highway Comm. v. Eden Cemetary Ass'n, 16 Ill. 2d 539, 158 N.E.2d 766 (1959); Litchfield & Madison Ry. Co. v. Alton & Southern R.R., 305 Ill. 388, 137 N.E. 248 (1922); Gaylord v. Sanitary District, 204 Ill. 576, 68 N.E. 522 (1903); Sholl v. German Coal Co., 118 Ill. 427, 10 N.E. 199 (1887); Chicago & Eastern Ill. R.R. v. Wiltse, 116 Ill. 449, 6 N.E. 49 (1886); Libbee v. Imhoff, 11 Ill. App. 2d 344, 137 N.E.2d 85 (1956). For United States Supreme Court cases in accord, see Berman v. Parker, 348 U.S. 26, 32 (1954); Madisonville Traction Co. v. St. Bernard Mining Co., 196 U.S. 239, 251-2 (1905); Missouri Pacific Ry. Co. v. Nebraska, 164 U.S. 403, 417 (1896); Cole v. La Grange, 113 U.S. 1, 6 (1885); Bd. of Commissioners v. Lucas, 93 U.S. 108, 114 (1876); Mills v. St. Clair County, 8 How. 569, 584 (1850).

men . . . have certain inherent and inalienable rights—among these are life, liberty, and the pursuit of happiness." This guarantee is similar to the due process clause, and the right to contract unfettered by unwarranted restrictions has been held to be guaranteed by this clause.[30]

One court has recently held that "as an unenumerated inalienable right a man has the right to acquire one of the necessities of life, a home for himself and those dependent upon him, unfettered by discrimination against him on account of his race, creed, or color."[31] The court deduced this proposition from the language of the Declaration of Independence that "all men are created equal."

If the equality which the Declaration of Independence assumes bans discrimination on account of race, creed, or color, why does it not ban discrimination based on age? Does it deny fundamental equality for a man to offer his house to persons over 35 but not to those under that age, or vice versa? If equality is the aim, why not forbid discrimination based on financial circumstances? Surely the merchant prince and the penniless pauper are equal within the meaning of the Declaration of Independence, and if this is the test, they should have equal rights to live in a mansion. If equality is the aim, why should a seller be entitled to discriminate in favor of the wise, the thrifty, the industrious, and the careful, and against the foolish, the spendthrift, the indolent, and the careless? Are the latter not also entitled to the inherent, inalienable rights which the Declaration of Independence proclaims to be self-evident?

It will not do to say that the seller is interested only in the color of the purchaser's money. He has declared otherwise; for he would not discriminate unless that were not so. Nor is it persuasive to declare that the statute is not taking "private property for private use without the consent of the owner" because "the owner of the real estate involved has announced of his own free will that he wants to dispose of his private property for the private use of a purchaser who meets the terms upon which the real estate is placed

---

30 Reid v. Smith, 375 Ill. 147, 30 N.E.2d 908 (1940).
31 Colorado Anti-Discrimination Comm. v. Case, *supra*, n.28 at ——.

on the market."[32] One of those *terms*, and a most important one to the seller or landlord, may be the ethnic background of the buyer or tenant. This term may indeed be more important than the price, financial responsibility of the other party, or any other term of the contract. If the state can eliminate one term, it can eliminate all, and dictate all aspects of the transaction.

If acquiring property is an inalienable right regardless of the ability to meet the terms of the seller's offer, then why should not a pauper be able to offer his penny and buy a $100,000 home? Why should not a 16-year-old child have equal rights to buy with an adult? Why may any conditions be placed in a sale or lease which someone may not be able to meet? The mere statement of the proposition refutes its reasonableness.

Moreover, if an inalienable right to buy property includes the right to disregard the terms of the seller's offer, why does not the inalienable right to sell property include the right to disregard the terms of the buyer's offer? If the state has the right to tell a seller that he must not be interested in the color of the buyer's skin because that is irrelevant, why cannot the state tell the buyer that he must not be interested in the color of the seller's house because this, too, is irrational? All a state need find is that too many people refuse to buy red brick buildings, that owners thereof have a hard time selling them, and that therefore buyers should be forbidden to discriminate against such buildings. The result would be to give the state power to fix any term of any transaction.

The inalienable right of acquiring property has a long, common-law background. It consists of the right of a willing buyer to buy from a willing seller, and the right of a willing seller to sell to a willing buyer, without government interference. Both are thereby placed on an equal footing with each other and all other people. These rights are inherent, inalienable, and self-evident. To place the government's thumb in the balance is a negation, and not an affirmation, of equality.

(d) *Police Power and Housing Needs.* Tracing the origins of the claimed power to pass antidiscrimination legislation is like

---

[32] *Id.* at ——.

playing "This Is the House that Jack Built." A Colorado case[33] relies on a Massachusetts case,[34] which in turn relies on a California case,[35] which rely on two New Jersey cases[36] which rely on a law review article[37] and a U.S. Civil Rights Commission Report[38] which in turn rely on nothing at all except sheer speculation.

One law review article traces a variety of ills to overcrowding, which in turn is traced to housing restrictions, with not so much as a shred of evidence to support it.[39] The numerous "For Rent" signs on buildings and in real estate brokers' offices in Chicago's colored areas, the multitude of advertisements in the Chicago Defender, and the substantial vacancy ratios in Chicago's Negro districts, belie the assertion of lack of housing. Recent figures show that "doubling up" has been reduced to the vanishing point,[40] and there is an utter dearth of valid data to demonstrate that inferior Negro housing conditions are not caused by lower income[41] and, in some cases, by the careless habits of the tenants themselves.[42]

A recent survey of Negro housing in ten midwestern cities by a corporation which insures such housing came to the conclusion

---

33 *Ibid.*

34 Massachusetts Commission Against Discrimination v. Colangelo, 182 N.E.2d 595 (Mass. 1962).

35 Burks v. Poppy Const. Co., 57 Cal. 2d 463, 20 Cal. Reptr. 609, 370 P.2d 313 (1962).

36 Jones v. Haridor Realty Co., 37 N.J. 384, 181 A.2d 481 (1962); Levitt & Sons v. Division Against Discrimination, 31 N.J. 514, 158 A.2d 177 (1960).

37 Van Alstyne & Karst, *State Action*, 14 Stan. L. Rev. 3, 47 (1961).

38 1961 U.S. Comm. on Civil Rights Rept., Book 4, p. 1.

39 *Supra*, n.37.

40 Between 1950 and 1960 in Chicago doubled-up white households were reduced from 86,285 (5.9% of the total) to 23,826 (1.4%) and nonwhite households from 26,725 (17.5%) to 8,336 (3.3%) according to U.S. Census figures.

41 Although the median rental for apartments which whites paid in Chicago was $91 and the median rental which Negroes paid was $88 according to 1960 Census figures, these figures likewise showed that overcrowding was far more prevalent in Negro areas than in white areas. Thus, Negro families paid almost the same amount for apartments, but crowded far more people per room into them. To reduce overcrowding would require expansion of the number of rooms per family. Census figures show that in 1960, Chicago's white population had a median income of $7,680 and paid 18.9% for living quarters, while Chicago's Negroes had a median income of $4,786 and paid 27.3% for living quarters. Thus even with an inadequate number of rooms Chicago's nonwhite budget allots a substantially larger portion of its budget for housing than does its white population. Hence, to compensate for lower income, a larger proportion of income must be allocated for rent and a smaller number of rooms must be taken. Thus, low income seems to be the key to Negro overcrowding.

42 This fact can be verified by talking to any real estate broker active in lower-income nonwhite areas. See N.Y. Times, April 29, 1962, p. 82, col. 3, for the case of a New York City landlord who bitterly placed his Harlem apartment houses up for sale because his tenants were so destructive that "he did not know what more the tenants could do 'except demolish the buildings.'"

that in seven of them there was no nonwhite housing shortage, that in two cities the Negro market was "oversold," and that in only three cities was there an estimated unfilled Negro housing demand.[43] And even in the cities where there was supposed to be an unfilled demand, it was not shown that the demand was caused by people who could in fact pay the going price. Thus, the picture painted of discriminatory restrictions causing overcrowding and slums which has so uncritically and unthinkingly been swallowed whole by several courts recently as justification for restrictions on basic property rights, is at best a distortion and in all probability a fabrication. This must be the first instance in American jurisprudence when judicial notice was taken of nonexistent facts.

Discussion of new housing fares no better. The conclusion of the U.S. Civil Rights Commission that "new housing, by and large, is available only to whites"[44] is, as applied to Chicago, a myth, and a drive down South Park or Cottage Grove Avenues in Chicago, or into the new Negro suburbs,[45] is enough to destroy this fantasy if one will keep his eyes open.[46]

Moreover, even if there was a need for housing by particular individuals, the broad statutes proposed and enacted in other jurisdictions could not be justified since they dispense with any showing of need. Antidiscrimination laws operate whether the individual already has a house or even wants to purchase the property as an investment. The seller is completely at the mercy of the applicant even if the latter offers to purchase out of caprice or spite. Statutes which place one party's economic relationship at the mercy of another are constitutionally invalid.[47] The business relationships of two private parties do not affect the public wel-

[43] Midwest Minority Housing Markets 7 (A Special Report by Advance Mortgage Corp., Dec. 1, 1962). Cities which the report claimed still had an unfilled Negro housing demand were Chicago, Cleveland, and Milwaukee. Pittsburgh, Indianapolis, Grand Rapids, Detroit, and Cincinnati had an adequate Negro housing supply, while Columbus and Dayton actually were oversupplied with nonwhite housing.

[44] Supra, n.38.

[45] For a recent discussion of this subject, see "Negro Suburbia," Chicago Sun-Times, Nov. 15, 1962, pp. 30-32.

[46] There is ample evidence that Chicago is not unique in the construction of new nonwhite housing. See N.Y. Times, July 1, 1962, Sec. 8 (Real Estate), p. R. 11, col. 1, for an article on 800 nonwhite homes in a $10,000,000 development being built near Washington, D.C. See also Midwest Minority Housing Markets, supra, n.43.

[47] Illinois Hospital Service Inc. v. Gerber, 18 Ill. 2d 531, 165 N.E.2d 279 (1960).

fare,[48] and the legislature cannot give the property of one person to another to compensate the latter for any special disability he may be under.[49]

If discrimination in housing may be banned, why not ban discrimination in the sale of food, clothing, medicine, automobiles, and all other necessities of life? And if discrimination on ethnic grounds may be forbidden, why not forbid it based on age, marital status, financial or social standing, or any other ground? Singling out ethnic discrimination in housing is unconstitutional because "if the legislature should undertake to provide that persons following some lawful trade or employment shall not have capacity to make contracts or receive conveyances . . . or in any other way to make such use of their property as was permissible to others, it can scarcely be doubted that the act would transcend the bounds of legislative power."[50]

Moreover, the groups advocating such legislation justify it, not as a "good housing for Negroes" statute, but to achieve residential integration.[51] As the Illinois Supreme Court has declared: "The law will not allow the rights of property to be invaded under the guise of a police regulation, for the promotion of health [safety or welfare], when it is manifest that such is not the object and purpose of the regulation."[52]

(e) *Separation of Powers.* Article III of the Illinois Constitution provides for the division of the state government into three branches, and requires that no part of one branch "shall exercise any power properly belonging to either of the others." Under this section, it has been held that the legislature may not delegate through a vague statute the power to prescribe standards to an administrative agency,[53] preclude the courts from independently reviewing both the factual as well as legal basis for an administrative determination,[54] and permit administrative agencies to

---

48 Frazer v. Shelton, 320 Ill. 253, 50 N.E. 696 (1926).
49 People v. Chicago, M. & St. P. Ry. Co., 306 Ill. 486, 138 N.E. 155 (1923).
50 Eden v. People, 161 Ill. 296, 307, 43 N.E. 1108 (1896).
51 See Chicago Urban League Report, Chicago Sun-Times, Dec. 14, 1962, p. 32, cols. 1-6.
52 *Supra,* n.50.
53 Boshuizen v. Thompson & Taylor Co., 360 Ill. 160, 195 N.E. 625 (1935).
54 Commerce Comm. v. Cleveland, C.C. & St. L. Ry. Co., 309 Ill. 165, 140 N.E. 868 (1923).

establish penalties or remedies for violation of a statute not specified therein.[55]

The enforcement provisions of one anti-discrimination law in housing in Colorado have already been held unconstitutional as conferring on an administrative commission the power to fashion remedies.[56] It would seem that administrative enforcement of anti-discrimination legislation in Illinois would meet the same fate.

Conclusion. It must never be forgotten that an antidiscrimination law in housing deprives the owner of property in contemplation of law. This is clearly illustrated by *City of Chicago v. Wells.*[57] Here, the Illinois Supreme Court struck down an ordinance which compelled property owners to subdivide property into 25-foot lots. It said: "The ordinance in question does not deprive appellant of her land, but it does deprive her of her control and dominion over it. . . . Property, in its broader sense, is not the physical thing which may be the subject of ownership, but is the right of dominion, possession and power of disposition which may be acquired over it. The right of dominion, possession and power of disposition over a tract of land includes the right of an owner to subdivide it in such a way as he sees fit or to leave it unsubdivided."[58] This applies to discrimination, and for this reason, as well as all of the others above set forth, antidiscrimination legislation in private housing is at war with our most fundamental notions of property rights.

---

[55] Reid v. Smith, 375 Ill. 147, 30 N.E.2d 908 (1940); Cleveland, C.C. & St. L. Ry. Co. v. People, 212 Ill. 638, 72 N.E. 725 (1904).
[56] Colorado Anti-Discrimination Comm. v. Case, —— P.2d —— (Colo. 1962).
[57] 236 Ill. 129, 86 N.E. 197 (1908).
[58] *Id.* at 132-3.

SOME SOCIAL AND PSYCHOLOGICAL DETERMINANTS OF INTERGROUP RELATIONS IN CHANGING NEIGHBORHOODS

JOSHUA A. FISHMAN*

I. *Overt Behavioral Responses*

BOTH THE POPULAR and the technical literature attests to the fact that the most immediate and widespread reaction to the entry of Negroes into hitherto all-white middle class residential districts (outside of the South) is one of withdrawal. This withdrawal is very frequently of such a hasty and chaotic nature that it has been appropriately characterized as *panicky*. However, there are also circumstances under which the exodus of whites is *initially* of a slower and calmer variety. This is most usually the case when either public or private low-rental or rent-controlled housing is concerned which cannot easily be duplicated or improved upon at a similar cost. So far, the major evidence for nonwithdrawal behavior as an *initial* white reaction to the entry of Negroes comes from developments that have been planned as integrated communities from the very first. This is an entirely different context for integrated housing than the one in which Negroes enter already established communities populated only by whites. In planned integrated communities selection factors are obviously operating that bring to them only such white families as do not oppose a racially integrated community or cannot afford to live in any other

* B.S. 1948, M.S. 1948, Univ. of Pennsylvania; Ph.D. 1953, Columbia Univ. Research Asst. (1951-2), Senior ·Research Associate and Educational Psychologist (1952-4), Dept. of Research, Jewish Education Comm.; Research Asst. (1955-6), Asst. Director and Director of Research (1956-8), College Entrance Examination Board, Inc.; Visiting Professor of Psychology, City College of New York, 1957-8; Associate Professor of Human Relations and Psychology, Univ. of Pennsylvania, Director of Research, A.M. Greenfield Center for Human Relations, Univ. of Pa., 1958-60; Dean and Professor of Psychology, Graduate School of Education, Yeshiva Univ., 1960-date. President, Applied Social Division, New York State Psychological Assn., 1962-3. This article, originally subtitled "An Introduction to the Bridgeview Study," concerns a study dealing with Bridgeview, New Jersey, a relatively new and privately financed suburban community within easy commuting distance of New York City. The study itself was conducted jointly by Eleanor Leacock, Martin Deutsch, and Joshua A. Fishman, with grants from the Society for the Psychological Study of Social Issues, Anti-Defamation League, New World Foundation, Albert M. Greenfield Center for Human Relations, Bridgeview Community Conference, and American Jewish Committee. This introduction was originally presented as a paper at the 16th International Congress of Psychology, held at Bonn, Germany, August 1960, and is reprinted by permission from 40 Social Forces, No. 1, October 1961. The introductory material, tables, conclusion, summary and appendix of bibliography are omitted.

of similar quality. Planned integrated communities commonly plan to maintain a balance between various population groups via so-called "benign quotas," a form of "democratically inspired" *controlled occupancy*. Such communities have not existed for a sufficient length of time, nor have they been studied in sufficient detail, to permit any discussion of their long-term stability. At the moment, it seems that some are continuing according to their original design, whereas in others withdrawal tendencies have become noticeable in conjunction with the natural turnover of occupancy. There is, finally, still another early reaction pattern to Negro entry into a hitherto all-white community (as well as to housing in an already integrated neighborhood). This is the tendency for some white individuals actually to seek out housing in districts where both Negroes and whites are present. Although ideological factors have been found to play some role in this last-mentioned phenomenon, proximity to place of employment or to shopping and recreational areas, economic factors (most frequently accompanied by a *lack of concern* for racial problems rather than any strong social-equalitarian commitments) seems to be of much greater moment.

Although all of the above-mentioned overt response patterns do exist, the white withdrawal pattern is certainly the dominant one, both as an *immediate* and as a *long-term* reaction. This white withdrawal is only infrequently accompanied by violence, threats of violence or grosser social pressures. Within time reciprocal visiting and interracial social functions become commonplace. Nevertheless, it is important to note that each group admits to certain dissatisfactions with the ostensibly pleasant behavioral patterns that are established.

In Bridgeview we noted that the hold-outs from reciprocal visiting were mostly whites who had already visited in the homes of Negroes but who had not yet had Negroes to their own homes. This implies both Negro initiative in issuing invitations and in seeking to establish interracial social relations as well as a hanging back on the part of whites. Actually we have considerable evidence that Negroes are much more eager for interracial social relations than are whites. Negroes more frequently want to be warm neighbors, and they more frequently prefer that their neighbors, Negroes and whites alike, be warm and friendly rather than casual and polite. Negroes believe that interracial social relations have not sufficiently increased in number. Whites on the other hand, are less eager for interracial social relations, believe that interracial social functions have grown greatly in number and are generally much less eager to give or to receive warm neighborly behavior— particularly where Negroes are involved. For whites a varied social world exists outside of the interracial residential community. For most Negroes, the social world outside of the interracial residential community is limited to the Negro ghettos which they are seeking to escape.

.II. *Concomitant Attitudinal Responses*

A number of studies indicate that the overt behavioral response made by whites to either an existing or a potential interracial community in terms of moving away or remaining, is not a dependable indication of their interracial attitudes. Thus it seems useful to distinguish between withdrawal for "normal family cycle reasons" (change of job, increase or decrease in size of household), withdrawal due to illfounded fears and beliefs (e.g., fears of physical danger), withdrawal due to status concern or sensitivity to social pressures from outside the residential community, and withdrawal due to acknowledged or verifiable antipathy toward Negroes or other minorities. Withdrawal due to reasons of the latter type may actually be relatively infrequent although this is not to say that most whites do not harbor anti-Negro prejudice at an unconscious level quite inaccessible to extinction on the basis of daily life experiences. Be this as it may, the other grounds for withdrawal from an existing or potential interracial neighborhood (family cycle, erroneous beliefs, and social sensitivity) undoubtedly contribute to the departure of many whites whose departure we would not predict if we were to be concerned with interracial or intergroup attitudes alone. The reverse proposition is also true, namely that those whites remaining in such communities are not all free from anti-Negro prejudice. In any case, the reasons for white departures are likely to be complex. Where social and personal insecurities exist democratic ideological commitments are more likely to weaken.

Family Cycle Factors

Because of the generational concentration typical of many older metropolitan as well as newer suburban neighborhoods, "normal family cycle" factors have played an important role in the entry of Negroes and other minorities. In older white neighborhoods established many years ago, the removal of adult offspring to homes of their own and the death of parents result in "normal" vacancies. In white communities of intermediate age, many vacancies result from the accelerated pace of removal to the suburbs. In nearer suburban areas, many vacancies are a result of the need for larger quarters as family size increases or as job advancement and social mobility dictate. In view of the greatly increased Negro middle class, its sadly inadequate housing, and its more vigorous rejection of the Negro urban ghetto, there is obviously a great demand on the part of Negroes for the very homes being vacated by whites. It is equally obvious that the Negro entrants are socially and economically well-suited to occupy the new housing they have obtained.

Because of this last-mentioned fact, and because of the lesser saliency of anti-Negro sentiments, it is not surprising to find that most attitudinal and behavioral measures of Negro-white relations subsequent to the period of initial entry of Negroes show largely positive or, at the very least, neutral results. Whites commonly find that they get along well with their Negro neighbors, that these neighbors and their children are decent, well-behaved people, that they care for and improve upon their property to a degree equal to or greater than that of the whites themselves—in short, that they possess all of the middle class virtues, perhaps even with a vengeance. This has even been found to be the case in those communities where the initial entry of Negroes was met by opposition and hostility. Nevertheless, a discrepancy between attitudes and behaviors frequently still obtains largely because of intragroup social pressures.

Attitudes in Relation to Behaviors

The possibility of discrepancy between attitudes and behaviors is clearly demonstrated in our Bridgeview data which enables us to compare blocks that vary in racial composition. The blocks which Negroes entered first were, after three years, predominantly Negro blocks by the time that our study got underway. One might expect that the few whites remaining on such blocks would be attitudinally and ideologically favorably disposed toward Negroes, if only as a result of the self-selection which remaining on such blocks entails. Actually, we find the highest F scores of our entire white sample on these blocks, the smallest rate of pre-Bridgeview involvement in general or intergroup organizational work, the highest rate of thinking about moving away, the greatest inclination to interpret the departure of a white family as an indication that a "panic" was underway and the least interest in interracial socializing. Notwithstanding these many negative attitudes these whites remained on their blocks after two or more white panics had swept away most of their original white neighbors. Of course these same white residents also hold a few positive attitudes toward Negroes and toward life in an interracial neighborhood. However, the outstandingly positive blocks in this connection are the all white ones, into which no Negro has as yet moved. Nevertheless, it was predictable that were Negroes to move into such blocks most whites would sooner or later move away. Indeed, that is exactly what *is* happening on some of these blocks at this very moment.

Social Status Factors

Thus, it would seem that there are individuals who are predominantly negative attitudinally who nevertheless remain in an interracial community that is becoming progressively more Negro, at the same time that there are individuals who are predominantly positive who nevertheless move away. How is this to be explained? In Bridgeview a nonattitudinal factor, occupational status, seemed to be involved. Whites with manual occupations tended to remain even when attitudinally negative. Perhaps they could not as easily find comparable housing or residential proximity to New York within their means anywhere else. Whites with nonmanual occupations tended to be oriented outwards, i.e. toward leaving the community, even when attitudinally positive toward its current interracial features. Their greater financial means provide them with the flexibility of leaving whenever Negroes become either too numerous or too close with respect to their own personal standards.

More consistent interactions between type of residential block, attitudes, and occupational status are, of course, also observable. Several good examples of these are found among Negroes living on predominantly Negro blocks. On such blocks upper occupational Negroes are more frequently attitudinally negative and oriented toward leaving. Perhaps these blocks are now too Negro to satisfy their status aspirations. Lower occupational Negroes on these same blocks are most frequently positive attitudinally and oriented toward staying. For them Bridgeview is still a suburb and a good bit better than the all-Negro or predominantly Negro neighborhoods that they left behind them when moving to Bridgeview. Thus, one man's paradise lost is another's paradise gained just as one man's "sour grapes" are another's "sweet lemons." On the whole, however, Negroes remain much more positive toward themselves, their neighbors, and the entire community regardless of all the vicissitudes of interracial living. After all is said and done an interracial suburban neighborhood is a step-up for most Negroes. Any white who is appreciably concerned for his status in the larger white world (of family, friends, employers, etc. who do not live in interracial communities) may conclude that for him such a community is a step-down. Whether or not he will do anything about it may then depend upon his financial means and the intensity of his status strivings.

The Drift Toward Increased Negro Occupancy

Notwithstanding all of the harmonious experiences and positive attitudes that interracial communities have so consistently been found to afford, the process of white withdrawal nevertheless slowly but steadily continues in neighborhoods where benign quotas, or other controls are not enforceable. As a result, the interracial nature of the community is quietly undermined, as each white withdrawal is more likely than not replaced by a Negro entrant. This erosion process has been explained largely on the basis of status concerns on the part of whites whose major social roots are normally in a world that does not accept the legitimacy of interracial life and ascribes to it a lower social status. That social status concerns are dominant in this context rather than prejudice per se seems indicated by data on propinquity of Negro entrants. Attitudinally, a Negro living down the block should be objected to as much as one living closer at hand. However, the status loss is much greater in the latter case than in the former. There is evidence that the closer the Negro-owned house is to any given white-owned house the more likely that the white owner will move and the more likely that he will be replaced by a Negro. Another contributing factor to the erosion of white occupancy in interracial neighborhoods may be related to the approaching adolescence and sexual maturity of children. As yet this factor has been little studied, but it seems likely that it too should be distinguished from the more ordinary forms of anti-Negro prejudice. As a result of the initial panic and the subsequent, more "respectable" erosions, a point is reached after which the community is felt to have "turned" or "gone Negro." This point varies as to its numerical definition, but it need not be synonymous with an actual preponderance of Negroes and may even be less than the proportion of Negroes in the general population. After this point is reached, there is once more a quickening of white withdrawal, stampeded by and contributing to the fear of "being left in the minority."

III. *Interminority Relations*

The "turning point" may be considered as a point near the end of a long line of attempts to stabilize interracial communities. At the very outset the neighborhood must be defined by someone as an appropriate one for a Negro to enter. When this definition is made by the Negro entrant himself, it is likely to be based upon appraisals of both the physical and the human components of the neighborhood under consideration. In the great majority of cases Negroes have entered neighborhoods contiguous to those that have long been defined as Negro. On the other hand, there are also many cases, particularly in the suburbs, of leap-frogging quite a distance from previously Negro neighborhoods. The expansion of Negro housing had frequently been into neighborhoods that had most recently been middle or lower-middle class Jewish neighborhoods. Both the degree of the social opposition to be encountered in such neighborhoods and their stage in the "normal family cycle" may often be such as to present particularly attractive vacancies for Negro home-buyers. Even though urban Negro-Jewish tensions have a long history and have lately begun to increase, it may even be that Negro entry into suburbs is also more frequent in those communities that have been "opened up" by the previous entry of Jews. Bridgeview seems to be an instance of this kind.

Jews arrived in great numbers in Bridgeview immediately after the Second World War as a result of their own efforts to find better and less ghettoized housing. Within a few years the Jewish populations grew from a minor number to over 10,000 (roughly a quarter of the total population and appreciably more than this fraction in certain neighborhoods). The "old line" reaction to the Jewish influx included moving away (after "selling out" at a profit) and social rejection, but in each case the reaction was far less severe than that which subsequently obtained in the face of the Negro "invasion." Although Negroes did not move into the predominantly Jewish sections of Bridgeview, there developed a general view that Jews either facilitated or were more favorable toward the entry of Negroes into Bridgeview. This view is widespread among both whites and Negroes, and—within the white group—among Jews as well as non-Jews. This may be due to the fact that Jews were particularly active in organizing and maintaining the Bridgeview Community Conference (BCC), an interracial neighborhood organization whose goal was to stem white panics and departures and bring about a stable interracial neighborhood. Jews also constitute a high percentage of the few whites who remained on predominantly Negro blocks. Attitudinally Jewish residents of Bridgeview more frequently prefer warm relations with Negro neighbors, more frequently characterize interracial relations in a positive way, have the lowest F scores, and more frequently engage in reciprocal visiting with Negroes. Although minority empathy may play some role in each of these manifestations, it also bears pointing out that Jews more frequently had general and intergroup relations organizational experience before moving to Bridgeview, and those most conspicuous in the BCC and as holdouts on predominantly Negro blocks frequently held adolescent-young adult membership in liberal-leftist political groups.

Quite obviously not all Jews were favorably disposed (or even relatively so) toward the Negro "invasion." Many Negro and white residents of Bridgeview report that a number of Jews were among the first to leave when the first Negroes moved in. These Jews are contrasted with the ones that have remained as being more status oriented, as having closer ties with family and friends outside of Bridgeview, and as being more oriented toward "middle class virtues, synagogue membership, parties, new cars." However, once again, not all of those with unfavorable orientations moved away.

A comparison of Jewish respondents scoring "high" and "low" on the F scale reveals the possibility of interesting and unsuspected aspects of authoritarianism (or its absence) in minority groups. Jewish subjects with "Low" F scores not only revealed the expected greater acceptance of Negroes, of interracial living and of non-Jews generally but also *a greater rejection* of their own (Jewish) group. They less frequently belong to Jewish organizations and more frequently suggest de-emphasizing Jewish identification as a means of increasing Jewish assistance to Negroes. Jewish "high" F subjects, on the other hand, reveal not only the expected lesser acceptance of Negroes, of interracial living, and of non-Jews generally, but also *a greater acceptance of their own group.* Among Negroes the relationship between acceptance of one's "own group," acceptance of the "other" (white) group, and F scores is reversed. "Low" F Negroes reveal very thorough acceptance of their own group together with a tendency to reject whites (as unreliable allies, unimportant, etc.). On the other hand, "high" F Negro respondents reveal just the opposite combination of attitudes, i.e., they reject their own group but accept (and aspire for acceptance from) the "other" group. Nevertheless these trends are reminiscent of Kurt Lewin's well-known observations on minority group leadership, and they imply that general authoritarianism theory developed for white Protestant Americans may need minor alterations and emendations to cope with the problems of self-identification of minority group members. Depending on the relative permeability of majority society for various minority groups and depending on the ideological-philosophical orientations in vogue amongst them, F scores may have varying implications for own-group and other-group attitudes.

IV. *Realtors, Clergymen, and Other Community Influentials*

The initial definition that a given neighborhood is appropriate for Negro entry may not be made by a Negro at all. There are instances in which Realtors have made this definition, have introduced Negro occupants into hitherto all-white communities, have exerted themselves to frighten whites into leaving and have then benefited by the increased turnover of homes as panic and erosion ensue. There are indications that when Realtors act in this manner they make as carefully reasoned (or rationalized) a choice of neighborhood as when the initial definition is made by Negro families themselves. Neighborhoods without residents of some power, authority, or influence, either because of their recency or because of the nature of the social class occupying them, and neighborhoods contiguous to heavily Negro districts may be the most likely targets for this type of Realtor definition. In Bridgeview both of these sets of factors were operative among a large group of Realtors not all of whom were personally opposed to stable integrated neighborhoods. However, even those who were not opposed to integrated neighborhoods were not sufficiently in favor of them to refrain from tactics intended to panic white residents. Thus Realtors act not only as the "gate keepers" of statusful neighborhoods but also as "gate crashers" of nonstatus neighborhoods.

Another group of considerable potential influence in the establishment of interracial patterns is the clergy. Most national church groups have adopted statements or programs supporting racial equality. By referring to these statements and by relating them to religious principles of brotherly love and ethical behavior clergymen can first ease the acceptance on incoming minority members and then work toward bringing about a more stable and balanced interracial neighborhood. Of course, churches as a whole and clergymen as individuals will differ widely in the degree to which they will interpret a social issue as being relevant to their religious concerns. In Bridgeview, e.g., none of the "low church" clergymen (Baptist, Methodist, Evangelical, Christian Science, Reformed, and Jehovah's Witnesses) interpreted social issues as being relevant to their personal concerns or to those of their church, whereas almost all of the "High Church" clergymen (Episcopalian, Congregationalist, Presbyterian, and Lutheran) did. In general, as compared with Low church clergymen, the High church clergymen more frequently viewed racial integration as a major social problem. They consistently showed a more positive attitude toward Negroes and advocated less social distance between the races, and they more frequently sermonized about the local inter-racial housing issue. All in all, however, clergymen—even High church clergymen—played a rather minor role in the housing situation, and none became actively involved in attempts to stabilize the community. Members of the BCC, and actually only a few of them, were the only ones about whom it can justifiably be said that they actively attempted to stem the tide of white exodus. Unfortunately, BCC members were not as effectively organized as the Realtors nor did they have as much stature in the community as the clergy. As a result, their actual influence on the course of events was quite negligible.

V. *Neighborhood Associations*

The white residents of a neighborhood into which Negroes already have begun to move quickly develop a sensitivity to the direction and rate at which their area is changing. Their definition of whether "the neighborhood is going Negro" has been found to depend not only on the number of Negro entrants, but also on the opinions of self-styled "two-time losers" who have experienced Negro entry into previous areas of residence, on the opinions of Realtors as to the likelihood of a decline in property value, on the number of transfer requests on the part of teachers in local schools as well as on evaluations of the excellence of these schools, on change in crime and delinquency rates, on changes in public services such as police protection, playground maintenance, garbage collection, etc., and on the reports and activities of voluntary "neighborhood associations." There has yet been only very meager research on this last-mentioned factor, the neighborhood association. Nevertheless, its importance has been recognized and some of its problems have already been outlined. Although such associations have largely failed to achieve racially stable interracial communities, they have often succeeded in the important tasks of slowing the process of population turnover and in developing more intimate and positive Negro-white relations. However, the disparate composition of their membership and their long-range organizational ineffectiveness frequently produce tensions and disappointments within their ranks.

The Bridgeview Community Conference was formed after

one white panic had already spent its force. Its organizers were liberal whites who favored a stable interracial community for themselves and their children. These individuals remained the major activists of the organization until its dissolution some five years later. Their efforts to actively involve Negroes in the organization met with only partial success. The Negroes who were attracted to the BCC had less organizational experience and less time to offer. Many were high F individuals who were more concerned with the maintenance of community services and the preservation of standards of decorum and property values than with the ideological re-education of whites who might leave. Whereas white BCCers derived their major satisfaction from organizing intergroup relations discussions, and preparing or distributing printed material on the merits of interracial communities, Negro BCCers derived major satisfaction from the interracial social affairs (for adults or children) that the BCC occasionally sponsored. Negro BCCers often felt that white members were interested in spending time and effort on "just talk" whereas white BCCers were disappointed that Negroes did not share, nor even recognize, the altruism and high mindedness that motivated them but, instead, were interested in such "frivolous" affairs as interracial parties and shows.

Thus whites did not grasp the central importance of social equality and intimacy to Negroes as proof of sincere (behavioral) interracial good will. On the other hand, Negroes were often not in a position to appreciate the abstract, philosophical and guilt-relieving dedication of white BCCers to lectures, discussions, meetings, and other educational and hortatory undertakings. In addition, conformist and middle class behaviors and tastes were aspects of the surrounding white world that white BCCers rejected, both intellectually and behaviorally. Many Negro BCCers, on the other hand, were proud finally to have attained middle class status and all of its accouterments. All-in-all, the ideological-cultural gap between large groups of white and Negro BCCers was far too great for amicable and effective organizational procedure. In addition, most Americans lack personal and organizational experience of dedication to long-range ideological goals. A Red Cross drive and a political campaign are both short-term undertakings toward concrete and philosophically innocent goals that are realistically possible of attainment. The maintenance of a stable interracial community is far more difficult, far more drawn out, and conceptually more involved. BCCers were never quite sure just what goals to set for themselves, how or whether various undertakings contributed to these goals, and when or why they failed or succeeded. As the Negro influx continued, several white BCCers also moved away, thus hastening its demise. The problems of the BCC can serve as excellent case material for other such groups thoughout the United States.

VI. *The "Image" of the Neighborhood*

Bridgeview today is still going through panics as Negroes continue to enter hitherto all-white blocks, and as whites continue to flee from them. On substantially mixed and predominantly Negro blocks, a slower erosion of the white population also continues. Nevertheless, on these latter blocks, a fairly harmonious and, at times, genuinely accepting interracial *modus vivendi* has been attained, without unpleasant "incidents" of any kind and without deterioration of neighborhood appearance or real estate values. If Bridgeview has failed to become the stable interracial neighborhood that some had hoped, this seems to be due to status needs, status fears, and status pressures far more than to the antipathy or prejudice of its white residents.

In many ways modern American suburbs epitomize basic American cultural values and aspirations. The Jewish middle class and the rapidly growing Negro middle class eagerly pursue these values and aspirations, and this pursuit inevitably leads them to suburbia. However, their presence in suburbia is inimical to the status needs and values of many who are (or who can more easily pass as) "old American." In fact, their presence is often inimical to the very image of what a suburban community should be like. Jews and Negroes represent the city and all of the dirt, grime, haste, sweat, and unloveliness of city life. Thus, their arrival not only lowers the status value of a neighborhood, but for many it also cancels the suburban image of a suburb. As long as flight to uncontaminated areas is possible and feasible, it will be resorted to.

INTERRACIAL HOUSING AND THE LAW:
A SOCIAL SCIENCE ASSESSMENT

CLAIRETTE P. ARMSTRONG,[†] RALPH W. ERICKSON,[††]
HENRY E. GARRETT[*] AND A. JAMES GREGOR[**]

I. *Introduction*

EVER SINCE THE FIRST "sociological brief" prepared by Louis Brandeis and Felix Frankfurter made its appearance in 1908,[1] social science has played an increasingly influential role in the judicial process of our nation.[2] Judicial assessments have become

[†] B.A. 1908, Barnard College; M.A. 1909, Columbia Univ.; Ph.D. 1931, New York Univ. Chief Psychologist, Psychiatric Div., Bellevue Hospital, New York City, 1924-6; Lecturer in Psychology, Bellevue Medical School, 1924-6; Chief Psychologist, Boston Psychopathic Hospital, 1926; Chief Psychologist, Children's Court and Domestic Relations Court of New York City, 1926-1946. Life Fellow, American Sociological Society, American Psychological Assn., New York Academy of Sciences (Chairman, Psychological Section, 1948-49) (Vice-President, 1948); Associate Fellow, New York Academy of Medicine. Author: 660 Runaway Boys: Why Boys Desert Their Homes (1932), and articles in numerous psychological journals and publications.

[††] B.A. 1922, M.A. 1928, Ph.D. 1937, University of Minnesota. Instructor, Rochester Jr. College, 1929-30; Instructor in Psychology, Hibbing Jr. College, 1930-42; Personnel Consultant and Clinical Psychologist, U.S. Army, 1942-6; Associate Professor of Psychology and Head of Testing Service, Carleton College, 1946-7; Professor of Psychology and Head of Department, Mississippi State College, 1947-date. Fellow, American Psychological Assn.

[*] A.B. 1915, D.Sc. 1954, Univ. of Richmond; M.A. 1921, Ph.D. 1923, Columbia Univ. Instructor in Psychology (1923-6), Asst. Prof. (1926-35), Asso. Prof. (1935-43), Professor of Psychology, 1943-56, Head of Psychology Dept., 1941-56, Columbia Univ. Former Visiting Professor, U. of Cal., U.C.L.A., U. of So. Cal., U. of Hawaii, U.N.M., U. Fla., U. of Va. Expert Consultant, Secretary of War, 1940-44; Member, Committee on Classification of Military Personnel and advisor to The Adjutant General, 1940-5. Director (1943), President (1944), Eastern Psychological Assn.; President, Psychometric Society (1943); President, N.Y. State Assn. for Applied Psychology (1940); Member of Council (1933-5, 1939-41), President (1945), American Psychological Association; Vice-Chairman (1940), Nat. Research Council. Author: Statistics in Psychology and Education (1926, 1937, 1947, 1953); Great Experiments in Psychology (1930, 1941, 1951); Psychological Tests, Methods and Results (1933); Psychology (1950); General Psychology (1955); Testing (1959). General Editor, American Psychology Series.

[**] B.A. 1952, M.A. 1959, Ph.D. 1961, Columbia Univ. Instructor, 1952-8, Reader, 1958-9, Columbia Univ.; Instructor, 1960-1, Washington College; Assistant Professor, 1961-date, University of Hawaii. Irwin Edman Scholar, Columbia Univ. Lecturer, Graduate Dept. of Social Relations, Johns Hopkins Univ. and Peace Corps. Member, Institut International de Sociologie; American Sociological Assn.; Secretary, International Association for the Advancement of Ethnology and Eugenics. Paper before XIXth International Congress of Sociology (Mexico City, 1960). Staff Member, American Journal of Psychiatry, Sociology and Social Research, Sociological Quarterly, Science and Society; Assistant Editor, Mankind Quarterly.

1 Mueller v. Oregon, 208 U.S. 412 (1908).

2 Cf. Fischman, *The Role of Social Science in Desegregation: A Symposium* 7 (Anti-Defamation League, 1958); See Calhoun v. Atlanta Board of Education, 188 F. Supp. 401, 409 (N.D. Ga. 1959). Compare, however, Pettigrew, *Social Psychology and Desegregation Research*, 16 American Psychologist 105-112 (No. 3, 1961).

increasingly "functional," "pragmatic" rather than "analytic." The sociological brief, decked out in the paraphernalia of social science, with its trappings of historic, economic, statistical and sociometric data, has to a significant extent replaced the brief accoutered in the austere garb of legal reasoning and established precedent.[3] When the Supreme Court, in 1947, took the four restrictive covenant cases under consideration the principal briefs by the Negro plaintiffs veritably bristled with references citing sociological material systematically and strategically "planted," upon the counsel and direction of NAACP lawyers and consultants, in suitable journals for years prior to the actual adjudication.[4]

The Supreme Court decision of 1948 concerning restrictive covenants[5] marked but one victory in the overall program on the part of private, and ultimately public agencies to make racially homogeneous housing impossible. Originally acting as a regulative to assess the social impact of private contractual commitments, as in the restrictive covenant case, social science research has been employed to provide a rationale for proscriptive legislation, in many cities and some states, making unlawful the exercise of personal preference in the letting of private housing units. The rationale justifying such a regulative and proscriptive program includes considerations (1) turning on problems which attend the maintenance of homogeneous neighborhoods, i.e., the impediment it offers to free market competition and subsequent dislocations (the inferiority and curtailment of units available to non-whites)[6] and (2) assessing the socioeconomic and personality impairments suffered both by those who "segregate" and those who are segregated.[7]

The law has been employed to foster an action program the

---

[3] Cf. Cardozo, *The Nature of the Judicial Process* 102 (1921).

[4] Cf. Meeting of NAACP Lawyers and Consultants on Methods of Attacking Restrictive Covenants, September 6, 1947 (Mimeographed Minutes, NAACP Files), p. 2; Vose, *NAACP Strategy in the Covenant Cases*, 6 W. Res. L. Rev. 130, 143 (1955).

[5] Shelley v. Kraemer, 334 U.S. 1 (1948).

[6] Cf. Weaver, *The Negro Ghetto* (1948); Abrams, *Forbidden Neighbors* (1955); Rose, *The Negro in America* 209-212 (1948); Deutsch, *Problems and Progress of Research in Housing in its Bearing Upon Race Relations*, 5 Inventory of Research in Racial and Cultural Relations 65, 89-90 (Univ. of Chicago, Mimeo., Nos. 2, 3, Winter-Spring, 1953).

[7] Abrams, *op. cit. supra* note 6, at 283; Deutsch & Collins, *Interracial Housing* (1951); Deutsch, *op. cit supra* note 6, at 81, 86; Wilner, Walkley & Cook, *Residential Proximity and Intergroup Relations in Public Housing*, 8 Journal of Social Issues 45 (1952).

tactics, nature and ultimate end of which have, purportedly, been defined in social science research. Since social science has served as a regulative in the judicial process as well as a tool in formulating public policy, it becomes incumbent upon its practitioners (1) to bracket whatever motivating factors, values, preferences and prejudices, originally generated the interest that leads to research and consequently, (2) to accord themselves rigorously to the relatively well-defined canons of scientific inquiry, to undertake research under reasonably well-defined control conditions and to interpret their data with the caution and precision requisite to a scientific enterprise.

That these considerations have not been clearly borne in mind is an evident fact. Dr. Bernard Rosenthal, of Division of the Social Sciences of the University of Chicago, has tendered the following pronouncement: "I realize that there is a profound need today to obtain certain conclusions in social science because we have a certain program of social action. Most social researchers are liberals, and this is the wave of the future, but one must clearly distinguish between scientific research and social value; and it seems to me that in much research going on in this area, this distinction has not been made clearly."[8]

There is some evidence that such biases do in fact intrude themselves upon race relations research, contaminating what should be objective conclusions. The obligation of the social scientist, that is, to conduct his research as a scientist, entails the necessity that he confine the function of his own values and preferences to personal motivation and not permit them to influence the results of his inquiry. Why a man undertakes research in a specific area is a matter of little concern as long as whatever motivates him does not impair his competence as a scientist. Unfortunately there is some evidence to indicate that ethical, political and social crotchets have not only provided the original impetus for race relations research but have also influenced purported conclusions.[9]

II. *The Need for Housing by Negroes*

We are not concerned here with the problem of adequate housing *per se*. The authors entertain as a *value* the commitment

---

[8] Deutsch, *op. cit supra* note 6, at 89.

[9] Cf. van den Haag, *Social Science Testimony in the Desegregation Cases—A Reply to Professor Kenneth Clark*, 6 Vill. L. Rev. 69 (1960).

that every human being has the right to adequate housing. This tentative assessment is concerned, rather, with whether the available social science data gives any indication that racial integration forced either as a public policy, through social pressure or moral suasion has ameliorated or can be expected to ameliorate the conditions in which the American Negro finds himself. When our nation cannot adequately meet the real need for adequate housing on the part of white and non-white citizens alike an economic problem of no mean proportion is thereby created. But it bears upon our concern here in only a tangential fashion. What concerns us is the suggestion, made by a number of research specialists, that the problem of adequately housing America's non-white minority is inextricably linked with racial integration.

In spite of the spectacular housing gains made by Negroes between 1950 and 1960,[10] they still have not quite caught up to white standards either in quantity or quality.[11] In some areas, Negro housing shortages have been eliminated,[12] and in such areas, there is no shortage to be removed by integration, which could have as its sole motive social engineering. In others, the low income of Negroes[13] may require special enabling legislation to stimulate the construction of adequate, but low rent dwelling units.[14] In discussing the influence of integration on Negro housing needs, we are herein referring to those areas where a shortage of housing still remains, because in other areas, since there is no shortage, there is no need to cure it by integration.

When this is borne in mind it becomes evident that the in-

[10] Between 1950 and 1960, the percentage of doubled-up white households decreased 5.1% to 1.4%; doubled-up Negro households decreased from 12.6% to 3%, according to census figures. *Midwestern Minority Housing Markets* 25 (Special Report by Advance Mortgage Corp., Dec. 1, 1962). In the same period, white use of housing in New York City went from 3.2 persons per unit to 2.88 persons per unit; non-white use went from 5 persons a unit to 3 persons a unit. N.Y. Times, Dec. 31, 1961, p. 35, col. 1.

[11] Half of the non-white renters and one-third of the non-white homeowners live in substandard housing. A disproportionately large percentage of such substandard housing is found in the South. N.Y. Times, March 23, 1961, p. 26, col. 6.

[12] *Midwestern Minority Housing Markets* reported that the Negro housing shortage had been eliminated in Cincinnati, Columbus, Dayton, Detroit, Grand Rapids, Indianapolis, and Pittsburgh, and that a backlog of Negro demand remained only in Chicago, Cleveland, and Milwaukee.

[13] Bedell, *Employment and Income of Negro Workers, 1940-1952*, 76 Monthly Labor Review 596-601 (1953); Perlo, *Trends in the Economic Status of the Negro People*, 16 Science and Society 115-150 (1952).

[14] Cf. McGraw, *The Neglected Tenth of Housing* (paper presented at Atlantic City, New Jersey, July, 1948).

sistent policy of "integrating" public housing is clearly at fisticuffs with real Negro needs. As we shall see, it has been established that the maintenance of "stable interracial communities" in public housing has required the overt or covert adoption of "benign" or "benevolent" quotas restricting the availability of low cost dwelling units to non-white applicants in an effort to maintain "optimum integration" and thereby prevent the evacuation of whites.[15] Under such "quotas" the incidence of non-white occupancy is fixed at an arbitrary maximum—further non-white applicants are turned away irrespective of need. The confusion of two problems, that of adequate housing for non-whites and that of residential segregation, has led to harrowing contradictions in public policy— part of the general "crisis" in public housing.

"Benevolent quota systems" have been used covertly in public housing executive offices ("securing a representative cross-section of the population") in order to bring to whites and non-whites the presumed benefits of interracial contact—"without such controls there is no reason to expect any substantial success in maintaining mixed occupancy. . . ."[16] This has been true in as "liberal" a state as New York.[17] These policies for which standard euphemisms have been coined: "optimum non-white occupancy," "controlled occupancy" the "quota system" and so forth, are clearly designed to engineer "integration" and not to materially assist the American Negro in obtaining adequate housing. Even should adequate housing exist, the Negro is denied access by an arbitrary quota system. Where adequate housing does not exist needed public housing has been frequently curtailed because such housing was planned for areas predominantly occupied by non-whites (as has been the case in New York, Chicago, Philadelphia and Columbus, Ohio) and would, hence, be "segregated." In Buffalo the objection to the construction of low rental housing in the most distressed Negro areas turned on the contention that such housing could not be "integrated."[18]

[15] Jahoda & West, *Race Relations and Public Housing*, 7 Journal of Social Issues 132 (No. 2, 1951).

[16] Wolf, *The Invasion-Succession Sequence as a Self-Fulfilling Prophecy*, 13 Journal of Social Issues 19 (No. 4, 1957); Cf. the New York experience, Wood, *The Small Hard Core; The Housing of Problem Families in New York City. A Study and Recommendations* 19 (Citizens' Housing and Planning Council of New York, Inc., 1957).

[17] Cf. N.Y. Times, July 4, 1960, p. 1.

[18] Cf. *Another Northern City Runs into Race Problem*, U.S. News and World Report, April 18, 1958, p. 90.

The concern in such instances is obviously not with providing adequate housing for the most distressed elements of our citizenry, but rather with fostering a program of racial integration in housing. In the service of the fancied benefits which attend interracial contact the free access to available low-rental dwelling units is denied to Negroes. Since Negroes are disproportionately represented among the lower economic groups, restricted access to low-rental public housing builds up pressure in Negro communities which seeks outlet in peripheral white neighborhoods. The consequence is to initiate what has become an all but universal pattern of invasion-succession sequence in the standard metropolitan areas.[19]

Denied access to low-rental public housing projects, Negroes are forced to pay a higher average price for properties, in the areas into which they expand, than would whites during the first stage of ethnic "invasion."[20] The policy of the "benign quota" thus plays into the hands of the unscrupulous real estate dealer, who, faced with a neighborhood giving evidence of depreciation, abetted by "anti-discrimination" legislation, proceeds to "tip" it. That such regulative and/or proscriptive legislation functions in this way seems evident from whatever facts are available. Even such well-meaning efforts as that of the Supreme Court concerning restrictive covenants resulted in increased segregation of non-whites.[21] What it did do was to open areas insulated by restrictive covenants to manipulation. The fact is that the most immediate and widespread reaction to Negro entry into racially homogeneous residential districts outside the South has been one of withdrawal.[22] "The process of white withdrawal . . . slowly but steadily continues in

19 Grodzins, *Metropolitan Segregation*, 197 Scientific American 33-41 (No. 4, October, 1957).

20 "Negroes paid 28% to 51% in excess of prices paid by white buyers for 1 and 2 dwelling-unit structures during invasion." Schietinger, *Racial Succession and Value of Small Residential Properties*, 16 American Sociological Review 834 (No. 6, December, 1951).

21 Cowgill, *Trends in Residential Segregation of Non-Whites in American Cities, 1940-1950*, 21 American Sociological Review 56 (1956).

22 Cf. National Community Relations Advisory Council, *Guide to Changing Neighborhoods* (1956); Fauman, *Housing Discrimination, Changing Neighborhoods, and Public Schools*, 13 Journal of Social Issues 21-30 (No. 4, 1957); Kerckhoff, *A Study of Racially Changing Neighborhoods*, 3 Merrill-Palmer Quarterly 15-50 (1957); McDermott & Dennis, *Helping the Panic Neighborhood: A Philadelphia Approach*, 28 Interracial Review 131-135 (1955).

neighborhoods where benign quotas, or other controls are not enforceable."[23]

On the pretext of fostering "residential racial integration" Negro access to available low-cost public dwelling units is curtailed irrespective of the fact that the Negroes as a group are, because of their low economic status, those to whom the bulk of the low-cost housing should be made available. Negroes are driven, by the pressure of increased non-white inmigration, natural increase and the inaccessibility of public housing, into all-white neighborhoods[24] where (1) during the period of transition they are forced to pay anywhere from 28% to 51% more than whites for comparable units, (2) suffer the ignominy of more or less systematic white rejection;[25] to ultimately (3) find themselves in a resegregated community, since all the evidence indicates that the vast majority of communities have such a "tip-point," i.e., the most liberal and tolerant of whites will ultimately abandon a neighborhood where the incidence of Negro occupancy transcends that critical point.[26]

The "benign" quota system in public housing, entertained to engineer "successful" integration, drives non-whites, who because of their low economic status are in direst need, into the white community, where their entrance is facilitated by legislation proscribing "discrimination." Under these conditions the non-white, in his eagerness to obtain adequate housing denied him in low-cost public dwellings, facing the reluctance of whites, irrespective of formal legislation, to provide suitable private dwell-

---

[23] Fishman, *Some Social and Psychological Determinants of Intergroup Relations in Changing Neighborhoods: An Introduction to the Bridgeview Study,* 40 Social Forces 46 (No. 1, October, 1961).

[24] Coe, *Non-White Population Increases in Metropolitan Areas,* 50 Journal of the American Statistical Association 283-308 (No. 270, June 1955).

[25] Cf. Rosenthal's comments on the nature of white avoidance even in "stable interracial communities" in Deutsch, *op. cit. supra* note 6, at 90. Cf. Fishman, *Bridgeview, An Interracial Suburban Community. V. Intergroup Relations; the Attitudinal and Behavioral Levels.* (Manuscript, 1960). Fishman, *op. cit. supra* note 23, at 44.

[26] Cf. Leacock, Deutsch & Fishman, *The Bridgeview Study: A Preliminary Report,* 15 Journal of Social Issues 30-37 (No. 4, 1959. "This process of 'tipping' proceeds more rapidly in some neighborhoods than in others. White residents who will tolerate a few Negro neighbors, either willingly or unwillingly, begin to move out when the proportion of Negroes in the neighborhood or apartment building passes a certain critical point. This 'tip-point' varies from city to city and from neighborhood to neighborhood. But for the vast majority of white Americans a 'tip-point' exists. Once it is exceeded, they will no longer stay among Negro neighbors." Grodzins, *op. cit. supra* note 19, at 34.

ing units, will be forced to pay as much as 50% more than would whites for similar accommodations. Ultimately whites evacuate the neighborhood and the cycle is complete. The non-white is re-segregated and the area deteriorates.

III. *Results of Negro Dispersal*

The socioeconomic impairments suffered by Negroes under these conditions are obvious. To those herein briefly discussed must be added the reduced opportunity for small scale Negro entrepreneurs to maintain an economically viable market for their services under conditions prevailing in the standard metropolitan areas. The only areas in which the Negro professional and entrepreneurial class has maintained a toe-hold in American enterprise are those in which he has enjoyed an insulated advantage of servicing a racially homogeneous community.[27] In "transitional" neighborhoods Negro business suffers in competition with established white concerns. Negroes do not return to the old neighborhood to patronize Negro business.[28] Similarly, in transitional neighborhoods in the standard metropolitan areas, the Negro clergy finds it difficult to maintain the integrity of their congregations. Since the Negro church provided a disproportionately high percentage of Negroes with status[29] the threat which attends even temporarily mixed neighborhoods weighs heavily on the established minority middle class.

The bulk of the Negroes, occupying lower class status, suffer under current policies because they are denied access to the little housing which is within their means. They are forced into peripheral white residential areas to pay inordinately high prices for available accommodation, to subsequently suffer the ignominy of being the ultimate cause of white withdrawal. The Negro entrepreneurial and quasi-professional class suffers as a consequence of the threat to racially insulated neighborhoods which afford him

---

27 Cf. Walker, *The Negro in American Life* 46 (1954); Simpson & Yinger, *The Changing Patterns of Race Relations*, 15 Phylon 327-345 (1954); Davis, *The American Negro's Dilemma: The Negro's Self-Imposed Predicament* 109 (1954).

28 Cf. Brussat, *Incidental Findings on Urban Invasion*, 16 American Sociological Review 94-96 (1951).

29 Cf. Myrdal, *An American Dilemma, The Negro Problem and Modern Democracy* 940 (1944); Kinzer & Sagarin, *The Negro in American Business: The Conflict Between Separatism and Integration* 158 (1950).

a market for his commercial or professional wares. The only segment of the Negro community not immediately threatened by serious socioeconomic disabilities is that identified as "the new Negro middle class," those who hold civil service positions, clerical and quasi-professional positions under the prevailing conditions of economic boom and full employment. Significantly enough, organizations like the National Association for the Advancement of Colored People draw their principal support from this small but articulate section of the Negro community.[30] Negroes of the lower class, who have suffered all the disabilities which attend urban "integration" programs, have been increasingly drawn into protest organizations which advocate not increased interracial contact but racial separation.[31] These protest movements, advocating racial separation, have been the only Negro organizations that have succeeded in attracting anything like mass participation.[32] They have been characterized by express hostility toward the "social insinuation" programs they conceive to be so much at variance with their real needs.[33]

IV. *Reasons for White Withdrawal*

White withdrawal which is, for all intents and purposes, the universal response to non-white intrusion, has been treated in a curious way in the professional literature. Generally it is ascribed to "irrational" motives, the consequence of "low mental health,"[34] and yet because of the universality of the pattern it would be singular indeed if such were the case. As a matter of fact a more sophisticated analysis indicates that while whites have learned locutions appropriate to "tolerance" and consequently belie their verbal attitudes by their overt behavior, they have clear and sufficient *rational* motives for abandoning a neighborhood where non-white occupancy exceeds a critical ratio.

[30] Cf. Wynn, *The NAACP Versus Negro Revolutionary Protest* (1955); Frazier, *The Negro Middle Class and Desegregation*, 4 Social Problems 291-301 (No. 4, 1957).

[31] Cf. Lincoln, *The Black Muslims in America*, 72, 74 (1961); Essien-Udom, *Black Nationalism: A Search for an Identity in America* 61, 98, 112, 259 (1962).

[32] *Id.* at 102; Cronon, *Black Moses: The Story of Marcus Garvey and the Universal Negro Improvement Association* (1955).

[33] Lincoln, *op. cit. supra* note 31, at 146-155; Essien-Udom, *op. cit. supra* note 31, at 302. N.Y. Times, April 23, 1963, p. 20, col. 3.

[34] Cf. Deutsch & Collins, *op. cit. supra* note 7, Appendix A.

In areas occupied by middle-class families one of the primary family goals is an adequate education for their children, since status is by and large a function of the adequacy of the individual's education. White parents have been known to use the incidence of Negro students as an index of a neighborhood school's educational competence. Whatever the ultimate cause, Negro pupils as a group function at a lower level of academic performance.[35] In the Southeast, at the twelfth-grade level, this deficit is as large as four full years below standard.[36] In the New York metropolitan area Negro and Puerto Rican children at the eighth-grade level score at least two full years below national norms in reading and arithmetic achievement.[37] Where inmigrants are from the South these disabilities are particularly striking. Even where the non-white children are long-time city residents reduced efficiency characterizes their mean performance.[38] As such, the disposition to vacate an area on the part of middle-class whites having children of public school age is perfectly rational.[39] Interestingly enough, there are but few investigations in the literature treating this very real problem even though it is one of the principal reasons for middle-class white withdrawal from racially mixed neighborhoods.[40]

In lower-class neighborhoods, where the real or fancied competence of the public schools is not accorded such a high priority

35 Cf. Osborne, *Racial Differences in Mental Growth and School Achievement: A Longitudinal Study*, 7 Psychological Reports 233-239 (1960); Osborne, *School Achievement of White and Negro Children of the Same Mental and Chronological Ages*, 2 Mankind Quarterly 26-29 (No. 1, July-Sept., 1961). For an exhaustive account of psychological test results of Negro performance see Shuey, *The Testing of Negro Intelligence* (1958); Dreger & Miller, *Comparative Psychological Studies of Negroes and Whites in the United States*, 57 Psychological Bulletin 361-402 (No. 5, Sept., 1960); Deutsch, *Minority Group and Class Status as Related to Social and Personality Factors in Scholastic Achievement: Monograph Number Two* (Cornell, 1960).

36 Cf. Osborne, "Racial Difference in School Achievement," *Mankind Monographs* (Edinburgh, Scotland, 1962); Osborne, *Racial Differences in Mental Growth and School Achievement*, 7 Psychological Reports 233-239 (1960).

37 Public Education Association, *The Status of the Public School Education of Negro and Puerto Rican Children in New York City* 24 (1955).

38 Garrett, *Negro-White Differences in Mental Ability in the United States*, 65 Scientific Monthly 329-333 (No. 4, 1947).

39 ". . . a commonly expressed fear of parents in middle class changing areas is that school standards will 'go down' if a substantial number of Negro children enroll. If we believe that deprivation and enforced psycho-social isolation, with subsequent unfavorable effects upon the self-image, have indeed interfered with the development of many Negro children, we should be the last to insist that these fears are entirely groundless and therefore irrational." Wolf, *op. cit. supra* note 16, at 17.

40 Fauman, *op. cit. supra* note 22.

level, the inmigration of lower-class Negroes brings with it the disabilities which attend the increased presence of a group collectively characterized by inordinately high rates of delinquency, crime, sexual immorality and communicable disease.[41] The reduced mobility of economically impaired whites forces them to remain in threatened communities.[42] They tend to remain in neighborhoods threatened with substantial Negro occupancy because they can not avail themselves of comparable housing at reasonable proximity to the place of employment.[43] This could only breed a free floating hostility which materially increases the real threat of racial and non-racial violence in the standard metropolitan areas.

V. *The Rational Basis for Homogeneous Neighborhoods*

The deterioration of the standards of local schools, the increased incidence of delinquency and crime, greater public health hazards, regular exposure to a group which, because of conditions prevailing in its subculture, is characterized by lax sexual morality, broken homes and minimal academic aspirations, would seem to provide, in general, sufficient rational motive for white flight. And yet there are further considerations which weigh in the deliberations leading to evacuation of a heterogeneous neighborhood.

Sociologists have long appreciated the fact that men are animated by a disposition to seek out those they fancy similar to themselves. This has been characterized as a generic fact of social life: "The manifest tendency of . . . groups is to value their distinctive traits, be they physical or cultural, to make interpersonal selection on the basis of perceived similarity, and to enter into selective associations, associations of preference, the obverse of which is the latent or manifest avoidance of those groups which are,

---

41 Cf. Frazier, *The Negro in the United States* 376, 649 (1949); Frazier, *The Negro Family in the United States*, chapt. VI (1951); Weyl, *The Negro in American Civilization*, chapt. XVIII (1960); Fox & Volakakis, *The Negro Offender in a Northern Industrial Area*, 46 J. Crim. L., C. & P.S. 641 (1956); Axelrad, *Negro and White Institutionalized Delinquents*, 57 American Journal of Sociology 569 (1952); Fox, *Intelligence, Race and Age as Selective Factors in Crime*, 37 J. Crim. L. & C. 141 (1946); Kephart, *The Negro Offender: An Urban Research Project*, 60 American Journal of Sociology 46-50 (1954).

42 Fishman, *op. cit. supra* note 23, at 43.

43 *Id.* at 45. Cf. Weaver, *Integration in Public and Private Housing*, 304 Annals Am. Academy Pol. & Soc. Sci. 95 (1956).

in lesser or greater degree, dissimilar."[44] This dispositional trait has been identified as a "constant" by Niceforo, as a high-order generalization in his law of "attraction of similars and the repulsion of dissimilars."[45] It has been empirically assessed in a number of studies, in a number of micro-sociological situations.[46]

Such a disposition manifests itself in an emotional conceptualization of the group of which the individual is a member. The conscious recognition of the psychic feeling of belongingness renders the individual comfortable in the presence of members of his preferred association and uncomfortable in their absence or in the presence of out-group members.[47] It is a natural tendency for men to enter into associations of limited membership—such self-regarding associations characterize social life.[48] The tendency to associate with a select group becomes increasingly emphatic when the relationships are primary, rather than secondary.[49] The circumstances which attend living in the same building, or in the same neighborhood, engender contact on a primary level—which by and large explains why approximately 80% of the American people favor some form of homogeneous housing accommodation.[50]

Each group, whether that group be economic, religious, national or ethnic, entertains certain values to which it commits itself, which are preferred and which it would instill in its children. Whatever those values happen to be, they lend substance to group

44 Gregor, *The Dynamics of Prejudice*, 3 Mankind Quarterly 79-88 (No. 2, Oct-Dec., 1962); cf. Gregor, *On the Nature of Prejudice*, 52 Eugenics Review 217-224 (No. 4, Jan., 1961).

45 Niceforo, *Schematico profilo di una sociologia generale in cinquanta paragrafi*, 11 Rivista Italiana di Economia, Demografia e Statistica par. 10 (No. 3-4, July-Dec., 1957); cf. Marotta, *Il pensiero sociologico di Alfredo Niceforo*, 1 Rassegna Italiana do Sociologia 83 (No. 2, April-June, 1960).

46 Cf. Davitz, *Social Perception and Sociometric Choice of Children*, 50 Journal of Abnormal and Social Psychology 175 (No. 2, March, 1955); Lundberg & Dickson, *Inter-Ethnic Relations in a High School Population*, 58 American Journal of Sociology 1 (No. 1, July, 1952); Lundberg & Dickson, *Selective Association Among Ethnic Groups in a High School Population*, 17 American Sociological Review 23-35 (No. 1, Feb., 1952); Warrington & Blaisdell, *Unconscious Attitudes as Correlates of Sociometric Choice in a Social Group*, 47 Journal of Abnormal and Social Psychology 790-796 (1952).

47 Cf. Elmer, *Identification as a Social Concept*, 39 Sociology and Social Research 103-109 (No. 2, Nov.-Dec., 1954).

48 Cf. Gregor, *Corrado Gini and the Theory of Race Formation*, 45 Sociology and Social Research 175-181 (No. 2, Jan., 1961); Lundberg, *Some Neglected Aspects of the "Minorities" Problem*, Modern Age 285-297 (Summer, 1958).

49 Cf. Gordon, *Ethnic Groups in American Life*, Daedalus 263-285 (Spring, 1961).

50 Cf. Jahoda, *Race Relations and Mental Health*, Race and Science 487 (1961).

life, to preferred associations, and it would seem that parents have a legitimate right to foster in their offspring the values that have given meaning and content to their own lives. There are matters of taste and preference each group may seek to foster, concepts of belief, morals and etiquette peculiar to themselves that they wish to see live on in their children. Men live in preferred associations of limited compass and each association is animated by its own values.

Whatever we know of attitude formation in children indicates that attitudes, at specific developmental stages, are articulated by and large in the interaction with a peer-group[51] in the neighborhood school, for example, or the neighborhood itself. Children with well-established primary systems developed by virtue of parent-child and subsequently peer-group interaction, are fundamentally more secure than children beset by the psychological tensions of adjusting to a variety of diverse and perhaps conflicting value systems.[52]

Primary value systems are the consequence of the tolerably well understood process of developmental identification. The child assimilates the values shared by his primary family group. Suggestibility, the capacity to identify, is an innate capacity which enables the child to assimilate the acquired experiences of others.[53] Insofar as the child has within him this tendency to do as others do, so he adopts the mores, values, beliefs and customs of those with whom he interacts. As the child ventures into the community his contact with secondary groups, should those groups entertain values other than his own, can not only undermine the coherency of his value system but can generate real psychic tension. The parent must face the dilemma of seeing his child abandon cherished group values or suffer the debilitating psychological consequences of attempting to adjust, at a critical period of maturation, to diverse, and sometimes mutually exclusive values. In an environment in which self-regarding groups, animated by distinct values, come into sustained contact, a child is beset by making one

[51] Cf. Berenda, *The Influence of the Group on the Judgments of Children* (1950).
[52] Cf. Thompson, *Child Psychology: Growth Trends in Psychological Adjustments* 552-589 (1952).
[53] Hadfield, *Childhood and Adolescence* 122 (1962).

or the other adjustment. The exposure to such diversity, while it may stimulate and enrich the life of the mature individual, may very well impair the life of the child and the adolescent. Should any group, be it a class, a religion, a national or ethnic minority, seek to foster its values in its children, it would seek, quite rationally, to maintain the class, religious, national or ethnic integrity of the environment in which the child develops in order to insure the continuity and coherency of moral, aesthetic or religious training. The values of the middle class in America differ in substantial and critical respects from those of the lower class,[54] the values of Catholics differ from those of Protestants, those of Jews as a group from those of Negroes as a group. Parents have a right to raise their children in an environment in which there is a reasonably high order probability that those with whom their child will enter into contact will share their fundamental values. It is reasonable to expect that a group which shares a common culture, history and heritage will share substantially the same values. For a family to seek such an environment, compatible with the fostering of its select values, is, in essence, reasonable. And this is, in fact, what occurs in the pluralism of American democracy.[55] There is an interaction of ethnic, class and religious selective association. Where groups evince high social visibility, preferential association follows racial or ethnic lines in spite of religious or class similarities.[56] There is some evidence that the differences which obtain in child rearing practices between the Negro middle class and the white middle class, for example, would tend to justify the social distance which is, in fact, maintained. For if contemporary theories of child-rearing practices and their influence on personality formation and subsequent value commitments are correct, we would expect systematic differences to characterize Negroes and whites irrespective of their class and religious similarities.[57]

Where high social visibility is not evident, religious exclusiveness may operate to maintain residential homogeneity. In any

---

[54] Cf. Carroll, *Relation of Social Environment to the Moral Ideology and Personal Aspirations of Negro Boys and Girls*, 53 The School Review 30-38 (No. 1, Jan., 1945).

[55] Gordon, *op. cit. supra* note 49, at 280.

[56] Cf. Westie & Westie, *The Social-Distance Pyramid: Relationships Between Caste and Class*, 63 American Journal of Sociology 190-196 (No. 2, Sept., 1957).

[57] Cf. Davis & Havighurst, *Social Class and Color Differences in Child Rearing*, 11 American Sociological Review 709 (No. 6, Dec., 1946).

event the seeking out of kind is not only a natural disposition of man as a social animal, but is the consequence of a rational assessment on the part of parents with respect to their obligations in affording their children the most propitious environment for healthy psychological development and the fostering of treasured values.

Finally, the argument that self-segregation is psychologically harmful because it induces a superiority complex is completely devoid of merit. If whites labor under a superiority complex as a consequence of segregating themselves from Negroes, then the citizens of the United States suffer similarly by segregating themselves from the rest of mankind, and the Catholics suffer a similar complex by separating themselves in their church from others. Every group in society, which evinces preference for its own members, would labor under a similar disability. Such preferences characterize group life and there is no empirical evidence that whites, or any other component group in the complex of groups which constitute society, are disabled by such hypothetical complexes.[57a] Such an argument rarely rises above the level of an *ad hominem* appeal and warrants but little attention.

We have here focused on the disposition to evacuate racially mixed neighborhoods largely because contemporary anti-discrimination legislation is patently designed to engineer *racial* integration. What we have tried to indicate in this brief discussion, is that the effort to maintain the relative homogeneity of a neighborhood, or vacate when that homogeneity no longer obtains, may be perfectly rational. The decision to evacuate a racially mixed neighborhood may be motivated by any of a number of considerations. That many of the motives are perfectly rational cannot be gainsaid. Nor can the desire to maintain some degree of residential homogeneity, in and of itself, be adjudged irrational and/or detrimental to the public interest.

VI. *Intra-Racial Preference*

The systematic attempt to force integration in housing has engendered a host of problems not easily dismissed. Many of the

[57a] Cf. Medalia, *Myrdal's Assumptions on Race Relations: A Conceptual Commentary*, 40 Social Forces 223 (1962); Campbell, *Moral Discomfort and Racial Segregation— An Examination of the Myrdal Hypothesis*, 39 Social Forces 228 (1961).

assessments of these housing experiments are characterized, it seems, by wishful thinking, exhortation and cant. The fact is that the disposition to preferential association is a generic social fact.[58] In the instance of contact between groups of high social visibility[59] in situations of high salience, an almost inevitable consequence is at best withdrawal, at worse, open violence. Hofstaetter, in his factorial analysis of cultural patterns in the United States found a correlation of .97 obtaining between the incidence of Negroes in the total population and the intensity of discrimination.[60] What this means in effect is that "neither better and more widespread education nor a rise of the standard of living affect racial discrimination directly. Racial discrimination, however, is a function of the relative frequency of the element discriminated against."[61] The increased incidence of Negro occupancy will directly increase the disposition of whites to flee. The express reasons given for evacuating may range from those of "normal family cycle reasons" (change of job, increase or decrease in size of household) to acknowledged or verifiable antipathy toward Negroes. "Withdrawal due to reasons of the latter type may actually be relatively infrequent although this is not to say that most whites do not harbor anti-Negro prejudice at an unconscious level quite inaccessible to extinction on the basis of daily life experiences. [62]

Such considerations must give us pause. If, as a matter of fact, the natural disposition of groups, ethnic, religious or economic, to enter select associations,[63] particularly with respect to residence, is magnified when out-groups are characterized by high social visibil-

58 Lundberg, *op. cit. supra* note 48; Gordon, *op. cit. supra* note 49.

59 "Since members of different racial groups, like white people and Negroes, look significantly different, they have a very strong tendency to consider each other not only as looking but also as being different and, consequently, as belonging to two different groups. . . . They have this very strong, possibly irresistibly strong, tendency, whether they are explicitly aware of it or not, whether they honestly admit it or hypocritically deny it, whether they would be able to define what this 'being different' means or not. This means also that this basic sociosensory perception of difference in physique plays a powerful role in the conscious, and probably still more powerful role in the unconscious, group identification." Ichheiser, *Sociopsychological and Cultural Factors in Race Relation,* 54 American Journal of Sociology 396 (No. 5, 1949).

60 Hofstaetter, *A Factorial Study of Cultural Patterns in the U.S.,* 32 Journal of Psychology 105 (1951).

61 *Id.* at 108; cf. Pettigrew, *op. cit. supra* note 2, at 109.

62 Fishman, *op. cit. supra* note 23, at 44.

63 *Supra,* n.44.

ity, as is the case with the Negro, we would expect "integrated" communities to maintain their "stability" only under the aegis of some express controls, "benign" or "ethnic quotas."[64] As we have suggested, these controls could only serve to limit the availability of low-cost housing to those most expressly in need. More than that, the first sanguine reports of "successful social experiment" even with respect to such contrived situations have given rise to considerable reservations. Successes were, in fact, reported as a consequence of poorly conducted research.[65] Early reports of "success," the consequence of "research in a field where the adequate scientific foundations of fact and theory have not been laid . . ." did, in effect, result in "science for propaganda, however good one may feel this propaganda" leading social science into a "miasma of unverified fact, nebulous concepts, and strong compulsion to prove what we would all like to believe should exist."[66]

Where controls do not exist, white withdrawal is either rapid, bordering on panic, or erosive. Whatever its pace, the results are almost everywhere and ultimately the same, resegregation. In the period of transition the Negro is forced to pay a significantly higher price for housing and the Negro entrepreneurial and professional class loses access to a unified and insulated market. Whites flee to the suburbs and the central core of the standard metropolitan areas deteriorates into slums. To attend these disabilities the Negro faces the full realization that the promised "integration" is a false hope. The futility and frustration which attends this process cannot be gauged. There is good presumptive evidence that Negro aggressiveness and disposition to violence is a function of this systematic frustration and disillusionment.

VII. *Integration as a "Human Value"*

While all this must be, and has in a variety of places been, said, there still remains one of the most compelling arguments in the "liberals' " repertory of exhortations: that of "human values." The argument is that "segregation" *per se* does irreparable damage

---

[64] Cf. Bell & Willis, *The Segregation of Negroes in American Cities*, 6 Social and Economic Studies 59-75 (No. 1, 1957).
[65] Cf. Rosenthal in Deutsch, *op. cit. supra* note 6, at 90.
[66] *Id.* at 91.

to the Negro personality. Its converse, that the psychodynamic impairments suffered by the Negro are materially reduced in "integrated" situations, is by-and-large presumed. In fact, there is little probative force to such arguments.

Only under special circumstances have Negroes made inroads into white communities under conditions approximating normalcy. A professional or quasi-professional Negro family may occupy a residence in a middle-class white community without precipitating serious community tension. Rarely, for example, does the appearance of a single, professional or quasi-professional Negro family precipitate flight, particularly in a neighborhood whose population has been long established. But under such conditions the Negro is an exceedingly small minority. What little evidence is available indicates that Negro children brought up under such circumstances develop xenocentric orientation, that is, they regularly accept white preferences and prejudices and systematically reject their own race. "Causes for a stronger white than Negro identification are multiple. Strongest among them, however, seems to be an early childhood spent as a member of the single Negro family in a white neighborhood, plus the factor of the usual middle class attempt of the parents in such a situation to gloss over the 'race problem.' "[67] Wherever the individual Negro family succeeds in successfully "integrating" a neighborhood he condemns his children to systematic exposure to white racial preferences, particularly those least amenable to ameliorative influence: aesthetic standards. "The most obvious, but none the less detrimental, obstacle to the growth of a secure self-system among Negro children is the blind acceptance of white racial prejudices and measuring one's personal worth by the degrees of proximity to white complexion or other Caucasian features. These evaluations of skin color and other physical features, however, do not affect the Negro child directly before he comes in close contact with white children. . . ."[68] As Myrdal early pointed out, the Negro's "integration" into the white community can only succeed in making him increasingly aware,

---

[67] Brenman, *The Relationship Between Minority-Group Membership and Group Identification in a Group of Urban Middle Class Negro Girls*, 11 Journal of Psychology 195 (1940).

[68] Dai, *Some Problems of Personality Development Among Negro Children*, in *Personality in Nature, Society and Culture* 451 (Kluckhohn, Murray eds., 1949).

in a negative sense, of the fact that he is a Negro. "Their color valuation is only one instance, among many, of the much more general tendency for the Negro people, to the degree that they are becoming acculturated, to take over the valuations of the superior white caste. In other spheres this process can, on the whole, be regarded as a wholesome and advantageous adjustment. . . . In this particular respect, however, a conflict emerges which is unsolvable, as the average Negro cannot effectively change his color and other physical features. If the dark Negro accepts the white man's evaluation of skin color, he must stamp himself as inferior. If the light Negro accepts this evaluation, he places himself above the darker Negroes but below the whites. . . . The conflict produces a personality problem for practically every single Negro. And few Negroes accomplish an entirely successful adjustment."[69]

We know something of the psychodynamic ravages of this kind of "acculturation" enhanced by "successful integration." It is not unusual for the syndrome of psychotic Negroes to include color denial.[70] Middle-class Negroes are notoriously out-group orientated.[71] Negro children in "integrated" school situations show a marked preference for whites when compared to those from schools where white contact is minimal. While 80% of Negro children from racially homogeneous schools indicate a preference for their own skin color only 20% of the Negro children from biracial schools show a similar preference.[72] Moreover, Northern Negro children from "integrated" communities show marked in-group rejection.[73] In Northern areas where inter-racial contacts are systematically fostered, Negro children show marked out-group preferences (74%) and in-group antagonisms (24%); over half (57%) manifest feelings of inferiority toward whites.[74] As we have indicated, the evidence indicates that Negroes develop these psychosocial impairments as a consequence of systematic contact with whites, particularly during critical phases of personality formation.

[69] Myrdal, op. cit. supra note 29, at 699.

[70] Cf. Myers & Yochelson, Color Denial in the Negro, 11 Psychiatry 39-46 (No. 1, 1948); Lind, The Color Complex in the Negro, 1 Psychoanalytic Review 404 (1914).

[71] Marks, Skin Color Judgments of Negro College Students, 38 Journal of Abnormal and Social Psychology 370-372 (No. 3, 1954); cf. Frazier, op. cit. supra note 30.

[72] Cf. Clark, Prejudice and Your Child 44 (1955).

[73] Clark & Clark, Racial Identification and Preference in Negro Children, in Readings in Social Psychology 551-560 (Swanson, Newcomb & Hartley, eds., 1952).

[74] Goodman, Race Awareness in Young Children 62 (1952).

Negroes, on the other hand, raised in all Negro communities, tend to have less negatively toned affective response to whites and tend to have a "much higher regard for Negroes"—a "more favorable . . . expression toward [their] race."[75]

All that non-discrimination in housing can reasonably mean is equality of access in regards to cost, financing, terms and credit requirements. That equality of treatment in access to housing can be creditably linked with tortured notions about heterogeneous neighborhoods is but little supported by whatever facts are available, and, it would seem such a forced wedding of the two concerns is, in significant measure, harmful. The compulsory maintenance of "integrated" public housing does violence to the legitimate demand on the part of non-whites to adequate low-rental dwelling units, driving Negroes into the open market where they are disadvantaged in the competition with whites only to find themselves, ultimately, resegregated. In the course of transitional or "controlled" integration, their children are exposed to all the psychodynamic impairments which beset minority groups possessed of socio-perceptual traits of high visibility in protracted contact situations. *The most notable response to these prevailing conditions, the result of concerted efforts to compel "integration," has been the organization of Negro protest groups, of unmatched vitality, demanding racial separation.*[76]

VIII. *Unimportance of Segregation in Housing*

That a considerable portion of the social science community has badly analyzed the situation can most charitably be ascribed to the fact that they labor under the influence of an anterior commitment of some compelling sort. The vague and ambiguous evidence and artless argument used to support the insistent demand for "integration" can only be the consequence of such an influence. A poll of psychologists and sociologists elicited a response, bordering on unanimity, that "enforced segregation had detrimental effects on the segregated groups."[77] Such a poll has little intrinsic

75 Hill, *Race Attitudes in Oklahoma's All-Negro Community*, 7 Phylon 268 (No. 3, 1946).

76 Cf. Lincoln, *op. cit. supra* note 31; Cronon, *op. cit. supra* note 32.

77 Cf. Abrams, *op. cit. supra* note 6, at 283; Deutcher & Chein, *The Psychological*

merit. It is admitted that "there is little in the scientific literature on the precise effects of prejudice and discrimination on the health of personality," and "unfortunately for scientific accuracy and adequacy, thoroughly satisfactory methods of determining the effects of prejudice and discrimination on health of personality have not yet been devised."[78] If this is the case, it is difficult to conceive what evidence is employed by "most social scientists" in formulating their considered judgments.

In all such loose discussions the variables attending "segregation" are not assessed. If "segregation" *per se* were the primary causative variable in psychological impairment, we would expect to be able to isolate its influence everywhere. Such is not the case. In a number of areas in the world where "segregation" obtains, and status differential is evident, the minority groups show none of the disabilities of the American Negroes.[79] On the other hand, in Brazil, where *de jure* residential segregation has never, for all intents and purposes, ever existed, and *de facto* segregation does not obtain, non-whites show some of the same personality impairments evinced by American Negroes.[80] Professor Bruno Bettelheim has contended in fact that "There is no scientific evidence that racial segregation damages the human personality,"[81] and Professor van den Haag objected to the suggestion that there is any substantial scientific evidence that segregation, *per se*, impairs the personality.[82] There is no probative evidence that residential segregation, *per se*, impairs the personality. There is, in fact, some evidence that residential segregation, providing an insulated environment for the maturation of a coherent self-system on the part of the Negro child, may actually be a positive advantage.[83]

Effects of Enforced Segregation: A Survey of Social Science Opinion, 26 Journal of Psychology 259-287 (1948).

[78] Clark, *The Effects of Prejudice and Discrimination*, in *Personality in the Making* 136, 139 (Witmer & Kotinsky, eds., 1952).

[79] Cf. Gillin, *"Race" Relations Without Conflict: A Guatemalan Town*, 53 American Journal of Sociology 337-343 (No. 5, 1948).

[80] Cf. Willems, *Racial Attitudes in Brazil*, 54 American Journal of Sociology 402-408 (No. 3, 1949); Bastide & van den Berghe, *Stereotypes, Norms and Interracial Behavior in Sao Paulo, Brazil*, 22 American Sociological Review 689-694 (No. 6, 1957).

[81] Cf. Clark, *The Desegregation Cases: Criticism of the Social Scientist's Role*, 5 Vill. L. Rev. 224, 236 (1959-60).

[82] Ross & van den Haag, *The Fabric of Society* 164 (1957).

[83] "Where the social group of the racially subordinate individual is highly organized and integrated as in the Little Italies or Chinatowns, or in many Southern Negro com-

To indissolubly embroil the problem of adequate housing for America's non-white minority with affirmative integration is to do a grave disservice to those it would ostensibly assist. There is some evidence that such an assessment[84] has been forthcoming from the responsible community. James Conant's well received book *Slums and Suburbs* clearly distinguishes the problem of adequate schooling from the problematic issue of "integrated" schooling. Similarly the legitimate Negro demand for adequate housing must be separated from the ill-defined and apparently ill-considered problem of "integrated" housing. That the law has been mustered to the service of such a program is perhaps a commentary on the dangers inherent in the extension of the concept of "expert testimony" to cover the immature disciplines of the social sciences,[85] but also those inherent in social action programs designed to "engineer" attitudes and coerce "folkways" through the legal machinery of the state.

IX. *Conclusion*

What is suggested here is that social science research delivers no unequivocal conclusions with respect to the merit, feasibility and socio-psychological implications of racially homogeneous or heterogeneous housing. Public officials and private persons should, as a consequence, be aware that the personal preferences of the investigator have ample room to operate as a significant factor in interpreting the available data. At their best the social science disciplines can tender reasonably high order predictions concerning the collective and individual consequences of specific action programs only in specific situations. Broad generalizations are at best hazardous. Finally, to suggest that social science data supports, without qualification, the programs designed to racially integrate public and private housing is mistaken, sometimes mischievous and frequently harmful to those most in need of succor.

munities, its members will usually have relatively less psychological conflict over their racial status." Davis, *Racial Status and Personality Development*, 57 Scientific Monthly 358 (1943).

[84] Cf. Friedman, *The White Liberal's Retreat*, Atlantic Monthly 42-46 (Jan. 1963).

[85] "Those who have attempted to evaluate action programs in race relations since the war are almost unanimous in repeating this fundamental point: we simply do not know which premises are standing up and which deserve to be jettisoned." Bradbury, *Evaluation of Research in Race Relations*, 5 Inventory of Research in Racial and Cultural Relations 102 (Univ. of Chicago, Mimeo., Nos. 2, 3, 1953). Cf. Freeman, *Theory and Strategy in Race Relations*, 30 Social Forces 77-87 (October, 1951).

ANTI-DISCRIMINATION LEGISLATION:
A BRITISH VIEW

Editorial Note: This article represents portions of a debate conducted in the House of Lords on May 14, 1962 on a proposed Racial Discrimination Bill banning discrimination based on race, color or religion in hotels, lodging houses, restaurants, and places of amusement. The bill was ultimately denied a second reading (defeated). While much of the debate is not relevant to the topic of this symposium, some parts are. Those portions are reprinted below by permission.

LORD MILVERTON:[1] . . . For instance, he said that if we do not legislate, if we do not approve this Bill, then we shall be advertising to the world that we condone, if not sympathise with, discrimination. I cannot accept the validity of that argument. It surely is the duty of the government, and the duty of ourselves, to exercise our judgment in matters of this kind, irrespective of any misrepresentation or misunderstanding which may occur as the result of our judgment. . . .

. . . I have given the subject a good deal of study during my life and my experience throughout the world has been that racial discrimination is a universal defect in human relations. It seems often to be based on a mental stereotype, a fixed mental picture of another group. It is not merely, as the noble Lord himself said, a colour question. It is apt to be mingled with religion, culture, and economic differences and opposing social traditions and differences of outlook of every kind . . . .

. . . Prejudice against foreigners, let us accept it as a fact which has run through the centuries, is world-wide. All nations have it, in greater or lesser degree. Sometimes, it is true, it is mixed with a number of feelings, estimable enough in themselves, such as a consuming pride in national achievement. But let us not forget that prejudice is an attitude of mind, which may or may not lead to discrimination. Discrimination is action. For instance, a racial riot or a restriction of amenities or privileges is but the active rationalisation of a dislike that is already there. We know

---

[1] Arthur Frederick Richards, 1st Baron Milverton. G.M.G. 1933; K.G.M.G. 1935; G.C.M.G. 1942; Knight of St. John. B.A. 1907, Oxford Univ. Governor of North Borneo, 1930-3; Governor of Gambia, 1933-6; Governor of Jamaica, 1938-43; Governor of Nigeria, 1943-7. In writing to the editor by letter of July 10, 1962, giving permission to have his remarks reprinted, he stated about anti-discrimination legislation in housing: "My own view is that all such specific legislation is fundamentally unsound and likely to intensify the prejudice which it aims to eliminate."

that there are cultural differences. We know that individuals are not equal in intelligence, and surely it is reasonable to assume that the forces which have shaped evolution have not produced equality in the average mental agility in associated groups of men known as races. Different habits require,time and patience to tolerate, and resentment is inevitable if a community is asked to absorb more than a certain number of an alien culture in one area at a given time.

That, I suggest with respect, is the answer to the noble Lord, Lord Walston, when he made reference to-day to the Commonwealth Immigrants Bill which we recently passed. The point is that that Bill was precisely aimed at a reduction of the likelihood of a growth of prejudice in this country as a result of our trying to assimilate too quickly too large a number of people of a different way of life. For prejudice, as the right reverend Prelate has said, the only remedy is education in the broadest sense—the understanding of other societies, the realisation that we are all human and the appreciation of the common ancestry of mankind.

For many reasons, which time does not permit me to go into now, many racial groups have started late in the ever-increasing speed of modern human development. As Philip Mason has pointed out in his extremely interesting book entitled *Common Sense About Race*:

"It took 10,000 years to learn a new way of polishing a flint arrow-head, while a modern fighter aircraft is obsolete almost before it comes off the drawing board." It is no wonder that the backward races are bewildered and also desperately anxious to avail themselves of modern knowledge and training and prove themselves as fundamentally capable of advance as those races now so far ahead of them. They are naturally, too, resentful of any rigid separation which corrupts and strains good will and hampers such advance.

The noble Lord who sponsored this Bill believes that the proper remedy is legislation and that this can be an effective remedy. One of his earliest predecessors was Alexander the Great, who, in a famous proclamation, advocated the acceptance of the idea of human equality. And from Alexander the Great down through the centuries to the French Revolution and the American Declaration of Independence, this ideal has been proclaimed and never realised. It has not yet been achieved. Efforts have been made to accelerate the recognition of the brotherhood of man and the Churches have lent their voices in support of it. As the right reverend Prelate has said, great progress is being made, but I suggest that progress has been, and must be, slow when one is changing how men think.

The question remains: can the law alter race relations? In the main, I differ from the noble Lord, Lord Walston; I do not think it can. It can, at best, help to create a climate in which the only effective agents, the hearts and minds of men, can change, influenced in a slow, evolutionary manner by social forces and education. There is, I believe, relatively little discrimination in this country, as the right reverend Prelate has suggested, and it will diminish—it is, I suggest, taking it by and large, diminishing now —too slowly for most of us who would wish it to go faster, but it is one of those things in which an unwise attempt to accelerate its pace would probably defeat our object.

The United States of America have been mentioned. The United States have had a long experience in this matter of legislative attempt to control prejudice and prohibit discrimination. Law unquestionably is often an appropriate and effective mode of regulating behaviour, but I suggest that we cannot successfully legislate against feelings. As W. G. Sumner, the American, once said: "Stateways cannot change folkways." I am inclined to believe in this comment: in the case of prejudice, where a law is backed by the community, it is unnecessary, and where it is opposed by the community, it is futile.

New York laws have for long outlawed discrimination in jury service; in the right to practise law; in the admission to public schools, places of public accommodation, resort or amusement; in insurance rates and benefits; in public employment and employment in utility companies and in firms fulfilling public works contracts; in admission to tax exempt non-sectarian education institutions; in civil service, public housing, labour unions, public relief, defence industries, and in the sale and delivery of alcoholic beverages. But the real impact on life has been relatively ineffective. Americans have rather a way of encouraging high-souled legislation, so long as they are left the freedom to disregard it or ignore it.

The Bill before us, if I may say so, is pure compulsion: it is neither educational nor cautious. . . . It is effective by a Government with the things that are solely under its control, but I suggest that it is highly improper to use compulsion of that kind to inflict upon the general public any matters which are not under Government control. That course of action—the outlawing of discrimination by administrative rules—might spread the custom and habit of toleration; it could—indeed, it does—steadily undermine and destroy the prejudice from which discrimination springs. Discrimination of the kind dealt with, for instance, in Clause 2 of this Bill is difficult to define or prove, and evasive tactics would be extremely easy. I do not know who would administer the Bill if it became law, and I do not think it makes administrative sense. It would not promote good will, and it would, in practice, constitute a grave invasion of private liberty.

. . . My own view is that the Government should set a public example in its own sphere and should not attempt to force tolerance by intolerant legislation. My Lords, I think this is a bad Bill, narrow in conception and impossible in administration and execution. It relies on naked compulsion and, because I believe in the aims and objects of this Bill as much as the noble Lord who introduced it, I think that it should be denied a Second Reading.

VISCOUNT MONTGOMERY OF ALAMEIN:[2] . . . Of course, we have had many references to what has been said in the United States. I have for some time been a student of the racial problem in the United States. It is well known that it is stated in the American Declaration of Independence that all men are created equal. Personally, I have never agreed with that statement. But I

[2] Field Marshal Sir Bernard Law Montgomery, 1st Viscount Montgomery of Alamein. G.C.B., D.S.O. LL.D. 1945, Queens University, Belfast; LL.D. 1945, St. Andrew's University; D.C.L. 1945, Oxford Univ.; LL.D. 1946, Cambridge Univ.; LL.D. 1946, Toronto Univ.; LL.D. 1946, McGill Univ.; LL.D. 1946, Glasgow Univ.; D.C.L. 1946. Edinburgh Univ.; D.C.L. 1946, Dalhousie Univ.; D.Sc. 1946, Louvain Univ.; D.Sc. 1946, Liege Univ.

think we must be clear on what that famous sentence means. For instance, I suppose in the secondary schools of this country there may be one million boys, or fewer—I do not know what the figure is—but no one can seriously believe that all those boys are created with equal possibilities of brain power. The mark of a machine is sameness, but in human life and nature the mark is difference.

There is no doubt we will all believe that every human being is a soul of equal value in the sight of God. That is quite clear. But that does not mean that we are created with equal talents, and the hard fact is that all men are not created equal. As they grow up into men and women they become less equal. Of course, that does not detract from the general proposition that there should be equality of opportunity in so far as it is humanly possible to give it, and in this country of course we have it. We have the principle of one man one vote, one woman one vote, and all we are asked to give in return for having our affairs regulated for us by the Government is a modest contribution in the form of taxation.

To come now to the question of colour, I read that years ago, in 1854, Abraham Lincoln, who was the great emancipator, said that while he would not hold a negro in slavery, they could not be made equals. That is what he said, and that doctrine would seem to prevail in the United States today. I was staying with a farmer in the Northern Transvaal recently when an American reporter turned up. He said to the farmer, "Well, how is your *apartheid* getting on?" The farmer replied, "All right, thank you. How is yours?" My travels have taken me to most countries in the world which are inhabited by black people, brown, yellow, white, everybody. In this changing world the white man can no longer look on the black man as clay for the moulding, or as a docile object of his policy. The problem to-day surely is to find the best way towards a new relationship of friendship and mutual respect between emergent black races and the white man.

I do not think that that new relationship will be found by asserting that there is no essential difference between white and black. The hard fact is that peoples of different colours cannot be converted into a homogeneous whole by Acts of Parliament, nor by the exhortations of idealists. The distaste and the discriminations which exist may be due to prejudices which have no justification in science or ethics. But the prejudices are there; they are strong and they are deep-rooted. Statesmen must make allowances for them or their policies will be stultified. Of course, science may insist that all human beings are potentially equal. Science will say that, but history would suggest that, like the animals on George Orwell's farm, some are more equal than others. I do not believe that we can get rid of these injustices and discriminations by entrenching laws about them in the Statute Book. That is where I think they went wrong in South Africa.

I agree very much indeed with what was said by the Lord Bishop of London. Today in our country black and white are free to meet and to mix or not, as they choose. Is that not the best way? Is it not best to let time bridge the gap which exists? I think it will be disastrous to the bridging of the gap if the solution is to be found in the views of idealists, or if we give way to abstract generalities, or base our approach to the problem on emotional feelings. Surely the practice of government by a host of regulations tends to leave out the one essential in government—indeed, its essential basis—which is the good will of the people. If we make laws and put them on a Statute Book we must be able to enforce them. The laws in this Bill could not be enforced. I would suggest that on that count alone the Bill fails. I have a great regard for the noble Lord who moved the Second Reading, and I listen with tremendous interest to everything he says in this House. I greatly hope he will agree that a discussion such as we are having now will do so much to clear the air that the Bill is best withdrawn. If the House were divided on this Bill I would feel in my conscience that I must vote against it.

LORD SALTOUN:[3] . . . I think that if we give this Bill a Second Reading it is very likely to rouse the very spirit we seek to allay. . . .

3 Alexander Arthur Fraser, 19th Baron Saltoun of Scotland. In writing to the editor by letter of July 14, 1962, giving permission to have his remarks reprinted, he stated: "With respect to the housing question it seems to me to be very much a question of the normal conduct to be expected of any particular type of tenant than a question of colour. If the normal treatment of a house to be expected from the members of any particular race is likely to injure the structure or depreciate the value of the house, or to injure the neighborhood so as to militate against the letting of other neighboring houses, or to constitute a nuisance, I cannot see that a general reluctance to let to such persons could properly be called racial discrimination."

I think, with regard to the categories of persons mentioned in Clause 2, that we are trying to punish them for what other people do. I will give an example, which must be in your Lordships' memory. Two years ago some Spanish gypsy dancers came over here to give performances. I forget how long they were here, but on one occasion I went along to see them. They obtained lodgings in an hotel, but, through some unreasonable prejudice conceived against Spanish gypsies, all the other inhabitants of the hotel threatened to leave unless the Spanish gypsies left.

The proprietor of the hotel was faced with such a grievous loss that, although I do not think they could have been compelled by law to do so, he begged the gypsies to go. I remember it well, because I was so horrified that we started considering what we could offer them by way of alternative accommodation. Before anything could be done, however, fortunately some other Briton stepped in and gave them accommodation, which they occupied during the rest of their stay. The point I am trying to make is that it was not the proprietor of the hotel who was at fault, but his customers. If he had defied his customers he might have lost his business. Therefore I really object to this Bill because it is punishing A for what B has done, and I think that that is a strong objection.

. . . Here is a case where I think the Bill would punish a man for what was in his mind. A publican has, from time immemorial, had the right to turn anybody off his premises without actually giving any reason at all. Now you are going to argue as to what is in his mind. Clause 1, line 3, uses the expression that the person is denied "facilities or advantages on the ground of the colour, race or religion of that other person." The noble Lord, Lord Walston, has, perfectly rightly, not used the words "expressed ground," because that would defeat his Bill altogether. Therefore, this is a Bill which is going to impose a penalty on a man on the ground of what was in his mind. . . .

. . . If there is any possibility of persuading a judge or a jury of what was in a publican's mind when he asked a man to leave his premises, there will be a great danger of miscarriage of justice, because one can never be quite certain—a jury may be wrong, a judge may be wrong. I will go further and say that you are opening the door wide to a very unpleasant class of blackmail. I could very easily construct a story (which would quite likely prove to be a true story if this Bill were to go through) which would show how that would work.

Moreover, I would say that while the Bill is ostensibly going to attack prejudice on colour, race, or religion, it is probably going to arouse it and intensify it all the more, because—I do not know; I am not clever enough to be sure—I think that I could run a restaurant with great success in complete defiance of this Bill, without the smallest difficulty. That being so, here you have a Bill which can be defied, can be set at nought, one which will not effect the purposes which it is intended to effect and which will give a possible opening to quite horrible crimes. I regard blackmail as a thoroughly horrible crime. I hope, therefore, that the House will not give it a Second Reading. If a Bill of this kind ought to be passed, it ought to be passed by the Government after mature consideration of all the factors involved, and after very careful and well-founded judgment. In that case, it might be possible to have a Bill which would not do more harm than good. In my opinion, this Bill will do more harm than good.

LORD MERRIVALE:[4] . . . My Lords, it seems to me that such a Bill as we have before us to-day, as has been mentioned by other noble Lords, would be difficult to enforce. If I understood the noble Lord, Lord Walston, rightly, he said that hotelkeepers or innkeepers cannot, under Common Law, refuse refreshment or accommodation to travellers. My Lords, when a booking is made through an agency—for instance, Cook's or American Express— the name of the person is mentioned, but not the colour of his skin. Also, when a traveller calls at a hotel and is told, "I am very sorry, but the hotel is full and there is no accommodation," what action can he take? I presume none whatsoever either now or under this Bill. I do not suppose that, under this Bill, he could ask to see the hotel register, or the register or bookings; nor could he check to see whether or not all the rooms had occupants.

4 Jack Henry Edmond Duke, 3rd Baron Merrivale. Dulwich College, Ecole des Sciences Politiques. In writing to the editor by letter of July 26, 1962, giving permission to have his remarks reprinted, he referred to the "conflict between legislation to prevent discrimination and refusal or denial of the fundamental human rights and rights of property."

It seems to me, too, that this Bill could infringe upon the rights of the individual. For instance, under the Bill, the owner of a lodging-house could be placed in a very difficult position. It might be that other tenants or residents in his lodging-house objected to a coloured person coming in, and that the landlord had admitted a coloured person because he was not prejudiced. Should he then lose his livelihood? That is why I agree with what the noble Lord, Lord Saltoun, said, that, in effect, we should be legislating for one class of person, when it is the other class of person who would be committing an offense.

VISCOUNT MASSEREENE AND FERRARD:[5] My Lords, I, like the rest of your Lordships, entirely sympathise with the motives of the noble Lord, Lord Walston, in introducing this Bill. I think all of us in this House, and the majority of the people in this country, deplore discrimination of any kind, and especially racial discrimination. But, of course, the prevention of discrimination really goes deeper than mere legislation. Wherever you look you have discrimination. We have prejudices in human character which go back for thousands of years, and racial discrimination is probably one of the strongest instincts of the human race. To find discrimination you have only to look at the trade union and the closed shop. Where could you have greater discrimination?

I would even go so far as to say that the noble Lord is himself introducing discrimination by this Bill; that he is discriminating against the free choice of hotel proprietors and restaurant keepers as to the clients they will have on their premises. I think it was the noble Lord, Lord Walston, who mentioned that there were certain golf clubs, which I have not come across personally, where Jews were not elected. I realise that this Bill is not about clubs, but I was in Brighton once, and I went into a hotel and was asked to extinguish my cigarette because it happened to be a Jewish special day in the calendar. Of course, I extinguished it, and had no objection to extinguishing it, but that hotel proprietor's hotel was chiefly for Jewish people, presumably because he preferred having

---

[5] John C. T. F. W-M. Skeffington, 13th Viscount Massereene and Ferrard. In writing to the editor by letter of July 5, 1962, giving permission to have his remarks reprinted, he stated that "traditional rights of property and liberty of association will be frittered away, in fact destroyed, if such a Bill as the Racial Discrimination Bill ever becomes law."

Jewish customers, and he was perfectly entitled to do so. But if this Bill became law, he could not have only his known clientele; he would, for instance, be scared to refuse me. If he did, I could then say to him: "This is racial discrimination."

I think this would be an extremely hard law to enforce. I have heard some people say that we shall have racial discrimination until all the world is coffee-coloured. Personally, I am inclined to agree with the right reverend Prelate, the Lord Bishop of London, that, with education, time and tolerance, gradually it will disappear. But what I am concerned about is that we shall not bring the law into disrepute. We already have on the Statute Book many laws which extremely law-abiding citizens often disobey. You have only to take the case of the 30 miles an hour speed limit. I frequently break that. I do not wish to break it, but I just cannot help breaking it. I think that if this Bill were on the Statute Book it would be broken the whole time, and I will shortly tell your Lordships why.

How is Clause 2 to be enforced? If a coloured man, or a man of Jewish religion or any other religion, goes to a hotel, the proprietor may refuse him on genuinely good grounds. The man may then think he is being refused on racial or religious grounds. First, he would have to prove that the proprietor refused him on racial or religious grounds. That would be extremely difficult, because the hotel proprietor could say: "This man was rather insulting." Or he could have a list of fictitious hotel bookings. He could have friends who booked rooms in their names—stooges who would be hand in glove with him—and it would be extremely difficult to prove.

Another objection is that hotels, especially our great hotels in London, have their known clientele. I may go to a hotel and the proprietor may refuse me because he does not like my face. But if a coloured man went to the same hotel, the proprietor would not dare to refuse him, because he was coloured and the proprietor would be afraid of an action against him. This Bill would really work unfairly against white people. My noble friend Lord Merrivale has pointed out that a gang of white youths could be turned out of a dance hall for being rowdy, but a gang of black youths, who could be equally rowdy, would make it very difficult for the proprietor, who would be extremely careful about turning them out.

The noble Lord, Lord Walston, said that in various States of America there is legislation doing away with all racial discrimination in hotels and public places. I have been to America a good deal, and if they have these laws they do not work. Every summer an increasing number of American tourists come over and pour dollars into this country. Though I do not approve of it, as your Lordships know, a great many Americans dislike coloured people, and if our great hotels in the West End have preference for coloured people—and it would amount to that—we are going to lose a great deal of our dollar tourist trade.

* * * *

If this Bill is given a Second Reading and is eventually passed into law as it is worded it is going to be unfair to property owners. Different races have different domestic habits. I am not saying whose habits are the best, but some people prefer not to have another race living next door or occupying the same premises. This depreciates some properties a great deal and owners have no redress at all. After all, property owners pay the rates and a great deal of the taxation of the country, and I consider they ought to have some consideration. I honestly think that we might just as well have a Bill to provide that all men between twenty and thirty must prefer blondes and all men between thirty and forty must prefer brunettes. This Bill is almost as absurd as that. The noble Lord, Lord Hemingford, has said that we have laws to prevent treason and pornography. But treason is extremely unnatural to the average human being, and so is pornography. One cannot compare the two things. I think that that is an impractical argument. I will vote against the Second Reading of this Bill, because it takes the freedom of choice from the property owner and the hotel keeper and because it is impractical. It would be evaded all the time and bring the law into great disrepute.

THE LORD CHANCELLOR:[6] . . . Now may I ask your

6 David P. M. Fyfe, 1st Viscount Kilmuir. B.A. 1922, D.C.L. 1953, Oxford Univ.; LL.D. 1947, Univ. of Liverpool; LL.D. 1954, Univ. of Manitoba; LL.D. 1955, Univ. of Edinburgh; LL.D. 1955, Univ. of Wales; LL.D. 1956, St. Andrew's Univ.; LL.D. 1960,

Lordships to consider one or two points in the Bill? The difficulty of the matter is shown when we come to Clause 1. It defines dis-. crimination as the refusal, withholding or denial to any person of facilities or advantages "on the ground of the colour, race or religion of that other person." Your Lordships will appreciate that refusal or denial of facilities is not to be an offence in itself, for, of course, plainly that would be an invasion, not only of the rights of property, but of the fundamental human rights of any human person. It is to be made an offence only if the refusal or denial is carried out for a particular reason, namely, on the grounds of colour, race, or religion. It is the Government's view that, where a person seeks to exercise discrimination in the circumstances set out in the various clauses of the Bill, it will, as my noble friend Lord Saltoun said, rarely be possible, whatever the suspicion may be, to show in such a way as to satisfy a court of law in criminal proceedings that his reason for the refusal or denial of facilities is in fact on the ground of colour, race or religion. If that be so, then the clause is ineffective in achieving the purpose for which it is designed.

* * * *

Now let me take Clause 2, which prohibits the exercise of discrimination by occupiers of various premises. All your Lordships, whether lay or lawyer, have the matter exactly right—that apart from the Common Law obligation on the hotelkeeper who is an innkeeper, other persons have at the moment the occupier's Common Law right to refuse admission to any person and to request any person to leave their premises, without giving a reason. To begin with, the clause would be a serious infringement of their right, and could be justified only if there was evidence of a widespread wrong and reason to suppose that the Bill's provisions would have some practical effect in righting that wrong.

My noble friends Lord Massereene and Ferrard and Lord Merrivale pointed out the real difficulty that exists on this point.

Univ. of Chicago; LL.D. 1960, George Washington Univ.; LL.D. 1960, Columbia Univ.; LL.D. 1960, Ottawa Univ. Hon. Fellow of Balliol College, Oxford Univ. 1954. P.C. 1945; G.C.V.O. 1953; F.R.C.S.E. 1955. Solicitor-General 1942-5; Attorney-General 1945; British Deputy Chief Prosecutor at Nuremberg Trial 1945-6; Lord High Chancellor of England 1954-1962.

The occupier of such an establishment may well have grounds other than personal prejudice for excluding certain categories of persons. He may find their presence leads to disorder. As my noble friends pointed out, the disorder may be in a white gang or in a black gang. But as my noble friends pointed out, and as my noble friend Lord Saltoun reinforced, what a very difficult situation it would be—I am not exaggerating—for the person who is trying to keep order in a dance hall if he turned out a black gang! I have had experience of being in charge for three years of the police forces of this country, and I know the difficulty it would cause the police.

* * * *

Then one comes to the point that was made by the right reverend Prelate the Lord Bishop of London, that to prove a case of discrimination on grounds of colour it might be necessary to bring evidence of the treatment of a number of coloured people and also of a number of white people of similar social status who have received different treatment. Assuming that the evidence could be obtained, there might have to be an organised attempt on the part of a number of coloured people to obtain it by co-ordinated attempts to gain admission. But, in such a delicate matter, such action might well have the reverse effect to that intended by the noble Lord, Lord Walston, in introducing this Bill— namely, the fostering of racial antagonism where none existed before. . . .

Again, I know that my noble friend Lord Arran put this as a sort of quantification of infringements of principle, but I find it very difficult to say that someone who lets off to people all the rooms in her house as bed-sittingrooms, or what-have-you, should not be entitled to say, "I am a Welsh woman and I want Welsh lodgers"; or, "I am a Scots woman and I want Scots lodgers"; or, let us say, "I am a woman from Northern Ireland and I want Northern Irish lodgers." I do not know; I have not the gift of noble Lords to my left, of sweeping aside these principles and not being afraid to infringe them because they think greater good may thereby come. Principle, I assure your Lordships, is not something which can safely be played with, and the same applies to the other clause.

I put it quite shortly. What your Lordships are asked to do today on the other clause, concerning the lease, is to finance your own altruism at the expense of, it may well be, quite poor people who own property. What you are asked to do—and there is no question about this; I am not overstating it at all—is to pass legislation to say that if someone believes and honestly believes, and it is corroborated, that her property will decline in value because certain houses are occupied by people of other races she is not to be entitled to prevent that. Of course, there are various methods by which she could seek to do it if she took legal advice, but what the Bill is aimed at is that she should not be entitled to do it. I should like to try to persuade my noble friend Lord Arran to believe there is basis in my words, whether he accepts it or not. I ask him to consider that.

Is the way to say "All right. In the interests of this fine ideal, I am going to make it impossible for a widow who owns three houses, which bring her in her entire income, to prevent them from depreciating in value"? There is a lot to be said for the fact that it is a fine ideal but there is a lot to be said against, as I say, financing your ideals by taking from other people money which they may not be able to afford. That is the difficulty that we are in. In all these cases one has to prove the criminal offence; one has to do it in a way which, in my view, would be very likely to increase the absurdity rather than diminish it; and at the end of the day one would find that the case was impossible to prove and therefore that the Act was not enforceable.

*   *   *   *

One comes back to this. As I said, the problem of racial discrimination is basically one of personal human relationships, always a delicate matter and particularly so when a large number of people come here from countries with different climates and economic and social backgrounds. Legislation could not, in itself, prevent discrimination on the part of individuals in their private dealings with coloured people, and indeed the Bill makes no attempt to do so. But from these personal and private dealings between neighbours, workmates, and children, arise the public attitude and behaviour towards coloured people in general, which the Bill seeks to control. In the Government's view, this problem is not solvable by legislation. There is, unfortunately, no shortcut answer. Only patient education of public opinion by example and expressions of view by responsible individuals and bodies can achieve lasting results. We have heard twenty expressions of view by responsible individuals against racial discrimination this afternoon. Social habits must be determined by education and by the manifold influences that help to mould our tolerant British society. It is on this basis that I suggest to your Lordships that you should, while acknowledging the sincere motives that have prompted the noble Lord to introduce the Bill, deny it a Second Reading.

COMMENTS ON O'MEARA v. WASHINGTON STATE BOARD AGAINST DISCRIMINATION

FOREWORD TO COMMENTS

The subject of anti-discrimination legislation in housing is a matter of much public concern at the present time. Cases in this area are therefore of general interest, and warrant careful study and comment.

Comments on this subject from responsible individuals contribute to a general understanding of the whole area, and are to be welcomed as adding to public knowledge. The judges, law professors, lawyers, social scientists, and others who have contributed to this symposium by giving the public the benefit of their comments and experience have added to the much needed full discussion in this area and therefore have advanced the public interest.

J. Howard McGrath[*]

Editor's Note: In *O'Meara v. Washington State Board Against Discrimination,* 58 Wn. 2d 793, 365 P.2d 1 (1961), the Supreme Court of Washington held that state's law forbidding discrimination in publicly-assisted housing to be unconstitutional. In so deciding, the court split three ways. Three justices held that the distinction between owners of property who received government assistance and those who did not was arbitrary because the former were no more likely to discriminate than the latter, and hence the classification violated the equal protection clauses of the federal and state constitutions. Two concurring justices held the statute unconstitutional as violative of the due process clause, the clause forbidding a person from being "disturbed in his private affairs, or his home invaded," the clause providing that "private property shall not be taken for private use," the separation of powers clause, and the original jurisdiction of the courts clause of the Washington State constitution. Four justices dissented on the grounds that the classification was reasonable and the act was a reasonable exercise of the police power to eradicate housing discrimination as a "major social problem."

COMMENT ON O'MEARA:
ALL-POWERFUL GOVERNMENT

The theory that government can and must use its tremendous coercive power to solve every problem of society and its members,

* Ph.B. 1926, LL.D. 1941, Providence College; LL.B. 1929, Boston Univ.; M.Sc. 1942, Bryant College; LL.D. 1942, Manhattan College; D.Sc. 1942, R.I. College of Pharmacy; Ed.D. 1942, R.I. College of Education; LL.D. 1943, Duquesne Univ.; LL.D. 1943, Holy Cross College; LL.D. 1943, La Salle College; LL.D. 1943, National Jewish Theological Seminary of America; LL.D. 1943, National Univ.; LL.D. 1943, R.I. State College; LL.D. 1943, St. Mary's College. Attorney-General of the United States, 1949-1952; United States Senator from Rhode Island, 1947-9; Solicitor-General of the United States, 1945-6; Governor of Rhode Island, 1941-45; U.S. Attorney for the District of Rhode Island, 1934-40. Member of the Rhode Island Bar.

from racial and religious prejudice to agricultural over-production and from unmarried mothers to the price of steel, appears to be accepted by a majority of politicians and the public in some of our more populous states. That such a theory in operation leads inevitably to the all-powerful state with tyrannical authority over its citizens does not deter those who are intent solely on capturing the votes of enough pressure groups to win elections.

Characteristically, the politicians who practice this theory talk almost entirely about goals and very little about the means of achieving the goals. This or that thing is evil or wrong or unfair, therefore government must eliminate or correct it, regardless of how much government must stretch the Constitution or interfere with the rights and freedoms of individuals to accomplish its objective. They and sometimes we as voters forget that means are as important as goals, and that means which violate the rights and freedoms of even a small minority can step by step erode away the rights and freedoms of all.

One would think that with all the current examples of tyranny which operate on this theory, whether communist, fascist or a variant of one or the other, we in the United States would be vigilant against being led down the same blind alley. Certainly, the men who framed our Constitution, having just fought a bloody war for freedom, were well aware of the danger to liberty inherent in all-powerful government. They not only limited the powers of government to those specified, but added the checks of independent legislative and judicial branches.

That these checks on autocratic exercise of executive power no longer function as they should is abundantly clear from a reading of the *O'Meara* decision of the Washington State Supreme Court. True, the Court, by a bare majority of 5 to 4, declared unconstitutional a 1957 statute declaring it an unfair practice and a misdemeanor (a crime, in other words), to discriminate against anyone in the sale or rental of publicly-assisted housing on account of race, creed, color or national origin.

The state legislature enacted the statute quoted in the decision as follows:

The right to be free from discrimination because of race,

creed, color or national origin is recognized as and declared to be a civil right. This right shall include, but not be limited to:

. . . .

(3) the right to secure publicly assisted housing without discrimination.

That this kind of gobbledegook should appear in a criminal statute is in itself a disgrace to the legislative process and demonstrates how misunderstood is the true function of government. Just how can a judge or jury decide what motivates an individual who refuses to sell or lease his home to another individual? Maybe he just didn't like the prospective buyer. Or are we no longer free in this country to like or dislike whom we please?

The right to discriminate, to choose one's neighbors, friends and associates, is about as essential to individual freedom as any you can name. And when you discriminate in choosing your companions, you automatically discriminate against anyone and everyone else who might desire ardently to be your dearest friend. No one in a free society can be guaranteed any right not to be discriminated against in these areas. It would deprive others of their more essential right to discriminate, a fact of life which the Washington State Legislature overlooked.

The Court decision, aside from the concurring opinion of Justices Mallery and Ott, is an even more amazing document to be written by judges under oath to support and defend the Constitution, which in this instance means to protect individual rights and freedoms against attempts by Government to overreach its limited powers. The legal part of Justice Foster's majority opinion could have been covered in a few paragraphs. It found the statute unconstitutional on the narrow ground that the classification of government-assisted housing was arbitrary and capricious and violated the equal protection clauses of the state and federal constitutions. The rest of the opinion is a political apology for the decision, emphasizing agreement with the goal the statute sought to achieve.

Justice Mallery, in his concise and lawyerlike concurring opinion, had no difficulty in citing five other constitutional provisions which the statute violated and probably could have found others. It is clear from his opinion that Justice Mallery recognizes the fallacy in "liberal" propaganda that human rights are somehow endangered by and must take precedence over property rights. The right to own and use property is a human right and is as essential to individual freedom as any. Our current "liberals" overlook the fact that the right to own and use property was one of the vital distinctions between freemen and serfs and slaves in the Middle Ages.

Most disturbing, however, was Justice Rosellini's dissent in which three other justices concurred. The essence of his opinion is that since the goal is worthy in his view, the plain English of the Constitution must be stretched and distorted sufficiently to validate it. His philosophy can be deduced from this illuminating paragraph:

> The police power extends not only to the preservation of the public health, safety and morals, but also *to the preservation and promotion of the public welfare.* The police power is an attribute of sovereignty, an essential element of the power to govern and a function that cannot be surrendered. It exists without express declaration, and *the only limitation upon it is that it must reasonably tend to correct some evil or promote some interest of the state,* and not violate any direct or positive mandate of the Constitution. (Emphasis supplied.)

If that is not a blueprint for a police state, then I do not understand plain English. Given that mandate and another few decades of erosion of the Constitution, and a good lawyer could justify the repetition here of virtually all the governmental decrees of Communist Russia or Nazi Germany which turned their citizens into vassals of all-powerful police states.

JOSEPH H. BALL*

COMMENT ON O'MEARA: OPINIONS ABROAD

One of the arguments frequently heard for elimination of traditional rights is that permitting discrimination or freedom of choice in housing will make other countries refuse to deal with us, or throw them into the arms of the Communists. Various statements appear in the daily newspapers from time to time that

---

* Former United States Senator from Minnesota (1940-49).

if there is discrimination in housing, African countries will refuse to deal with us, go and take Russian aid, and so forth. In the case of *O'Meara v. Washington State Board Against Discrimination*, the following statement appears in one of the opinions:

> It may be noted also that elimination of discrimination is necessary for the sake of America's relations with the rest of the world. Our standing with the so-called uncommitted peoples of the world suffers seriously because of the continued discrimination and segregation practiced in America.

Any legislation or executive orders issued on any subject in this country should not be determined by what any foreigners may think. We should have a proper respect for their opinions, but we must preserve our freedom of choice. This is something that all responsible American citizens, both colored and white, I believe will insist upon.

The foreign relations of other countries are determined primarily by their own internal policies and needs, and not by our internal policies. Foreign trade, internal and international business, economics, and the like are more likely to influence a country's policies than its views of the internal policies of other countries. Liberia, Haiti, and Ethiopia, to take three examples, had friendly relations with the United States during a long period of time when rigid segregation of Negroes was in force, and even when there was an occasional lynching in the South, although their governments no doubt strongly disapproved of this. Diplomats of these countries lived in Washington when it was segregated without serious incident.

It is high time that the public in this country awaken to the fact that property rights are human rights and must be protected just as fervently as any other rights. If they are not so protected all other rights will be lost, including the right of equality before the law of differing races, creeds, and colors. I do not believe we can impose discrimination or non-discrimination by statute. It must be done by lifting the morals of the public. This applies uniquely to housing, where property interests are especially private.

Basic property rights and rights to freedom of choice lie at the foundation of our system of government. It is neither necessary nor desirable that we change our basic domestic policies because someone abroad might disapprove of them.

SPRUILLE BRADEN*

COMMENT ON O'MEARA:
BRITISH VIEW OF FOREIGN POLICY

The points made in this case are the usual ones being employed in America and Britain today. They are, nevertheless, fallacious. The fact of the matter is that foreign countries do not arrange their internal policies to suit the prejudices of the Western nations. For example, when I was a professor in India I was not allowed to have beef in the central provinces because a state law had been passed making it a capital offence to kill the cow and eat beef in that state. When it was rumored that the Moslems, in their quarter, had brought in some beef from Gabalpur, the mobs rioted and burnt down the bazaar, killing many of the Moslems. Moreover, all High Class Hindus will not eat, even at the same table, with a foreigner. In fact, once Doctor Misra, Vice Chancellor of Sangour University, would not eat at the same table with Professor West and me, even though it was an official University function. According to his standards of Hinduism, he would have been polluted if two unbelievers were eating in his presence.

No nation can organise its internal affairs for the benefit of foreigners of totally different ways of life; consequently, doing so is interpreted as complete weakness on the part of America, Britain, or any other Western power which commences to do so, when at the same time it has not called upon the Hindus, for example, to allow us when living in their country to eat beef, eat in their presence, or drink alcohol. What these people demand for themselves, therefore, and which I do not deny them, the Western peoples have equally the right to demand, that is, the freedom of choice to do as they wish within their own community, according to the laws of that community.

* Ph.B. 1914, Yale Univ.; LL.D. 1938, Univ. of Buenos Aires; LL.D. 1939, Johns Hopkins Univ.; LL.D. 1946, Clark Univ.; LL.D. 1946, Allbright Coll.; E.D. 1947, Mont. Sch. of Mines. Assistant United States Secretary of State, 1945-7; U.S. Ambassador to Argentina, 1945; U.S. Ambassador to Cuba, 1942-5.

My own experience in dealing with Indians in official positions is that they are not at all impressed by this kind of "window dressing." Short of giving up every privilege which we have, they are not interested at all. When it is realised that the average workman at present is getting about 60 rupies in India (about four pounds or twelve dollars per month), it is quite clear that, if we want to come to terms with these people on the basis of currying favour, we would have to reduce our own standard of living and upgrade theirs until we all have the same standard. This would mean, for the Americans and British, a less than what we would consider subsistance standard. Short of this, they are not at all interested in what I have called this "window dressing" legislation.

I do not believe that Afro-Asian nations, in ultimate, will make any decision as to which side they are on because of legislation of a restrictive nature or otherwise, concerning Afro-Asians in our own countries. They will be fundamentally concerned with local issues in arriving at their decisions. Britain has, for example, given untold wealth to countries like Ghana and Egypt. This does not, however, prevent these countries from working consistently against Britain, which has no colour bar and in which country citizens are treated as absolute equals, and compromising all the time with Russia. The decisions which Afro-Asians are likely to make in any crisis will depend upon one of two things: (1) the military might which the parties concerned are able to field; and (2) what will benefit most of the politicians at the heads of each of these countries at the time of crisis. I do not believe that any other considerations will be weighed. Therefore, to disorganise our own internal arrangements and bring them into press publicity as a consequence, so that they can be employed as propaganda against us, towards meeting the requirements of Afro-Asian ideology, and weaken ourselves in every possible way as a consequence of this, is not likely to serve the very ends that these people suggest it will—that is—to placate the Afro-Asians.

The energy spent in explaining ourselves to the Afro-Asian Group and advising people to follow policies alien to their own tradition, in order to please the Afro-Asians, could well be spent in projecting our standards upon them. That is, in fact, what the Russians do. They project their standards upon these people, while they follow an entirely independent policy at home. For example, Africans who have been to Russia, after having studied in places under Western influences, such as London, complain of the colour bar exercised against them in Russia. If we were exercising the same wisdom as the Russians in this respect, and going our own way, there would be no basis of complaint by Africans as to their treatment in any white country, be it capitalist or Marxist! However, what we have set out to do is to enter into competition with Russia to see who can give these people the most. In order to outbid the Russians, we are, actually, trying to force our own peoples to follow a mode of existence alien to their tradition. In so far as we are doing that, we are, in fact, committing a worse crime than the Russians.

ROBERT GAYRE
of Gayre and Nigg*

COMMENT ON O'MEARA: FOREIGN POLICY

In *O'Meara v. Washington State Board Against Discrimination*,[1] the Supreme Court of Washington split three ways in overturning a statute compelling integration in publicly assisted housing. Three justices held the classification invalid, two forthrightly

---

* M.A. 1934, Univ. Edinburgh; D.Pol.Sc. 1943, Palermo Univ.; D.Phil. 1944, Messina Univ.; D.Sc. 1944, Naples Univ. Baron of Lochoreshyre; Chief of Clan Gayre; Chamberlain to the Prince of Lippe. Knight of the Sacred Military Order of Constantine St. George of Naples; Knight Commander of the Cross of Merit (Military Division) of the Sovereign Military Order of Malta; Knight Commander of the Order of Lippe; Knight Grand Cross with Collar of the Military and Hospitaller Order of St. Lazarus of Jerusalem; Knight Grand Officer of the Crown of Italy. Member: Instit. des Studios Politicos, Madrid; Inst. Int. de Sociologie; National Academy of Science of India; Colegie Brasileiro de Genealogia; Acad. of Sc., National Society, Naples; Pontaniana Acad.; Peloritana Acad., Messina; Acad. of Palermo. Consultore pro lingua anglica, Collegio Araldico, Rome; Guest of Honor, South African Genetics Society Congress, 1962; Fellow, Institute of Arts and Letters (Switz.); Fellow of the Inst. Ital. du Geneal. e Arald.; Hon. Academician Acad. de Genealogia y Heraldica 'Mota Padilla,' Mexico; Hon. Associate Member, Royal Hungarian Society of St. Ladislas; Vicente Vignau Prizeman of Inst. Intern. de Gen. y Her., Madrid. Holder of: Bronze Medal, Collegia Araldico, Rome; Silver Medal of Merit, Military and Hospitaller Order of St. Lazarus of Jerusalem; Silver Medal of Ist. Intern. di Genealog. e Arald., Rome. Lt. Col., Royal Artillery; Educational Adviser to the Allied Military Government of Italy; Director of Education to the Allied Control Commission for Italy; Chief of Education and Religious Affairs, German Planning Unit. Supreme Hq. of the Allied Expeditionary Force (W.W. II). Former Professor of Anthropology and Head of the Post-Graduate Dept. of Anthropo-geography, Univ. of Saugor, India. Copyright © 1963 by Robert Gayre.

1 58 Wash. 2d 793, 365 P.2d 1 (1961).

recognized that the statute violated fundamental rights of property and liberty, and four justices dissented on the ground that the statute was valid.

Of special interest in this case is a remark in the first opinion which one finds repeatedly urged as justification for laws and court decrees requiring integration. The court said: "It may be noted also that elimination of discrimination is necessary for the sake of America's relations with the rest of the world. Our standing with the so-called uncommitted peoples of the world suffers seriously because of the continued discrimination and segregation practiced in America."[2]

This statement is by no means an isolated expression. Antidiscrimination legislation in the District of Columbia has been urged on the ground that African diplomats could not get homes where they wanted, and hence would get a bad impression of the United States.[3] Since African diplomats should not have more privileges than ordinary American citizens, it has likewise been urged that such legislation should be extended to cover everyone.[4] The same grounds have been urged for banning discrimination in restaurants and all sorts of other business places.[5]

The asserted position, that compulsory integration by government is necessary to preserve America's position of leadership in the free world, and to prevent other countries of the so-called African-Asian bloc from becoming hostile to the United States, naturally raises two questions. These are: (1) should American internal policy be dictated by the views of other countries; and (2) do these so-called uncommitted nations maintain the same attitude, and permit their domestic policies to be dictated by our standards? An answer to either of these questions in the negative should lay to rest once and for all the argument so often heard that foreign policy must ultimately determine domestic policy, instead of the reverse.

---

2 *Id.* at 796, 365 P.2d at 3.

3 N.Y. Times, April 13, 1962, p. 22, col. 1; *id.*, March 26, 1962, p. 21, col. 4; *id.*, July 9, 1961, p. 15, col. 3; *id.*, May 26, 1961, p. 21, col. 5.

4 *Id.*, April 14, 1962, p. 25, col. 7; *id.*, July 11, 1961, p. 18, col. 3.

5 *Id.*, Oct. 8, 1961, p. 56, col. 3; *id.*, Sept. 27, 1961, p. 3, col. 6; *id.*, Sept. 26, 1961, p. 5, col. 3; *id.*, Sept. 14, 1961, p. 1, col. 8.

The first argument, at the time of the framing of the United States Constitution, would have struck the framers as preposterous. The fundamental law was framed by Americans for Americans, at a time when the crowned heads of Europe looked upon our institutions as radical innovations. Had our internal policy been permitted to be dictated by the views of almost any other civilized nation of the time we would have chosen a king with large, if not unlimited powers, instead of a president, a national legislature of carefully enumerated powers, an independent judiciary, and states with a large group of reserved powers. The Bill of Rights could hardly have impressed European ambassadors and their sovereigns favorably, and other republican institutions were equally ill-suited to the idea of conformity with foreign views.

The United States Constitution contemplates that internal policy shall be made for the benefit of Americans, and not to please or conform to foreign views in any particular whatsoever. Were this otherwise, the Constitution would give foreign ambassadors seats, at least, if not votes, in the Congress, as delegates from territories are given seats. The President's constitutional duties, which he performs through the State Department, are to represent America to foreign nations,[6] and not to represent foreign nations to the United States. The theory that compulsory integration at home is necessary for American relations with other countries is quite inadmissible, for the simple reason that it contemplates that which in law cannot exist. The function of American law is to enlarge and protect individual rights and liberties, and if any other country finds the rights we hold dear to be obnoxious, then it is the duty of the State Department and other agencies of foreign policy to persuade and convince such other countries that the protection of these rights is part of the American way of life which we are not, for reasons of policy too deeply rooted to be cast aside for any considerations of temporary popularity in so-called "uncommitted nations" or in any other place whatsoever, prepared to abandon now or in the future for whatever gain may be offered, here or abroad. If a fraction of the energy were spent explaining the reasons why we have adopted the internal policy we have as is devoted to apologizing for it, we might find that

[6] United States v. Pink, 315 U.S. 203 (1942).

these "uncommitted nations" would realize that our own policy which is best suited to our own conditions does not disqualify us from the esteem abroad that we desire.

But assuming that considerations of foreign policy should move our lawmakers, have we not as a minimum the right to expect that foreign countries which demand that we observe their standards reciprocate by observing ours? The United States Supreme Court will not enforce foreign judicial judgments unless foreign courts reciprocate;[7] why should we concern ourselves with foreign judgments of public opinion except on the same basis? The adage about not throwing stones when one lives in a glass house seems peculiarly appropriate here.

When we look at foreign standards, we find little reciprocity of respect for our opinions indeed. Most of these so-called "uncommitted nations" have authoritarian one-party dictatorships with little remotely resembling free elections as we know them in this country. In Ghana, for example, political opponents are jailed or exiled. In a number of Arab countries, military cliques rule in fact when they do not rule in name as well. India's aggression over unanimous American disapproval shared by all shades of political opinion in this country against Goa, and Indonesia's strong-arm tactics in virtually seizing Netherlands New Guinea, are too fresh in the minds of Americans to permit moralizing from those sources. Less well known, but equally significant, are the laws of Indonesia and the Philippines which discriminate against the Chinese minority far more drastically than Negroes have faced in this country since the Civil War.

If governmental standards of these so-called "uncommitted nations" are dubious bases for criticizing American internal policy, then personal standards give even less warrant for casting stones at others. Shall we tailor our internal policy to please the Congolese soldiers who committed mass rape on 15 white women after having rounded up their husbands?[8] Are we really that interested in the opinions of Kenyan businessmen who use government loans and grants to buy more wives, so that they can produce more fe-

7 Hilton v. Guyot, 159 U.S. 113 (1895).
8 N.Y. Times, Nov. 7, 1961, p. 1, col. 2.

male children who will be sold as brides to male suitors?[9] Do we want to bother impressing Congolese spectators at football games of whom their own minister of sports said: "The referees, judges and players are frequently attacked by spectators. Moreover, some become so excited that they burn automobiles and loot houses."[10]

A recent dispute in Gabon, formerly a province of French Equatorial Africa, is a fitting comparison with the pronouncements of those who would conform American internal policy to foreign whims. In September 1962, Gabon's team defeated the French Congo in a soccer match by 3 to 1. In a return match held in Brazzaville, the score was reversed. However, Congo fans thought it should have been 5 to 1, and that the two goals nullified by an umpire from a neutral state were proper. After the game, they rioted. Gabonese held this against the Congo. Also held against the Congo was the fact that when Gabon scored first, the Congolese band failed to play a fanfare, traditional when either side scores.

Retaliation was quickly forthcoming. In Libreville, capital of Gabon, thousands of irate Gabonese stoned cars, burned homes, and beat up Congolese citizens resident there. The Gabon government then expelled 3,000 Congolese.

In Brazzaville, capital of the Congo, Gabonese citizens sought refuge with the police in fear of revenge being taken on them. The Congo President appealed for calm. "It is in such times of challenge that a nation is forged and a country becomes great," he said. He also declared a day of national mourning. All this occurred over two points in a soccer match.[11]

Are these the people we want to impress? If so, why? Why should we worry about our standing in the eyes of such people? Can we possibly even justify considering their standards at all? Will that not drag down rather than raise our own standards?

Americans will do much better to stop being self-conscious about the things others think about us, and stop taking international Gallup polls and worrying about each fractional rise or fall

9 *Id.*, May 9, 1962, p. 60, col. 2.
10 *Id.*, Nov. 26, 1961, p. 3, col. 2.
11 *Id.*, Sept. 23, 1962, p. 1, col. 7.

in our popularity or foreign image. Let us instead do what is right for Americans by preserving our constitutional heritage. In that way, we will not only preserve our own liberties, but in the long run, by steadfastly adhering to principle, gain the admiration and emulation of thinking people everywhere.

JOHN D. GRAVES*

HERBERT C. SANBORN**

COMMENT ON O'MEARA: CLASSIFICATION

The opinion in the *O'Meara* case inspires a consideration of the question of the constitutionality of the various types of legislative acts and governmental regulations designed to prevent discrimination on the basis of race, color or religion in the sale or rental of housing units.

There would seem to be four possible types of such legislation: (1) enactments which in terms forbid all land owners to engage in such discrimination; (2) statutes prohibiting all owners of a specified number of contiguous housing units from engaging in discrimination; (3) legislation prohibiting such discrimination by all owners of property the construction or purchase of which has at any time been financed by government funds; and (4) legislation or regulation which imposes the prohibition as a restriction on property the purchase or construction of which may be financed with government funds accepted by an owner of the property after the effective date of the statute or regulation.

It is apparent that none of these four types of legislation can be constitutionally justified on the theory that it is an exercise of the power of eminent domain if for no other reason than that they make no provision for compensation to the landowner. If

* B.A. 1927, LL.B. 1929, Columbia Univ. Member of the New York Bar.
** Ph.B. 1896, Boston Univ.; A.M. 1897, Tufts Coll.; Jacob Sleeper Fellow at Univ. of Heidelberg, 1900-2, Univ. of Berlin, 1903, Univ. of Halle, 1904, Univ. of Munich, 1906-8; Ph.D. 1908, Univ. of Munich; Member Psychologisches Institut, Univ. of Leipzig, 1908-9. Professor of Philosophy and Psychology, Vanderbilt Univ., 1911-42, and head of dept. Author: The Function of History in Liberal Education (1951); Dingler's Methodical Philosophy (1952); The Problem of Language (1952); Communism and the Problem of Academic Freedom (1953); The International Conspiracy (1954); Thucydides on History of Philosophy (1956); The Meeting Point of Philosophy and Psychology (1957).

they can be supported at all it is on the theory that they are within the police power. It is, of course, fundamental that the exercise of the police power must have a reasonable and rational relationship to the protection of the public health, safety, or welfare. It is equally fundamental that if a statute enacted under the police power is so framed that it affects one class of persons differently from other classes, the equal protection of the laws clause contained in most constitutions requires that there must be, between the classes that are treated differently, some natural and substantial difference germane to the subject and purpose of the legislation.

If each of the four types of legislation listed above is subjected to the test of constitutionality established by these principles of constitutional law, the following conclusions will result:

There can be little question that any legislative body could reasonably come to the conclusion that it is for the public welfare to prevent discrimination on the basis of race, color or religion in the sale or leasing of housing units and that legislation is necessary to prevent that discrimination. Accordingly, there should not be any question about the validity of a statute which prohibits discrimination by all landowners in either the sale or rental of all property. As regards the other three types of legislation, the question is somewhat more involved because in each of those types the legislation classifies property and calls for different treatment of the various classes.

The second type listed above is the sort of statute which prohibits discrimination by any owner of more than a prescribed number of contiguous housing units. To treat these landowners as being in a class different from those who own a lesser number of contiguous units may well be justified either on the ground that the owner of large multiple dwellings is more likely to be tempted to discriminate or on the ground that those people who are most likely to be discriminated against are most apt to flock to multiple dwellings. These differences between classes of landowners are logical and germane to the purpose of the legislation.

So, too, with regard to the fourth type of regulation, that in which discrimination by landowners who have received aid in

financing their properties from government funds after the enactment of the statute or regulation: True such landowners are put
in a class to be treated differently from others but they are different from others in that by accepting government financing they
have consented to be treated differently.

The situation with reference to statutes which prohibit discrimination solely by landowners who have received government
financing at any time is quite different. The distinction between
landowners who have received government financing at any time
and all other landowners is not a difference which is germane to
legislation against racial or religious discrimination. As is pointed
out in the *O'Meara* opinion: "There is no reason to suppose that
persons with FHA mortgages on their homes are more likely to
discriminate against minority groups than those who have conventional mortgages or no mortgages or those who are purchasing
under contract." Consequently legislation of this fourth type
should be held offensive to the equal protection of the laws clause
in the constitution.

Legislation of types (1), (2) and (4) should be held constitutional whereas that of type (3) should be held unconstitutional.

ERNEST A. INGLIS*

COMMENT ON O'MEARA: MORALITY

The *O'Meara* case, which held the Washington State law
against discrimination in housing to be unconstitutional, contains,
in one of the opinions, the following statement: "The practice of
discrimination is utterly inconsistent with the political philosophy
upon which our institutions are based, and with the moral principles which we inherit from our Judeo-Christian traditions." This
statement raises some interesting questions in terms of basing a
legal determination on "moral principles."

Moral principles are, of course, beliefs. They are not scientifically provable facts. If a person were to urge in support of a

---

* Ph.B. 1908, D.C.L. 1943, LL.D. 1954, Wesleyan Univ.; LL.B. 1911, Yale Univ.
Chief Justice of the Supreme Court of Errors of Connecticut (Ret.).

law that "I believe thus-and-so, and we should therefore enact my belief into law," he would at once be met with the reply: "But I believe the opposite. Why shouldn't my belief be enacted into law?" It could hardly be contended that 51% of the people could force 49% to conform to every majority belief, or that such a law would be consistent with traditional American notions of minority rights or liberties under the Constitution.

Since this leads to a dead end, people will say: "God demands thus-and-so." The short answer to this is: "How do you know?" The reply that "I believe God demands it" is subject to the same infirmity: "I believe the converse."

People therefore turn to the views of religious leaders, saying: "94.628% of all religious leaders say thus-and-so is immoral, the converse is moral, and I strongly recommend the converse." The problem is that this still is the affirmation of a belief.

If someone were to urge the proposition that 90% of all religious leaders smoke X-brand cigarettes or drive Y-brand automobiles, and hence X and Y were the only moral brands, the position would be held untenable. Yet such unanimity would likewise demonstrate a strong belief. The fact that a belief in a course of action is sufficiently strongly held so that a religious leader is willing to characterize it as a "question of morality" does not detract from its essential quality as a belief.

But it may be argued that religious leaders smoke cigarettes and drive automobiles, not out of a question of morality, but out of personal preference or utility, whereas their views on integration are based on morality. This again, however, is a "bootstraps operation." It depends on the power to define the problem. If we define it as one of "taste," "social or political utility," or as something other than morality, the views of religious leaders lack any greater persuasive power than those of businessmen, bankers, doctors, lawyers, or anyone else, and in the case of a particular field, requiring expertise, such as housing, perhaps they carry considerably less weight than those expert in the field, such as Realtors. To permit a religious leader to define a question as one of morality, in which he presumably has greater expertise, is to permit him to translate a belief that a question involves moral considerations into the very fact at issue, and to prove the proposition by assuming the premise. Underlying the definition is still a *belief*, subject to the same infirmities as all other beliefs.

The reason why the problem is insoluble, and must inevitably lead to a dead-end, is that moral standards are necessarily subjective.[1] No clearer illustration of the law's difficulty in applying moral standards can be found than in those immigration, naturalization, and deportation statutes dealing with "good moral character" or "moral turpitude."[2] In a lengthy dissent in *Jordan v. De George*,[3] Mr. Justice Jackson first asked:

> Can we accept "the moral standards that prevail in contemporary society" as a sufficiently definite standard for the purposes of the Act? This is a large country and acts that are regarded as criminal in some states are lawful in others. We suspect that moral standards which prevail as to the possession or sale of liquor that has evaded tax may not be uniform in all parts of the country, nor in all levels of "contemporary society." How should we ascertain the moral sentiments of masses of persons on any better basis than a guess?[4]

He then pointed out:

> Irrationality is inherent in the task of translating the religious and ethical connotations of the phrase into legal decisions. The lower court cases seem to rest, as we feel this Court's decision does, upon the moral reactions of particular judges to particular offenses. . . . The guiding line seems to have no relation to the result reached. The chief impression from the cases is the caprice of the judgments. How many aliens have been deported who would not have been had some other judge heard their cases, and vice versa, we may only guess. That is not government by law.[5]

He concluded:

> We should not forget that criminality is one thing . . .—and that morality, ethics, and religious teachings are another. Their relations have puzzled the best of men . . . it shows on what treacherous grounds we tread when we undertake to translate ethical concepts into legal ones. . . . We usually end up by condemning all that we personally disapprove and for no better reason than that we disapprove it. In fact, what better reason is there?[6]

1 See Hughes, *Morals and the Criminal Law*, 71 Yale L.J. 662 (1962).

2 8 U.S.C. §§ 1182(9), 1251(a)(4), 1427(a)(3). See Note, *Naturalization—Good Moral Character as a Prerequisite*, 34 Notre Dame Law. 375 (1959).

3 341 U.S. 223 (1951).

4 *Id.* at 238-9.

5 *Id.* at 239-240.

6 *Id.* at 241-2. See also State v. Musser, 118 Utah 537, 223 P.2d 193, 196 (1950): "In the final analysis, each individual has his own moral codes, private and public, and what acts might be considered as injurious to public morals are as numerous as the opinions of man."

Not only is the use of contemporary moral standards entirely subjective, but its ascertainment is equally so. Judge Learned Hand has posed the problem very well:

> Even though we could take a poll, it would not be enough merely to count heads, without any appraisal of the voters. A majority of the votes of those in prisons and brothels, for instance, ought scarcely to outweigh the votes of accredited churchgoers. Nor can we see any reason to suppose that the opinion of clergymen would be a more reliable estimate than our own.[7]

The short of the matter is that to enact or sustain anti-discrimination legislation based on moral notions, or even to use such notions in discussing this type of legislation, is to base law on the quicksand foundation of shifting popular feelings held, not by the community at large, but by a greater or lesser proportion of them, and at all times disapproved of by a significant segment of society. Such a law has the inherent vice of widespread popular disapproval, and, like prohibition, invites evasion, contempt of the law, and an eventual variance between law and community standards so wide as to bring the legal system into disrepute.[8]

ANDREW PORTOGHESE*
E. F. W. WILDERMUTH**
CORNELIUS GREENWAY***
JOHN M. SCHOFIELD****

[7] Schmidt v. United States, 177 F.2d 450, 451 (2d Cir. 1949).

[8] See N.Y. Times, Dec. 2, 1961, p. 25, col. 3, where the Rev. Dexter L. Hanley, S.J., Professor of Law at Georgetown University Law School "described as bad legislation . . . an old Connecticut law that makes criminal the practice of artificial birth control or the dissemination of information about it. . . . 'Of course, I maintain . . . that the practice of birth control is morally wrong, but . . . the unenforceability of such a law could lead to disrespect for law in general,' " he said. And see N.Y. Times, Nov. 12, 1961, p. 122, col. 3, reporting a Fund for the Republic Report, "Religion and American Society," which says: "Because Americans hold diverse views on what is moral, attempts to legislate a religious group's view of morality, in addition to preaching it, have been 'spectacular failures,' . . . 'These statutes . . . are tainted with the moralism that corrupts the law. Because they are unenforceable, and do not reflect the existing concensus of the citizens who live under them, they have brought law itself into disrepute.' "

* B.S. 1956, Univ. of Alabama; M.D. 1960, Tufts College of Medicine; O.D.-D.O.S. 1963, Mass. College of Optometry. Copyright © 1963 by Andrew Portoghese and E. F. W. Wildermuth.

** Member of the New York Bar.

*** B.S. 1925, S.T.B. 1928, Tufts Univ.; D.D. 1941, St. Lawrence Univ.; LL.D. 1946, Lincoln Memorial Univ.; LL.D. 1948, Lincoln College; D.H.L. 1960, Wagner College. Minister, All Souls Universalist Church, Brooklyn, New York, 1929-date.

**** B.S. 1938, Univ. of Illinois. Member of the South Carolina Bar. Minister since 1953; President, Committee for Christian Universalist Churches, 1961-date; President, Georgia Universalist Convention; Editor, The Christian Universalist; former Editor, The Universalist Herald.

COMMENT ON O'MEARA: HISTORICAL INACCURACY

In this case, the court alleged that "elimination of discrimination is necessary for the sake of America's relations with the rest of the world." The objection to this observation is not primarily that it is false, which in my opinion it is, but that it introduces considerations which should be irrelevant to judicial decision. The task of the court was to judge the constitutionality of a statute. Whether the law conduces to results pleasing to foreign nations is irrelevant to its constitutionality. When such considerations are introduced, a state or federal constitution becomes superfluous since it is interpreted arbitrarily in terms of extraneous considerations. Finally, judges of a supreme court are neither trained nor qualified to forecast the foreign-policy effects of legislation. When they seek to do so (or rather reiterate the currently fashionable clichés in the foreign policy area), they violate the fundamental American precepts of constitutional separation of powers.

The court's statement in the same case that "the practice of discrimination is utterly inconsistent with the political philosophy upon which our institutions are based, and with the moral principles which we inherit from our Judeo-Christian Traditions" is contrary to the historic record.

The first point to make is that *discrimination* is defined (*The Oxford English Dictionary*, 1961 edition) as "the perceiving, noting or making a distinction or difference between things." Those who do not discriminate between the true and the false are incapable of logical thought; those who cannot discriminate between the good and the bad, or the better and the worse, are without any sense of morals or values.

When the court states that racial discrimination is contrary to the basic American philosophy, it forgets that none of the Founding Fathers considered the Negroes as citizens or as capable of being members of American society or as being persons to whom the safeguards of the Constitution and the Bill of Rights applied. Thomas Jefferson, James Madison and Abraham Lincoln were convinced that the Negro was so inferior by nature that he could not form part of the American community as a citizen and urged therefore that his emancipation be coupled with his immediate deportation from the United States. Jefferson urged these views in his *Notes on Virginia*, Madison in his correspondence and Abraham Lincoln on many occasions, notably in his Cooper Union Speech and in his First Annual Message. The record on this matter is so clear that one is amazed to find educated people falsifying it. The judges of the State Supreme Court are entitled to advance racial equality and non-discrimination as their personal preferences; they are not entitled to falsify the views of the dead in order to gain a spurious historical support for their prejudices.

The belief that non-discrimination is inherent in the Judeo-Christian tradition is also a falsification of historic fact. Jewish law discouraged intercourse with Gentiles on terms of equality and in many instances categorically forbade it. The Jewish theocratic system was based on concepts of human inequality and eugenic reproduction.

In the Christian doctrine, Jesus ordered his disciples to avoid the Samaritans, "But go rather to the lost sheep of the house of Israel." (*Matthew* X:5 & 6). After the death of Jesus, St. Paul in effect eliminated the distinction between Jew and Gentile, but he retained the concept of inherent human inequality and discrimination among men. This view was expounded clearly in his analysis of the powers, capacities and duties of the members of the Church whom he called "the body of Christ" (*I Corinthians* XII:4-31). This conception of the basic inequality of man is fundamental to the Christian Church and was expounded on many occasions by such theologians and Patristic Fathers as St. Augustine and St. Thomas Aquinas. The entire Calvinist theology is based on predestination, an inequality foreordained by God. Moral conduct in the Calvinist system requires *discrimination* between those predestined for salvation and those predestined for damnation.

Thus, the statements made by the justices of the Supreme Court of Washington concerning the relationship of discrimination to American institutions and to the Judeo-Christian tradition are entirely false, historically inaccurate and devoid of merit.

Judges do not increase the public reputation of their calling by abandoning considerations of law and constitutionality in their decisions in favor of dogmatic generalizations concerning specialized areas in which they lack any special competence.

NATHANIEL WEYL*

* B.Sc. 1931, Columbia Univ. Economist, A.A.A., 1933-4; Economist in charge, Latin American Research, Federal Reserve Bd., 1940-1; Spl. Asst. and Asst. Director, Board of Economic Warfare, 1941-3; Chairman, Interdepartmental Balance of Payments Committee, 1945-7; Economist, Comm. for Refugee Settlement in Surinam, 1948. Author: The Reconquest of Mexico (1939); Treason (1950); The Battle Against Disloyalty (1951); Red Star Over Cuba (1960); The Negro in American Civilization (1960); The Geography of Intellect (1963).

COMMENTS ON MARTIN v. CITY OF NEW YORK

Editor's Note: In *Martin v. City of New York,* 22 Misc. 2d 389, 201 N.Y.S.2d 111 (1960), a trial court judge in New York City held the city's ordinance forbidding discrimination in private housing to be constitutional. The court conceded that the ordinance interfered with the landowner's property rights in his business and property, and might lessen his rental income because of inability to rent to others. However, the court gave the following rationale for the law: "It is now believed that many of our problems arising from the diverse nature of our population will be brought nearer solution by integration." And it concluded that although plaintiff's business might suffer, "it is an additional instance where the individual must yield to what legislative authority deems is for the common good."

COMMENT ON MARTIN: GOOD HOUSING

Martin v. City of New York represents the philosophy that it is the function of government to pass anti-discrimination legislation in housing, and that such legislation will solve both housing problems and problems relating to relations between the races. In the 1959 Report of the United States Commission on Civil Rights, I stated as follows:

> We yield to no one in our goodwill and anxiety for equal justice to all races, in the field of housing as elsewhere. A good home should be the goal of everyone regardless of color, and the Government should aid in providing housing in keeping with the means and ambitions of the people. Government aid is important where public improvements have displaced people and where slums become a liability to the community. This does not mean, however, that the Government owes everyone a house regardless of his ambition, industry, or will to provide for himself. When generosity takes away self-reliance or the determination of one to improve his own lot, it ceases to be a blessing. We should help, but not pamper. But there remains a financial limit beyond which the Government cannot go.

> In dealing with the problem of housing, we must face realities and recognize the fact that no one pattern will serve the country as a whole. . . . Suggestions keyed to integration rather than housing, . . . if carried out in full, will result in delay and in many cases defeat of adequate housing, which is our prime objective. The repeated expressions, . . . "open housing," "open market," and "scatteration" suggest a fixed program of mixing the races anywhere and everywhere regardless of the wishes of either race and particular problems involved. The result would be dissention, strife, and even violence evident in sections where you would least expect it.

> To us it is not only wise, but imperative that biracial committees be set up in different sections to provide areas for adequate housing in keeping with just requirements for the people involved. This can be done; it is being done in different sections such as

Atlanta, Ga., in keeping with the wishes of both races. This responsibility, however, must be met in a positive, courageous, and constructive manner in keeping with the requirement at the local level.

The foregoing statement is as valid today as when it was made. The suggestions made therein, rather than anti-discrimination laws, will reduce racial friction and promote better housing for all.

JOHN S. BATTLE*

COMMENT ON MARTIN: PSYCHOLOGICAL ASSUMPTIONS

The *Martin* case, which upheld the constitutionality of New York City's ordinance forbidding discrimination in private housing, the earliest one in the country, is based, in its final analysis, on this rationale, expressed therein: "It is now believed that many of our problems arising from the diverse nature of our population will be brought nearer solution by integration." On this altar, the most fundamental rights of property and freedom of choice and association are sacrificed. Principles as old as the common law itself are cast aside for sociological experimentation with people.

The use of passing social science or economic fads to alter basic constitutional principles to accord with judicial approval of these fads is not new in American jurisprudence. As early as 1905, in *Lochner v. New York*,[1] Mr. Justice Holmes protested that "The 14th Amendment does not enact Mr. Herbert Spencer's Social Statics."[2] More recently, Mr. Justice Frankfurter pointed out:

> Adam Smith was treated as though his generalizations had been imparted to him on Sinai. . . . The result was that economic views of confined validity were treated by lawyers and judges as though the Framers had enshrined them in the Constitution. This misapplication of the notions of the classic economists and resulting disregard of the perduring reach of the Constitution led to Mr. Justice Holmes' famous protest in the Lochner Case against meas-

---

* LL.B. 1913, Univ. of Virginia; LL.D., Hampden-Sydney Coll.; LL.D., Univ. of Richmond; LL.D., Wake Forest Coll.; LL.D., William & Mary Coll. Member, U.S. Commission on Civil Rights, 1959-61; Governor of Virginia, 1950-4. Member of the Virginia Bar.

1 198 U.S. 45 (1905).
2 *Id.*, at 75.

uring the Fourteenth Amendment by Mr. Herbert Spencer's Social Statics. . . . Had not Mr. Justice Holmes' awareness . . . gradually prevailed, there might indeed have been "hardly any limit but the sky" to the embodiment of "our economic or moral beliefs" in that Amendment's "prohibitions."[3]

But while the Courts were abdicating their role as guardian of fundamental rights of liberty and property, on the pretext that such rights were committed solely to legislative mercies, they gradually assumed the role of promoter of sociological and psychological experiments with people. If Adam Smith was dethroned, Myrdal was crowned in his stead.[4]

The "scientific" material used to promote integration makes even its friends wince. Professor Edmond Cahn declared that he "would not have the constitutional rights of Negroes—or of other Americans—rest on any such flimsy foundation as some of the scientific demonstrations in these records [in the segregation cases]."[5] Commenting on how new and imprecise the social sciences are, he added:

Today's sanguine asseveration may be cancelled by tomorrow's new revelation—or new technical fad. . . . It would be quite another thing to have our fundamental rights rise, fall, or change along with the latest fashions of psychological literature. . . . Recognizing as we do how sagacious Mr. Justice Holmes was to insist that the Constitution be not tied to the wheels of any economic system whatsoever, we ought to keep it similarly uncommitted in relation to the other social sciences.[6]

Professor Cahn has already demolished beyond repair the social scientific evidence used to support integration through government fiat.[7] One can hardly resist quoting such topical headings of his as "opinion based on opinion based on etc.,"[8] or "if facts may prove inconvenient, shun them."[9] His quotation of one of the leading social scientists cited by the Supreme Court is masterful:

Let there be no mistake. I have myself had occasion to argue in another connection that facts are not established scientifically by

3 American Federation of Labor v. American Sash & Door Co., 335 U.S. 538, 543 (1949).
4 Brown v. Board of Education, 347 U.S. 483, 494, n.11 (1954); Hughes v. Superior Court, 339 U.S. 460, 463 (1950).
5 Cahn, *Jurisprudence*, 30 N.Y.U.L. Rev. 150, 157-8 (1955).
6 *Id.* at 167.
7 Cahn, *Jurisprudence*, 31 N.Y.U.L. Rev. 182 (1956).
8 *Id.* at 189.
9 *Id.* at 190.

holding a poll among scientists concerning their preferences. Nor can issues of fact be settled by surveys of scientists' opinions.[10]

Professor Ernest van den Haag has gone even further, and demonstrated that the social scientific evidence commonly used to support government-sponsored integration, in fact, if anything, supports the converse. He has observed:

> It is often assumed that prejudice springs from ignorance and is reduced by knowledge and contact. This is certainly the case if the prejudice has no source but misinformation. Yet, misinformation often is the effect and not the cause of prejudice which itself springs from a variety of social and psychological sources. Information, or contact, is no cure where misinformation is the effect and not the cause of prejudice. The slaughter of the Jews in Germany was not due to ignorance or preceded by segregation or avoided by contact. In times past, hundreds of thousands of harmless old women were burned as witches. The people who accused them of being witches, who saw them riding through the air, etc., were their neighbors, villagers who had known them long and well. Clearly, contact produces as much as it reduces prejudice. And divorce cases suggest that even prolonged and intimate contact can produce hostility, contempt and prejudice just as well as affection, respect, and knowledge.[11]

And he reached the following astounding conclusion:

> I am forced to the conclusion that Professor Clark misled the courts. Whether it be granted that his tests show psychological damage to Negro children, the comparison between the responses of Negro children in segregated and in nonsegregated schools shows that "they do not differ" except that *Negro children in segregated schools "are less pronounced in their preference for the white doll" and more often think of the colored dolls as "nice" or identify with them.* In short, if Professor Clark's tests do demonstrate damage to Negro children, then they demonstrate that the damage is *less* with segregation and *greater* with congregation. Yet, Professor Clark told the Court that he was proving that "segregation inflicts injuries upon the Negro" by the very tests which, if they prove anything—which is doubtful—prove the opposite.[12]

One would think that with the social science arguments in favor of government-sponsored integration so completely devastated, the courts would abandon them, Yet, surprisingly, this is not the case. Courts continue to give their "lesson in democracy"[13]

10 *Ibid.,* quoting Chein, *What Are the Psychological Effects of Segregation Under Conditions of Equal Facilities?,* 3 Int'l J. Opinion and Attitude Research 229, 230 (1949).
11 van den Haag, *Social Science Testimony in the Desegregation Cases—A Reply to Professor Kenneth Clark,* 6 Vill. L. Rev. 69, 70 (1960).
12 *Id.* at 77.
13 Taylor v. Board of Education, 191 F. Supp. 181, 187 (S.D.N.Y. 1961).

based on thoroughly discredited and exploded "experimentation," and opinions, based on more opinions, based on still more opinions,[14] and enshrine the results of this intellectual crystal-ball gazing into fundamental constitutional notions.

Martin is but another example of this enshrinement. It proceeds from undemonstrated hypothesis to unwarranted conclusion. The hopeful assumption that integration will solve intergroup problems lacks even sufficient basis to be used as a non-coercive policy. To raise it to the level of a fundamental norm which can overthrow deeply-rooted constitutional guarantees of association and private property is a manifest distortion of any rational governmental aim.

CHARLES C. JOSEY*
ROBERT E. KUTTNER**
FRANK C.J. McGURK***

COMMENT ON MARTIN: CHANGING CONCEPTS

Martin v. City of New York[1] tested the constitutionality of a newly created police power given the City of New York to be used to compel an unwilling landlord to let apartments to Negroes. The landlord rested his case upon the rule that both parties must agree to the formation of a contract of lease just as they do in the making of all contracts. He picturesquely asserted that ancient prerogative of landlords to lease only to acceptable tenants, even though the acceptance be limited to redheaded women. The same theory is expressed thus in *Browning v. Slenderella Systems:*[2] "if one chooses to operate a boarding house. . . , it can be done with

[14] In re Skipwith, 14 Misc. 2d 324, 180 N.Y.S.2d 852 (1958).
* A.B. 1913, Wake Forest Coll.; A.M. 1918, Ph.D. 1921, Columbia Univ.; Instructor and Asst. Prof. of Psychology, Dartmouth Coll., 1921-3; Professor of Philosophy and Psychology, 1923-32, Head of Dept., 1932-9, Univ. of South Dakota; Head of Dept. of Psychology, 1939-date, Butler Univ. Author: The Role of Instinct in Social Philosophy (1921); The Social Philosophy of Instinct (1922); Race and National Solidarity (1923); The Psychology of Religion (1927); Psychology of Normal People (1940); The Psychological Battlefront of Democracy (1944); Psychology and Successful Living (1948).
** B.S. 1950, City College of New York; Ph.D. 1958, Univ. of Connecticut. Instructor, Creighton Univ. School of Medicine. Copyright *1963, by Robert E. Kuttner*.
*** B.S. 1933, M.A. 1937, Univ. of Pennsylvania; Ph.D. 1951, Catholic Univ. of America. Professor of Psychology, Villanova Univ.

[1] 22 Misc. 2d 389, 201 N.Y.S.2d 111 (1960).
[2] 54 Wn. 2d 440, 341 P.2d 859 (1959).

a clientele selected according to the taste or even the whim of the landlord. There is no analogy between a public housing project . . . wherein Negroes have equal rights, and a private home where there are no public rights whatever and into which even the King cannot enter."[3] A tenant's possession is exclusive even as to the landlord; hence the forced quartering of Negroes upon white owners is a taking of private property for private use and violates a constitutional right.

The *Martin* opinion overruled the need for mutual agreement in the formation of a contract, a doctrine that has been universal from time immemorial, and upheld the constitutionality of authorizing a city commission to exercise the power of eminent domain for private use under the guise of it being an exercise of the police power. The direct and immediate effect of the *Martin* case upon the law of contracts is to make contracts to which only Negroes consent enforcible by this new police power vested in an administrative agency of the city. This constitutes a clean break with the prevailing law of contracts and eminent domain and in addition it ousts the courts of their original jurisdiction over real property.

The theory supporting this new police power deserves comment. It is true, as the opinion says, that courts have upheld the constitutionality of building construction restrictions and regulations as a permissible exercise of the police power for the purpose of promoting safety, sanitation, health and comfort. These regulations are not the subject of negotiation or contract between the city and the individual builder. They are totally unrelated to the subject of leases or the identity of the tenants of the buildings.

The *Martin* opinion cites them as the legal precedent upon which it relies. The only thing they have in common is that they are both exercises of the *police power*. The new concept is that only a police power label is needed to circumvent the Constitution; a similarity of facts is no longer necessary to constitute a precedent.

The basis for the theory that the police power can make and

[3] *Id.* at 869.

enforce contracts against the will of a party is explained in one
article[4] that if a party is willing to contract at all and his willingness to deal becomes known, it is the prerogative of the police
power to make a contract for him by designating any Negro it
chooses as the other contracting party. The article is a criticism
of *O'Meara v. Washington State Board Against Discrimination*.[5]
O'Meara had offered to sell his home by advertising in a newspaper. He refused, however, to sell to a Negro applicant, who
thereupon invoked the Washington State police power, which is
a counterpart of the New York police power here in question.
The Board ordered O'Meara to sell to the Negro. This was not a
taking of property according to the writers' theory thus expressed:

> *However, the Board order, in fact, only regulates the disposition
> of property voluntarily sought to be relinquished, instead of ap-
> propriating to the public use property sought to be kept. Conse-
> quently, the kind of interference involved in O'Meara is an
> exercise of the police power, not the power of eminent domain—
> the "taking" clauses govern only the latter.*[6]

The writers do not assert that housing a Negro is a public
use. Apparently their theory is that the constitutional bar to the
taking of property for private use applies only when it is sought
to be accomplished by a proceeding in eminent domain. If the
police power is used instead, it is not a taking of property as to
"the disposition of property voluntarily sought to be relin-
quished." In other words, a willingness to deal when once established enables the board under the police power to make and
enforce a contract of conveyance to any Negro it designates as the
other contracting party. To dispense with voluntary consent to
the formation of contracts is to impose police power regimentation upon every financial aspect of life.

The writers, of course, have only rationalized the action of
the courts in upholding use of the police power in an expanding
field of Negro legislation relating to the most sensitive areas of
freedom. Thus a Negro can call upon the board to exercise its
police power to compel a party either to work for him or to hire
him at the Negro's election whenever a general willingness to deal

4 37 Wash. L. Rev. 131 (1962).
5 58 Wn. 2d 793, 365 P.2d 1 (1961).
6 *Supra* note 4, at 144.

has been expressed in a want ad or otherwise. In *Browning v. Slenderella Systems*,[7] where the court upheld a Negress' right to compel the service of a white woman who had advertised, it was only a dissent which said: "When a white woman is compelled against her will to give a Negress a Swedish massage, that, too, is involuntary servitude."[8]

The specific police power here in question was created to coerce integration in the field of housing. The *Martin* opinion says:

> It is now believed that many of our problems arising from the diverse nature of our population will be brought nearer solution by integration. These have been found constitutionally unobjectionable. The interference with private business is just as great but it has had to yield to *changing concepts* of what the state can and should do.[9] (Emphasis supplied.)

These "changing concepts" of constitutional rights in private property deserve comment. Conceding that time makes ancient good uncouth and that provision for amendment in all constitutions were made in recognition of that fact, still constitutions are no more than mere statute law if they do not give stability and preserve the essential rights and freedoms against the assaults of militant pressure blocks. The brave new statesmanship does not deny this directly. Instead, its gimmick is to assert the exemption of the police power from the constitutional prohibitions. Each succeeding decision provides a base for the next departure from the clear meaning of constitutional language. Ultimately, reference to the Constitution will be futile because the law will have become all decision and no Constitution. Since the *Martin* case strikes down the oldest and most indispensable attributes of private property, namely, control and possession, it could hardly do other than rely upon the doctrine of "changing concepts." We are now in the third "change."

Our constitutions naturally embodied their contemporaneous concepts. The original one has been called "rugged individualism." President Hoover stated it most tersely in his last campaign, to the effect that it is the duty of the people to support the govern-

---

7 *Supra* note 2.
8 *Id.* at 869.
9 *Supra* note 1, at 391.

ment, not the duty of the government to support the people. That concept was reversed in 1933, when it was considered to be a proper function of government to concern itself with the economic affairs of the people to the end that they should not starve in the midst of plenty through no fault of their own.

This 1933 concept was dubbed the *"Welfare State"* by reluctant taxpayers. They only had a pocketbook of objection to it, however, since it left intact all of the traditional freedoms and preserved all the constitutional property rights of the individual. The tax burden of the welfare programs was heavy but the State itself administered the programs and particular individuals were not singled out and drafted to execute them at their private expense.

The Welfare State met the problem of sub-standard Negro housing with F.H.A. financing, housing projects, slum clearance, etc. The Negroes' housing relations were with the government. No property right of any individual was subjected to Negro whim. Thus the Welfare State adhered to that ancient credo of Liberty that the State can best promote the common good by protecting the interest and rights of the individual.

The crowning achievement in man's long climb to freedom was the designation of the individual as the unit for whom constitutional rights were created. He is shielded from encroachment by majorities and militant minorities. He is even protected from the government itself for in truth and in fact freedom inheres in those restraints upon sovereignty which are implemented on behalf of the individual by an independent judiciary.

Contrast the concept of freedom of the individual under the Welfare State, with the Police State concept of the *Martin* case. The Police State solves the problem of sub-standard Negro housing by quartering Negroes upon private property. When a Negro singles out an owner and puts the finger on him, the Police State commandeers the property for him. This is a taking of property for private use since both possession and control of it pass to the Negro tenant. Between depreciation of the property and/or rent control which the Police State has sanctioned, financial loss, which may occur, is merely, the *Martin* opinion says, ". . . additional instance where the individual must yield to what legislative authority deems is for the common good." Hitler never said it better.

The N.A.A.C.P. identifies the "common good" as *integration*. All other features of Negro legislation are mere details or supporting arguments. This is demonstrated in *Price v. Evergreen Cemetery Company*,[10] wherein it was said:

> In view of the cemetery's long-standing segregation restrictions, it could not sell the Negro appellants a burial plot in "Babyland." The white parents who have relied upon the white restriction in question have acquired a right to the association of their own race exclusively. It is this specific right of segregation which this particular case in a series was brought to eliminate. Let it be noted that herein there is no refusal of sepulchre to a Negro nor any complaint as to the quality of available burial plots.
>
> The cemetery representative tried earnestly to show and sell appellants a burial plot in a children's section of the cemetery where both white and Negro children were interred. The appellants refused to even look at it. They insisted on burial in "Babyland" and brought this action for injuries to their feelings because they were not permitted to intrude upon the white children segregated therein. Obviously, if Negro children were admitted to "Babyland," its white exclusiveness would be gone, and it would be in the same category as the unsegregated section which was rejected by the Negro appellants. The appellants' grievance is the mere *existence of any exclusive section* for white children into which Negroes cannot intrude at will. In view of the fact that the respondent cemetery provides unsegregated facilities of equal quality for the general public, including Negroes, there is no other possible issue herein than that of compulsory total desegregation in cemeteries.[11]

The police power technique which was specifically sanctioned in the *Martin* case may not at this instant constitute a massive assault upon the traditional freedoms of association and of privacy but it sets an approved working pattern for assaults from so many angles that their unopposed combination and extension will eventually amount to a police state in fact as well as in theory. Every element of the pattern is incompatible with freedom. One of its worst features is the police power to make contracts. Housing and labor contracts will be joined by many other kinds in due course. It cannot be doubted that contracts create and condition the most important of the aspects of life that are outside of a man's

10 57 Wn. 2d 352, 357 P.2d 702 (1960).
11 *Id.* at 704.

skin. Certainly, all of the necessities of life are the subject of contract. A wide intrusion of the police power into the field of contract would mark the end of liberty as Patrick Henry knew it, for he who has no choice (the right and power of discrimination in all private and individual matters) has no liberty. Such a one is but the tool of the State.

The significance of the *Martin* case is that it strips the white man of the constitutional protection of his rights without due process. The struggle in the courts is substantially over. Only the inevitable extensions of the *Martin* rule remain. It is the green light for the N.A.A.C.P. It transfers the struggle to the political arena where anything goes which can muster enough votes. As was said in *Price,*

> It remains to be seen how resistant our ancient liberties of private association will be to the variety of mass pressures being mobilized by the N.A.A.C.P. It is, indeed, a concerted and aggressive force to be reckoned with. Experience has shown that an aggressive minority can frequently exact special privileges from an indifferent majority. It may be that the realization of the Negro dream of compulsory total togetherness is just around the corner.[12]

JOSEPH A. MALLERY*
JAMES B. McGHEE**
I. BEVERLY LAKE***
ROBERT E. LEE****

COMMENT ON MARTIN: SELECTION OF TENANTS

In this New York case the owner of residential property held for rental attacked the constitutionality of a statute which forbids the owners of multiple dwellings to deny accommodations to any person on account of race, color or religion. The owner asserted

12 *Id.* at 705.
* LL.B. 1926, Univ. of Washington. Justice of the Supreme Court of Washington (Ret.).
** Chief Justice of the Supreme Court of New Mexico (Ret.).
*** B.S. 1925, Wake Forest Coll.; LL.B. 1929, Harvard Univ.; LL.M. 1940, S.J.D. 1947, Columbia Univ. Professor of Law, Wake Forest Coll. Law School, 1932-51; Asst. Atty. Gen. of North Carolina, 1952-5.
**** B.S. 1928, LL.B. 1928, Wake Forest Coll.; M.A. 1929, Columbia Univ.; LL.M. 1935, S.J.D. 1941, Duke Univ. Instructor (1929-36), Asst. Prof. (1936-42), Professor of Law (1942-5), Temple Univ.; Dean and Professor of Law, Wake Forest College School of Law, 1946-50, Professor since 1950. Author: Advanced Business Law (1934); Cases on Contracts (1937, 1940, 1948); Law of Contracts (1946, 1948).

his right to determine for himself what persons, or classes of persons, were desirable tenants; and he specifically objected to renting to Negroes. His refusal arose from no personal hostility to the race, but from the belief that occupancy by colored persons rendered his property less attractive to other tenants, thereby decreasing its rental value.

This is not one of those which may be called "civil rights" cases and which involve, for example, racial discrimination in the use of public facilities and accommodations and which have invoked the application of the Fourteenth Amendment of the Federal Constitution. The case now discussed bears a kinship to those which involve the validity or enforceability of provisions in deeds or contracts for the sale of real property which restrict its sale or occupancy to persons of a certain race. These cases, which are numerous, have quite generally upheld the validity of covenants forbidding the sale or lease of property to Negroes.[1]

The reasoning on which these decisions rest is that it is not contrary to public policy for the owners of property to place such restrictions on its use and that they involve transactions between individuals to which the Fourteenth Amendment has no application. The decisions of the several state courts heretofore cited are reinforced by the Supreme Court of the United States in *Corrigan v. Buckley*,[2] which involved specifically the validity of restrictions on the sale of property to Negroes. In answer to the contention that such conditions were violative of the Fourteenth Amendment the Court said:

> And the prohibitions of the Fourteenth Amendment "have reference to state action exclusively, and not to any action of private individuals." Virginia v. Rives, 100 U.S. 313; United States v. Harris, 106 U.S. 639. "It is state action of a particular character that is prohibited. Individual invasion of individual rights is not the subject matter of the Amendment" . . . It is obvious that none of these Amendments prohibited private individuals from entering into contracts respecting the control and disposition of their own property; . . .[3]

---

[1] See Parmalee v. Morris, 218 Mich. 625, 188 N.W. 330 (1922); Meade v. Dennistone, 173 Md. 295, 196 Atl. 330 (1938); Ridgeway v. Cockburn, 163 Misc. 511, 296 N.Y. Supp. 936 (1937). See also 162 A.L.R. 180, 114 A.L.R. 1237, 66 A.L.R. 531, 38 A.L.R. 1183, and 9 A.L.R. 120, and the cases cited therein.

[2] 271 U.S. 323 (1926).

[3] *Id.* at 330.

It seems plain, therefore, that any approval of the statute here challenged must be found within the powers of the state to enact such legislation. It is to be regretted that the court's opinion did not discuss this phase of the case more fully. It contents itself merely by referring to laws regulating rental housing in respect to type of construction, sanitary facilities, number of occupants, etc., and assuming that because such laws have been upheld this one must also be approved. The analogy is not apt. The other laws mentioned are plainly for the protection of the health and safety of tenants and of the public. Even the zoning ordinances regulating the type and use of structures in defined areas find their basis in consideration of the public good. It is in this failure to recognize the difference between acts affecting the public welfare and those matters of purely private concern that I think this decision is at fault.

The sole question here is the right of a landlord to rent his property to such tenants as he thinks desirable and whose tenancy will assure him of a more certain income, where no question arises as to the health or safety of his tenants or of the public. Many residential properties are leased only to selected tenants. We are all familiar with those which deny occupancy to families with small children, seeking thereby to avoid the costs of upkeep arising from the destructive nature of youngsters and avoiding the complaints that their boisterous conduct might evoke from other tenants. Other landlords limit their rentals to elderly persons, finding them to be more satisfactory tenants than younger, more active, pleasure-seeking couples. I know of no case where the right of a landlord to exercise such choice has been denied.

Justification for this legislation, if there can be any, must be found in the powers reserved to the state by the provisions of the Tenth Amendment to the Federal Constitution. The broad terms of the Amendment no doubt cover a vast and unopened field of legislation and might be taken to imply that a state can do anything it wants to so long as it does not conflict with the Federal Constitution. But it would seem that there are certain natural and inherent rights which an individual has in his property and of which he cannot be deprived. Among these are the right to utilize it as he chooses so long as he does not interfere with the safety or health or comfort of his neighbors or the public.

The Court's opinion concludes with the statement that even if the compulsion to admit Negro tenants results in lessening the rental income of the property, nevertheless this "is an additional instance where the individual must yield to what the legislative authority deems is for the common good."

Without conceding that this statute advances the public good, it may be pointed out that the argument is the same as that on which the right of eminent domain is based. And if it be true that the effect of this statute is to lessen the rental income of the property, then the owner has had a valuable property right taken from him without any provision for the payment of that just compensation which is provided for in the constitution of every state in the Union. Even were there no other reason, this, in this writer's opinion, is sufficient to render the law invalid.

JOHN PAUL*

COMMENT ON MARTIN: RIGHT OF PROPERTY OWNER

In considering whether the ordinance involved in the *Martin* case is constitutional and enforceable, it is necessary to begin with the fundamental proposition that our government is founded upon a *system of free enterprise*. Accordingly, every individual under the protective shield of the Constitution of the United States has the right to own property, both real and personal, and to use it as he sees fit, so long as he does not interfere with the lawful right of his neighbors in the use and enjoyment of their property, or use it in a manner that would endanger the public safety, health, morals or the general welfare of the community.

The right to the lawful use of property by its owner constitutes its only economic or monetary value to him. To completely deprive him of its use completely destroys its value to him. And

* B.S. 1903, Va. Mil. Inst.; LL.B. 1906, University of Virginia. Judge of the United States District Court for the Western District of Virginia (Ret.), 1932-1962; U.S. Atty., W.D. Va., 1929-31; Spl. Asst. to U.S. Atty. Gen., 1924-5; Member of the U.S. House of Representatives, 1921-3.

any act on the part of the federal, state or municipal government which deprives the owner of its use, in whole or in part, amounts to a taking of said property to the extent of the use of which he is deprived.

Such taking can be lawfully accomplished under the power of eminent domain, provided it is for a public use and provided the owner is justly compensated therefor; or the owner can be deprived of the use of improvements upon realty under the police power of the state, without compensation, when the owner puts it to a use which constitutes a danger to the *public safety, health, morals or general welfare* of the community in which the property is located.

Neither the federal, state nor municipal governments have the power to prohibit or place limitations upon the use of property by its owner other than under the exceptions and for the reasons above stated, i.e., unless it constitutes a danger to the public safety, health, morals or general welfare of the community. Even modern zoning ordinances are justified by the courts upon the ground that they affect the general welfare of the community and that the common good thereby achieved outweighs any loss occasioned by the limitation of use of the individual owner incurred by such zoning ordinance. In fact, legislative bodies predicate their right to pass such ordinances upon the ground that it is for the general welfare of the community.

Aside from the above exceptions, any limitations placed upon the use of private property by federal, state or municipal governments create a liability for damages to the owner for its loss in value as a result of such limitation. And any destruction of its value by such action without just compensation constitutes a taking of property "without due process of law" under the provisions of Articles V and XIV of the United States Constitution. Any legislative act purporting to be under the police powers of the state which shows upon its face that it is arbitrary and which is in fact wholly unrelated to the public safety, health, morals or general welfare of the community is not sustainable in law.[1]

1 Hadacheck v. Sebastian, 239 U.S. 394 (1915); City of Tucson v. Arizona Mortuary, 34 Ariz. 493, 272 Pac. 923 (1928).

One of the cardinal principles of the freedoms secured to us under our Federal Constitution is that we have the privilege to choose our associates and to associate or not to associate with whomsoever we please and to contract or refuse to contract with whomsoever we please in matters relating to our own property. These rights were never successfully challenged until the United States Supreme Court in *Brown v. Board of Education*[2] and *Bolling v. Sharpe*[3] by judicial legislation and sociological theories *a la* Myrdal decided otherwise. Since then numerous erroneous public statements have been made by public officials high in the echelons of our Federal government to the effect that those decisions constitute *the law of the land* when in fact they are at the most the law of the case. The decisions in this field of discrimination against minority races have been broadened to the point of absurdity. The decision under discussion is an example of this view and of ignoring fundamentals.

An ordinance providing in substance "that because a man is a Negro he is not ipso facto an undesirable tenant" not only invades the property rights of the owner of such property but it is an invasion of his right to sell or lease it to whomsoever he pleases or not to sell or lease it if he desires. And there is the rub. Who has the right to determine whether a tenant is desirable or undesirable? An apartment house is not affected with a public interest. Therefore, the public cannot interfere unless it is used for a purpose which endangers the public health, safety, morals or general welfare of the community. Certainly the *refusal* to rent property to anyone, whether plutocrat or pauper, black or white, gangster or gentleman, does not endanger the safety, health, morals or general welfare of the community where it is kept in a sanitary condition.

The ordinance here in question undertakes to define and control the desires and the business judgment of property owners in the City of New York. Martin determined that a Negro would be undesirable under the circumstances as a tenant. He was the only person who could possibly be interested. In arriving at this,

---

2 347 U.S. 483 (1954).
3 347 U.S. 497 (1954), a District of Columbia case decided the same day as Brown v. Board of Education, *supra*.

he considered the profit and loss side of his ledger and he desired to continue to keep his units rented. His judgment dictated he could not rent to a Negro and keep them rented. Neither his personal desires nor his business judgment relating to the management of his property can be controlled by others so long as it is a lawful use nor can it be controlled by any branch of the government, federal, state, or municipal. If we bear in mind the attributes inherent in the ownership of real property under the system of free enterprise and under the Federal Constitution, in my opinion, we cannot escape the conclusions reached above.

It may be conceded, *arguendo,* that from the standpoint of the Negro involved it may have seemed unfair to refuse to rent him an apartment. But even equity, if involved, must follow the law, and the legal rights of the owner to rent or not to rent would prevail. That right rests upon the rock-bottom foundation that the property belonged to him and to no one else and that his right to control its lawful use was and is paramount to the whims or caprice, the desires or dissents, the needs or even the legal rights of all others including the federal, state or municipal government within which it is located.

The question of desirability or undesirability or the business judgment of the individual concerning the management of his property does not fall within the sphere of legislative regulation or control, unless carrying his desires and judgment into execution amounts to a violation of criminal law or injuriously affects the public health, safety, morals or general welfare of the community.

In the exercise of his business judgment, Martin violated no criminal law. His act did not and could not affect the public health, safety, morals or general welfare of the community. His refusal to rent did not change the status quo of his property at all. Therefore the New York City ordinance here involved is clearly in violation of the constitution and for that reason and others stated above it is void and the decision is therefore erroneous.

M. T. PHELPS*

* LL.B. 1912, Vanderbilt Univ. Chief Justice of the Supreme Court of Arizona (Ret.).

COMMENT ON MARTIN: INTEGRATION

Martin v. City of New York held the New York City local law which banned discrimination in private housing in New York City to be a constitutional exercise of government power. The basis for this holding is that the state may interfere "with his property rights in his business" and encroach "on free enterprise or the rights of private property" because "the individual must yield to what legislative authority deems is for the common good." What is that "common good?" In a nutshell, it is: "It is now believed that many of our problems arising from the diverse nature of our population will be brought nearer solution by integration." The justification for curtailment of our most sacred rights of property, free enterprise, and freedom of choice and association is integration as a solution to intergroup relations.

The problem with the solution is that, assuming the desirability of the end, the means are utterly foreign to American constitutional principles. Two United States Supreme Court decisions point this out clearly. The first one, *Meyer v. Nebraska*,[1] arose shortly after the First World War. A massive wave of immigrants came to the United States from Europe between 1880 and 1914. Nebraska and twenty-one other states passed laws restricting the teaching of foreign languages, since language instruction was one of the traditional mainstays of minority perpetuation in Europe.[2] The Attorney General of Nebraska argued in support of the law:

> The object of this legislation . . . was to create an enlightened American citizenship in sympathy with the principles and ideals of this country, and to prevent children reared in America from being trained and educated in foreign languages and foreign ideals before they have had an opportunity to learn the English language and observe American ideals.[3]

Without even reaching the question as to whether the perpetuation of subcultural patterns was socially desirable, the Supreme Court struck down the statutes as an undue infringement on liberty and in effect held that freedom to choose to perpetuate

---

1 262 U.S. 390 (1923).
2 Cf. Matter of Catalonian Nationalist Club, 112 Misc. 297, 184 N.Y.S. 732 (1920).
3 262 U.S. at 394.

the values had constitutional protection, regardless of the desirability of the choice. The Court held:

> It is also affirmed that the foreign-born population is very large,
> that certain communities commonly use foreign words, follow
> foreign leaders, move in a foreign atmosphere, and that the chil-
> dren are thereby hindered from becoming citizens of the most
> useful type, and the public safety is imperiled.
>
> That the state may do much, go very far, indeed, in order to
> improve the quality of its citizens, physically, mentally, and mor-
> ally, is clear; but the individual has certain fundamental rights
> which must be respected. . . . Perhaps it would be highly advan-
> tageous if all had ready understanding of our ordinary speech,
> but this cannot be coerced by methods which conflict with the
> Constitution—a desirable end cannot be promoted by prohibited
> means.
>
> . . . .
>
> In order to submerge the individual and develop ideal citizens,
> Sparta assembled the males at seven into barracks and intrusted
> their subsequent education and training to official guardians. Al-
> though such measures have been deliberately approved by men of
> great genius, their ideas touching the relation between individual
> and state were wholly different from those upon which our insti-
> tutions rest; and it hardly will be affirmed that any legislature
> could impose such restrictions upon the people of a state without
> doing violence to both letter and spirit of the Constitution.
>
> The desire of the legislature to foster a homogeneous people
> with American ideals . . . is easy to appreciate. . . . But the means
> adopted . . . exceed the limitations upon the power of the state,
> and conflict with rights assured to plaintiff in error.[4]

In *Pierce v. Society of Sisters*,[5] the issue was even more sharply
drawn. When the State of Oregon passed a law requiring all children to attend public school during some part of the day, its governor also used the melting pot argument to sustain the state's
restriction of private and parochial schools. He declared:

> The voters of Oregon might have felt that the mingling together
> during a portion of their education, of the children of all races
> and sects, might be the best safeguard against future internal dis-
> sentions and consequent weakening of the community against
> foreign dangers.[6]

A unanimous Supreme Court, including Justices Holmes and
Brandeis, struck down this statute as an infringement on individual liberty, here again without feeling the necessity of going into

4 *Id.* at 401-2.
5 268 U.S. 510 (1925).
6 *Id.* at 525.

the desirability of perpetuating a particular religious or cultural
point of view. The Court said:

> The fundamental theory of liberty upon which all governments
> in this Union repose excludes any general power of the state to
> standardize its children by forcing them to accept instruction from
> public teachers only. The child is not the mere creature of the
> state. . . .[7]

Lest it be thought that this case turned on freedom of religion, it is clear that the co-appellee Hill Military Academy was
not engaged in propagating any religion at all. Moreover, Roman
Catholics in Oregon were still free to attend their own church
and send their children to religious school after secular education
was over for the day. Rather, the law was designed to prevent
educational segregation of children on the basis of religion, economic class, or ancestry, by their parents. The Supreme Court's
decision upholding the right of parents to segregate their children
to instill in them their group subcultural values is a significant
limitation on the *Martin* theory.

The fallacy of *Martin* from a constitutional point of view is
that it assumes, contrary to *Pierce*, that human beings are mere
creatures of the State and may be subjected to government-imposed
experiences of intergroup living if the State deems this best for
public welfare and harmony regardless of their own wishes. The
rationale of anti-discrimination legislation as expressed in the
opinion is that individuals can be subjected to experiences or
persons or ideas so as to change their thinking or outlook on life
regardless of their own free will if government so requires. Such
a philosophy of "community brainwashing" is by no means unknown in modern history. The judicial organs of National Socialist Germany frequently expressed this point of view.[8] In the
United States, where government exists for the individual, and

---

[7] *Id.* at 535.

[8] In Gardner, *Liberty, the State, and the School*, 20 Law and Cont. Prob. 184, 190-1
(1955), there is reprinted in n.19 a decision of the District Court, Waldenburg, Silesia,
Germany, rendered November 2, 1937, entitled "Parents Who Use Their Educational
Influence on Their Children in Such a Manner as to Bring These Children into Open
Conflict with the National Socialist Idea of Community Abuse Their Right of Guard-
ianship." This decision, reported in *Deutsche Justiz* (Official Gazette of the German
Administration of Law, Bulletin of the Department of Justice), Ausgabe A, No. 47,
p. 1857, Berlin, Nov. 26, 1937, reads in pertinent part as follows:

The parents of the children belong to the sect of International Bible Students. Like
all Bible Students, this sect is concerned not only with purely religious matters but also
deduce from their religious premises the necessity to deny the simplest and most self-

not the converse, a doctrine that government may subject individuals to compulsory association has an alien ring. The *Martin* rationale denied the whole fabric of our fundamental constitutional assumptions, and is therefore inconsistent with due process of law in its most basic sense.

EDWARD P. SCHARFENBERGER[*]

evident duties towards the State and the German people. Obstinately they refuse, even on solemn occasions, to take part in the German salute, and by doing so express their disagreement with the principles upon which the new German state rests. Purposely they put themselves outside the German community. The father admits openly that even in case of war he would refuse to take up arms. The philosophy which the parents espouse is inimical to the will to resist by armed force, and, therefore, capable of impairing the foundations of the State.

This conviction of the parents is also transmitted to the children. Of course, the parents have denied this during the hearing; they have declared that they did not influence the children's general view of life. But such an attitude, as encouraged by the Bible Societies, dominates the whole of life. It is a matter of practical experience that such a philosophy of life, expressing itself daily in the narrow family circle, influences the children, even though it is not put in express words. Indubitable evidence has also been introduced to prove that in this case such active influence actually exists. The father, when admonished by the court, had to admit that he had already been penalized for not sending his children to National Socialist festivals. The father, in this connection, also made the plausible statement that his children did not care for such meetings, and that they themselves had expressed the desire to be excused from going. This statement only goes to prove the strength of the influence which actually originates from the parents; and, furthermore, the degree to which the children have already succumbed to such influence.

This statement of fact compels us to the following juristic considerations:

If parents through their own example teach their children a philosophy of life which puts them into an irreconcilable opposition to those ideas to which the overwhelming majority of the German people adheres, then this constitutes an abuse of the right of guardianship as expressed in Par. 1666 of the Civil Code. This abuse of the power of guardianship endangers to the highest degree the welfare of the children, inasmuch as it ultimately leads to a state of mind through which the children will some day find that they have cut themselves off from the rest of the German people. To avert such danger the Guardianship Court has to take the necessary steps according to Par. 1666 of the Civil Code. A permanent remedy in this respect can only be found if the right of guardianship over the person is withdrawn from the parents, because only through such withdrawal can we be sure that the evil educational influence of the parents is eliminated and broken.

In accordance with the opinion of the Guardianship Court, the following must be admitted: the law, as a National Socialist form of State order, entrusts German parents with the right to educate only on condition that this right is exercised in a manner which the people and the State have a right to expect—a condition which is not specifically expressed by the law but which must be considered as something self-evident. Here in particular we have to remember that all education must have as its ideal aim the creation of the belief and conviction in children that they are brothers forming a great nation; that they are molded into the great union of the German people together with all other German comrades through the sameness of their fundamental ideas. Whoever in the exercise of a purely formal right to educate his children evokes in those children views which must bring them ultimately into conflict with the German community ideal does not comply with those self-evident presuppositions. Therefore, out of purely general considerations the right to educate must be denied to such a person without the necessity of having to refer to the implicit presuppositions of Par. 1666 of the Civil Code.

[*] LL.B. 1954, Brooklyn Law School. Member of the New York Bar. Copyright 1963 by Edward P. Scharfenberger.

PROHIBITION AND ANTI-DISCRIMINATION LEGIS-LATION IN HOUSING—THE MORAL AND PSEUDO-SCIENTIFIC APPROACH IN LEGAL THINKING

I. *Introduction*

There is no question that discrimination in housing has become a major civil rights issue throughout the nation. In discussing the issue of anti-discrimination legislation in housing, much has been said which sounds strikingly similar to discussions about prohibition of liquor. This comment will compare thinking in legal materials related to legislation against discrimination in housing with the similar thinking in connection with prohibition legislation. The purpose of this analogy is to discover whether the same type of thinking pervades both areas.

Generally, most social legislation is based on economic principles. For example, unemployment compensation is based on the need of the unemployed wage-earner for public support.[1] Likewise, low-rent public housing is based on the inability of the tenants to pay the going market rental for housing.[2] In each of these cases scientifically objective economic data leads to the conclusion that the need for the measure involved exists.

There have been instances, however, where legislation was passed which was based primarily on moral and pseudo-scientific concepts. Prohibition appears to be an example of such an attempt to legislate morality. Throughout the prohibition era, glittering generalities were used to provide reasons for prohibition legislation. Such bold statements as prohibition prevents crime, disease, slums, and economic depression were used in support of this legislation. It appears that some of the same pseudo-social scientific type of thinking is presently being used to justify anti-discrimination legislation in housing. A similarity in moral declarations can also be found. This article will make a comparison between thinking in the two areas illustrating this fact.

II. *Legislative Materials*

In comparing the legal thinking behind prohibition and anti-discrimination legislation, resort may be had to both legislative history and statutory preambles. Anti-discrimination legislation is so new that only several states have enacted it. For them, legislative history in the form of printed debates is lacking, and preambles or statements of purpose must be resorted to. The basic patterns of thinking about prohibition, however, are reflected in national legislation and hence in legislative debates which are extant.

---

[1] Stewart Machine Co. v. Davis, 301 U.S. 548 (1937).
[2] Allydonn Realty Corp. v. Holyoke Housing Authy., 304 Mass. 288, 23 N.E. 665 (1937).

The culmination of the prohibition drive in America, which had its roots long before the turn of the twentieth century,[3] was the Eighteenth Amendment, ratified in 1919. An examination of the Congressional Record reveals two underlying concepts for the basis for the proposed amendment. These concepts are: (1) to maintain the strength of the nation by elimination of crime, disease, vice and poverty, (2) to retard the growth of an evil which morally effects the individual and society as a whole.

The argument that enactment of prohibition would cure crime, disease, and poverty was much urged during the debates on the adoption of the Eighteenth Amendment. The following generalized statement by Congressman Edwin Y. Webb of North Carolina illustrates this position well:

> Government is but the organized forces of the nation formed for strengthening its power and advancing its life. Its highest aim is to suppress those agencies which have a tendency to sap and weaken the nation's strength, to suppress vice and crime in order that the nation may, unrestrained by these evils, go forward in its efforts for greater liberty, freedom and achievement; that it may raise itself into a higher civilization more nearly approaching our ideal of a perfect government.
>
> The use of intoxicating liquor for beverage purposes has long attracted the attention of our leading statesmen, and with great unanimity has been condemned as one of the greatest agencies for evil and crime that is now retarding our national growth.[4]

During the debates in the House of Representatives, other Congressmen expressed similar sentiments.[5] To the argument that people were entitled to drink, members answered that people should not be permitted to pursue "a course that leads to poverty, weakness, and disease."[6] In refuting the argument that prohibition would restrict personal freedom, Representative Addison T. Smith of Arkansas declared:

> Under ordinary conditions, those engaged in the liquor traffic make no apology for their business, but when cornered they fall back upon the stale arguments of "personal liberty" and the alleged right of the individual to do as he pleases. This argument is

---

[3] 12 Encyclopedia of The Social Sciences 500 (1934).

[4] 56 Cong. Rec. 426 (1917). He also said: "The use of alcoholic liquors for beverage purposes has long been regarded as a great national evil, which physically, mentally, and morally unfits man for his greatest usefullness." *Id*. at 427.

[5] *Id*. at 442. Congressman Richard W. Austin of Texas, for example, declared: "A law which has emptied the jails in Tennessee and virtually wiped out the criminal side of the dockets of the courts will do the same thing in every State in the American Union. King Alcohol has filled the world already with enough misery, with enough murders, with enough insane people, with enough unhappy wives and unfortunate children."

[6] *Id*. at 441 (Cong. William J. Graham of Illinois). Congressman M. Clyde Kelly of Penn. said: "They have weighed the arguments of blear-eyed defenders of personal liberty and have decided that the personal liberty which means wrecked lives, destruction of property, disease, crime, and degeneracy is a menace to the public welfare and should be outlawed." *Id*. at 437.

so absurd that it is scarcely worth answering. The first law of society is that individuals shall not be permitted to do that which, although considered beneficial to themselves, may be injurious to others or to the community at large.[7]

Thereafter, upon listing traditional examples of the use of the police power, he concluded:

> Why, then, should there be any reluctance in restricting the sale of alcoholic liquors when their baneful effects on health and life are acknowledged by every disinterested person. We legislate to prevent the spread of poverty, crime, and disease. The use of intoxicating liquors produce all of these, and are we not justified in legislating to prevent the progress of its devastating influence?[8]

A third example of the same sort of generalizations likewise comes from an Arkansas Congressman. In supporting passage of the amendment he told the House:

> Who are for whiskey? Those who make fortunes out of it. Who are against it? The mothers of the land, because it destroys their loved ones. The ministers, because liquor undoes what they do. The officers of the law, because alcohol is the unapproachable chief of all causes of crime. The doctors advise against it because there is no more potent source of disease. The judges are against it because of its appalling record of misery, pauperism and crime. Statesmen are against it because it is a menace to stable government. Educators are against it because it is a grim threat to every child in the land.[9]

In the Senate the amendment was supported on the same grounds. For example, Senator Beckham of Kentucky declared:

> It has been shown by overwhelming evidence that when so used even in moderate quantities, it is a positive injury to the human system. It weakens the body, it blurs the mind, it invites disease and it destroys the soul of man. It produces more pauperism, more crime, more sorrow than all other causes combined.[10]

In addition to the elimination of the evils mentioned above, moral precepts were urged as a reason for enacting prohibition. For example, Congress-

---

7 *Id.* at 442. He also said: "I am sure that there is not a Member on this floor, be he for or against this resolution, who does not admit to himself that the liquor traffic is and always has been the cause of a large proportion of the crime, poverty, and inefficiency throughout the land."

8 *Ibid.* See also *id.* at 462.

9 *Id.* at 451, Cong. John N. Tillman. See also the statement of Cong. Thaddeus H. Caraway of Arkansas, at p. 431, that "Vice, poverty, and ignorance are its handmaids, and these will curse the world as long as we permit the manufacture and sale of intoxicating liquors."

10 55 Cong. Rec. 5653 (1917). See also the statement of Senator John F. Shafroth of Colorado at page 5657: "The U.S. census report shows that the number of crimes committed in prohibition States is far less than in the States where liquor is sold. It is the saloon that attracts the criminal, and it is the saloon that lures so many of the young men of our country to their destruction."

man Alben W. Barkley of Kentucky, later to be Vice President of the United States under President Truman, declared:

> We know that the manufacture and sale of intoxicating liquors have been responsible for more things that degrade and debase humanity than any other cause, and we might with equal truth say than all other causes combined . . . , that it dissipates the mental vigor of our race, that it warps, debauches, and finally destroys the moral perceptions of those who are its devotees.[11]

Concurring with this point of view, Representative M. Clyde Kelly of Pennsylvania likewise urged the House to adopt the amendment for moral reasons. He said:

> The adoption of this amendment today will be a pledge of moral progress to the world. . . . It will show that this House dares to meet a great moral, social, and economic problem involving a mighty financial interest and that it trusts the people with the solution.[12]

Probably the best illustration of the fact that prohibition was motivated, at least in large part, by the then current concepts of morality, is the fact that opponents of the measure urged the House of Representatives not to attempt to legislate morality on the ground that this would be both illegal and unworkable.[13] In reply to this, the successful proponents of the measure declared that, having failed to obtain temperance by persuasion they were now justified in passing legislation.[14] The Senate was likewise told that, "Liquor traffic is an evil . . . from the moral point of view."[15] "Hu-

---

[11] 56 Cong. Rec. 459 (1917). He also said at page 458: "But no man who is jealous of his reputation for moral or intellectual integrity will any longer attempt to defend or justify the continuance of the saloon or the liquor traffic in this Nation upon any ground of principle, either moral, social, or political."

[12] *Id.* at 438. See also the statement of Representative Edwin Y. Webb of North Carolina, at p. 427, as follows: "The religious world has found that [liquor] undermines the morals of the Nation. The business world has found that it weakens the intellect. . . . The courts of the country find it the cause of crime and justify this conclusion by the records of their criminal courts."

[13] See for example the statement of Congressman George S. Graham of Penn., who told the House: "You may say this is a moral question, and I will grant you for the sake of argument . . . but you have no right to legislate in behalf of the accomplishment of a moral reform by adopting illegal measures to accomplish your purpose. When men become fanatical in any movement they become unreasonable. Men have been known to try to make others religious by violence, by the sword and the flame." *Id.* at 464.

[14] Rep. Webb said: "Opponents of the prohibition cause tell us our fight is all wrong; that it is a moral issue and we should appeal to the individual to restrain himself. . . . We have already tried moral suasion. Godly men for all these years have preached temperance to the people . . . but they still find that their weaker wards stumble on their journey through life and succumb to this frailty of humanity when faced by the alluring invitation of an open bar room. . . . Since we have not been successful in keeping our weaker brother from whisky, let us try keeping whisky from our weaker brother." *Id.* at 427.

[15] 55 Cong. Rec. 5646 (1917). (Sen. Thomas Sterling, S.D.).

manity, decency, good government and civilization demand prohibition," a Senator said during the debates.[16]

The prevailing feeling that prohibition was an enactment of morality was used to justify the denial of property rights implicit therein. As one Senator declared:

> Let the rights of property be considered more sacred than the rights of humanity, if you will, but in this great day of struggle let us at once rise to the level where moral sacrifices are made.[17]

When we turn to anti-discrimination legislation, we find very similar statements in legislative declarations. For example, the preamble to the first anti-discrimination ordinance affecting private housing, passed in 1957 in New York City, declared:

> In the City of New York, with its great cosmopolitan population consisting of large numbers of people of every race, color, religion, national origin and ancestry, many persons have been compelled to live in circumscribed sections under substandard, unhealthful, unsanitary and crowded living conditions because of discrimination in housing. These conditions have caused increased mortality, morbidity, delinquency, risk of fire, intergroup tension, loss of tax revenue and other evils. As a result, the peace, health, safety and general welfare of the city and all its inhabitants are threatened.[18]

To the same effect, a statement found in a Pennsylvania statute forbidding discrimination in housing informs the reader:

> The practice or policy of discrimination against individuals or groups by reason of their race, color, religious creed, ancestry, age, or national origin . . . foments domestic strife and unrest, threatens the rights and privileges of the inhabitants of the Commonwealth, and undermines the foundations of a free democratic state. . . . [Discrimination in housing] compels many individuals to live in dwellings which are substandard, unhealthful and overcrowded, resulting in . . . juvenile delinquency and other evils, thereby threatening the peace, health, safety and general welfare of the Commonwealth and its inhabitants.[19]

A county ordinance in Maryland lists an equally sweeping group of

---

16 *Id.* at 5588 (Sen. Wesley L. Jones, Wash.). Sen. Beckham declared: "No one can now stand before an intelligent audience and defend the existence of the saloon. . . . Prohibition is not only a moral but also an economic blessing to any State that adopts it." *Id.* at 5654. And a leading advocate of prohibition, Sen. William S. Kenyon, of Iowa, proclaimed at p. 5639: "the American saloon has no conscience. It never did a good act or failed to do a bad one."

17 *Id.* at 5646 (Sen. Lawrence Y. Sherman, Ill.). He also said: "Drunkenness is the monarch of all human vices. Other evils are its mere satellites."

18 5 New York City Code & Charter, § W41-1.0 (Supp. 1960).

19 43 Purdon's Pa. Stat. Ann., § 952. See also Deering's Calif. Code, Labor, § 1141 (discrimination "foments domestic strife and unrest"); 5 R.I. Stat., § 28-5-2 (same); Wisc. Stat. Ann., § 111.31 (same); Smith-Hurd Ill. Ann. Stat., § 851 (discrimination causes "conflicts and controversies resulting in grave injury to the public safety, health and welfare").

evils caused by discrimination. Its preamble states: "the practice of discrimination . . . causes breaches of the peace, intensifies conflicts between groups and individuals, threatens the peace and good order of the County, . . . subjects many County inhabitants to indignities, hardships, and deprivations which are detrimental to their physical and mental health, increases juvenile delinquency, . . . reduce[s] the revenues and increase[s] the costs of the County government . . . , undermines the foundations of a free and democratic County . . . and whereas substantial numbers of foreign persons visit Montgomery County . . . and such discriminatory practices against such persons have in the past and may in the future adversely affect the relationship of the United States with other nations of the world."[20]

In addition to sweeping findings of a social science nature made in anti-discrimination legislation, unmistakable moralizing has found its way into these statutes. For example, a number of laws declare that "discrimination threatens not only the rights and proper privileges of its inhabitants but menaces the institutions and foundations of a free democratic state."[21] The Virgin Islands goes further, saying:

> Whereas it is the cultural and democratic heritage of the people of the Virgin Islands to respect the human and civil rights of all people and to judge all persons according to their individual merit without reference to race, creed, color, or national origin; and to cherish the racial equality, harmony, and goodwill that exists in the Virgin Islands; and

> Whereas racial discrimination, segregation, and other forms of bias and bigotry are not part of the way of life of the people of the Virgin Islands.[22]

Likewise, Indiana talks of discrimination's "incompatibility with American

---

[20] Ordinance 2-120, Montgomery Co., Md., 7 R.R.L.R. 263 (1962). Ordinance 615, § 1, City of Braddock, Pa., approval May 3, 1955, 1 R.R.L.R. 742 (1955), declares that discrimination "unjustly condemns large groups of this Borough to depressed living conditions which breed crime and vice, juvenile delinquency and disease, thereby causing great injury to the public safety, public health, and general welfare of this Borough." The same declaration is found in Ordinance 237, Pittsburgh, Pa., 4 R.R.L.R. 195 (1958). Moreover, this ordinance says that discrimination compels people "to live in circumscribed, unhealthy, unsafe, unsanitary and overcrowded living conditions . . . [which cause] increased mortality, disease, crime, vice, and juvenile delinquency." See also F.E.L., St. Paul, Minn., 2 R.R.L.R. 702 (1957); F.E.P.L. Bakersfield, Calif., 2 R.R.L.R. 1026 (1957). The 1959 U.S. Com. on Civ. Rts. Rept., p. 4, likewise declared that the results of discrimination were "high rates of crime, fire, juvenile delinquency, crime and social demoralization among those forced to live in such conditions."

[21] Kans. Gen. Stat., § 44-1001; Minn. Stat. Ann. § 363.12; N.J. S.A., § 18:25-3; N.Y. Executive Law, § 290; Ore. Rev. Stat., § 659.020; R.I. Stat. § 28-5-2; Wash. Rev. Code, § 49.60.010; 10 Virgin Is. Code, § 1.

[22] 10 Virgin Is. Code, § 1. See also Statement of N.Y.C. Bd. of Ed., Aug. 31, 1960, 5 R.R.L.R. 911 (1960): "This has been a natural consequence of the morality of our American heritage and of our Judeo-Christian tradition. In the process each group not only itself benefited from this blending but also has contributed to the enrichment of our culture and the growth of our country."

principles of equality and fair play, and violation of the brotherhood of man,"[23] while a New York State Code of Fair Practices justifies banning discrimination because "our spiritual heritage proclaims the supreme worth of the individual."[24]

From a comparison of the legislative materials set forth here, it can be seen that much of the legislative thinking which culminated in prohibition legislation is used in anti-discrimination legislation. Some of the phraseology is strikingly similar. This indicates that legislators have approached both subjects with the same sort of moralistic and pseudo-scientific ideas in mind.

III. *Case Analysis*

In analyzing those cases dealing with the liquor traffic, once again one finds that regulations are justified on the twin grounds of prevention of crime, disease, poverty, and sundry social evils, and the promotion of morality. Sweeping language runs like a dominant thread throughout all of these decisions from the earliest reports.

For example, in the *License Cases*,[25] Chief Justice Taney indicated that liquor was "calculated to produce idleness, vice, or debauchery,"[26] while Justice McLean referred to it as a "vicious indulgence."[27] Justice Woodbury noted that laws restricting the sale of liquor "reduce family expenditures, secure health, lessen pauperism and crime."[28] Justice Grier declared liquor "to be pernicious in its effects, and the cause of disease, pauperism, and crime,"[29] and furthermore asserted that "misery, pauperism, and crime . . . have their origin in the use or abuse of ardent spirits," a diminished consumption of which would make a state "the gainer a thousandfold in the health, wealth, and happiness of the people."[30]

Likewise, speaking for the court in *Mugler v. Kansas*,[31] Justice Harlan declared: "we cannot shut out of view the fact, within the knowledge of all, that the public health, the public morals, and the public safety, may be endangered by the general use of intoxicating drinks; nor the fact, established by statistics accessible to everyone, that the idleness, disorder, pauperism, and crime existing in the country are, in some degree at least, traceable to this evil."[32] Justice Gray, in a dissent in *Leisy v. Hardin*,[33]

---

23 Ind. Laws of 1961, Ch. 208, § 7.
24 5 R.R.L.R. 932 (1960).
25 46 U.S. (5 How.) 504 (1847).
26 *Id.* at 577.
27 *Id.* at 591.
28 *Id.* at 627
29 *Id.* at 631.
30 *Id.* at 632.
31 123 U.S. 623 (1887).
32 *Id.* at 662.
33 135 U.S. 100 (1890).

declared that "Common experience has shown that the general and unre-stricted use of intoxicating liquors tends to produce idleness, disorder, dis-ease, pauperism and crime."[34] Finally, in *Crowley v. Christensen*,[35] Justice Field, speaking for a unanimous United States Supreme Court, stated:

> By the general concurrence of opinion of every civilized and Chris-tian community, there are few sources of crime and misery to society equal to the dram shop, where intoxicating liquors, in small quantities, to be drunk at the time, are sold indiscriminately to all parties applying. The statistics of every state show a greater amount of crime and misery attributable to the use of ardent spirits obtained at these retail liquor saloons than to any other source.[36]

State courts likewise used sweeping language to justify prohibition legislation. The Illinois Supreme Court said that prohibition was a "means of ridding society of the demoralizing effects of drunkenness, and of the social and economic waste of an organized traffic producing insanity, pov-erty, and crime."[37] The Kansas Supreme Court declared that liquor is "the prolific source of disease, misery, pauperism, vice and crime."[38] In Maryland it was stated that control of the liquor traffic would "prevent intemperance, crime and pauperism, and the . . . disorders in society."[39] The Nebraska Supreme Court held that liquor was "productive of pauper-ism, vice, misery, and crime."[40] And a federal court characterized an in-toxicated individual as "a brute," and "a worthless excrescence."[41]

Prohibition of liquor was not only justified in case reports on the ground that this measure would sweep away social evils, but also because it would promote morality. Justice McLean referred to control of liquor traffic as a "great moral reform,"[42] and stated that "the state regulation has a salu-tary tendency on society, and is founded on the highest moral considera-tions."[43] Probably one of the best illustrations of the moral underpinnings of prohibition in legal thinking is found in a federal judge's charge in Georgia. He declared:

---

[34] *Id.* at 159. He also declared that prohibition was within a state's "undoubted power to protect its inhabitants against the evils, physical, moral and social, attending the free use of intoxicating liquors."

[35] 137 U.S. 86 (1890).

[36] *Id.* at 91.

[37] People v. Alfano, 322 Ill. 384, 153 N.E. 729, 730 (1926).

[38] State v. Durein, 70 Kans. 13, 80 Pac. 987, 989 (1905).

[39] Fell v. State, 42 Md. 71, 81 (1874).

[40] Pleuler v. State, 11 Nebr. 547, 10 N.W. 481, 488-9 (1881). See also State ex rel. Wilkinson v. Murphy, 237 Ala. 332, 186 So. 487, 496 (1939) (regulation of liquor "to protect the community from crime and the burdens of pauperism"); State v. Stucker, 58 Iowa 496, 12 N.W. 483 (1882) (prohibition prevents "intemperance, pauperism, and crime"); State v. Bixman, 162 Mo. 1, 62 S.W. 828, 832 (1901) (same); Longmire v. State, 75 Tex. Cri. R. 616, 171 S.W. 1165, 1167 (1914) ("prevention of crime").

[41] Weil v. Calhoun, 25 Fed. 865, 874 (N.D. Ga. 1885).

[42] License Cases, 46 U.S. (5 How.) 504, 588-9 (1847).

[43] *Id.* at 591.

I have not discussed the moral phases of this great question, but merely those which seem to be legal and political. If the laws which the people of our state have enacted are enforced, the chief happiness to inure to those we love is the consciousness that henceforth, if we expel the demon of the still from our borders, confidence and peace will reassume their place in happy homes among those dear objects of our love, dearer to us "than are the ruddy drops that visit our hearts." Once there was within my own memory no such thing in all the borders of this Southland as that unspeakable crime, the bare mention of which will stir a fever in the blood of age, and make the infant's sinews strong as steel. It will disappear from our civilization when the brain of the docile African, even of the lowest order, is no longer infuriated and rendered careless or desperate of consequences by the drink he absorbs. In his furtive wanderings on the lonely roads, or in his solitary lair in the forest, the poisonous cardiac stimulant drives the blood of the savage in swift pulsations to his compressed or maddened brain, and then—no matter how desperate the chance or certain of detection—the crime is committed. This it is which has ranked the people of Georgia, save perhaps in one or two great cosmopolitan cities, in the serried ranks of those who have determined that the sale and furnishing of liquor shall stop within our borders. The politicians did not do it. They framed a platform for local option. The representatives of the people stamped the planks of this platform into nothingness. It is a revolution, and it will not stop with Georgia, nor do I believe it will stop with the South. Even now the senior senator of this state has invoked the powerful aid of Congress to fulfill the purpose of this people. Lives will become irradiant by its presence. Gentle woman reassumes her rightful station as a regnant queen. The prayers of good men in great cities, amid the dim religious light of great churches, are heard that it may prosper. And in country churches, in the shades of gigantic oaks, or amid the sighing pines, the prayers and the song worship of the simple, earnest servants of the oldtime religion, as they roll away amid the aisles of the forest, are a thank-offering of a long suffering and a sorely troubled people that strong drink has been forever banished from our state.

I have confidence, gentlemen, that you, who are selected from the thoughtful, the conscientious, the reflecting, the home-loving, the God-fearing, the patriotic people of Georgia, will give such consideration to this great topic as will advance the cause of temperance, justice, right, and home.[44]

Cases dealing with anti-discrimination and related topics display a strikingly similar parade of glittering generalities. Here again, one finds an all-encompassing collection of evils which the statute will cure, and undertones of moralistic fervor which occasionally break through to the surface.

Pseudo-social scientific findings abound in sweeping terms. One case tells us:

Discrimination against Negroes in the sale and rental of housing accommodations results in inadequate housing for them and in

[44] In re Charge to Grand Jury, 162 Fed. 736, 741 (S.D. Ga. 1908).

segregation in housing. They are thus compelled in large numbers to live in circumscribed areas under substandard, unhealthy, unsanitary and crowded living conditions. These conditions in turn produce disease, increased mortality, unstable family life, moral laxity, crime, delinquency, risk of fire, loss of tax revenue and intergroup tensions. Standards of sanitation have to be sacrificed because strict enforcement of building and health codes will simply make a great many people homeless. All these things imperil the tranquillity of a community.[45]

The California Supreme Court has announced: "Discrimination in housing leads to lack of adequate housing for minority groups and inadequate housing conditions contribute to disease, crimes, and immorality."[46] And on a very different level, *Martin v. City of New York*,[47] declared that: "It is now believed that many of our problems arising from the diverse nature of our population will be brought nearer a solution by integration."[48]

Moralistic structures are equally broad. We are told that integration is "a lesson in democracy,"[49] that non-discrimination is "a civil right basic to human dignity,"[50] that opponents of integration are "fickle to our democratic way of life,"[51] and that such discrimination is "unreasoned prejudice."[52] One judge declared:

[45] Jones v. Haridor Realty Corp., 37 N.J. 384, 181 A.2d 481, 485 (1962). In Levitt & Sons v. Division Against Discrimination, 31 N.J. 514, 158 A.2d 177, 186 (1960), the court said; "There is ample support for a conclusion that lack of adequate housing for minority groups, an effect of discrimination, causes crime and disease-breeding slums."

[46] Burks v. Poppy Const. Co., 57 A.C. 503, 20 Cal. Rept. 609, 370 P.2d 313, 317 (1962). In Massachusetts Commission Against Discrimination v. Colangelo, 182 N.E.2d 595, 599-600 (Mass., 1961), the court stated: "Discrimination in multiple dwellings and contiguously located housing might tend to restrict Negroes to a relatively small area and perhaps to encourage slum conditions through density of population." And in O'Meara v. Washington State Board Against Discrimination. 58 Wash. 2d 793, 796, 365 P.2d 1, 3 (1961), the court quoted a lower court judge's observations that the effects of discrimination in housing, "in terms of social, economic, and psychological damage to the community, are well known. Segregated housing, in particular, is linked intimately with substandard, unhealthy, unsafe living conditions with resultant fire and health hazards. It undoubtedly contributes to instability in family life, moral laxity, and delinquency."

[47] 22 Misc. 2d 389, 201 N.Y.S.2d 111 (1960).

[48] *Id.* at 391, 201 N.Y.S.2d at 112.

[49] Taylor v. Board of Education, 191 F. Supp. 181, 187 (S.D.N.Y. 1961). See also Ming v. Horgan, 3 R.R.L.R. 693, 697 (Super. Ct. Sacramento Co., Calif., 1958) ("when one dips one's hand into the Federal Treasury, a little democracy necessarily clings to whatever is withdrawn").

[50] Williams v. Hot Shoppes, 110 U.S. App. D.C. 358, 293 F.2d 835, 847 (1961). See also City of Highland Park v. F.E.P.C., 364 Mich. 508, 111 N.W. 797, 800 (1961): "It is an effort to transpose into law that cherished portion of the American dream which is referred to in the pregnant phrase 'equality of opportunity.'"

[51] Evans v. Ennis, 281 F.2d 385, 389 (3d Cir., 1960).

[52] City of Highland Park v. F.E.P.C., 5 R.R.L.R. 1125, 47 L.R.R.M. 2044 (1960). In Swanson v. Commission on Civil Rights, 6 R.R.L.R. 841, 842 (Conn. Super. Ct., 1961), the court said that an anti-discrimination law in housing would "help eradicate bias." And Justice Frankfurter, in Railway Mail Assn. v. Corsi, 326 U.S. 88, 98 (1944), said that "a State may choose to put its authority behind one of the cherished aims of

I cannot believe that a man's mortal remains will disintegrate any less peaceably because of the close proximity of the body of a member of another race, and in that inevitable disintegration I am sure that the pigmentation of the skin cannot long endure. It strikes me that the carrying of racial discrimination into the burial grounds is a particularly stupid form of human arrogance and intolerance. If life does not do so, the universal fellowship of death should teach humility. The good people who insist on the racial segregation of what is mortal in man may be shocked to learn when their own lives end that God has reserved no racially exclusive position for them in the hereafter.[53]

A leading example of moralizing is found in *New York State Commission Against Discrimination v. Pelham Hall Apts.*,[54] the earliest decision concerning an anti-discrimination law in housing. Here the court said:

[W]e, as a people do hold firmly to the philosophy that all men are created equal. Indeed, discrimination against any individual here on account of race, color or religion is antagonistic to fundamental tenets of our form of government and of the God in whom we place our trust.[55]

In a more recent case, a court declared:

The practice of discrimination is utterly inconsistent with the political philosophy upon which our institutions are based and with the moral principles which we inherit from our Judeo-Christian traditions. . . . It can and must be eliminated . . . in order that the majority may be brought to act in a manner consistent with the principles which they profess.[56]

Thus it can be seen that cases involving both prohibition and anti-discrimination legislation both use sweeping social science conclusions and strong moralistic strictures. In some cases, the language is strikingly sim-

American feeling by forbidding indulgence in racial or religious prejudice to another's hurt."

53 Long v. Mountain View Cemetery Assn., 130 Cal. App. 2d 328, 330, 278 P.2d 945, 946 (1955), quoted with approval in Erickson v. Sunset Memorial Park Assn., 259 Minn. 532, 108 N.W.2d 434, 436 (1961). See also Progress Development Corp. v. Mitchell, 182 F. Supp. 681, 706 (N.D. Ill., 1960) mod. on oth. gr., 286 F.2d 222 (7th Cir. 1961) ("The attitude of some of the Village residents was deplorable. . . . Fear gripped the community and fear is the very base and foundation of hate and intolerance"). And Justice Musmanno, in his dissent in In Re Girard's Estate, 386 Pa. 548, 127 A.2d 287, 330 (1956), said: "The Majority Opinion quotes over and over the line which is slightly revolting to me that a man's prejudices are a part of his liberty. From a philosophical point of view I would say that a prejudiced person may have the right to hurt himself through the indulgence of his prejudices, but he has no right to affect the liberty of others."

54 10 Misc. 2d 334, 170 N.Y.S.2d 750 (1958).

55 *Id.* at 757. In a Statement on Grosse Point, the Attorney General of Michigan said: "I condemned this system [of discrimination] as being morally corrupt," and "the system is wholly immoral." 5 R.R.L.R. 567 (1960).

56 O'Meara v. Washington State Board Against Discrimination, supra n.46. See also City of St. Paul v. F.W. Woolworth Co., 2 R.R.L.R. 626 (Mun. Ct., St. Paul, Minn., 1956) ("since we may legislate on morals").

ilar, as if the same subject were being discussed. Here again, therefore, evidence of similar thinking is apparent.

IV. *Legal Writers*

In turning to legal writers in textbooks and periodicals, we find that the pattern set out above is duplicated. Once again, broad social science findings and moral preachments abound in the literature on both prohibition and anti-discrimination legislation. Even the most eminent legal writers justified prohibition as a means "for the prevention of intemperance, pauperism, and crime."[57] Sweeping declarations were made as to the drastic diminution of crime which would follow the enactment of laws regulating or stopping the liquor traffic.[58] Even Booker T. Washington was pressed into the fray to prove that Negro crime would be reduced by prohibition.[59] As one writer declared:

> [W]ise judicial thought has largely established the truth that a business whose chief progeny is pauperism and crime, and whose inevitable tendency is to unfit its victims for domestic and civic usefulness, is not entitled to the beneficence of constitutional provisions designed by the founders of government for the protection of legitimate property and wholesome liberty.[60]

Moreover, it was admitted that prohibition constituted the "power to impose upon the minority the sentiments or prejudices of the majority of the community, as to what is morally right or good."[61] The control of liquor traffic "is a question of public expediency and public morality,"[62] one writer declared, adding:

> It is an intolerable incongruity that a thing which unmistakably results in the poisoning of the very fountains of government should flourish under the protection of that which it would destroy.[63]

In turning to legal writing on anti-discrimination legislation in housing, the same species of sweeping social science declarations are to be found. One article informs us that "there is no need at this late date to spell out or prove the existence of a relationship between racial and religious discrimination in housing and the existence of a whole train of serious social evils, slums, crimes, juvenile delinquency, health dangers, etc., which flow from such discrimination."[64] Another writer stated:

[57] Cooley, *Constitutional Limitations* 718 (6th ed. 1890); Freund, *Police Power* § 204, p. 193 (1904).

[58] Trickett, *The Era of Law Enforcement*, 40 Chi. L.N. 141, 145-6 (1907); Note, 128 L.T. 555 (1909).

[59] Washington, *Negro Crime and Strong Drink*, 3 J. Cri. L. & Crim. 384 (1912).

[60] Slaymaker, *Governmental Control of the Liquor Traffic*, 56 Cent. L.J. 444, 445 (1903).

[61] Freund, *op. cit.* supra, n.57.

[62] Slaymaker, *op. cit.* supra, n.60, at 447.

[63] *Id.* at 445.

[64] Foster & Rabkin, *The Constitutionality of Laws Against Discrimination in Pub-*

[T]he minority groups excluded are confined to their ghettos providing the worst housing at the greatest cost with resultant hazards to the health and welfare of the persons excluded. . . . It is generally accepted that these areas are synonymous with areas of disease and ill health, crime and juvenile delinquency, personal, family and social disorganization.[65]

A recent article also declares:

The Negro who strives to live by the social and ethical standards of the majority must reside, nonetheless, in the neighborhood of poverty, filth and vice. . . The distortion of social values in the Negro neighborhood is manifest in higher crime rates, and in relatively greater expense to the community in required police, fire and health services.[66]

And it has been stated, to the same effect, that "these non-white minorities can find housing only in overcrowded slum areas and live under substandard conditions with the inevitable concomitant—a high incidence of delinquency, vice, crime, and disease."[67]

Ample moralizing can also be found. We are informed that anti-

licly-Assisted Housing, 6 N.Y.L.F. 38, 53 (1960). See also Abrams, *Discrimination and the Struggle for Shelter*, 6 N.Y.L.F. 3, 6 (1960): "[A] housing famine now confronted the newly in-migrating minorities in the cities. It was affecting their opportunities in life, their educational patterns, their aspirations, and their children's prospects."

65 Linder, *The Social Results of Segregation in Housing*, 18 Law. G. Rev. 2, 3 (1958). See also the model statute in 18 Law. G. Rev. 28 (1958), which contains the same statements. And note Van Alstyne & Karst, *State Action*, 14 Stan. L. Rev. 3, 47 (1961): "Standards of sanitation have to be sacrificed; if building codes are enforced strictly, a great many people will simply be without homes. Disease rates are notoriously higher under such circumstances than for the rest of the population. Crime and delinquency similarly rise."

66 Groner & Helfell, *Race Discrimination in Housing*, 57 Yale L.J. 426, 428-9 (1958). See also Scanlan, *Racial Restrictions in Real Estate-Property Values Versus Human Values*, 24 Notre Dame Law. 157, 159-160 (1949): "Many studies have demonstrated beyond cavil the menace to health, to morals, and to the general decency of cities, the plague spot for racial exploitations, frictions, and riots, the media for crime, juvenile delinquency and prostitution, and the proportionally greater expense to the community in required police, fire, and health services, which a policy of legalized ghetto housing has caused."

67 Saks & Rabkin, *Racial and Religious Discrimination In Housing: A Report of Legal Progress*, 45 Iowa L. Rev. 488, 491 (1959). There are several student notes to the same effect. See Note, 26 Ford. L. Rev. 675, 679 (1958); Note 28 Geo. Wash. L. Rev. 758 (1960) (discrimination causes "loss of taxable income to the cities, coupled with higher incidence of crime, illness, poverty, and juvenile delinquency"); Note, 107 U. Pa. L. Rev. 515, 526 (1959) (Anti-discrimination laws will "wage a frontal attack against slum areas, which are caused in part by the inability of great numbers of people to purchase or rent elsewhere"). In Note, 12 Rutgers L. Rev. 557, 566 (1958), a most expansive purpose of the statute if found, for we are told that anti-discrimination laws in housing will result in "the elimination of slum areas as a means of decreasing health, fire, and density problems and achieving an aesthetic improvement in physical facilities; the encouragement of depressed groups to develop themselves; the eradication of racial frictions resulting from ignorance and a paucity of inter-group contact; the cure and avoidance of the psychological problems which are the cognates of segregation; the enrichment of the majority culture by blending it with the cultures of the various minorities."

discrimination legislation results from "heightened moral pressures that look upon such discrimination as a negation of American ideals."[68] An article on the subject stated that "The pervasive gap between our aims and what we actually do is creating a kind of moral dry rot which eats away at the emotional and rational basis of democratic beliefs. This moral decay has on the whole been aided by the law of discrimination in housing."[69] And a third legal author quoted another writer as saying: "When smug, complacent idolators of the *status quo*, or so-called defenders of property rights deny to any human being the opportunity to live on terms of honest objective equality, they are denying the Son of God."[70]

V. *Conclusion*

A comparison of the thinking about prohibition and anti-discrimination legislation in legal sources, be they statutory materials, cases, or legal books and periodicals, reveals striking similarities of concept. In both instances, a whole series of evils is attributed to liquor and discrimination; in both, sweeping reforms are predicted in the wake of the proposed regulations. To the practice sought to be banned, the widest collection of the ills of society is attributed. Ending the practice in each case, the materials tell us, will usher in undreamed of social betterment and progress. Sometimes the very terminology used is the same, as if the writers were all writing about the same subject.

In advocacy of both prohibition of liquor and prohibition of discrimination, moral influences are strikingly evident. Here again, terminology is remarkably consistent. The same moralistic appeals are used in proclaiming the virtues of both species of legislation.

It can therefore be concluded that the moral and pseudo-scientific approach in legal thinking concerning prohibition of liquor and anti-discrimination legislation in housing is in fact the same. The concepts, the ideas, the ideals, and even the terminology is practically identical. Fifty years of time alone separates the two.

C. E. MARSHALL
P. J. FASONE
L. S. DOTSON

[68] Saks & Rabkin, *op. cit.* supra, n.67 at 523.
[69] Groner & Helfell, *op. cit.* supra, n.66 at 450.
[70] Scanlan, *op. cit.* supra, n.66, at 159, n.5, quoting the remarks of Most Rev. Bernard J. Sheil, Auxiliary Bishop of Chicago, in Sheil, *Racial Restrictive Covenants* 25-31 (1946). Scanlan also says: "Moreover, we shall leave for theologians the appraisal of the moral dilemma involved in tolerating what have been aptly termed the 'legalistic concentration camps of America.'" *Id.* at 160.

THE EFFECT OF INTEGRATION ON CRIME AND SLUMS

The purpose of this study is to determine whether integration has any effect on the rate of crime or the growth of slums. In order to study this, one must determine whether mixed neighborhoods show a lower crime rate than do homogeneous neighborhoods. In addition, a determination must also be made as to whether a formerly all-white neighborhood, which becomes mixed, shows any increase in the number of sub-standard dwellings.

I. *Effect on Crime*

To determine what effect integration of a neighborhood has on the crime rate, two districts in Chicago, Fillmore and Woodlawn, were selected for detailed study.[1] Woodlawn, in 1950, had a substantial non-white population, and between 1950 and 1960, showed an increase in the non-white population. In 1950, Fillmore had very few non-white residents, but by 1960, most of the inhabitants were Negro.

The overall arrest figure in Chicago for 1958, the last year in which published detailed figures were made available, shows that whites accounted for 55% of the arrests, Negroes accounted for 39% of the arrests, and the balance is attributable to others.[2] The 1960 census report shows that Chicago has a white population of 76% and a non-white population of 24%, which adjusted to a 1958 figure on the basis of the 10-year population shift, would give a 78%–22% ratio.[3] Thus, whites had an arrest ratio of 70% to their population ratio, while non-whites had an arrest ratio of 177% to their population ratio.

Turning to the Fillmore District, in 1950 whites constituted 95% of the population, and non-whites made up only 5%.[4] The total number of major offenses was 2,176.[5] In 1959, the last year in which the old reporting system of the Chicago Police Department was in effect, the total number of major offenses was 3,733.[6] In 1960, when a new comprehensive reporting

1 In December, 1961, police districts in Chicago were altered. This study was based on the old districts.
2 Annual Report of the Police Dept. of Chicago 11 (1958). The others included Indians, Orientals, and persons not classified in the report. It might be noted that as the percentage of Negro residents in Chicago has risen, their share of arrests has likewise risen. In 1955, the percentage was 63% white, 30% Negro; in 1956 it was 58% white, 33% Negro; and in 1957 it was 58% white, 36% Negro. See Annual Report of the Police Dept. of Chicago for 1955, p. 19; *id.* for 1956, p. 17; and *id.* for 1957, p. 11.
3 1960 Annual Report, Chicago Plan Commission 40. In 1950, Chicago had a white population of 86% and a non-white population of 14%. This represents an 18% shift in ten years, or an average shift of 1% each year.
4 1950 Chicago Crime Commission Rept. 1 (mimeograph). The total population was 161,839.
5 *Id.* at 5.
6 1960 Chicago Crime Commission Rept. 4 (mimeograph).

system was used, 8,888 major offenses were reported.[7] Thus, integration of the neighborhood was accompanied by a significant rise in the number of major offenses reported.

In 1960, the Fillmore District had a population of 70,944 whites and 152,176 non-whites, making the new ratio 68%–32%.[8] Thus, non-whites accounted for 79% of the arrests, and whites for 21%. The number of arrests included 1,019 whites, 3,723 Negroes and 132 others.[9] Thus, notwithstanding the integration of the neighborhood, whites had an arrest ratio of 66% to their population ratio, while non-whites had an arrest ratio of 115% to their population ratio.

Of more significance is the ratio between population and crime with the city and with other districts. In 1960, Fillmore reported 7% of the city's major offenses with only 6% of its population.[10] In 1950, with 4.3% of the population, it reported only 3.9% of the major offenses.[11] Thus, here again we find that the change in the neighborhood has not decreased the amount of crime.

Turning to Woodlawn, in 1950 this district had a white-Negro ratio of 66%–34%.[12] The total number of major offenses reported was 3,176.[13] In 1959, the last year of the old reporting system, the total number of offenses was 3,114.[14] Thus, the crime rate remained almost static, as contrasted with the soaring crime rate in Fillmore, which, during the same period, was undergoing a period of integration.

In 1960, the Woodlawn District had a population of 27,995 whites and 93,696 non-whites, a new ratio of 23%–77%.[15] The number of arrests included 719 whites, 6,160 Negroes, and 187 others.[16] Whites therefore accounted for 10% of the arrests; non-whites accounted for 90% of arrests. The arrest ratio to population of whites was 43%; in the case of Negroes it was 117%.

In 1960, Woodlawn reported 4.9% of the city's major offenses with 3.4% of the population.[17] In 1950, with 3.5% of the population, it reported 5.7% of the major offenses.[18] Some of this is no doubt due to the

7 Ibid.
8 Interview with D. T. Blackiston, member of the South-East Chicago Commission. These figures were obtained from census and Police Dept. source compilations.
9 Ibid.
10 1960 Chicago Crime Commission Rept. 4 (mimeograph).
11 1950 Chicago Crime Commission Rept. 1 (mimeograph).
12 Ibid. The total population was 128,088.
13 Id. at 5.
14 1960 Chicago Crime Commission Rept. 4 (mimeograph).
15 Interview, supra, n.8.
16 Ibid.
17 1960 Chicago Crime Commission Rept. 4 (mimeograph).
18 1950 Chicago Crime Commission Rept. 4 (mimeograph).

police augmentation and saturation campaign initiated by the South East Chicago Commission and the University of Chicago to protect persons connected with the university.[19] For a while, the campaign significantly depressed the rate of offenses in the Woodlawn District, although most recent figures indicate that it is now beginning to rise again.[20]

As a control area, the 40th police district, between the Chicago River and Lake Michigan, and Devon and Lawrence Avenues, was examined. This area was over 99% white in 1950, and over 95% white in 1960. It is comparable in size to Woodlawn.[21] It has about 3.7% of the city's population. In 1950, it had 2.2% of the reported major offenses, and in 1960 this rose to only 2.8%.[22] Thus, the crime rate here has remained well below the average for the whole city.

From the above analysis of two mixed districts, it can be seen that integration of a neighborhood cannot be said to have a tendency to reduce the crime rate therein. In fact, integration sometimes increases the crime rate. It would appear that the undue proportion of non-white crime is reflected in an integrated neighborhood as in the city as a whole. No reduction thereof can be attributed to integration.

II. *Effect on Slums*

To determine the effect of the movement of Negroes into a formerly all-white area on the growth of slums, eight community areas having the greatest change in racial composition between 1950 and 1960 were studied. A comparison was then made between the change in the number of substandard and delapidated units of housing in these areas between 1950 and 1960 and the over-all city change.[23] While both figures are set forth, since the figure for substandard housing includes not only dilapidated housing, but also housing lacking adequate plumbing facilities, which cannot neces-

[19] See Memorandum of D. T. Blackiston to Julian H. Levi, Sept. 15, 1958, and Memorandum of Julian H. Levi, Executive Director, S.E.C.C., to Board Members, March 16, 1959.

[20] Chicago Crime Commission reports indicate that the number of major offenses committed in the Woodlawn District was as follows: 1950, 3176; 1951, 3807; 1952, 4091; 1953, 3119; 1954, 2767; 1955, 1918; 1956, 1557; 1957, 1515; 1958, 2172; 1959, 3114. In 1960, under the new reporting system, it was 6385. The same pattern was shown in the Hyde-Park police district, which includes the other half of the University of Chicago, in which the same campaign was used.

[21] *Ibid.* Its population of 135,656 changed little in ten years.

[22] *Ibid.*

[23] These figures come from a mimeographed report of the Research Section, Chicago Dept. of Urban Renewal, May 1962, entitled: "Housing Quality; Condition and Plumbing Facilities, City of Chicago, by Community Area, 1950-1960." The term "dilapidated" was defined as follows: "Dilapidated units do not provide safe or adequate shelter; they have one or more critical defects, or have a combination of intermediate defects in sufficient number to require extensive repair or rebuilding, or are of inadequate original construction." Substandard housing was defined to include dilapidated housing or housing which lacks hot or cold running water or private toilet or bath.

sarily be classified as a "slum," it is obvious that the figure for dilapidated housing is far more significant.

Chicago as a whole improved its housing picture greatly between 1950 and 1960. In 1950, 22% of the total number of housing units was substandard, while by 1960 only 14% of the units were so classified. The percentage of dilapidated units throughout the city fell from 6% to only 2½% in the ten-year period.

Not only was there a percentage decline in terms of the total number of units of housing, but there was an absolute decline as well. The number of substandard units in 1950 was 246,251; in 1960 it was 169,664, a drop of 76,587. The elimination of dilapidated units was even more pronounced; in 1950, 65,447 such units could be found, while in 1960, only 30,926 such units existed, a drop of 34,521. The percentage of substandard housing in 1960 of the 1950 figure was 69%; the same same figure for dilapidation is 47.3%. Thus, a failure of any of the neighborhoods to keep pace with the city average would tend to show that integration could be equated with substandard housing even if the number of substandard or dilapidated dwellings did not rise or even declined somewhat.

Four neighborhoods which changed from all-white to all-Negro between 1950 and 1960 were studied. These were Kenwood, Chatham, Englewood, and Greater Grand Crossing. Three neighborhoods, East Garfield Park, North Lawndale, and Woodlawn, changed from half-Negro to all-Negro. Hyde Park changed from white to half-Negro.

East Garfield Park and North Lawndale are both directly west of the Loop. In 1950, 33% of the housing in East Garfield Park was substandard, and 10% was dilapidated, while in 1960 the figures were 30% substandard and 4.7% dilapidated. The number of substandard units in 1960 was 89% of the 1950 figure; the number of dilapidated units was 43%. Thus, while the latter figure is slightly better than the city average, the reduction in substandard units is 20% less than the city average.

In 1950, 16% of the housing in North Lawndale was substandard, and 4.9% was dilapidated. In 1960, the comparable figures were 14% and 3.8%. The percentage of substandard housing in 1960 of the 1950 figure was only 97.6; the decline in dilapidated housing was to only 86.4% of the prior total. In both cases, this is far less than the city average, and shows that the percentage of slum dwellings had not yielded to city efforts as much as it has in other neighborhoods.

Kenwood and Hyde Park are both immediately to the north of the University of Chicago; Woodlawn lies directly to the south thereof. All three areas face Lake Michigan, and have substantial amounts of housing for faculty and students at the university.

In 1950, 26% of the housing in Kenwood was substandard and 1.7%

was dilapidated. In 1960, 21% was substandard and 2.6% was dilapidated. However, hidden in those figures, which reflect a large amount of new building, is an increase of 6% in the number of substandard units and 76% in the amount of dilapidated housing. This is a complete reversal of the city trend, and represents one out of the only eight neighborhoods in Chicago's 76 neighborhoods which showed an increase in the number of dilapidated units of housing.

Another one of these eight neighborhoods which showed an increase in dilapidation is Hyde Park. In 1950, 16% of the housing was substandard, and in 1960, this figure had been reduced to 14%. However, in 1950, only 2.6% of the housing was dilapidated, while in 1960, this figure rose to 4.1%. Thus, the 1960 substandard figure was 90% of the 1950 figure, but there was a 50% increase in dilapidation. Here again, one finds a dramatic reversal of the city-wide trend.

About 37% of Woodlawn's housing in 1950 was substandard and 4.6% was dilapidated. By 1960, 30% was substandard and 3.7% was dilapidated. The number of substandard housing units had been reduced to 92% of the former total and the number of dilapidated housing units was reduced to 91% of the prior total. Here again, the reduction was less than the city average.

Englewood and Greater Grand Crossing are located in south central Chicago. In 1950, 21% of the total housing supply in Englewood was substandard and 5.6% was dilapidated. In 1960, 14% was substandard and 3.8% was dilapidated. The 1950 figures therefore declined to 68.7%, almost exactly the city average, in substandard housing, and to 60.5% in dilapidated housing, somewhat worse than the city as a whole for that period. However, it might be noted that Englewood fronts on a predominantly white area, and contains a significant amount of middle-income non-white housing.

A similar picture is found in Greater Grand Crossing. In 1950, 11% of the housing was substandard and 3% was dilapidated. In 1960, 7% of the housing was substandard and the exact same percentage was dilapidated. Thus, while the 1950 figure declined to 68.7%, almost the exact city average, the dilapidation figure dropped to only 95.6%, a far smaller drop than the city average.

Chatham, the newest neighborhood to turn Negro, is located in south central Chicago below Greater Grand Crossing. It formerly was a white, middle-income or upper-middle-income area of predominately single family dwellings. In 1950, only 2.3% of the dwellings was substandard, and only 1% was dilapidated. This was far below the city average. By 1960, only .8% was substandard and .3% was dilapidated. Thus, the 1960 figure for substandard dwellings was 35% of the 1950 figure, and the figure for dilapidated dwellings was 30.4% of the prior total. This was considerably better than the city average. However, it might be noted that in 1950, there were a total of only 148 dilapidated dwellings, and in 1960, there were 45 such dwellings. The area has become a middle-income or upper-middle-income Negro area, and is one of the best Negro residential districts in Chicago. Thus, this area is not typical of Negro residential areas in Chicago.

III. *Conclusion*

From the above study, it would appear, that integration would not favorably affect either the crime rate or the growth of slums. Where the influx into a neighborhood consists of Negroes whose crime rate is high, the neighborhood shows a sharp increase in the crime rate. Where law-abiding Negroes move in to a formerly all-white neighborhood, the crime rate attributable to them does not increase. Thus, it can be said that Negroes carry into their new neighborhood their old attributes as far as crime is concerned. Integration will not reduce the crime rate among Negroes, nor will it increase that rate.

In respect to slums, the statistics show that in all but one of these neighborhoods which changed in between 1950 and 1960, the number of slums either grew or was reduced less than the city average. Chatham, above, showed a better record than the city as a whole, and here the number of slums to begin with was negligible.

From these figures, we may conclude that when there is an influx of lower-income Negroes into a neighborhood, there is a tendency for housing to become substandard. Only when the Negroes moving in are in the upper middle class will the neighborhood standards be maintained. Thus, integration of lower-income Negroes will tend to cause neighborhood housing decay, but this is not so in the case of upper-income Negroes. Therefore, here again it may be said that integration per se will not retard the growth of slums.

F. C. NIEMI
R. D. SLAYTON

TORT LIABILITY OF BLOCKBUSTERS

I. *Introduction*

Blockbusters have recently been much in the news.[1] New York promulgated a rule forbidding real estate brokers to engage in blockbusting,[2] and the Secretary of State of New York recently revoked the license of a

---

[1] N.Y. Times, Nov. 16, 1962, p. 19, col. 7; Aug. 31, 1962, p. 23, col. 8; Aug. 29, 1962, p. 31, col. 3; April 9, 1962, p. 49, col. 4; Oct. 22, 1961, p. 46, col. 1.

[2] *Id.*, May 24, 1961, p. 28, col. 2.

real estate broker for so doing.[3] Detroit passed an ordinance making it illegal for real estate salesmen to engage in blockbusting.[4] One New Jersey town has even regulated the kinds of signs to be used on houses put up for sale.[5]

Non-commercial blockbusters have also gained a degree of notoriety.[6] Their influence has been felt in some suburbs.[7] Efforts to curb their activities have taken the form of banning signs likely to be used by them.[8]

"Blockbusting" may be defined as the introduction into a block or small neighborhood of a person as a resident of a racial, religious, or ethnic background different from those living there where such introduction is calculated to annoy or disturb existing residents or with knowledge that it will annoy or disturb existing residents and with intent to use such introduction as part of a plan to further some other end. The commercial blockbuster uses such introduction as part of a plan to pressure residents of the area to sell their houses more cheaply to him by warning them of the future loss they may take on any sale, and to permit him thereby to make a larger profit on the resale. The non-commercial blockbuster typically consists of an organization designed to promote integration. Its plan usually consists of forcing residents of an area to accept integration by selling a home to a person existing residents do not want to live with, and then pressuring residents not to sell by warning them of the loss they may take on the sale. In both cases, the unprivileged infliction of mental distress constitutes the basis of the plan. In addition, frequently the plan will consist of a conspiracy carried out by a group of people working in concert.

This comment will explore possible bases of tort liability of blockbusters. In so doing, it will not deal with cases where an individual on his own buys a home where he is not wanted, but only where such purchase is part of an overall plan promoted by someone who has no interest in such purchase.

II. *Intentional Infliction of Mental or Emotional Distress*

As a general rule, modern cases recognize the intentional infliction of mental or emotional distress as a tort.[9] Such liability was first imposed

---

[3] *Id.*, Nov. 2, 1962, p. 1, col. 1; Oct. 20, 1962, p. 25, col. 1; Sept. 22, 1962, p. 13, col. 5.

[4] *Id.*, Nov. 22, 1962, p. 61, col. 6.

[5] *Id.*, Oct. 18, 1962, p. 42, col. 4.

[6] *Id.*, Aug. 7, 1962, p. 18, col. 6; Oct. 11, 1961, p. 41, col. 4; Oct. 8, 1961, p. 123, col. 3.

[7] *Id.*, March 19, 1962, p. 1, col. 5; Dec. 5, 1961, p. 39, col. 1; June 30, 1961, p. 1, col. 2; May 21, 1961, p. 1, col. 2.

[8] Supra, n.5.

[9] Prosser, Torts 38 (2d ed. 1955); Anno, 64 A.L.R.2d 100; Prosser, *Intentional Infliction of Mental Suffering: A New Tort*, 37 Mich. L. Rev. 874 (1939).

on common carriers for abusive language used by their employees which caused embarrassment to passengers.[10] It was later extended to innkeepers,[11] owners of theatres,[12] amusement parks, [13] and public buildings.[14] Liability has also been imposed on perpetrators of cruel or humiliating pranks,[15] and upon public officials who used their official position to cause mental distress.[16] This tort has recently been applied to threats of economic injury,[17] and to the continuous sending of letters of ridicule which caused the recipient to become emotionally upset.[18]

In 1948, the revised Restatement of Torts recognized that the intentional infliction of mental distress was tortuous where the actor clearly crosses the bounds of social decency. It states that the act must be "one in which the recitation of facts to an average member of the community would arouse his resentment against the actor and lead him to exclaim 'outrageous!' "[19]

To determine whether blockbusting can constitute the tort of infliction of mental or emotional distress, we must decide whether the average person would consider this conduct outrageous. In so deciding, it is obvious that the course of conduct must be considered as a whole, rather than viewing isolated aspects thereof.

The commercial blockbuster uses mental distress as a tool of his trade. Where such distress is not sufficiently caused by the moving in of the family objected to, he incites it. Frequently, he sends other residents of the area letters or makes telephone calls warning them of the drop in the value of their home unless they sell due to the entrance of the family brought into the neighborhood. He fans the flames of natural apprehension and anxiety into a state of frenzy, and attempts to cause a community panic.[20] For this reason, such blockbusters are referred to as "panic peddlers." Their scheme is to move into the neighborhood a family objected to by the residents there, inform them of the movement, warn them of the drop in the value of their homes and in the ensuing panic buy the homes cheaply. He then resells the homes later at large profit. Thus, he makes a profit on emotional distress caused by him.

[10] Chamberlain v. Chandler, 5 Fed. Cas. 413 (No. 2575) (C.C. Mass. 1823).
[11] Milner Hotels v. Dougherty, 195 Miss. 718, 15 So. 2d 358 (1943).
[12] Planchard v. Klow Erlanger Theatres, 166 La. 235, 117 So. 132 (1928).
[13] Davis v. Tacoma Rwy. & Pwr. Co., 35 Wash. 203, 77 Pac. 209 (1904).
[14] O'Conner v. Dallas Cotton Exchange, 153 S.W.2d 266 (Tex. Civ. App. 1941).
[15] Great Atlantic & Pacific Tea Co. v. Roch, 160 Md. 189, 153 Atl. 22 (1930).
[16] Johnson v. Sampson, 167 Minn. 203, 208 N.W. 814 (1926).
[17] Curnett v. Wolf, 244 Ia. 683, 57 N.W.2d 915 (1953).
[18] Halio v. Lurie, 15 App. Div. 2d 62, 222 N.Y.S.2d 759 (1961).
[19] Restatement, Torts, § 46, Comment 9 (1948 Supp.).
[20] See Progress Development Corp. v. Mitchell, 182 F. Supp. 681, 706 (N.D. Ill. 1960). Cf. Ruiz v. Bertolotti, 37 Misc. 2d 1067 (1962) (Puerto Ricans threatened with physical violence so they will not buy house in white neighborhood, *held* actionable).

Emotional distress is also a stock in trade of non-commercial block-busters. They must publicize their activities to thrive. The natural dislike of the unwanted new neighbor is aggravated by the publicity given to his entrance. While such organizations do not need emotional harm as part of their plan of operation, they know that it will constitute an inevitable incident of their activities.

An average jury might certainly find such conduct outrageous without distorting community mores. It has been held that the use of emotionally disturbing methods to evict a tenant is actionable.[21] Likewise, the sending of dunning letters to a debtor or his neighbors or others with whom he had contact, or the making of unreasonable telephone calls to them, has been held to be actionable.[22] The conduct of a blockbuster may well be deemed no less outrageous than that of an insensitive creditor or an over-reaching landlord. It might well be that liability of a blockbuster could be founded on this traditional tort.

III. *Prima Facie Tort*

The relatively modern doctrine of prima facie tort imposes liability on actors who, without justification, do acts which, although lawful in themselves, are intended to or will, to the knowledge of the actor, inevitably cause temporal harm to another.[23] The major problem in applying the doctrine of prima facie tort to blockbusters is the issue of justification.

Legal justification in causing economic harm to another depends on "principles of policy," and it has been held that " 'fundamental assumptions in free enterprise,' including the belief that 'each business enterprise must be free to select its business relations in its own interest,' may justify or excuse the act of one who causes harm to another as a collateral consequence of his refusal to continue a business relation terminable at will."[24] Thus, justification has been found where one was protecting his own economic interests[25] or advancing his competitive position in business.[26]

Applying those principles to blockbusting, it appears that the harm

---

21 Emden v. Vitz, 88 Cal. App. 2d 313, 198 P.2d 696 (1948).

22 Curnett v. Wolf, 244 Iowa 683, 57 N.W.2d 915 (1953); LaSalle Extension University v. Fogarty, 126 Nebr. 457, 253 N.W. 424 (1934); Duty v. General Finance Co., 154 Tex. 16, 273 S.W.2d 64 (1954).

23 Forkosch, *Analysis of the "Prima Facie Tort" Cause of Action*, 42 Cornell L.Q. 465 (1957). See: U.S. Aluminum Siding Corp. v. Dun & Bradstreet, Inc., 163 F. Supp. 907 (S.D.N.Y. 1958); A. R. Barnes & Co. v. Chicago Typo. Union, 232 Ill. 424, 83 N.E. 940 (1908); Advance Music Corp. v. American Tobacco Co., 296 N.Y. 79, 70 N.E.2d 401 (1946); Ruza v. Ruza, 286 App. Div. 767, 146 N.Y.S.2d 808 (1955); Hibbard v. Halliday, 58 Okl. 244, 158 P.2d 1158 (1916).

24 House of Materials, Inc. v. Simplicity Pattern Co., 298 F.2d 867, 872 (2d Cir. 1962).

25 Reinforce, Inc. v. Birney, 308 N.Y. 164, 124 N.E.2d 104 (1954); Terry v. Dairymen's League Cooperative Ass'n, 2 App. Div. 2d 494, 157 N.Y.S.2d 71 (1956).

26 Spivak v. Delma Studios, 15 Misc. 2d 760, 181 N.Y.S.2d 877 (1958).

caused by commercial blockbusters, in depreciating the value of property adjacent to the house in which the unwelcome neighbor has moved, is ancillary and incidental to the advancement of his own economic interests. As such, the harm that he is causing stems directly from the advancement of his own business and the promotion of his own profits.

It is uncertain whether this profit motive would be held by a court to be sufficient justification for deliberately depreciating the value of the property. It has been held that a competitor may cut prices to put his opponent out of business.[27] On the other hand, it has also been held that one who improves his own land, and thereby causes damage to his neighbor's property through a foreseeable act, must compensate the latter for the damage done.[28] On the one hand, it may be argued that the residents of an area affected by blockbusting are not competitors of the blockbuster, but on the other hand, the latter may argue that they are fair game in our free enterprise economic system. What result a court would come to probably would be influenced by its general view of the economic desirability of the commercial blockbuster's activities.

Non-profit organizations engaged in integrating an area by blockbusting have no economic interests of their own to serve. Courts are likely to hold them to be officious intermeddlers. As such, they lack justification under the rules stated above, and probably would be held liable for the depreciation in the value of adjacent property which they cause.

IV. *Interference With Prospective Advantageous Relations*

Closely related to prima facie tort is liability for interference with prospective advantageous economic relations. At first, such tort was confined to acts harmful in themselves, such as violence,[29] but gradually liability was imposed for any unjustified interference with the prospective economic relations of another.[30] In the case of blockbusting, the consequent inability or greater difficulty of the residents of the area in selling their homes might be viewed as interference with prospective economic relations.

Of course, it may be argued that no examination of the blockbuster's scheme of operation is necessary because his act of buying the house and selling it to another is a lawful act and therefore the consequent damages which may occur to others are *damnum absque injuria*. It is true that no liability exists for the mere sale of a house to a neighbor whose racial, religious, or ethnic background makes him unwanted by residents of the

[27] Passaic Print Works v. Ely & Waller Dry Goods Co., 105 F.2d 163 (8th Cir. 1900).
[28] Young v. Darter, 363 P.2d 829 (Okla. 1961).
[29] Keeble v. Hickeringill, 11 Mod. 14, 103 Eng. Rep. 1127 (1707).
[30] Temperton v. Russell, [1893] 1 Q.B. 715; Tuttle v. Buck, 107 Minn. 145, 119 N.W. 946 (1909).

area,[31] and indeed, no state could constitutionally impose such liability.[32] However, when a lawful act becomes part of an unlawful scheme, liability may be imposed for the scheme even though the component acts, viewed in isolation, are lawful.[33] Moreover, "acts generally lawful may become unlawful when done to accomplish an unlawful end."[34] A good example of this is found in *United States v. U.S. Klans*.[35] Here, the Congress on Racial Equality was enjoined from engaging in so-called "freedom rides" in the South. The court declared:

> Those who sponsor, finance and encourage groups to come into this area with the knowledge that such publicized trips will foment violence in and around the bus terminals and bus facilities are just as effective in causing an obstruction to the movement of bona fide interstate bus passengers as are those defendants named in the Government's complaint . . . . The fact that this agitation on the part of the members and representatives of the Congress of Racial Equality, the Southern Leadership Conference, and the others named, is within the law of the United States and is activity that may be one of the legal rights belonging to these individuals as citizens of the United States, the right of the public to be protected from the evils of their conduct is a greater and more important right.[36]

The court was very careful to exempt from its order bona fide travelers in interstate commerce not engaging in the proscribed scheme, even though such travelers were doing exactly what the so-called "freedom riders" were doing. It said:

> This is not a restraining order enjoining individuals or groups who are traveling in interstate commerce through Alabama and through this district on bona fide trips. It is only directed to and against those organizations and individuals specifically named, or

---

31 Holbrook v. Morrison, 214 Mass. 909, 100 N.E. 1111 (1913); Stratton v. Conway, 201 Tenn. 582, 301 S.W.2d 332 (1957).

32 Barrows v. Jackson, 346 U.S. 249 (1953).

33 In United States v. Reading Co., 226 U.S. 324, 357-8 (1912), the court said:
"It is not essential that these contracts considered singly be unlawful as in restraint of trade. So considered, they may be wholly innocent. Even acts absolutely lawful may be steps in a criminal plot. But a series of such contracts, if the result of a concerted plan or plot between the defendants to thereby secure control of the sale of the independent coal in the markets of other States, and thereby suppress competition in prices between their own output and that of the independent operators, would come plainly within the terms of the statute, and as parts of the scheme or plot would be unlawful . . . . The scheme as a whole seems to us to be within reach of the law. The constituent elements, as we have stated them, are enough to give to the scheme a body and, for all that we can say, to accomplish it. Moreover, whatever we may think of them separately when we take them up as distinct charges, they are alleged sufficiently as elements of the scheme. It is suggested that the several acts charged are lawful and that intent can make no difference. But they are bound together as the parts of a single plan. The plan may make the parts unlawful."

34 Gomillion v. Lightfoot, 364 U.S. 339, 347 (1960).

35 194 F. Supp. 897 (M.D. Ala. 1961).

36 *Id.* at 904.

other like organizations or individuals acting in concert with them or acting as their agents or attorneys, that have been and are engaged in assisting, encouraging, financing and sponsoring groups and/or individuals in traveling in interstate commerce for the specific and announced purpose of testing and demonstrating.[37]

Since blockbusting is not the mere isolated act of selling a house to an unwanted new buyer, but constitutes an entire scheme of which this is only one part, the interference with the other residents' prospective purchasers due to making the area less attractive must be justified. As the Restatement of Torts declared: "one is privileged purposely to cause a third person not to enter into or continue a business relation with a competitor of the actor if (a) the relation concerns a matter involved in the competition between the actor and the competitor and . . . (d) the actor's purpose is at least in part to advance his interests in his competition with the other."[38]

If viewed as a competitor of the resident homeowners, a commercial blockbuster might be said to have a justification for engaging in his actions. However, a commercial blockbuster is not in reality a competitor of the other residents of the area. He is, in fact, a prospective purchaser of their homes. He is a competitor of other purchasers. His scheme is to drive away all other purchasers so he can purchase cheaply.

To justify interference with the homeowner's rights, the blockbuster must show that he is in direct competition with the homeowner.[39] Moreover, competition which may be deemed "unfair" will not come within the privilege granted to a competitor to intefere with prospective economic advantages.[40] As one court declared: "It seems clear that elementary principles of business ethics demonstrate the unlawfulness of Sander's conduct, and the law ought to insist on as high a standard of business morality as prevails among reputable businessmen."[41]

While no case has yet passed upon the point, it certainly may be argued that a blockbuster's tactics are something less than the "high standard of business morality" which "prevails among reputable businessmen." Certainly, if frightening ducks away on a competitor's pond by shooting at them is actionable as being unfair,[42] then it may be said that frightening prospective purchasers away by deliberately inducing an unwanted neighbor into the area and then creating alarm over this is likewise un-

---

[37] *Id.* at 906. To the same effect, see Douglas v. Congress of Racial Equality, 6 R.R.L.R. 1161 (U.S.D.C., S.D. Miss. 1961).

[38] Restatement, Torts, § 768 (1938). See also Prosser, Torts § 107 (2d Ed. 1955).

[39] Dunshee v. Standard Oil Co., 152 Iowa 618, 132 N.W. 371 (1911); Harper & James, Law of Torts, § 6.13 (1956).

[40] *Ibid.* See also Avins, *Inducing the Termination of Contract,* 24 Tenn. L. Rev. 1089 (1957).

[41] Sorenson v. Chevrolet Motor Co., 171 Minn. 260, 214 N.W. 754, 755 (1927).

[42] Keeble v. Hickeringill, 11 East 574, 103 Eng. Rep. 1127 (1707).

fair. Indeed, it has been held in early cases that an "action upon the case lies against one that shall by threats fright away his tenants at will."[43] Accordingly, a court might well find liability as a result of a commercial blockbuster's plan.[44]

A non-commercial blockbuster has no interest to serve. Its political or social views hardly justify it in interfering with the enjoyment by another of his property rights. The courts have never permitted one to interfere with another's economic situation for such reasons.[45] Moreover, the combination in the organization to engage in blockbusting is in itself a wrong. It has been held that although real estate owners might individually refuse to deal with Negroes, they could not combine in an agreement to so act.[46] By the same token, it would seem that although an individual could buy a house where he pleased regardless of the consequences to others, a conspiracy to obtain unwanted buyers might well be actionable. Certainly, the fact that such organizations infringe on the freedom of choice of existing residents to live with neighbors they like cannot be a ground for giving their activities favorable consideration. Here again, the conspiracy to drive away other purchasers and limit existing residents' freedom of association may well give rise to liability.

V. *Other Remedies*

Several other remedies may be briefly noted. If the commercial blockbuster is a licensed real estate salesman, and the applicable licensing statute contains a provision which would authorize revocation of his license for unethical conduct, his license might be revoked for blockbusting, as has already been done in one case in New York.[47] Moreover, civil liability might be based on this standard. Thus, an Illinois statute provides for revocation where the real estate broker has "demonstrated unworthiness or incompetency to act as a real estate broker or salesman in such manner as to safeguard the interests of the public."[48] It might be held that this provides a mandatory standard of conduct for such licensed persons and that violation thereof creates an appropriate civil remedy.[49]

Moreover, if blockbusting creates a threat of violence, it might be enjoined, either at the suit of the state or of any affected party.[50] Certainly,

---

43 *Id.* at 1128.
44 Harper & James, Law of Torts, § 6.11 (1956).
45 *Ibid.* Cf. Hitchman Coal & Coke Co. v. Mitchell, 245 U.S. 229, 252-261 (1917); In re Young, 29 Misc. 2d 817, 211 N.Y.S.2d 621 (1961).
46 Kates v. Lefkowitz, 28 Misc. 2d 210, 216 N.Y.S.2d 1014 (1961).
47 Supra, n.3.
48 Ill. Rev. Stat. ch. 114½, § 8(d)(11) (1961).
49 Dart v. Pure Oil Co., 223 Minn. 526, 27 N.W.2d 555 (1947); Morris, *The Role of Criminal Statutes in Negligence Actions*, 49 Colum. L. Rev. 21 (1949); Lowndes, *Civil Liability Created by Criminal Legislation*, 16 Minn. L. Rev. 361 (1932).
50 United States v. U.S. Klans, 194 F. Supp. 897 (M.D. Ala. 1961).

a resident of the area affected would be deemed an interested party for this purpose.

VI. *Conclusion*

While no court has yet passed on the point, it appears that civil remedies may exist for blockbusting. These remedies may be found within the scope of traditional tort actions, and some of the above-mentioned actions may prove to be helpful in this regard.

R. PECK
B. STRATTON

THE NEGRO HOUSING MARKET FROM A REAL ESTATE BROKER'S POINT OF VIEW: AN ILLINOIS SURVEY

I. *Introduction*

This article consists of the results of a survey taken of members of the Illinois Association of Real Estate Boards by the staff of the housing symposium. Realtors throughout the State of Illinois were included in the survey. Each received a questionnaire prepared by the Legislative Committee of the Illinois Association of Real Estate Boards and the housing symposium staff.

For the purposes of comparison the state was divided into three areas: Downstate, the suburbs of Chicago, using the normal thirty-five mile radius from Chicago, and the City of Chicago itself. Of those that received questionnaires in the downstate areas, 122 Realtors replied. From the suburbs a total of 85 questionnaires was received and from Chicago 92 questionnaires were tabulated.

The information requested was a breakdown of the type of housing found in the area of each Realtor as to price, type of dwelling and the occupation class found therein. Also sought was the price trend on these dwellings over a ten year period. Each broker was also asked what percentage of Negroes were in his area and if a demand for Negro housing existed there.

If the particular broker indicated that there were any number of Negroes at all residing in the area, he was then asked a series of questions as to whether any difficulties were encountered in gaining financing for the Negroes, whether there was opposition to Negroes in the area, and two questions dealing with what effect Negroes had upon the physical condition of a structure, i.e., whether it differed from habitation by white tenants. Also sought by these questionnaires was whether the brokers had encountered special difficulties in payment of rent or mortgage installments.

The purpose of this survey was to determine to what extent the Negro housing market differed from the overall housing market in Illinois. Thus the first question was designed to determine whether the price level, nature of house, or overall occupational categories of persons living in all-Negro or mixed areas differed from those living in other areas. The second question was designed to determine whether price trends in Negro areas or mixed areas differed from price trends generally in housing. The third and fourth questions, relating to percentage of and demand for Negro housing in the broker's area, were designed to establish the nature of the area involved. The fifth and sixth questions, concerning difficulty in securing financing for Negro purchasers and opposition to integration, were included to determine what difficulties a Negro homeseeker faced and, in addition, whether there was opposition to integrated housing in Illinois. The seventh question, relating to difficulties with Negro tenants or purchasers, was designed to determine whether discrimination was based on objective criteria in any instances. The last question, directed to alteration of maintenance costs of buildings occupied by Negroes, was asked to find out whether integration is likely to result in a decrease in maintenance and a corresponding deterioration of buildings.

Real estate brokers are generally the persons most intimately familiar with the housing market in their areas, especially used and rental housing. Moreover, not being parties to the real estate transaction in the typical case, they are generally the most detached and impartial observers available of the overall housing market picture. Accordingly, it is believed that their responses constitute the most reliable and unbiased presentation of the actual state of the Negro housing market available.

II. *Similarity of Negro Housing Market to Market As a Whole*

The first question asked was designed to elicit a determination as to the similarity of the Negro housing market to the overall market in Illinois. This question was further broken down into three categories: first, the price categories of housing in the area; secondly, the building type; and thirdly, the occupational classes of residents in the area. Table A shows the price category distribution. Part I deals with Chicago, Part II with the suburbs, Part III with downstate, and Part IV cumulates all of Illinois.

TABLE A. *Price Category Distribution: Part I, Chicago*

Percentage of Housing	Percentage of Negro Occupancy					
	None	.01-10	11-25	26-50	51-100	Total
Under $15,000						
0-20	49	12	2	2	4	69
21-40	3	5	2	—	1	11
41-60	1	3	—	—	2	6
61-80	—	—	—	—	4	4
81-100	—	—	—	—	2	2
$15,000-$25,000						
0-20	9	2	1	—	5	17
21-40	10	6	1	—	3	20
41-60	14	4	1	2	3	24
61-80	11	4	1	—	1	17
81-100	9	4	—	—	1	14
Over $25,000						
0-20	20	10	1	—	10	41
21-40	13	5	2	—	—	20
41-60	7	2	—	2	3	14
61-80	6	1	—	—	—	7
81-100	7	2	1	—	—	10
Total in Group	53	20	4	2	13	92

TABLE A. *Price Category Distribution: Part II, Suburbs*

Percentage of Housing	Percentage of Negro Occupancy					
	None	.01-10	11-25	26-50	51-100	Total
Under $15,000						
0-20	45	22	2	—	—	69
21-40	5	—	1	—	—	6
41-60	1	1	1	—	—	3
61-80	2	—	—	—	—	2
81-100	3	2	—	—	—	5
$15,000-$25,000						
0-20	14	5	1	—	—	20
21-40	6	5	1	—	—	12
41-60	17	5	1	—	—	23
61-80	10	8	1	—	—	19
81-100	9	2	—	—	—	11
Over $25,000						
0-20	25	12	2	—	—	39
21-40	11	6	1	—	—	18
41-60	9	3	—	—	—	12
61-80	4	2	1	—	—	7
81-100	7	2	—	—	—	9
Total in Group	56	25	4	—	—	85

TABLE A. *Price Category Distribution: Part III, Downstate*

Percentage of Housing	Percentage of Negro Occupancy					
	None	.01-10	11-25	26-50	51-100	Total
Under $15,000						
0-20	13	15	—	—	—	28
21-40	6	10	2	—	—	18
41-60	15	16	5	—	—	36
61-80	5	13	1	—	—	19
81-100	15	4	—	2	—	21

TABLE A. *Price Category Distribution: Part III, Downstate (Continued)*

Percentage of Housing	Percentage of Negro Occupancy					
	None	.01-10	11-25	26-50	51-100	Total
$15,000-$25,000						
0-20	20	16	—	2	—	38
21-40	13	25	7	—	—	45
41-60	12	9	1	—	—	22
61-80	6	6	—	—	—	12
81-100	3	2	—	—	—	5
Over $25,000						
0-20	48	53	8	2	—	111
21-40	3	4	—	—	—	7
41-60	3	1	—	—	—	4
61-80	—	—	—	—	—	—
81-100	—	—	—	—	—	—
Total in Group	54	58	8	2	—	122

TABLE A. *Price Category Distribution: Part IV, Illinois Total*

Percentage of Housing	Percentage of Negro Occupancy					
	None	.01-10	11-25	26-50	51-100	Total
Under $15,000						
0-20	107	49	4	2	4	166
21-40	14	15	5	—	1	35
41-60	17	20	6	—	2	45
61-80	7	13	1	—	4	25
81-100	18	6	—	2	2	28
$15,000-$25,000						
0-20	43	23	2	2	5	75
21-40	29	36	9	—	3	77
41-60	43	18	3	2	3	69
61-80	27	18	2	—	1	48
81-100	21	8	—	—	1	30
Over $25,000						
0-20	93	75	11	2	10	191
21-40	27	15	3	—	—	45
41-60	19	6	—	2	3	30
61-80	10	3	1	—	—	14
81-100	14	4	1	—	—	19
Total in Group	163	103	16	4	13	299

From an examination of the above table, it would appear that while there is a small tendency for Negro housing or housing in mixed neighborhoods to be somewhat cheaper than housing in white areas, this tendency is not very pronounced. The figures given show no radical dissimilarity, and while Negroes, by and large, are living in less expensive housing, there are neighborhoods of predominantly or substantial Negro population with a considerable amount of better housing.

The second part of the first question was designed to determine the type of building which predominated in each of the neighborhoods. Table B shows the distribution of type of dwelling involved.

TABLE B. *Building Type: Part I, Chicago*

Percentage of Dwellings	Percentage of Negro Occupancy					
	None	.01-10	11-25	26-50	51-100	Total
Single Family						
0-20	13	5	1	1	5	25
21-40	8	3	2	1	5	19
41-60	12	5	—	—	1	19
61-80	5	6	—	—	—	11
81-100	15	1	1	—	2	19
Multi 2-8						
0-20	28	8	2	1	4	43
21-40	13	9	2	1	5	30
41-60	6	1	—	—	3	10
61-80	5	1	—	—	—	6
81-100	1	1	—	—	1	3
Multi over 8						
0-20	39	13	1	—	4	57
21-40	8	5	2	1	5	21
41-60	1	1	—	—	2	4
61-80	1	—	—	—	2	3
81-100	4	1	1	1	—	7
Total in Group	53	20	4	2	13	92

TABLE B. *Building Type: Part II, Suburbs*

Percentage of Dwellings	Percentage of Negro Occupancy					
	None	.01-10	11-25	26-50	51-100	Total
Single Family						
0-20	—	—	—	—	—	—
21-40	—	—	—	—	—	—
41-60	2	—	—	—	—	2
61-80	5	3	2	—	—	10
81-100	49	22	2	—	—	73
Multi 2-8						
0-20	52	25	3	—	—	80
21-40	2	—	1	—	—	3
41-60	2	—	—	—	—	2
61-80	—	—	—	—	—	—
81-100	—	—	—	—	—	—
Multi over 8						
0-20	55	25	4	—	—	84
21-40	1	—	—	—	—	1
41-60	—	—	—	—	—	—
61-80	—	—	—	—	—	—
81-100	—	—	—	—	—	—
Total in Group	56	25	4	—	—	85

TABLE B.   *Building Type: Part III, Downstate*

Percentage of Dwellings	Percentage of Negro Occupancy					
	None	.01-10	11-25	26-50	51-100	Total
Single Family						
0-20	2	—	—	—	—	2
21-40	—	—	—	—	—	—
41-60	2	3	—	—	—	5
61-80	8	11	2	—	—	21
81-100	42	44	6	2	—	94
Multi 2-8						
0-20	48	53	7	2	—	110
21-40	3	4	1	—	—	8
41-60	3	1	—	—	—	4
61-80	—	—	—	—	—	—
81-100	—	—	—	—	—	—
Multi over 8						
0-20	52	58	8	2	—	120
21-40	2	—	—	—	—	2
41-60	—	—	—	—	—	—
61-80	—	—	—	—	—	—
81-100	—	—	—	—	—	—
Total in Group	54	58	8	2	—	122

TABLE B.   *Building Type: Part IV, Illinois Total*

Percentage of Dwellings	Percentage of Negro Occupancy					
	None	.01-10	11-25	26-50	51-100	Total
Single Family						
0-20	15	5	1	1	5	27
21-40	8	3	2	1	5	19
41-60	16	8	—	—	1	25
61-80	18	20	4	—	—	42
81-100	106	67	9	2	2	186
Multi 2-8						
0-20	128	86	12	3	4	233
21-40	18	13	4	1	5	41
41-60	11	2	—	—	3	16
61-80	5	1	—	—	—	6
81-100	1	1	—	—	1	3
Multi over 8						
0-20	146	96	13	2	4	261
21-40	11	5	2	1	5	24
41-60	1	1	—	—	—	2
61-80	1	—	—	—	3	4
81-100	4	1	1	1	1	8
Total in Group	163	103	16	4	13	299

From the above table, it can be seen that single family dwellings predominate overwhelmingly in the suburbs and in downstate Illinois. This holds true for both white and non-white areas, and there appears to be no significant difference between the two. In Chicago, however, a substantial percentage of the population lives in multi-family dwellings.

The percentage of those living with over eight apartments is small, and there appears to be no significant variation between Negro and white areas. However, it seems that a slightly smaller percentage of Negro areas have single family dwellings, and a somewhat larger percentage of those surveyed have small apartment houses with from two to eight apartments. Here again, the difference does not appear to be radical, but only a difference of a small percentage. The two areas as a whole, however, look substantially similar.[1]

The third and last part of the first question relates to the broad occupational class of people living in the areas serviced by those answering the survey. Table C shows the distribution of the occupational categories of these residents:

TABLE C. *Occupation Type: Part I, Chicago*

Percentage of Residents	Percentage of Negro Occupancy					
	None	.01-10	11-25	26-50	51-100	Total
Unskilled						
0-20	38	13	4	—	1	56
21-40	10	3	—	—	6	19
41-60	3	2	—	1	2	8
61-80	1	2	—	1	3	7
81-100	1	—	—	—	1	2
Skilled						
0-20	4	3	—	1	3	11
21-40	8	2	1	1	5	17
41-60	25	10	2	—	2	37
61-80	10	5	1	—	3	19
81-100	6	—	—	—	—	6
Professional						
0-20	28	13	1	2	10	54
21-40	11	2	1	—	3	17
41-60	11	3	2	—	—	16
61-80	3	1	—	—	—	4
81-100	—	1	—	—	—	1
Total in Group	53	20	4	2	13	92

TABLE C. *Occupation Type: Part II, Suburbs*

Percentage of Residents	Percentage of Negro Occupancy					
	None	.01-10	11-25	26-50	51-100	Total
Unskilled						
0-20	52	23	1	—	—	76
21-40	3	2	3	—	—	8
41-60	—	—	—	—	—	—
61-80	1	—	—	—	—	1
81-100	—	—	—	—	—	—

[1] This conclusion finds support in the recent 1960 census wherein it was found that the predominance of Negro citizens live in multi-family dwellings. See U.S. Census of Housing, 1960, Illinois, Final Report H.C. (1)-15, Table 10.

TABLE C. *Occupation Type: Part II, Suburbs (Continued)*

Percentage of Residents	Percentage of Negro Occupancy					Total
	None	.01-10	11-25	26-50	51-100	
Skilled						
0-20	17	9	—	—	—	26
21-40	13	4	—	—	—	17
41-60	12	5	3	—	—	20
61-80	13	4	1	—	—	18
81-100	1	3	—	—	—	4
Professional						
0-20	13	10	2	—	—	25
21-40	8	2	2	—	—	12
41-60	13	4	—	—	—	17
61-80	12	4	—	—	—	16
81-100	10	5	—	—	—	15
Total in Group	56	25	4	—	—	85

TABLE C. *Occupation Type: Part III, Downstate*

Percentage of Residents	Percentage of Negro Occupancy					Total
	None	.01-10	11-25	26-50	51-100	
Unskilled						
0-20	26	32	2	1	—	61
21-40	14	16	6	1	—	37
41-60	9	6	—	—	—	15
61-80	3	4	—	—	—	7
81-100	2	—	—	—	—	2
Skilled						
0-20	12	8	—	1	—	21
21-40	8	16	3	1	—	28
41-60	17	24	4	—	—	45
61-80	15	11	1	—	—	27
81-100	2	5	—	—	—	7
Professional						
0-20	36	38	6	—	—	80
21-40	12	13	2	2	—	29
41-60	3	5	—	—	—	8
61-80	—	2	—	—	—	2
80-100	3	—	—	—	—	3
Total in Group	54	58	8	2	—	122

TABLE C. *Occupation Type: Part IV, Illinois Total*

Percentage of Residents	Percentage of Negro Occupancy					Total
	None	.01-10	11-25	26-50	51-100	
Unskilled						
0-20	116	68	7	1	1	193
21-40	27	21	9	1	6	64
41-60	12	8	—	1	2	23
61-80	6	6	—	1	3	16
81-100	3	—	—	—	1	4
Skilled						
0-20	33	20	—	2	3	58
21-40	29	22	4	2	5	62

TABLE C.   Occupation Type: Part IV, Illinois Total (Continued)

Percentage of Residents	Percentage of Negro Occupancy					
	None	.01-10	11-25	26-50	51-100	Total
41-60	54	39	9	—	2	104
61-80	38	20	3	—	3	64
81-100	9	8	—	—	—	17
Professional						
0-20	74	51	9	2	10	146
21-40	31	27	5	2	3	68
41-60	27	12	2	—	—	41
61-80	15	7	—	—	—	22
81-100	16	6	—	—	—	22
Total in Group	163	103	16	4	13	299

The suburban group shows a low percentage of unskilled workers, an average percentage of skilled workers, and a high percentage of professionals. No marked difference appears in respect to the racial composition of the area, although it must be noted that in all areas the Negro population is under 10%. Downstate, a normal distribution of unskilled, skilled, and professionals appear. Here again, no marked racial difference appears, although, the number of predominately Negro areas is very small. In Chicago, however, an undue percentage of Negroes are unskilled, with a correspondingly lower percentage of skilled workers and professionals. This reflects the general racial pattern, and tends to show that the survey has reflected an accurate picture of the community as a whole.[2]

III. Price Trends in the Negro Housing Market

Brokers answering the survey were asked for information concerning price trends over a ten year period, both in single-family dwellings and in apartment houses. The distribution with respect to single-family houses has been broken down into Chicago, suburban, and downstate areas, with a cumulative total for all of Illinois. The distribution for apartment houses, however, has been consolidated into one state-wide table. The reason for this is that the number of apartment houses in the suburbs and in downstate Illinois is so small that these figures, standing alone would not be statistically significant. The cumulative total in respect to multi-family dwellings represents a majority of Chicago responses, since an average of 46% of responses come from Chicago. However, it might be noted as the table itself shows, that a majority of all brokers did not answer the question as to price trends in apartment houses.

Table D shows price trends in single family houses. Table E shows these price trends in multi-family dwellings.

[2] This finding corresponds with the general conclusion printed in the United States Census for 1960 to the effect that in Chicago, an overwhelming majority of Negroes are presently employed in unskilled occupations. See United States Census of Population, 1960. General Social and Economic Characteristics, Illinois. Final Report, T.C. (1)-15c, Table 78.

TABLE D. *Price Trends, Single Family: Part I, Chicago*

Price Trend	Percentage of Negro Occupancy					
	None	.01-10	11-25	26-50	51-100	Total
1952						
Up	26	11	3	1	7	48
Steady	9	2	—	1	2	14
Down	2	—	—	—	1	3
No Resp.	16	7	1	—	3	27
1953						
Up	27	13	3	1	7	51
Steady	6	—	—	1	1	8
Down	2	—	—	—	1	3
No Resp.	18	7	1	—	4	30
1954						
Up	27	12	3	1	6	49
Steady	5	—	—	1	1	7
Down	4	1	—	—	1	6
No Resp.	17	7	1	—	5	30
1955						
Up	30	12	3	1	7	53
Steady	4	1	—	1	—	6
Down	3	—	—	—	2	5
No Resp.	16	7	1	—	4	28
1956						
Up	26	13	3	1	6	49
Steady	9	1	—	1	—	11
Down	2	1	—	—	2	5
No Resp.	16	5	1	—	5	27
1957						
Up	26	11	2	—	6	45
Steady	8	2	1	1	—	12
Down	4	1	—	1	2	8
No Resp.	15	6	1	—	5	27
1958						
Up	24	7	1	—	5	37
Steady	9	3	1	1	2	16
Down	5	5	1	1	3	15
No Resp.	15	5	1	—	3	24
1959						
Up	12	6	1	—	4	23
Steady	17	5	—	1	3	26
Down	9	4	1	1	4	19
No Resp.	15	5	2	—	2	24
1960						
Up	11	4	1	—	3	19
Steady	8	5	—	1	1	15
Down	19	7	2	1	6	35
No Resp.	15	4	1	—	3	23
1961						
Up	11	3	1	—	3	18
Steady	9	4	—	1	—	14
Down	23	8	2	1	7	41
No Resp.	10	5	1	—	3	19
Total	53	20	4	2	13	92

TABLE D. *Price Trends, Single Family: Part II, Suburbs*

Price Trend	Percentage of Negro Occupancy					
	None	.01-10	11-25	26-50	51-100	Total
1952						
Up	13	9	—	—	—	22
Steady	4	—	—	—	—	4
Down	—	—	—	—	—	—
No Resp.	39	16	—	4	—	59
1953						
Up	16	13	1	—	—	30
Steady	4	1	—	—	—	5
Down	—	—	—	—	—	—
No Resp.	36	11	—	3	—	50
1954						
Up	17	12	—	1	—	30
Steady	3	2	—	—	—	5
Down	—	—	—	—	—	—
No Resp.	36	11	—	3	—	50
1955						
Up	18	10	—	1	—	29
Steady	3	3	—	—	—	6
Down	—	1	—	—	—	1
No Resp.	35	11	—	3	—	49
1956						
Up	18	12	—	1	—	31
Steady	3	1	—	—	—	4
Down	—	1	—	—	—	1
No Resp.	35	11	—	3	—	49
1957						
Up	20	10	—	1	—	31
Steady	6	4	—	—	—	10
Down	—	2	—	—	—	2
No Resp.	30	9	—	3	—	42
1958						
Up	14	7	—	1	—	22
Steady	12	6	—	—	—	18
Down	1	3	—	—	—	4
No Resp.	29	9	—	3	—	41
1959						
Up	13	4	—	1	—	18
Steady	10	10	—	—	—	20
Down	5	4	—	—	—	9
No Resp.	28	7	—	3	—	38
1960						
Up	9	3	—	1	—	13
Steady	10	5	—	—	—	15
Down	14	11	—	—	—	25
No Resp.	23	6	—	3	—	32
1961						
Up	6	—	—	1	—	7
Steady	9	5	—	—	—	14
Down	18	14	—	—	—	32
No Resp.	23	6	—	3	—	32
Total	56	25	—	4	—	85

TABLE D. *Price Trends, Single Family: Part III, Downstate*

Price Trend	Percentage of Negro Occupancy					
	None	.01-10	11-25	26-50	51-100	Total
1952						
Up	6	21	3	—	—	30
Steady	3	3	1	—	—	7
Down	—	1	—	—	—	1
No Resp.	45	33	4	2	—	84
1953						
Up	16	26	3	—	—	45
Steady	7	5	1	—	—	13
Down	—	2	—	—	—	2
No Resp.	33	25	4	2	—	64
1954						
Up	14	29	4	—	—	47
Steady	6	4	—	—	—	10
Down	1	2	—	—	—	3
No Resp.	33	23	4	2	—	62
1955						
Up	13	27	3	—	—	43
Steady	8	6	1	—	—	15
Down	—	2	—	—	—	2
No Resp.	33	23	4	2	—	62
1956						
Up	12	25	4	—	—	41
Steady	7	9	—	—	—	16
Down	2	2	—	—	—	4
No Resp.	33	22	4	2	—	61
1957						
Up	15	21	3	—	—	39
Steady	7	13	1	—	—	21
Down	1	4	—	—	—	5
No Resp.	31	20	4	2	—	57
1958						
Up	14	20	1	—	—	35
Steady	6	14	2	—	—	22
Down	3	6	1	—	—	10
No Resp.	31	18	4	2	—	55
1959						
Up	15	12	1	—	—	28
Steady	5	17	—	—	—	22
Down	4	12	3	—	—	19
No Resp.	30	17	4	2	—	53
1960						
Up	10	4	1	—	—	15
Steady	8	20	—	—	—	28
Down	7	20	3	—	—	30
No Resp.	29	14	4	2	—	49
1961						
Up	9	5	1	—	—	15
Steady	9	16	1	—	—	26
Down	9	24	2	—	—	35
No Resp.	27	13	4	2	—	46
Total	54	58	8	2	—	122

TABLE D. *Price Trends, Single Family: Part IV, Illinois Totals*

Price Trend	Percentage of Negro Occupancy					
	None	.01-10	11-25	26-50	51-100	Total
1952						
Up	45	41	6	1	7	100
Steady	16	5	1	1	2	25
Down	2	1	—	—	1	4
No Resp.	100	56	6	5	3	170
1953						
Up	59	52	7	1	7	126
Steady	17	6	1	1	1	26
Down	2	2	—	—	1	5
No Resp.	92	36	5	5	4	142
1954						
Up	58	53	7	2	6	126
Steady	14	6	—	1	1	22
Down	5	3	—	—	1	9
No Resp.	86	41	9	1	5	142
1955						
Up	61	49	6	2	7	125
Steady	15	10	1	1	—	27
Down	3	3	—	—	2	8
No Resp.	84	41	9	1	4	139
1956						
Up	56	50	7	2	6	121
Steady	19	6	—	1	1	27
Down	4	3	—	—	2	9
No Resp.	84	44	9	1	4	142
1957						
Up	61	42	5	1	6	115
Steady	21	19	2	1	—	43
Down	5	7	1	1	2	16
No Resp.	76	35	8	1	5	125
1958						
Up	52	34	3	—	5	94
Steady	27	15	3	1	2	48
Down	9	14	1	1	3	28
No Resp.	75	40	9	2	3	129
1959						
Up	40	22	2	1	4	69
Steady	32	32	—	1	3	68
Down	18	20	4	1	4	47
No Resp.	73	29	10	1	4	117
1960						
Up	30	11	2	1	3	47
Steady	26	30	—	1	1	58
Down	40	38	5	1	6	90
No Resp.	67	24	9	1	3	104
1961						
Up	26	8	2	1	3	40
Steady	27	23	1	1	—	52
Down	50	46	4	1	7	108
No Resp.	60	26	9	1	3	99
Total	163	103	16	4	13	299

TABLE E. *Price Trends, Multi Family: State-Wide*

Price Trend	Percentage of Negro Occupancy					
	None	.01-10	11-25*	26-50	51-100	Total
1952						
Up	18	23	4	1	4	50
Steady	5	3	—	—	3	11
Down	2	1	—	—	2	5
No Resp.	138	76	12	3	4	233
1953						
Up	28	25	4	1	5	63
Steady	3	6	—	—	2	11
Down	2	1	—	—	2	5
No Resp.	130	71	12	3	4	220
1954						
Up	29	29	4	1	4	67
Steady	2	2	—	—	1	5
Down	2	1	—	—	3	6
No Resp.	130	71	12	3	5	221
1955						
Up	30	27	4	1	4	66
Steady	3	4	--	—	1	8
Down	2	1	—	—	3	6
No Resp.	128	71	12	3	5	119
1956						
Up	29	28	4	1	6	68
Steady	4	4	—	—	1	9
Down	2	1	—	—	3	6
No Resp.	128	70	12	3	5	218
1957						
Up	27	22	3	1	5	58
Steady	5	7	1	—	—	13
Down	6	3	—	—	4	13
No Resp.	125	71	12	3	4	215
1958						
Up	126	19	12	2	5	211
Steady	25	11	2	1	3	50
Down	7	7	2	—	1	21
No Resp.	5	66	—	1	4	17
1959						
Up	16	14	1	—	3	34
Steady	11	6	—	—	2	19
Down	10	7	2	2	3	24
No Resp.	126	76	13	2	5	222
1960						
Up	13	8	—	—	3	24
Steady	10	10	1	1	—	22
Down	17	22	3	1	4	47
No Resp.	123	63	12	2	6	206
1961						
Up	9	7	—	—	2	18
Steady	5	3	1	—	1	10
Down	17	22	3	1	4	47
No Resp.	132	71	12	3	6	224
Total	163	103	16	4	13	299

The general price trends, in both categories of housing, show that in all portions of the state, housing prices rose steadily between 1952 and 1957. During 1958, prices leveled off, and then commenced a decline. Since 1958, prices of housing have generally declined, with a greater degree of steadiness in downstate Illinois.

Price trends of single family houses in areas with a preponderance of non-whites, in those which are mixed, and in predominately white areas, have remained the same. No significant difference has been found as a result of the racial composition of the neighborhood, as far as the trends are concerned. The same general trend appeared for apartment housing throughout the state. However, there appears to have been a weaker market for apartment houses in non-white areas than in white areas. Even during the period of a general price increase for apartment houses in white areas, a noticeable tendency existed for the prices of such dwellings in non-white areas to decline.

IV. *Demand For Negro Housing*

As one of the most important questions in the survey, this question was formulated to determine the actual demand for housing by Negroes in all three geographical areas, for it was theorized that if a strong demand for Negro housing existed in Illinois, such demand would first be brought to the attention of the real estate broker. In correlating the responses to the question with the distribution of Negro population, conclusions might be drawn as to which areas the demand was the strongest. However, since the question requested only a yes or no answer, the extent of the demand cannot be determined from the responses to this question.

Table F shows the distribution of the responses to Question Four divided into three geographical areas, including a state wide chart showing total figures.

TABLE F. *Question Four: Demand for Negro Housing: PART I, Chicago*

Response	Percentage of Negro Occupancy					
	None	.01-10	11-25	26-50	51-100	Total
Yes	5	5	3	2	13	28
No	40	15	1	—	—	56
No Resp.	8	—	—	—	—	8
Total	53	20	4	2	13	92

TABLE F. *Question Four: Demand for Negro Housing: PART II, Suburbs*

Response	Percentage of Negro Occupancy					
	None	.01-10	11-25	26-50	51-100	Total
Yes	—	6	4	—	—	10
No	48	19	—	—	—	67
No Resp.	8	—	—	—	—	8
Total	56	25	4	—	—	85

TABLE F. *Question Four: Demand for Negro Housing: PART III, Downstate*

Response	Percentage of Negro Occupancy					
	None	.01-10	11-25	26-50	51-100	Total
Yes	3	43	6	2	—	54
No	47	15	1	—	—	63
No Resp.	4	—	1	—	—	5
Total	54	58	8	2	—	122

TABLE F. *Question Four: Demand for Negro Housing: PART IV, Illinois*

Response	Percentage of Negro Occupancy					
	None	.01-10	11-25	26-50	51-100	Total
Yes	8	54	13	4	13	92
No	135	49	2	—	—	186
No Resp.	20	—	1	—	—	21
Total	163	103	16	4	13	299

The downstate figures indicate almost an equal number of affirmative and negative answers to the question, but with the highest number of affirmative answers coming from those areas which presently include .01-10% Negro population. The great majority of negative answers can be seen to have been elicited from those areas which are at present all white. This would seem to bear out some of the comments from downstate brokers that Negroes prefer "to stick to themselves" in rural communities.

There is a more pronounced result from suburban Realtors. First, it can be seen that no suburban area contains more than 10% Negroes. From the area as a whole, the overwhelming majority of brokers replied that there was no demand for Negro housing. Even in areas where there is some degree of non-white residence, there is still a lack of strong demand for Negro housing facilities. But here too, the greatest demand for homes is found in those areas where some Negroes are already living.

The Chicago responses follow much the same pattern. A large number of negative answers were returned from those areas where there are presently no non-whites living. As can be seen, the demand for housing increases as the percentage of Negro occupancy increases. For instance, all twelve brokers in the heavy 51-100% Negro areas also replied that the demand was present. Here again, as was true downstate, in the .01-10% Negro areas, a lack of appreciable demand is shown from these figures.

Thus the responses to this question show that the demand for Negro housing is greatest in areas where Negroes already are living. It would therefore appear that the non-white desire for integrated housing is not as pronouced as might have been thought.

V. *Difficulties Experienced in Securing Financing for Negroes*

This question was designed to find what obstacles, if any, were encountered by Negroes in financing a home purchase. Again, the real estate broker, as the middle man in the real estate transaction, was asked this question so as to eliminate the bias which might manifest itself were either the financial institutions or the purchasers asked. It would seem that financial strength of the purchaser is a key issue in the problem of sufficient housing.

In the table that follows, a compilation of answers to this question is presented in the yes and no form similar to that presented in Question Four relating to demand. This question also asked for an explanation of the broker's answers and thus a space was left on the questionnaire for comment. A selection of these comments is found in the appendix to this article. The reason for the large number of "no responses" to this question stems from the instruction in the questionnaire not to proceed with Questions Five through Eight if the answer to Question Three (percentage of Negro residents) was "none." As was stated previously, the majority of the questionnaires fell in this group. Reprinted below is Table G relating to responses to Question Five.

TABLE G. *Question Five: Difficulties in Financing: PART I, Chicago*

Response	Percentage of Negro Occupancy					
	None	.01-10	11-25	26-50	51-100	Total
Yes	2	6	2	2	5	17
No	1	2	2	—	7	12
No Resp.	50	12	—	—	1	63
Total	53	20	4	2	13	92

TABLE G. *Question Five: Difficulties in Financing: PART II, Suburbs*

Response	Percentage of Negro Occupancy					
	None	.01-10	11-25	26-50	51-100	Total
Yes	1	4	3	—	—	8
No	—	2	1	—	—	3
No Resp.	55	19	—	—	—	74
Total	56	25	4	—	—	85

TABLE G. *Question Five: Difficulties in Financing: PART III, Downstate*

Response	Percentage of Negro Occupancy					
	None	.01-10	11-25	26-50	51-100	Total
Yes	1	20	3	1	—	25
No	—	21	3	1	—	25
No Resp.	53	17	2	—	—	72
Total	54	58	8	2	—	122

TABLE G. *Question Five: Difficulties in Financing: PART IV, Illinois*

Response	Percentage of Negro Occupancy					
	None	.01-10	11-25	26-50	51-100	Total
Yes	4	30	8	3	5	50
No	1	25	6	1	7	40
No Resp.	158	48	2	—	1	209
Total	163	103	16	4	13	299

An evaluation of downstate results shows an almost equal percentage of yes and no answers regardless of racial composition of the neighborhood. Additional light is thrown on the problem from a reading of broker comments relating to Question Five found in the appendix. Of those that mentioned that difficulties were present, most replied that the problem lay in the poor credit rating and lack of income on the Negro's part. Most said, however, that if the non-white purchaser was qualified and had a sufficient down payment, the problem of financing the remainder of the purchase by a mortgage was relatively easy. Therefore, it would seem that very few problems downstate stem from failure to secure loans from savings institutions.

The suburban returns for Question Five are very sketchy but would seem to show that more brokers have difficulties in securing financing than otherwise. An analysis of the suburban comments relating to this question reveals a similar pattern to that found downstate.

The results from Chicago brokers to Question Five shows the same general balance between affirmative and negative answers. Although too small to be statistically significant, it is interesting to note that in areas with sparse Negro populations, it would seem that brokers encounter a considerable amount of difficulty in securing financing for Negro purchasers, while in concentrated Negro areas, there are a significant number of negative answers. From this it might be said that more difficulties are encountered where there is a small percentage of Negro residents, whereas in established Negro neighborhoods, the problems decrease relatively to other areas.

An appreciable number of Chicago brokers, in commenting on Question Five, pointed to the low income and consequent poor credit rating of Negroes, in explaining their difficulties in obtaining financing. But also in Chicago, comments further indicated that at least part of the problem in securing financing was due to the reluctance on the part of savings and loan associations to loan to non-white purchasers. Some brokers stated this problem more specifically by replying that the reluctance was especially strong when the purchaser was contemplating moving into an all-white neighborhood. This would seem to indicate that if these lenders do present a problem to the Negro purchaser, it is mostly when the purchaser is attempting a "blockbusting" transaction. Therefore, it would appear that the problems in securing non-white financing are at least equally the result of both purchaser and lender, and sometimes caused by the want of qualifications of the prospective purchaser or the nature of his contemplated purchase.

VI. *Opposition To Integrated Housing*

The purpose of the Sixth Question was to learn the extent of opposition to integrated housing throughout the State of Illinois. The broker, generally being the agent of the seller, would be expected to be conscious of his client's attitude towards the favored racial composition of the neighborhood, and what the residents have done as a result of this opposition. Therefore, it could be said that the broker's appraisal of local opposition to integrated housing would have some merit.

This question too is divided into an affirmative and negative response chart with a portion of the appendix devoted to a treatment of the responses to the latter part of this question. Listed below is Table H reflecting the intensity of opposition in all three geographical areas.

TABLE H. *Opposition to Integrated Housing: Part I, Chicago*

| Response | Percentage of Negro Occupancy | | | | | |
	None	.01-10	11-25	26-50	51-100	Total
Yes	6	10	3	2	7	28
No	1	2	1	—	5	9
No Resp.	46	8	—	—	1	55
Total	53	20	4	2	13	92

TABLE H. *Opposition to Integrated Housing: Part II, Suburbs*

| Response | Percentage of Negro Occupancy | | | | | |
	None	.01-10	11-25	26-50	51-100	Total
Yes	4	13	4	—	—	21
No	—	4	—	—	—	4
No Resp.	52	8	—	—	—	60
Total	56	25	4	—	—	85

TABLE H. *Opposition to Integrated Housing: Part III, Downstate*

| Response | Percentage of Negro Occupancy | | | | | |
	None	.01-10	11-25	26-50	51-100	Total
Yes	—	36	4	2	—	42
No	1	13	2	—	—	16
No Resp.	53	9	2	—	—	64
Total	54	58	8	2	—	122

TABLE H. *Opposition to Integrated Housing: Part IV, Illinois*

| Response | Percentage of Negro Occupancy | | | | | |
	None	.01-10	11-25	26-50	51-100	Total
Yes	10	59	11	4	7	91
No	2	19	3	—	5	29
No Resp.	151	25	2	—	1	179
Total	163	103	16	4	13	299

From the downstate communities, a large majority of brokers in the .01-10% Negro areas noted an opposition to integrated housing in their areas. Since the broker was not asked to answer Question Six if there were no Negroes in the area, the questionnaires from all white areas do not reflect whether there is opposition in those areas or otherwise.[3]

Comment from downstate brokers regarding Question Six falls into three patterns. The most common result of the opposition is flight by white neighbors after a Negro moves in. Secondly, other brokers indicated that opposition, usually in passive form, is present when the first Negro family moves in to an area, but it soon diminishes and opposition wanes. The third group of comments centered on the caution exercised on the part of the brokers to place Negro purchasers in areas where a minimum of opposition would arise therefrom.

Suburban response to Question Six also indicates a definite opposition to integrated housing. All of the questionnaires reporting no opposition were returned from areas where some degree of Negro population is already situated, although even in such areas most brokers reported opposition to integrated housing. Comments from suburban Realtors reveal that there is no organized opposition but that it consists mainly of conversation, protest meetings, and in some areas threatening phone calls to the new Negro purchasers. Taken as a whole, the comments appear to show that when integration occurs in the suburbs, the reaction is immediate and unorganized, but then ceases as time goes by.

Responses from Chicago to Question Six tend to show the same general opposition in all areas regardless of racial composition. Interestingly enough, even in heavily concentrated Negro areas, opposition to integrated housing continues to prevail, but with a higher relative number of "no opposition" comments being recorded. The most common remarks of the

---

3 Other indications of public opinion with regard to opposition to integrated housing were also sought. In the public opinion poll taken in Deerfield, Illinois, while Progress was contemplating establishing a controlled occupancy subdivision there (see Progress Development Corp. v. Mitchell, 182 F. Supp. 681 (N.D. Ill. 1960), aff'd, 286 F.2d 222 (7th Cir. 1961)), out of 4045 residents voting, 3507 were opposed to the integrated project while 460 voters indicated that they were in favor of the subdivision. See Rosen, *But Not Next Door* 97 (1962); N.Y. Times, Dec. 7, 1959, p. 25, col. 5.

Further, a telephone poll was taken by members of the staff to determine how Property Owners' Associations in Chicago stood with respect to open housing. These associations are predominantly civic organizations devoted to community or neighborhood problems such as conservation of property, improvement of housing conditions and special difficulties of the residents in the area such as financing. A total of 47 associations were contacted to determine whether they as a group had made a decision to support or oppose open occupancy. Fifteen of the organizations contacted either refused to answer or had not taken a collective stand on the question. Nineteen associations were on public record as being in favor of open or integrated housing. A number of these were located in Negro areas. The remaining thirteen associations openly opposed integrated housing as a group but there was no indication that these groups were operating actively to voice their opposition or to implement their feelings into positive action. Although it was not the announced purpose of any of these groups to dedicate all their efforts to achieving or opposing integration, it is thought that the opinions offered by these groups give some insight into how the population of Chicago regards the problem.

Chicago brokers were that the result of opposition is flight of the whites from the neighborhood. This would seem to show an almost absolute reluctance on the part of white citizens to consent to integrated living conditions in Chicago. Less frequently, comments mentioned include results such as community organizations to combat Negro entrance, the necessity for police protection for new Negro purchasers, and in some cases neighborhood riots. The whole tenor of these comments seems to represent an attitude of near panic at the thought of non-whites moving into the neighborhoods.

VII. *Special Difficulties Encountered With Negro Purchasers Or Tenants*

This question was designed to determine whether real estate brokers found any special difficulties in renting or selling to Negroes as distinguished from white clients. It was thought that responses to this question would settle the question as to whether the effect of Negro residence in a dwelling is any different from that of white occupancy. Brokers were therefore asked to list any special problems arising from occupancy by a Negro which differed from their experience with white purchasers. Selected comments to Question Seven have been reproduced in the appendix. Table I shows the numerical distribution of affirmative and negative answers to Question Seven.

TABLE I. *Special Difficulties Arising from Negro Purchasers: Part I, Chicago*

Response	Percentage of Negro Occupancy					Total
	None	.01-10	11-25	26-50	51-100	
Yes	2	5	2	2	9	20
No	2	5	2	—	4	13
No Resp.	49	10	—	—	—	59
Total	53	20	4	2	13	92

TABLE I. *Special Difficulties Arising from Negro Purchasers: Part II, Suburbs*

Response	Percentage of Negro Occupancy					Total
	None	.01-10	11-25	26-50	51-100	
Yes	1	3	3	—	—	7
No	—	6	—	—	—	6
No Resp.	55	16	1	—	—	72
Total	56	25	4	—	—	85

TABLE I. *Special Difficulties Arising from Negro Purchasers: Part III, Downstate*

Response	Percentage of Negro Occupancy					Total
	None	.01-10	11-25	26-50	51-100	
Yes	1	20	5	2	—	28
No	—	20	1	—	—	21
No Resp.	53	18	2	—	—	73
Total	54	58	8	2	—	122

TABLE I. *Special Difficulties Arising from Negro Purchasers: Part IV, Illinois*

Response	Percentage of Negro Occupancy					
	None	.01-10	11-25	26-50	51-100	Total
Yes	4	28	10	4	9	55
No	2	31	3	—	4	40
No Resp.	157	44	3	—	—	204
Total	163	103	16	4	13	299

Downstate responses to this question were nearly equally divided but with the larger percentage of brokers replying that they had encountered special difficulties in selling or renting to Negroes. It would seem that a larger percentage of brokers with experience in the 11-25% and 26-50% Negro areas were more inclined to report that Negroes presented more of a problem than was reported in the .01-10% Negro areas. Analysis of comments relating to this question revealed that the most prevalent problem with Negroes is that they are unable to keep up with mortgage or rent payments. However, there are fewer reflections of foreclosure or eviction, which would seem to indicate that payment is made at some time, although perhaps late. Also mentioned with some frequency was physical damage to property by Negroes.

Questionnaires returned from the suburbs show a similar split of affirmative and negative answers to Question Seven. Comments from suburban brokers were relatively sparse but they too most frequently mentioned delinquent payments and physical damage to property as their chief difficulties with Negroes.

Responses received from Chicago brokers to Question Seven fall into a similar pattern to that found both downstate and in the suburbs. An equal distribution of yes and no answers can be seen in the first three categories of Negro occupancy. A somewhat heavier percentage of yes answers appears in the 26-50% and 51-100% Negro areas. This would seem to indicate that those brokers who have more experience with Negro purchasers find that Negro clients present more difficulties than do white customers. The comments from Chicago brokers indicate that the problems encountered are generally physical damage to the realty, inability to make payments, and faster depreciation of the property. Overcrowding was mentioned quite often with the consequent result of quicker depreciation of the structures where this occurred. The comments as a whole reflect a genuine problem with the Negroes which is not present with the white purchaser. However, it should be added that some brokers emphasized that their experience with Negroes had been good with but a few exceptions. The point often set forth was that if Negroes are given a chance to acquire decent housing, they will take care of the property.

VIII. *Changes in Maintenance Costs Due to Negro Occupancy*

The final question was designed to determine whether the cost of maintenance increased after Negroes moved into a dwelling or whether the cost remained the same. The question was directed especially to those brokers who had clients that had experienced the effects of both Negro and white occupants upon maintenance costs. The responses to this question were divided into three categories, that of up, down, and no change. This was done to accurately reflect the change of occupancy upon the costs of maintenance. Comments to this question were also requested and a collection of these appear in the appendix to this article. Table J shows the distribution of responses to this question.

TABLE J. *Increase or Decrease in Costs of Maintenance: Part I, Chicago*

Response	Percentage of Negro Occupancy					
	None	.01-10	11-25	26-50	51-100	Total
Up	1	2	2	2	7	14
Down	—	—	—	—	—	—
No Change	1	2	2	—	6	11
No Resp.	51	16	—	—	—	67
Total	53	20	4	2	13	92

TABLE J. *Increase or Decrease in Costs of Maintenance: Part II, Suburbs*

Response	Percentage of Negro Occupancy					
	None	.01-10	11-25	26-50	51-100	Total
Up	—	—	1	—	—	1
Down	—	2	—	—	—	2
No Change	—	4	2	—	—	6
No Resp.	56	19	1	—	—	76
Total	56	25	4	—	—	85

TABLE J. *Increase or Decrease in Costs of Maintenance: Part III, Downstate*

Response	Percentage of Negro Occupancy					
	None	.01-10	11-25	26-50	51-100	Total
Up	—	—	—	—	—	—
Down	1	7	1	—	—	9
No Change	—	15	1	1	—	17
No Resp.	53	36	6	1	—	96
Total	54	58	8	2	—	122

TABLE J. *Increase or Decrease in Costs of Maintenance: Part IV, Illinois*

Response	Percentage of Negro Occupancy					
	None	.01-10	11-25	26-50	51-100	Total
Up	1	2	3	2	7	15
Down	1	9	1	—	—	11
No Change	1	21	5	1	6	34
No Resp.	160	71	7	1	—	239
Total	163	103	16	4	13	299

Downstate totals show a majority of responses recorded in the "no change" category. Especially significant is a total absence of any responses which found that an increased expenditure had occurred due to Negro occupancy. Also important is the fact that nine brokers from downstate communities had found that the expenditure actually decreased with a change to Negro occupancy. Comments to this question provide an answer to the numerical responses. Many comments brought out the point that maintenance expenditure remained the same or decreased because landlords were unwilling to pay the increased cost, with the result that the property depreciated. Some responses, however, clearly indicated that there was no difference in maintenance due to a change in occupancy from white to Negro.

Suburban responses, too, indicate that there is no marked increase in maintenance expenditures due to Negro residence in a dwelling. Most brokers responded that there was no significant change in cost outlay to maintain the structures in question. One suburban broker stated that Negro tenants were more careful of the property than were the previous white tenants. Some brokers, however, concurred in what downstate brokers had said by explaining that landlords were unwilling to increase maintenance costs after Negroes moved in and thus increased depreciation resulted.

The most significant fact about Chicago answers to Question Eight was that no broker was able to say that Negro occupancy decreased the costs of maintenance costs of their clients due to a changeover to Negro residents. Most Realtors did state that in their areas, regardless of racial composition, the landlords were forced to increase their payment for maintenance where Negroes were living.

An analysis of comments relating to maintenance in Chicago reveals that maintenance costs increase with Negro tenants unless the owner allows the buildings to depreciate to slum condition. The inference arises that if the same amount is spent for maintenance as was spent when whites lived in the buildings, the landlord will not be able to properly maintain the building. Also mentioned was a high degree of vandalism occurring in structures occupied by Negroes resulting in physical damage requiring higher maintenance costs. Most brokers with experience in this area were very positive as to the adverse effects upon dwellings by Negro residents. Here again, some brokers replied that in their experience, a change in occupancy had little effect upon the physical condition of the buildings.

IX. *Conclusion*

Although the results of the survey were not as conclusive as might be desired, they do afford a good insight into the Negro housing market in Illinois through the eyes of the people in the community most intimately familiar with its problems. The results should be helpful in any analysis of the effect of anti-discrimination legislation on the Negro housing market in this state.

DONALD M. ANDERSON
JOHN B. KINCAID

APPENDIX

Real estate brokers responding to the questionnaire were asked to write comments to questions 5, 6, 7, and 8. Below are reprinted selected representative comments made by them. No attempt has been made to check the accuracy of these comments, and, of course, all comments are those of the broker and do not necessarily represent the views of the authors of this article or of the housing symposium staff.

Question 5—Do you find that non-whites have difficulty in financing home purchases?

CHICAGO: "Limited number of lenders for Negro clients and weak backgrounds of purchasers."

"No difficulty if down payment similar to white buyer."

"They do not have acceptable credit references."

"They do not have enough down payment or they have too large monthly payments on a car or other merchandise."

"Unsteady earnings, past payment record, and my own refusal of unethical dealings. (Second mortgage, Kick-back, etc.)"

"Not from F.H.A.—too liberal—count entire wife's income regardless of age—in many cases causes foreclosure."

"No more difficulty than for white purchasers of comparable economic standing. The percentage of loan to value of building is even, but we do find some difficulty when the credit report reveals they are colored prospects paying on two or three signature loans."

"The main difficulty is that they do not have large enough down payments to warrant the same financing that whites have enjoyed for years."

SUBURBS, *Zion*: "Bad credit rating. Poor moral habits, failure to meet past financial obligations."

Wilmette: "We sold several properties this year and last without problem of any kind."

Waukegan: "They usually have a credit report showing they are poor risks."

Harvey: "Lack of sufficient down payment."

DOWNSTATE, *Kankakee*: "Not if they have 10% or more down and good credit."

"Problem is too few with down payment for older homes."

Springfield: "Banks and private money will not take risk on colored."

Pontiac: "Usually there has been a careless attitude on the part of the applicant, in past history, warranting such financial refusal."

Freeport: "Frequently their credit rating is so poor they cannot qualify for a loan."

Decatur: "Credit background usually spotty. Our credit goes back 25-30 years. Also finance companies refuse to loan to Negroes in all-white areas."

Freeport: "Primarily few have saved money for down payment and many seem to be over-committed financially, are not thrifty."

Rock Island: "Sales to Negro families have been by contract with seller or through two-thirds loans from lenders. No attempt made for low down payment government insured loans."

Centralia: "Not if they have a good credit rating. Not because they are black or white, but a larger percentage of Negroes are unreliable."

Kankakee: "No more than others—Usually works out as a contract sale."

Rock Island: "I have not had any of them that could pass a credit report or length of employment to qualify. My sales have been on a contract basis."

Question 6—What has been the result of opposition to integrated housing in your area, if any opposition exists?

CHICAGO: "Whites leave. Sometimes takes several years. School problems usually is final breaking point, plus loss of prestige."

"Could result in riot very easily."

"In instances where Negroes have moved into areas there has been violence and immediate action by home owners to move from the area. So-called "borderline" areas adjacent to areas occupied by Negroes are almost impossible to sell to Caucasians, and when sold prices are 10% to 25% below previous sales."

". . . The whites run and refuse to live with the Negro."

"Much resistance—Negroes have gotten 'round the clock' police protection for many months after they move in."

Suburbs, *Skokie*: "Thrown stones, threatening phone calls, hysterical meetings, dozen of sale signs, diminished interest on buyer's part."

Cicero: "A riot."

Hinsdale: "Local neighborhoods have pooled funds to buy property in question."

Downstate, *Springfield*: "Stiff opposition—generally accepted by Negroes."

Decatur: "If Negro moves into white area, most whites sell their properties, move elsewhere."

Freeport: "Unpleasant neighborhood talk and phone calls."

Champaign: "Pressure from neighbors has influenced the owner not to sell to Negroes."

Kankakee: "Complete panic by whites when 'block-busting' occurs. There is a four block by twelve block area completely unsalable to whites because of fear and unsalable to Negroes because of loyalty of the whites to their neighbors."

Question 7—Have you or your clients experienced any special difficulties with Negro tenants or purchasers?

Chicago: "Physical damage and over-occupancy. Hard to collect rents. Majority of rents show larger percentage of loss and eviction. Damage, over-occupancy, and high percent of wear and tear has been experienced. Inability to pay. Poor housekeeping in many instances requiring complete redecorating and repairs before rentable."

"They are usually not prompt in payment on mortgages, contracts, or rent."

"They usually cause physical damage to property."

"Lower level of earnings, relief and general non-concern of their debts make rent losses. High cost of eviction and non-recoverable by collection agents. Doubling up, non-supervision of children, no regard for appearance make for high repairs and operating costs. Heat and water bills far exceed normal."

"Very much so! Break windows repeatedly, hall lights stealing and over-all damage. Steal door checks, smash out screens, tear light fixtures out and shades. That is a little of what they do as tenants. As owners, we've had no trouble."

Suburbs, *Brookfield*: "Over occupancy, physical damage, and slow payment of rent."

Maywood: "Terrific rent loss from non-payments. Doubling up of families prevalent. Constant extensive damage of buildings by tenants."

Palatine: "Great difficulty in collection of monthly payments."

Downstate, *Springfield*: "Usually not good tenants—Careless and untidy—Will get delinquent if permitted."

Pontiac: "We are fortunate to have a better class of Negro citizen in the small town than often move to a larger city. To date, not much difficulty has resulted from either tenant or homeowner in this respect."

Rock Island: "Probably 40% of sales to colored have been, later on, the subject of foreclosure or at least under constant threat of foreclosure in an effort to collect payments due. This is true even where the seller contract holder is also colored."

Question 8—Have clients owning real estate occupied in whole or in part by Negroes altered the degree or amount of money spent on maintenance? If so, what changes and why since the change in occupancy?

Chicago: "The maintenance expense has gone up due to extra repairs caused by misuse of property by tenants. Halls cleaned and painted will be ruined in a few months. Light fixtures stolen, rear porches and railings broken, fences destroyed, impossible to keep decent lawn or parkway."

"Maintenance costs are much higher. (20%) A lot of owners get discouraged after a while and let their properties deteriorate. Children are not controlled and are the cause of much of the constant damage and destruction of property."

"The cost of maintenance in a Negro occupied building is 90% higher than a white occupied building, except where the white tenant is from some of the southern states, then the percentage is about 75% higher."

Suburbs, *Brookfield*: "They refused to spend money on decorating and make the repairs that are only necesssary. I have been told that it does no good to keep a place up, if you decorate in a short while it is a mess anyway."

Downstate, *Rockford*: "Most owners of properties seem to neglect care of property once rented to Negro tenants. However, most Negro buyers seem to neglect their property once they have purchased."

Kankakee: "They spend less money because Negroes have a tendency to be very careless in house or apartment upkeep."

SOME ASPECTS OF THE NEGRO HOUSING MARKET IN THE CHICAGO AREA

Any discussion of anti-discrimination legislation in Chicago necessarily involves the Negro housing market, for which it would primarily be designed. An exhaustive analysis of the Negro housing market in the Chicago area would require a book larger than this symposium. Therefore, this article will deal with certain selected aspects of the Negro housing market which seems most relevant to the issue of anti-discrimination legislation in housing.

I. *New Negro Housing*

In order to investigate new building in the Negro housing market, the authors interviewed fifteen builders active in the Chicago area in this market. This constituted most of the leading non-white builders in Chicago. The authors personally inspected some of the new homes built for non-white occupancy. In addition, public officials, such as village clerks, deemed most knowledgeable in this area, were interviewed, and inspection was made of some public records, such as plats and building permits, which were deemed relevant to this survey. The material set forth herein is a composite of the data obtained through this investigation.

Historically, the large majority of Chicago's Negro population has been located on the city's central and south sides. As can be expected, the overwhelming percentage of new Negro construction has taken place in Chicago's south side and in the southern suburbs. Suburbs with large amounts of new non-white construction include Robbins, Markham, East Chicago Heights, Chicago Heights, Dixmoor and Phoenix.[1] Minor amounts of new Negro housing have been built in northern and western suburbs of Waukegan, Evanston, North Chicago, and Maywood.

The amount of land available for non-white construction appears to depend on where the land is desired. Most of the builders who concentrate on construction in Chicago itself stated that good sites for large-scale construction are difficult to obtain or assemble. This is likewise true for white housing. However, some subdivisions for non-whites have been started on Chicago's South Side, and more are planned.[2] A few builders stated that land was no problem for them even in Chicago, and that they could get all the land they needed.

Most of the builders active in the suburban areas feel that there is enough land available for at least immediate needs. In Robbins, village officials estimated that sites for 700 new homes still existed. East Chicago

---

[1] There is an extensive article entitled "Negro Suburbia" in Chicago Sun Times, Nov. 15, 1962, pp. 30-32.

[2] Chicago Tribune, Nov. 4, 1962, part 2, p. 6, col. 5.

Heights had about ½ vacant acreage, or roughly 40 city blocks. Phoenix still had about 25% of its acreage available for building. One firm stated that it had over 300 excellent sites ready for construction in Markham. The village president declared that 1200 sites were still available. Harvey reported 15% of the land still undeveloped. However, there is indication from several sources that there is increasing resistance to further non-white building in the predominantly white suburbs of Harvey and Markham.[3] Also, one builder active in these suburban areas felt that there was an undersupply of good land sites for non-whites.

Builders interviewed have built about 3800 new homes for non-white occupancy in the Chicago area in the last five years.[4] East Chicago Heights had 38 homes and 26 apartments built in 1962 alone. Robbins had 137 homes built in 1960, 133 homes constructed in 1961, and 185 homes built or platted in 1962. In Phoenix, in the last three years, 81 homes have been erected. In Harvey, 117 homes and 11 apartments for non-white occupancy were built since 1960. Markham has 600 non-white homes, but the dates when they were built could not be obtained. In Chicago itself, one veteran builder sold 300 homes to Negroes last year, and stated that other large builders were planning similar subdivisions.[5]

Total figures for new Negro building are not available. However, one source estimates such building in the Chicago area at 1,000 new units of housing per year.[6]

Most of these homes are sold at prices ranging from $12,000 to $24,000, although a few have been built for as much as $35,000. One builder claimed that his organization was at times able to build and sell for less money to Negroes because of the higher cost of land in some white areas.

The authors casually examined a random sample of the buildings involved in this survey. Based on this minimal examination, it appeared that most of the homes were of comparable quality to those built for whites at the same price. However, in one instance the houses appeared to be of inferior quality.

---

[3] Midwest Minority Housing Markets 10 (Special Report by Advance Mortgage Corp., Dec. 1, 1962).

[4] The following individual totals were included in this figure: 800, 300, 100, 250, 200, 125, 500, 300, 30, 500, 106, 600.

[5] Supra, n.2.

[6] Supra, n.3. The Chicago Urban League estimated that between 1950 and 1958, 17,269 units, or 16% of all new housing constructed, was built for Negroes. Statement of Edwin C. Berry, Executive Director, Chicago Urban League, before the U.S. Civil Rights Commission, May 6, 1959, printed in U.S. Civil Rights Comm. Hearings 849 (1959). Presumably, this represents the fulfillment of a current demand. It might be noted that although the Federal Housing Administration's Chicago office keeps no lists of mortgagors by race, the office's regional director estimated that 1000 new Negro homes per year were being built and sold, and stated that a majority of the new Negro housing in the Chicago metropolitan area had FHA reinsured mortgages.

Ordinarily the purchases of these homes are financed by conventional mortgages. In some cases, however, the purchases are handled on a contract basis because the people desiring to buy do not have sufficient capital for a down payment. In other instances FHA and VA loans are used. Generally, the down payment required is between 10% and 20% of the purchase price, although some firms only require $500 or closing costs. The economic status of the people buying these homes would probably be considered that of a middle class white family with a gross income of between $6,000 and $7,000 per year. Even though these average incomes are substantial most of the builders interviewed agreed that their biggest marketing problems were lack of sufficient funds for a down payment and inadequate financial stability on the part of the prospective purchasers.

An important question posed to each of these builders interviewed was whether there was a shortage or surplus of new Negro housing in the Chicago area. This inquiry caused a diversity of opinion. Most builders felt that there was, over-all, an unfilled demand for new Negro housing. Conversely, two large Chicago builders stated that the Negro housing market has paralleled the white market, and has now reached the saturation point in the Chicago area. In fact, they declared that there was an oversupply of both new apartments for rent and houses for sale, with more new housing than the Negro market can absorb. They stated that there were new homes which remained unsold for as long as a year and a number of unrented apartments.

Without exception, all builders interviewed agreed whatever demand there is for new Negro homes is thwarted from substantial increase by the inability of families desiring such housing to afford the existing market price. In respect to those who were financially able to afford a new house at the prevailing market price, builders were ready and willing to build new housing for them, and, as noted above, construction was in fact in progress. Advertisements for new Negro housing appeared periodically in the Chicago Defender and the Chicago Sun Times.

R. A. WINKLER
G. L. BEPKO
P. GELDERMAN

II. *Savings And Loan Financing*

Savings and loan associations are prime sources of financing the construction or purchase of homes in the Chicago area. Ninety Chicago associations were written to for the purpose of obtaining a picture of financing of non-white housing in Chicago, of which nine, or only 10%, replied. The discussion herein is derived from letters and interviews from these nine institutions.[7]

---

[7] Of the institutions surveyed, Illinois Federal and Service Federal did about 95% of their business with Negroes. Hyde Park Federal did a great deal of business with non-whites, Chicago Federal did about 15% non-white business, and the others did only a minimal amount of non-white business.

Negroes do obtain home loans from the savings and loan associations which responded, but they must be qualified. A major problem on which several officers commented was the inadequacy of down payments which Negro families could offer. Many are in lower income brackets and cannot afford to save substantial sums of money.

The lower income brackets of most Negro families make the wife's income an important consideration in determining whether the association will consider the household financially able to carry the house. If the wife has a well-paying, steady job, this will be a substantial factor in obtaining a home loan for a non-white family. The need for the wife's income in turn makes family stability of prime importance in financing a non-white house. Several officers of associations commented on the disruptive influence of Negro marital problems on home financing, and one letter said that because non-white families were less stable, particular attention should be devoted to this aspect of the applicant.

Several officers of savings and loan associations indicated reluctance to finance Negro purchasing in white or transitional areas. The reason given for this was the fear that property values in such areas would not remain stable. Most purchasers in changing neighborhoods bought on contract, paying a higher purchase price.

The associations interviewed disclaimed any discrimination against Negroes. It was impossible to obtain any accurate information about discrimination in financing generally in the Chicago area. One possible element of discrimination, however, was commented upon by several association officers. They stated that it was their belief that credit standards were quite strictly enforced against non-white purchasers by other associations, and that special precautions were often taken to assure that only those Negro buyers who met these standards were given financing. Moreover, in addition to somewhat more exacting credit standards, one officer indicated that Negroes frequently had to pay $\frac{1}{4}\%$ to $\frac{1}{2}\%$ higher interest rates than whites because their property was considered of lower value and the risk was deemed greater. All officers, however, stated that no discrimination was made in down payments.

R. A. WINKLER

III. *Integrated Private Housing*

Chicago's four major planned integrated housing projects are Prairie Shores, located 2800 Blocks south of the loop along the lake front, Lake Meadows, situated immediately south of Prairie Shores, Chatham Park Village Co-op Apartments, on East 83rd Place, and University Apartments on East 55th Street adjoining the University of Chicago Campus.[8]

---

8 The materials for this survey are a composite of interviews with Homer Burcell, Manager of Chatham Park, Miss Joan Gelderman, Secretary to the Manager of University

Prairie Shores, built in 1958, Lake Meadows completed in 1953, and University Apartments, finished in 1960, were all part of urban renewal programs, and were subsidized through federal Title I assistance, being built on cleared land. Thus, the developers obtained the land for Prairie Shores and Lake Meadows at 50¢ a square foot, and "light, air and greenery were provided on a scale unmatched in Chicago. Investors were satisfied with a lower return on their equity than speculative builders could accept. The City held taxes down."[9] Lake Meadows was financed by a 35 million dollar sum from New York Life Insurance Co., and Prairie Shores cost 25 million dollars obtained from nearby Michael Reese Hospital, and private sources. Both were part of a joint area redevelopment program undertaken by the hospital and adjoining Illinois Institute of Technology to combat engulfing slums. University Apartments, part of the University of Chicago's Hyde-Park Kenwood redevelopment program, cost Webb-Knapp, Inc., and another source 9 million dollars. Chatham Village was privately built in 1941.

The only opposition has been some grumbling that too much land was being cleared for the projects. Thus, at the Lake Meadow's site, the formerly all Negro population was eliminated and the present total population is less than 50% of the former Negro population. A number of Negro businesses have also been eliminated.

Rents in Lake Meadows and Prairie Shores average $33 per room per month, compared with $42 to $65 or $70 in comparable Chicago multistory buildings.[10] However, in the exclusive "Lake Meadows 600" building, rents range from $83 for an efficiency to $350 for a 6½ room apartment. Efficiencies to two bedroom apartments in University Apartments range from $120 to $200 monthly. Chatham Park requires $290 to $490 down for a three to five room apartment, and carrying charges of $83 to $120 monthly.

At Lake Meadows, integration váries widely according to the building. The first 500 families were almost all Negro, but white occupancy gradually increased, so that today, about 75% of the project is Negro, with variances in Negro occupancy ranging from all Negro to 25% in the most luxurious building. Prairie Shores was 80% white in 1961 and is 75% white today.

The project manager indicated that "bargain rentals" were "the biggest factor in successfully renting the buildings. It was this . . . that per-

---

Apartments, Frank Livingston, Manager of Prairie Shores, and Colonel William Reardon, Manager of Lake Meadows. In addition, the composite includes a four article series on Lake Meadows in The Chicago Defender of Nov. 12, 13, 14, and 15, 1962, all page 4, and articles in the New York Times, Feb. 19, 1961, Real Estate, page R1, col. 1, and Washington Post, Nov. 24, 1960 Page E6.

9 Washington Post, Nov. 24, 1960, page E6, Statement of Ferdinand Kramer, the project's overall manager.

10 *Ibid.*

suaded many white families to sacrifice prejudice in favor of economic advantage."[11] He also stated that "A more integrated tenancy was the result of a rental campaign undertaken by the Kramer concern. Businesses, schools, and other institutions in the Chicago area were canvassed for prospective white tenants, and special tours were arranged to introduce the project, which was also advertised over local cultural FM radio stations."[12]

University Apartments has a 20% Negro occupancy. Integration was planned, with the University of Chicago Housing Bureau referring many tenants to this nearby project. Many occupants are connected with the University of Chicago, and a number of students reside in the buildings to be near the campus so that they may satisfy regulations of the University to be on campus for a fixed number of hours per day. The project manager estimated that 40% of the tenants work nearby. Chatham Park has a 95% Negro occupancy. Advertisements have also been directed to the University of Chicago campus.

Lake Meadows has 2009 apartments, of which 2/3rds to 3/4ths are Negro-occupied. The Negro population includes some of Chicago's wealthiest and most prominent Negroes. However, a majority of the Negro tenants are in the middle income group. The poor cannot afford to live there. Prairie Shores has 1700 apartments, of which about 425 are Negro-occupied. Here again, the Negro residents are well-to-do and middle class. University Apartments have 540 units, of which 135 are Negro-occupied. The average income here is $10,000. Chatham Park has 544 units, all but 41 Negro-occupied. All projects are heavily Democratic.[13]

The tenants of all of the above projects are closely screened. As a result, they are generally quite responsible and rarely default in rental payments or damage property. Evictions are few, and vacancies occur occasionally. Lake Meadows and Prairie Shores have waiting lists.

[11] New York Times, Feb. 19, 1961, Real Estate, page R1, col. 1.

[12] *Ibid.* See also 1961 U.S. Civil Rights Commission Report 104 (Book 4, Housing), stating: " 'In the early stages, by far the most difficult objective to attain was a fully integrated neighborhood,' Mr. Kramer said, even though the rentals were '40 percent below anything comparable in the city.' "

[13] Figures obtained at the Chicago Board of Election Commissioners show the following: 34th Precinct, 2nd Ward (Lake Meadows) vote in November, 1962 for U.S. Senator and State Treasurer respectively: Republican 94 and 104, Democrat 274 and 239. April 1962 primary had 42 Republicans and 157 Democrats. 29th Precinct, 2nd Ward (Prairie Shores), U.S. Senator and State Treasurer, Nov. 1962: Republican 22 and 20, Democrat 205 and 195. April 1962 primary, 13 Republicans, 264 Democrats. 22nd Precinct, 5th Ward (University Apts.) U.S. Senator and State Treasurer, Nov. 1962: Republican 80 and 81, Democrat 287 and 258. April 1962 primary, Republican 25, Democrat 143. 17th Precinct, 21st Ward (Chatham Park), U.S. Senator and State Treasurer, Nov. 1962: Republican 94 and 84, Democrat 262 and 247. April 1962 primary, Republican 32, Democrat 104. By way of contrast the Illinois statewide vote for U.S. Senator was as follows: Republican 1,961,202; Democrat 1,748,007. The state wide vote for State Treasurer was Republican 1,831,925; Democrat 1,776,090. The Cook County vote for U S. Senator was Republican 956,884; Democrat 1,007,947. The Cook County vote for State Treasurer was Republican 890,691; Democrat 1,027,059.

No quota systems are used at the projects. However, if an undue number of applicants of one race exists, the sponsors make special efforts to obtain applicants of the other race. Thus, at Prairie Shores, when white tenancy reached over 80%, the managers made a special effort to obtain a sufficient number of Negro applicants to maintain a racially integrated tenancy.

P. GELDERMAN

IV. *Used Negro Housing Market*

The bulk of Chicago's non-white housing is located on the west and south sides, with smaller areas in the suburbs. Printed herewith are four maps prepared by the Chicago Department of City Planning from 1960 U. S. Bureau of Census figures, the first map showing the distribution of Negro population. The second map shows the percentage of units with 1.01 or more persons per room. The third map shows the population per household, and the fourth map shows vacancy ratios.

The maps show that while most over-occupied housing is found in Negro neighborhoods, nevertheless such neighborhoods have high vacancy ratios. Moreover, other areas have as densely populated households as do Negro neighborhoods. This paradox tends to support the conclusion expressed by a number of real estate brokers that the supply of Negro housing is plentiful but that over-occupancy is caused by low income, which limits the number of rooms many non-white families can afford. In this connection, 1960 census figures revealed that the median white income in Chicago was $7,200, while the median Negro income was $4,700. As one study concluded: "A major factor in enforcing Chicago's housing segregation has been the high value of Chicago's houses—a median of $18,200 within the city, higher in the suburbs. That is a price at which less than 20% of Chicago's Negro families may prudently buy."[14]

[14] Supra, n.3 at 30. The census figures used in this section were tabulated by this report.

In the Chicago Sun-Times, March 4, 1963, p. 8, col. 2, there is presented a Chicago Urban League chart showing the percentage of non-white residents and the percentage of vacant rental units in 75 Chicago census community areas corresponding to those numbered areas on the accompanying maps. This chart, set forth below, shows that vacancy ratios are not unduly small in Negro areas.

COMMUNITY	Non-white Resid. (%)	% Vac. Apts	COMMUNITY	Non-white Resid. (%)	% Vac. Apts
1. Rogers Park	0.7	5.5	11. Jefferson Park	0.1	2.5
2. West Ridge	0.3	1.6	12. Forest Glen	0.1	15.8
3. Uptown	4.0	10.9	13. North Park	3.3	1.7
4. Lincoln Square	0.6	2.9	14. Albany Park	0.4	2.5
5. North Center	0.6	2.5	15. Portage Park	0.1	2.2
6. Lake View	3.2	6.9	16. Irving Park	0.3	2.0
7. Lincoln Park	4.8	5.8	17. Dunning	0.2	3.6
8. Near North Side	33.0	9.4	18. Montclare	0.1	4.1
9. Edison Park	0.5	4.7	19. Belmont Cragin	0.1	2.6
10. Norwood Park	0.1	3.9	20. Hermosa	0.1	3.3

The extent of the Negro housing supply can be gaged by a look at the classified advertisements in the Chicago Defender, the city's major Negro newspaper. A tabulation of the advertisements in the Daily Defender for November 1962 revealed a daily average of 276 and a median of 273 apartment-for-rent advertisements, and an average of 56 and a median of 52 houses for sale each day. The Weekend Defender had an average of 865 and a median of 911 apartment-for-rent advertisements, and an average of 176 and a median of 175 houses for sale. These figures, especially for apartments, are deceptively low, since in many cases a number of apartments in the same building were advertised generally. Of course, it must also be remembered that many apartments are not advertised in the Defender, but are advertised in other Negro publications, in local neighborhood papers, in real estate offices, or only by vacancy signs on the building itself. The same is true with respect to houses for sale.

A count of the classified advertising in the Chicago Sun-Times, a comparable tabloid newspaper of general circulation, for a typical day, November 28, 1962, revealed 502 apartment-for-rent advertisements and 125 house-for-sale advertisements. The weekend Sun-Times for November 18, 1962 contained 546 apartment-for-rent advertisements and 251 house-for-sale advertisements.[15] Thus, the amount of advertising in the Defender

21. Avondale	0.3	2.4	49. Roseland	22.7	2.4
22. Logan Square	0.8	4.9	50. Pullman	0.1	7.9
23. Humboldt Park	0.9	3.8	51. South Deering	0.8	3.4
24. West Town	2.3	6.5	52. East Side	0.1	2.9
25. Austin	0.2	2.8	53. West Pullman	0.2	3.5
26. West Garfield Pk.	16.4	6.8	54. Riverdale	90.2	0.7
27. East Garfield Pk.	62.0	7.4	55. Hegeswisch	0.4	3.8
28. Near West Side	54.4	5.6	56. Garfield Ridge	6.9	3.8
29. North Lawndale	91.4	4.1	57. Archer Heights	0.5	3.2
30. South Lawndale	6.0	4.3	58. Brighton Park	0.2	3.2
31. Lower West Side	1.3	8.1	59. McKinley Park	0.1	4.4
32. Loop	11.4	4.1	60. Bridgeport	0.3	4.9
33. Near South Side	77.3	5.0	61. New City	0.4	5.0
34. Armour Square	42.4	3.7	62. West Esldon	0.5	2.3
35. Douglas	92.6	2.6	63. Gage Park	0.1	3.1
36. Oakland	98.7	5.0	64. Clearing	0.1	6.2
37. Fuller Park	96.1	2.9	65. West Lawn	0.1	3.1
38. Grand Boulevard	99.5	2.5	66. Chicago Lawn	0.1	2.7
39. Kenwood	84.9	4.6	67. West Englewood	11.8	3.5
40. Washington Park	99.2	3.2	68. Englewood	69.2	4.3
41. Hyde Park	40.3	9.0	69. Greater Grand Cr.	86.2	2.9
42. Woodlawn	89.6	5.9	70. Ashburn	0.1	6.3
43. South Shore	10.4	3.8	71. Auburn Gresham	0.2	1.8
44. Chatham	64.0	5.8	72. Beverly	0.1	2.4
45. Avalon Park	0.4	2.9	73. Washington Heights	12.7	1.7
46. South Chicago	5.2	2.8	74. Mount Greenwood	0.1	2.3
47. Burnside	0.3	2.2	75. Morgan Park	35.2	2.4
48. Calumet Heights	0.2	4.5			

[15] The Chicago Tribune, the largest morning newspaper in Chicago of general circulation, and one of the nation's leading newspapers, had in its Sunday, Nov. 18, 1962 edition 1737 apartment-for-rent advertisements and 1932 houses for sale. The respective

PERCENT OF NEGRO POPULATION, IN CENSUS TRACTS, CITY OF CHICAGO, 1960

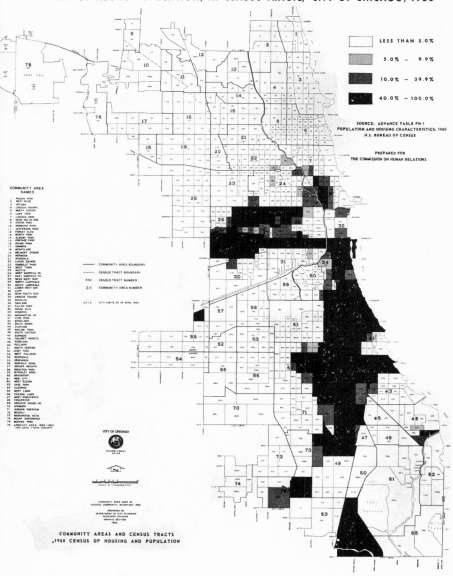

LESS THAN 5.0%

5.0% – 9.9%

10.0% – 39.9%

40.0% – 100.0%

SOURCE: ADVANCE TABLE PH-1
POPULATION AND HOUSING CHARACTERISTICS: 1960
U.S. BUREAU OF CENSUS

PREPARED FOR
THE COMMISSION ON HUMAN RELATIONS

COMMUNITY AREA
NAMES

——— COMMUNITY AREA BOUNDARY

- - - - CENSUS TRACT BOUNDARY

8-42   CENSUS TRACT NUMBER

33   COMMUNITY AREA NUMBER

NOTE   CITY LIMITS AS OF APRIL 1960

CITY OF CHICAGO

RICHARD J DALEY
MAYOR

SCALE IN THOUSAND FEET

COMMUNITY AREA BASE BY
CHICAGO COMMUNITY INVENTORY 1960
PREPARED BY
DEPARTMENT OF CITY PLANNING
RESEARCH DIVISION
GRAPHIC SECTION
1960

COMMUNITY AREAS AND CENSUS TRACTS
,1960 CENSUS OF HOUSING AND POPULATION

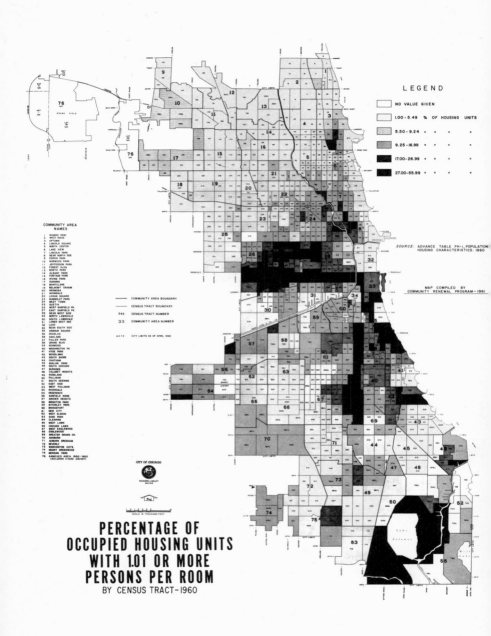

PERCENTAGE OF
OCCUPIED HOUSING UNITS
WITH 1.01 OR MORE
PERSONS PER ROOM
BY CENSUS TRACT-1960

LEGEND

	NO VALUE GIVEN
	1.00 - 5.49 % OF HOUSING UNITS
	5.50 - 9.24 " " " "
	9.25 -16.99 " " " "
	17.00 -26.99 " " " "
	27.00 -55.99 " " " "

SOURCE: ADVANCE TABLE PH-1, POPULATION
HOUSING CHARACTERISTICS: 1960

MAP COMPILED BY
COMMUNITY RENEWAL PROGRAM - 1961

COMMUNITY AREA
NAMES

1 ROGERS PARK
2 WEST RIDGE
3 UPTOWN
4 LINCOLN SQUARE
5 NORTH CENTER
6 LAKE VIEW
7 LINCOLN PARK
8 NEAR NORTH SIDE
9 EDISON PARK
10 NORWOOD PARK
11 JEFFERSON PARK
12 FOREST GLEN
13 NORTH PARK
14 ALBANY PARK
15 PORTAGE PARK
16 IRVING PARK
17 DUNNING
18 MONTCLARE
19 BELMONT CRAGIN
20 HERMOSA
21 AVONDALE
22 LOGAN SQUARE
23 HUMBOLDT PARK
24 WEST TOWN
25 AUSTIN
26 WEST GARFIELD PK.
27 EAST GARFIELD PK.
28 NEAR WEST SIDE
29 NORTH LAWNDALE
30 SOUTH LAWNDALE
31 LOWER WEST SIDE
32 LOOP
33 NEAR SOUTH SIDE
34 ARMOUR SQUARE
35 DOUGLAS
36 OAKLAND
37 FULLER PARK
38 GRAND BLVD.
39 KENWOOD
40 WASHINGTON PK.
41 HYDE PARK
42 WOODLAWN
43 SOUTH SHORE
44 CHATHAM
45 AVALON PARK
46 SOUTH CHICAGO
47 BURNSIDE
48 CALUMET HEIGHTS
49 ROSELAND
50 PULLMAN
51 SOUTH DEERING
52 EAST SIDE
53 WEST PULLMAN
54 RIVERDALE
55 HEGEWISCH
56 GARFIELD RIDGE
57 ARCHER HEIGHTS
58 BRIGHTON PARK
59 MCKINLEY PARK
60 BRIDGEPORT
61 NEW CITY
62 WEST ELSDON
63 GAGE PARK
64 CLEARING
65 WEST LAWN
66 CHICAGO LAWN
67 WEST ENGLEWOOD
68 ENGLEWOOD
69 GREATER GRAND CR.
70 ASHBURN
71 AUBURN GRESHAM
72 BEVERLY
73 WASHINGTON HGTS.
74 MOUNT GREENWOOD
75 MORGAN PARK
76 ANNEXED AREA 1950-1960
   (INCLUDING O'HARE AIRPORT)

—————— COMMUNITY AREA BOUNDARY
---------- CENSUS TRACT BOUNDARY
342 CENSUS TRACT NUMBER
33 COMMUNITY AREA NUMBER

NOTE CITY LIMITS AS OF APRIL 1960

CITY OF CHICAGO

RICHARD J. DALEY
MAYOR

SCALE IN THOUSAND FEET

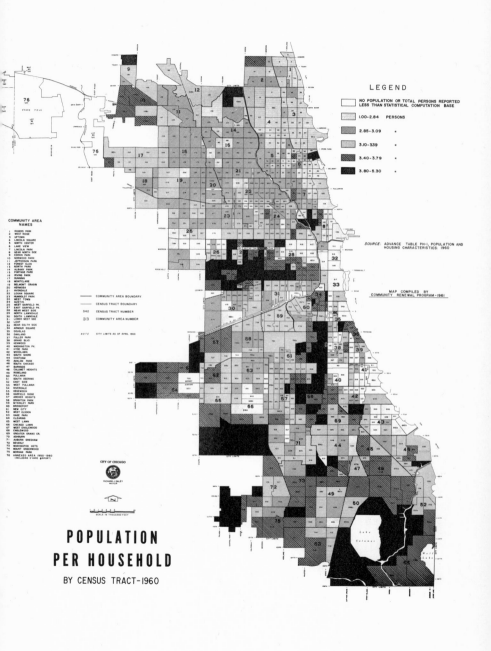

LEGEND

NO POPULATION OR TOTAL PERSONS REPORTED
LESS THAN STATISTICAL COMPUTATION BASE

1.00-2.84   PERSONS

2.85-3.09   "

3.10-3.39   "

3.40-3.79   "

3.80-5.30   "

SOURCE: ADVANCE TABLE PH-I, POPULATION AND
HOUSING CHARACTERISTICS: 1960

MAP COMPILED BY
COMMUNITY RENEWAL PROGRAM-1961

COMMUNITY AREA
NAMES

1   ROGERS PARK
2   WEST RIDGE
3   UPTOWN
4   LINCOLN SQUARE
5   NORTH CENTER
6   LAKE VIEW
7   LINCOLN PARK
8   NEAR NORTH SIDE
9   EDISON PARK
10 NORWOOD PARK
11 JEFFERSON PARK
12 FOREST GLEN
13 NORTH PARK
14 ALBANY PARK
15 PORTAGE PARK
16 IRVING PARK
17 DUNNING
18 MONTCLARE
19 BELMONT CRAGIN
20 HERMOSA
21 AVONDALE
22 LOGAN SQUARE
23 HUMBOLDT PARK
24 WEST TOWN
25 AUSTIN
26 WEST GARFIELD PK.
27 EAST GARFIELD PK.
28 NEAR WEST SIDE
29 NORTH LAWNDALE
30 SOUTH LAWNDALE
31 LOWER WEST SIDE
32 LOOP
33 NEAR SOUTH SIDE
34 ARMOUR SQUARE
35 DOUGLAS
36 OAKLAND
37 FULLER PARK
38 GRAND BLVD.
39 KENWOOD
40 WASHINGTON PK.
41 HYDE PARK
42 WOODLAWN
43 SOUTH SHORE
44 CHATHAM
45 AVALON PARK
46 SOUTH CHICAGO
47 BURNSIDE
48 CALUMET HEIGHTS
49 ROSELAND
50 PULLMAN
51 SOUTH DEERING
52 EAST SIDE
53 WEST PULLMAN
54 RIVERDALE
55 HEGEWISCH
56 GARFIELD RIDGE
57 ARCHER HEIGHTS
58 BRIGHTON PARK
59 MCKINLEY PARK
60 BRIDGEPORT
61 NEW CITY
62 WEST ELSDON
63 GAGE PARK
64 CLEARING
65 WEST LAWN
66 CHICAGO LAWN
67 WEST ENGLEWOOD
68 ENGLEWOOD
69 GREATER GRAND CR.
70 ASHBURN
71 AUBURN GRESHAM
72 BEVERLY
73 WASHINGTON HGTS.
74 MOUNT GREENWOOD
75 MORGAN PARK
76 ANNEXED AREA 1950-1960
    (INCLUDING O'HARE AIRPORT)

———— COMMUNITY AREA BOUNDARY

———— CENSUS TRACT BOUNDARY

342   CENSUS TRACT NUMBER

33   COMMUNITY AREA NUMBER

NOTE   CITY LIMITS AS OF APRIL 1960

CITY OF CHICAGO

RICHARD J. DALEY
MAYOR

SCALE IN THOUSAND FEET

POPULATION
PER HOUSEHOLD

BY CENSUS TRACT-1960

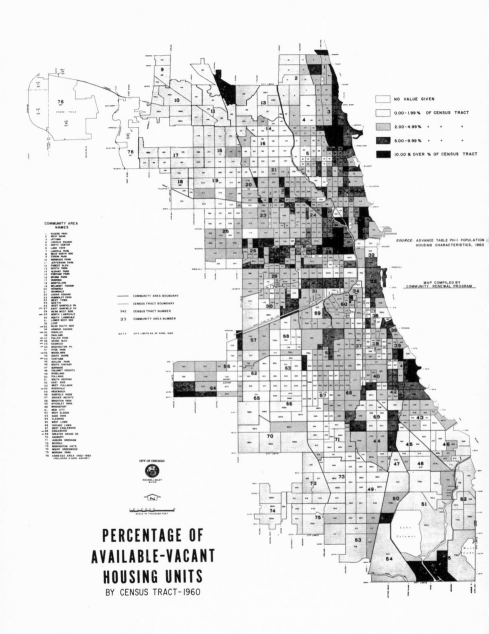

COMMUNITY AREA
NAMES

1 ROGERS PARK
2 WEST RIDGE
3 UPTOWN
4 LINCOLN SQUARE
5 NORTH CENTER
6 LAKE VIEW
7 LINCOLN PARK
8 NEAR NORTH SIDE
9 EDISON PARK
10 NORWOOD PARK
11 JEFFERSON PARK
12 FOREST GLEN
13 NORTH PARK
14 ALBANY PARK
15 PORTAGE PARK
16 IRVING PARK
17 DUNNING
18 MONTCLARE
19 BELMONT CRAGIN
20 HERMOSA
21 AVONDALE
22 LOGAN SQUARE
23 HUMBOLDT PARK
24 WEST TOWN
25 AUSTIN
26 WEST GARFIELD PK.
27 EAST GARFIELD PK.
28 NEAR WEST SIDE
29 SOUTH LAWNDALE
30 LOWER WEST SIDE
31 LOOP
32 NEAR SOUTH SIDE
33 ARMOUR SQUARE
34 DOUGLAS
35 OAKLAND
36 FULLER PARK
37 GRAND BLVD.
38 KENWOOD
39 WASHINGTON PK.
40 HYDE PARK
41 WOODLAWN
42 SOUTH SHORE
43 CHATHAM
44 AVALON PARK
45 SOUTH CHICAGO
46 BURNSIDE
47 CALUMET HEIGHTS
48 ROSELAND
49 PULLMAN
50 SOUTH DEERING
51 EAST SIDE
52 WEST PULLMAN
53 RIVERDALE
54 HEGEWISCH
55 GARFIELD RIDGE
56 ARCHER HEIGHTS
57 BRIGHTON PARK
58 MCKINLEY PARK
59 BRIDGEPORT
60 NEW CITY
61 WEST ELSDON
62 GAGE PARK
63 CLEARING
64 WEST LAWN
65 CHICAGO LAWN
66 WEST ENGLEWOOD
67 ENGLEWOOD
68 GREATER GRAND CR.
69 ASHBURN
70 AUBURN GRESHAM
71 BEVERLY
72 WASHINGTON HGTS.
73 MOUNT GREENWOOD
74 MORGAN PARK
75 MORGAN PARK
76 ANNEXED AREA 1950-1960
   (INCLUDING O'HARE AIRPORT)

——— COMMUNITY AREA BOUNDARY
——— CENSUS TRACT BOUNDARY
542 CENSUS TRACT NUMBER
33   COMMUNITY AREA NUMBER

NOTE   CITY LIMITS AS OF APRIL 1960

NO VALUE GIVEN

0.00-1.99 % OF CENSUS TRACT

2.00-4.99 %   "   "   "

5.00-9.99 %   "   "   "

10.00 & OVER % OF CENSUS TRACT

SOURCE: ADVANCE TABLE PH-1 POPULATION
        HOUSING CHARACTERISTICS, 1960

MAP COMPILED BY
COMMUNITY RENEWAL PROGRAM

CITY OF CHICAGO

RICHARD J. DALEY
MAYOR

SCALE IN THOUSAND FEET

PERCENTAGE OF
AVAILABLE-VACANT
HOUSING UNITS
BY CENSUS TRACT-1960

compares favorably with that in the Sun-Times, considering the fact that the City of Chicago, according to 1960 census figures, is 23.6% Negro and the Chicago metropolitan area, which these newspapers serve, is 14.8% Negro. These figures reinforce the statements of a number of real estate brokers interviewed, who said that there was an ample or good supply of non-white housing, or even that a surplus of Negro housing exists, and that the prime reason for the inability of Negroes to obtain good housing was lack of funds.[16]

Another index of the increasing housing supply available to non-whites is the virtual elimination of doubled-up households. The white 1950 figure of 5.9% was reduced to 1.4% by 1960, a reduction of 72.4%. The Negro figure for 1950 of 17.5% was reduced in 1960 to 3.3%, a drop of 68.8%, although the Chicago Negro population of about 509,000 in 1950 increased to 838,000 in 1960, while the white population dropped from about 3,112,000 in 1950 to 2,713,000 in 1960.

The quality of used Negro housing has been steadily improving. Substandard white owner-occupied houses declined from 12.2% in 1950 to 1.8% in 1960, while substandard Negro owner-occupied homes fell during the same period from 45.6% to 8%. Substandard white rented housing fell from 26.8% to 12.9%, while substandard Negro rented housing fell from 62.8% to 29%. During this same period, the Negro portion of Chicago's population rose from 14.1% to 23.6%, and the number of Negro households increased by 78%.

Moreover, while white home ownership rose from 646,000 units in 1950 to 915,000 units in 1960, a 42% rise, Negro home ownership rose from 24,700 units to 45,400 units, an 84% rise. One regional study concluded: "In every city of the region, Negro households in 1960 enjoyed housing conditions superior to those of the aggregate white households in 1950. The gap between average owner and renter conditions is now greater than that between the races. In all but one city, Negro home-owners are less likely today to live in substandard housing than white renters."[17]

DAVID M. TRUITT*

---

figures for Wednesday, November 28, 1962 were 453 and 261. Even here, the ratio of the Defender is quite favorable, except in respect to Sunday advertisements of houses for sale.

16 See supra, n.3 at 7, where the above report, based on 1960 figures, estimated that there was an unfilled Negro housing demand in 1960 in Chicago. However, in 10 midwestern cities which they surveyed, they concluded: "There is no housing shortage for either white or Negro . . . Doubling up and substandard housing are probably at all-time lows . . . In the non-white market, the supply of owner units is now more or less in balance with effective demand in 7 of the 10 areas we survey." It seems that this is now true of Chicago as well.

17 *Id.* at 25.

* B.A. 1955, Miami U. (Ohio); LL.B. 1962, Chicago-Kent College of Law. Member of the Illinois Bar. Real estate broker, former Associate Editor, Chicago-Kent Law Review.

PROPERTY VALUES IN CHANGING NEIGHBORHOODS

I. *Introduction*

During the last two decades, the rise in Negro ownership of homes in Chicago has been considerable. The proportion of Chicago's total ownership composed of nonwhites increased from 7.5% in 1940 to 15.7% in 1960. Likewise, the quality of nonwhite housing has been improving. In 1950 the median value of nonwhite homes in Chicago was $9,200, but by 1960 it had risen to $16,700. By way of contrast, between 1950 and 1960, white home ownership rose only 14% while Negro home ownership rose 130%. Likewise, the median value of white housing rose 48%, that of Negro housing rose 82%. Indeed, by the 1960 census, Negro median value lagged only $1,300 behind white median value of homes.[1]

The rise in Negro ownership of homes and increase in Negro middle class housing raises the problem of whether movement of Negroes into a formerly all-white neighborhood will effect property values. A recent book indicates that such effect is minimal, although the study was limited to single-family dwellings acquired by non-whites in areas not contiguous to established Negro neighborhoods.[2]

This author further examined the connection between property values and racial change in two Chicago neighborhoods adjacent to established Negro areas, since it is in such areas that racial change takes place. The results of this study are set forth below.

II. *Englewood*

In October 1961, the staff of the Chicago Commission on Human Relations examined the 29 homes in a block between 69th and 70th Streets and Yale and Princeton Avenues, researching transactions from 1955 onward. All had been acquired, directly or indirectly, by Negroes from their former white owners, although two were rented out.

Twenty-four homes were purchased on installment contract, but this number was reduced to 18 by 1961. Of the remaining six, five were paid up, and one was forfeited through the buyer's default.

The median value of these homes as indicated by the 1960 census was $16,500 to $19,000. However, non-resident speculators who sold these homes to Negroes on installment contracts paid the original white owners an average of $11,156, and resold them for an average of $19,216. Price increases ranged from 35% to 115%, averaging 73%.

1 "The Growing Negro Middle Class in Chicago," Research Report of the Chicago Commission on Human Relations, Sept. 1, 1962, p. 3.

2 Laurenti, Property Values and Race (1961); *passim*. See also Downs, "An Economic Analysis of Property Values and Race," 36 Land Economics 181 (1960).

This writer's check on the assessed valuation of these homes from 1954 to 1961 revealed an average increase of 20%. It cannot be determined whether this increase reflected an increase rental income from the house or was prompted by other factors, such as revised assessment schedules.

The 1960 census figures show 19 homes with 1.01 or more persons per room. Fifteen owners have sublet portions of their houses. The average monthly payments by Negro purchasers are $148, and evidently renting helps to meet them. Thus, to some extent it appears that the installment contracts made necessary by want of an initial down payment sufficient to attract conventional mortgage credit, result in high periodic payments which must be met by subdividing and renting portions of the house. This overcrowding in turn accellerates depreciation and deters conventional mortgage financing, resulting in higher rents and lack of down payments when the tenant desires to buy a house of his own. Thus, a vicious cycle is created by want of initial cash.

III. *Marynook*

Bounded by 83rd, 87th, Dorchester, and the Illinois Central Railroad tracks is a neighborhood of approximately 450 three to six-year-old single family homes. Schools, shopping centers, and medical facilities are nearby, and Avalon Park fronts on one side. Winding streets create a suburban atmosphere. The four basic types of homes were made to sell for approximately $19,000 to $22,000 six years ago when the majority of the homes were built.

Until March, 1962, the entire area was made up of white home owners. At that time, however, a Negro family purchased a home and moved in. The same month, three more did likewise. By December 1, 1962, a total of 57 known house transfers had taken place. In addition, fifteen to twenty houses have been rented during that time. The turnover rate, therefore, was approximately 17%. The estimated Chicago rate is approximately 5%.

A breakdown of the newly acquired owner-occupied homes shows 43 Negro, 7 White, 2 Japanese, 1 Filippino, and 4 Negro-white households. All the renting families are white except one which is Negro-white. These newcomers have comparable occupations to current residents. Some are professional personnel. A local Negro real estate broker estimated that the average income of the non-white families is higher than the whites. Approximately 50 homeowners either teach or work at the University of Chicago. The religious distribution of Marynook is 1/3 Catholic, 1/3 Jewish, and 1/3 Protestant.

Of relevance in comparison to the present purchase prices is the last six years' price fluctuation. The original selling range of $19,000 to $22,000 lasted about two years. Four years ago the average selling price for the same homes was between $25,000 and $30,000. Three years ago when nearby neighborhoods changed, a fear of Negro influx caused the market to drop sharply. Prices ranged from $18,000 to $19,000. The 1962 prices have remained fairly stable, ranging from $18,500 to $26,000, depending on the type of house.

The 1962 transfers revealed an average nonwhite purchase price of $22,310 and an average white price of $21,666. These figures disregard the type of house, which may be a factor. No homes have been bought on contract. However, down payments have been larger than average, with the balance financed by conventional mortgages.

A strong influential factor, the local Marynook Homeowners Association, has expended great efforts to keep the neighborhood stable and prevent panic during the period of change. Much effort and ingenuity has been put forth to find white buyers, and the cooperation of local white real estate brokers has been obtained. However, only three white purchases occurred during the last half of 1962, and white transfers are estimated by a local white broker to have declined 35%.

On the other hand, a local Negro broker claims to have three potential Negro buyers for every home which becomes available for sale in the area. This unbalanced market seems illustrated in the purchase prices. Since white buyers are scarce, they can command a lower price. However, many homeowners are unwilling to take a loss and therefore will sell to Negroes if no white buyer is available at a comparable price. The increase in rentals may be due to the reluctance of whites to buy in the area and their willingness to remain until the area turns if faced with no loss. The price stability may in great measure be attributed to the Homeowners Association's vigilance against "panic peddlers" (speculators).

But since the main problem has remained that of a scarcity of white buyers a few home owners, independent of the Homeowners Association, have formed an "investment" corporation to buy up homes and then to wait for white purchasers. Their activities are apparently in the embryonic stage. The same Negro real estate broker with a number of potential Negro buyers, however, feels that this action may be too late. He feels that the area will turn irrespective of the organizations and the sincerity of the white home owners. He advances one social-psychological theory: That whites cannot tolerate living next door to a Negro who is his financial superior.

IV. *Conclusion*

Laurenti's conclusion that the price of homes in a changing neighborhood remains relatively stable, absent conditions of panic, is born out by the Englewood and Marynook experiences. However, the white market in such an area diminishes almost to the vanishing point. The price structure is maintained by a Negro demand. To white homeowners the property is unsalable, and consequently, it takes much longer to find a purchaser. Where financing is conventional, Negro purchasers pay prices comparable to whites. Installment contracts, however, drive up the cost. As long as the Negro housing demand continues, property values will not decline because of a Negro influx. Should Negro demand abate, the price structure of such areas might weaken. On the other hand, a reverse influx could stabilize prices.

D. SLAYTON

AN ANALYSIS OF POSSIBLE IMPACT OF ANTI-DISCRIMINATION LEGISLATION ON THE HOME BUILDING INDUSTRY

I. *Introduction*

In February of 1962, builder members of the National Association of Home Builders were sent a questionnaire relative to their opinion as to the possible impact of a presidential executive order prohibiting racial discrimination in new housing. A total of 15,335 questionnaires were sent and 5,905 replies received. The answers to the questionnaire were tabulated by C-E-I-R, Inc., Washington Center, Arlington, Virginia, an independent research organization, and indicated that in the builders' opinion residential home construction would decline a total of 60% in the event such an order was in fact issued.[1]

The questionnaire sent to the members of the National Association of Home Builders was exceptionally brief and offered the builders little opportunity to state their reasons for anticipating such a drastic drop in residential home building activity. As a result, the survey as submitted to the President contained the following statement of opinion by the research organization in their summary of findings: "It would appear appropriate to view some of the more drastic predictions as emotionally placed, particularly in the light of the facts of limited actual FHA-VA dependence by many builders."

In the research organization's notes on the survey, the following comment was made:

In particular, there is a latent but important question concerning the possible relationship of respondents' varying degrees of emotional reaction to the structure of the resulting sample. It is possible that those most emotionally involved would have had a greater tendency to respond than those to whom the situation presented less of an emotional stimulus. In the absence of pretesting

[1] See N.Y. Times, July 9, 1962, p. 31, col. 2.

and of interviews in depth, this probable bias *must* (emphasis added) be regarded as real.

Another question . . . relates to the relative framework of factual basis which underlines the quantitative responses concerning building outlook under a potential anti-discrimination order.

On November 20, 1962, the President signed an executive order barring discrimination in new housing financed directly with Federal funds. It is very possible that the predictions of the membership of N.A.H.B. relative to a drastic decline in residential home construction, as a consequence of such an order, were greatly minimized by the absence of reasons for such a decline and the research organization's personal interpretations of psychological and emotional factors.[2]

The purpose of this article is to examine some of the economics of the home building industry in an effort to determine whether the views expressed by the builders in the above survey have a factual basis, and the relationship of such factors with either the executive order or state anti-discrimination legislation. It should be noted at the outset that there is a vast difference in the economic problems of the builders of apartment dwellings, the small volume home builder, and the large volume home builder.

II. *The Apartment Builder*

It is very doubtful that the presidential executive order or state anti-discrimination legislation will have a drastic effect on this type of building activity for several reasons. First, the actual cash equity investment of the builder is but a fraction of that required by the volume home builder. Since mortgages are calculated, to a large extent, on anticipated rent rolls a builder can many times in apartment construction "mortgage out" with the result that little or none of his capital is tied up for an extended period.

Secondly, much apartment building is initiated with the objective of selling the complete building as a package to a potential investor. As a result, the builder is not faced with the possible long term effect of an anti-discrimination order or legislation on the rent rolls.

Thirdly, apartment dwellers are considerably more mobile than the purchaser of individual homes. The renting of an apartment typically re-

2 Wall St. Journal, Dec. 28, 1962, p. 1, col. 6, carries a long article on builders' cutbacks because of the presidential order. It states: "President Kennedy's anti-bias housing order, little more than a month old, already is bringing cutbacks in the 1963 plans of many home builders. This early evidence comes from interviews with 54 builders from all parts of the country. The findings tend to confirm the fears of industry leaders and to refute claims of Federal officials that the impact of the order on construction will be all but nil." As an example, it states: "George Arquilla, a leading Chicago builder, says he has reduced his proposed housing construction by about half and has laid off 50% of his former 300-man work force."

quires no equity outlay and usually involves a relatively short term lease. It is thus a fairly simple matter for the lessee of an apartment unit to change his residence in the event he becomes dissatisfied with his neighbors. This is in marked contrast to the plight of the individual who has made a substantial equity investment in a private home and who then desires to make a move to a different location.

III. *The Small Volume Builders*

Here again it is doubtful if either the presidential executive order or anti-discrimination legislation will drastically effect the builder of 10 to 25 homes per year. Typically, a builder in this volume category is building on scattered, fully improved sites located in established neighborhoods and areas. The character of such areas has been established over a considerable period of years, and the prospective home buyer will have less reason for fear of a drastic change in the area than if he purchased in a completely new subdivision. It would appear that the major effect of the presidential executive order or anti-discrimination legislation could well be a considerable increase in the price of such scattered building sites due to a decrease in volume building, with a resulting price increase to potential home buyers. A further reason for not anticipating a drastic reduction in volume as regards the small volume home builder is on their comparative lack of reliance on either FHA or VA financing.

IV. *The Volume Builder's Operations*

Since World War II, the home building industry has undergone a considerable transformation. From an individually operated small scale craft operation the industry has, during the last 20 years, grown to a large scale assembly line production. It has been estimated that almost 90% of new housing construction activity is being provided by a handful of builders over 250 homes per year. In the home builders survey mentioned above only 233 builders out of 5,905 respondents indicated that they expected to build in excess of 250 homes in 1962.

The reason the large volume home builder has been able to produce such large percentage of new housing construction has been his ability to produce on a volume basis more home for less money, through volume purchasing power, effective use of labor-saving equipment, marketing research, and last, but most important, by his ability to develop large tracts of raw farm land into residential home sites. It is in connection with this type of building operation that the presidential order and possible state anti-discrimination legislation will have the most drastic effect.

As noted above, the volume home builder effects economies in a variety of ways. However, many of the more apparent economies are offset by increased overhead costs. For example, volume purchasing savings may be offset by the need to hire a purchasing agent. Volume sales are offset by increased commissions and advertising expenses. Volume production may be partially offset by increased cost of supervisory personnel. As a result, it has been in the field of purchasing and developing raw land in which the volume builder has been able to effectuate maximum economies.

In the purchase of an unsubdivided tract of raw land, a builder is faced with a wide range of economic and mechanical problems. Of initial importance is the determination of the basic price bracket in which the builder desires to build, or which is required in the area. If the area surrounding the tract is substantially developed, the builder is allowed, from a practical standpoint, little choice. For example, if the surrounding area is developed with homes in the $15,000 to $25,000 classification it would be foolhardy for a builder to attempt to market homes in the $40,000 to $50,000 bracket. On the other hand, if the surrounding area is developed with homes in higher price brackets, municipal building codes and land use zoning requirements are usually specifically designed to prevent the construction of lower cost housing.

A determination of the price bracket of the homes to be built on any particular tract of land, based on the above factors, will establish a proper price for the acreage involved. It is generally recognized that from 20% to 25% of the sales price of a single family dwelling represents the land on which it is located. Therefore, in an area having an average home value of $20,000, scattered subdivided lots within the area and with all improvements such as community water, sewer systems, roads, etc., will range from $4,000 to $6,000 per site. In order for the volume builder to be competitive with the small volume home builder purchasing such scattered lots, the volume builder must be able to purchase and develop the raw farm land in such a way that his unit cost per subdivided lot will be less than the price of scattered subdivided lots already in the same area.

A 40 acre tract, about the minimum that can be economically developed, will contain from 3 to 5 lots per acre of land, depending on local zoning requirements. On-site improvement costs for streets, sidewalks, sanitary sewer facilities, water facilities, public utilities, etc., are estimated in the Chicago area at approximately $30 per lineal foot. Assuming lots on both sides of a street, the improvement cost for a 50 foot lot is therefore, approximately $750. If it were possible to secure 200 lots from a 40 acre tract the builder's on-site improvement cost would therefore be $150,000. In addition, there must be calculated administration, engineering, legal, interest charges, etc. These miscellaneous indirect costs have been estimated to run from 30% to 50% of the end cost of the finished subdivided lot. Therefore, for a lot having an end value of $3,500 the builder can anticipate costs over and above raw land and on-site improvements of approximately $1400 per site. This sum added to the on site improvement cost of $750 would result in a total of $2,150 per site. Subtracting this figure from a desired value of $3,500 would enable the builder to économically pay $1,350 per site for the raw land, or a total of $270,000 for a 40 acre tract.

While raw land for subdivision purposes is acquired in a variety of ways, the most common method calls for the payment of 29% of the purchase price at the time of execution of the contract of purchase, with the balance in three or four equal annual payments with interest on the unpaid balance at approximately 6% per annum. The 29% figure has become fairly standardized as being the basis on which the seller can report the sale for income tax purposes on an installment basis.

Two methods are commonly used by attorneys to protect the seller from a possible default on the part of the buyer-builder. The first is a so-called "cushion" arrangement wherein the seller, in return for the 29% down payment conveys only 10% of the land involved. In the event of default at any time prior to the complete performance by the buyer, the balance of the initial deposit is forfeited as liquidated damages. The second method is to give a buyer-builder a full release of land in relationship to the down payment but require that the builder start his development at the farther-most corner of the parcel. The second method requires the builder to install in advance a sizeable amount of on site improvements on land to which he does not have title. In the event of a default these improvements inure to the benefit of the seller.

Under either of the above two methods a builder, to purchase a 40 acre tract for homes in the $20,000 price bracket, would be required to make an initial equity investment for the raw land of $78,300. In the event a "cushion" is required, the builder will receive for his down payment approximately $27,000 worth of land. As noted above, the balance would be held to insure the complete performance of his contract to purchase. If the contract designates that the builder start at the farther-most section of the tract, a comparable sum of money will be tied up until the complete performance of the contract by reason of the installation of improvements in advance.

Because of the huge cost involved, most subdivided tracts are developed in separate units. On a four year development of a 40 acre tract a builder might develop each year only 50 lots. As noted above, the improvement cost for 50 such lots would be approximately $107,500. Many Illinois municipalities require that such improvement money be deposited in advance with the municipality to insure completion. Some, in addition, require an additional deposit of 15% over and above the contract price of the improvements.

From the above data it can be seen that a volume builder entering into the development of a 40 acre tract of farm land must be prepared to invest a minimum of $78,300 as a down payment on the land in addition to improvement costs of $107,500, or an overall initial investment of $185,000. Since these figures represent an anticipated volume of only 50 homes per year, it is readily apparent that the builder of 250 or more homes per year can anticipate initial cash investments in excess of $500,000.

V. *Effect of Presidential Order*

It should be obvious that anyone who has the intelligence to acquire from $150,000 to $500,000 in the first place, would not risk such an amount of cash without first making a thorough analysis and determination of the ultimate success of his venture. Detailed market studies, current housing trends and availability, transportation and school facilities, location of industry and shopping centers, etc., are just a few of the factors taken into consideration and directed toward the end question of whether or not the planned homes can be sold to the buying public. In addition, the builder's own optimism or pessimism about a given area and his impression of the strength of the prospective market play an important role in the builder's decision to embark on a new subdivision program. Not only must the volume builder determine the overall market, but, in addition, must make a fairly accurate estimate of the volume of homes he will be able to sell in a given period. In addition to interest on his land purchase and construction loans, the volume builder is necessarily faced with substantial overhead costs in the form of superintendents, salesmen, accounting and secretarial help, etc. A builder with a fixed overhead cost of $50,000 a year must necessarily sell 50 homes per year to maintain a unit overhead cost of $1,000 per unit. If he miscalculates the speed at which his homes will sell and is able to sell only 10 homes in a year, it is apparent that his overhead cost per unit would amount to $5,000 and result either in his homes being over-priced, or the builder suffering a loss on each sale and resulting bankruptcy.

Moreover, assuming an unpaid balance on the land of $200,000, and 50 constructed homes costing $20,000 with unpaid construction mortgages of $15,000 each, plus $50,000 tied up in improvements, the builder will be carrying loans totalling $1,000,000. The interest on this alone, at 6%, is $60,000, so that if at the end of the year, 40 homes remain unsold, the builder has a net interest deficit of $48,000. Thus, each of these 40 homes must be raised $1,200 more simply to cover the interest.

It is the opinion of the writer that it was the economic factors mentioned above but not expressed in the home builder's questionnaire, rather than emotional factors which caused the members of the N.A.H.B. to estimate a 60% decline in the home building industry in the event an executive order or other anti-discrimination law was passed. It is suggested that the volume home builder is like any other mass producer of consumer goods. He is more concerned with the ultimate sale of his product to the consumer, rather than the background, color or religion of the particular consumer.

It is doubtful that the executive order issued by the President will have any *immediate* effect on the home building industry. Builders who are obligated by contract to purchase large tracts of land will undoubtedly complete their projects, rather than suffer the penalties for breach of their purchase contracts. Since the presidential order affected only homes financed by FHA and VA programs, it can be assumed that many builders will investigate the possibility of using conventional financing for the homes remaining in their projects.

The most drastic effect of the presidential executive order or state anti-discrimination legislation will probably be felt four or five years from now. The initial result will be the reluctance of volume builders to initiate plans for new developments to be started several years hence. This is particularly true if the presidential order is extended to include conventional mortgages not insured by the FHA or VA. The present order, the threat of extension to conventional financing, plus possible state legislation, is necessarily going to force the volume builder contemplating the investment of hundreds of thousands of dollars to ask himself one simple question, "If by reason of the presidential order or legislative act, I am forced to sell one of my first homes in a new subdivision to a Negro family, will I be able to sell the balance of my homes in the development with the speed needed to sustain my operation and justify my capital investment?"

While no amount of statistical data offered to prove that the presence of a Negro family does not have an adverse effect on white demand would probably have much affect on the personal conclusion reached by the individual volume builder, there is substantial evidence that initial occupancy by a Negro family would adversely affect white demand. In the book, "The Demand for Housing in Racially Mixed Areas," by Chester Rapkin and William G. Grigsby, a block by block study in West Philadelphia revealed that in 1955 out of 286 homes purchased by white families in an integrated area, only two were acquired next door to an already resident Negro family. The study further shows that white demand for housing in integrated areas declines sharply in relation to the number of non-whites in the area. A single family in a large geographic area might have only a slight affect on white demand, which is also influenced by such factors as proximity to work, familiarity with the area, etc. Each additional non-white family, however, caused an increasingly sharp decline in white demand. Since the decline in white demand is much greater than Negro demand, one of two results must occur. Either the neighborhood will become all Negro or, in the event prices are beyond reach of the Negro demand, the homes will remain unsold until prices are reduced to the level of the Negro purchasing power. Short of government control on where a family shall live, the opening up of new area by means of legislative action will result in a depression of home values in most areas.

Further, according to the above study, part of the drop off of white demand is based on the *anticipation* of greater Negro occupation rather than the occupation that in fact exists. It appears that the demand would not drop off as sharply if the white population would not fear or anticipate a complete turnover of the area.

Faced with the above, the volume home builder must anticipate the effect on his subdivision program if one of the first homes in his area was sold to a Negro family. If whites hesitated to buy for fear that the entire area could become Negro, the builder risks forfeiture of his investment capital and prospective bankruptcy.

Finally, a reluctance on the part of the volume builder to initiate new programs will result not only in the loss of thousands of jobs for carpenters, brick layers, laborers, electricians, plumbers, etc., drastic reductions in outlays for building materials, supplies, appliances but, in addition will increase the cost of housing to all purchasers—Negro and white alike. As noted earlier, a decline in volume building operation will force the potential home seeker to custom build on existing scattered home sites. It can be anticipated that the demand for such sites in established areas will greatly increase their price to the detriment of the home buying public.

R. J. ANDERSON

APPENDIX

The report of the tabulation set forth a number of tables. Those most pertinent to this article are set forth below.

TABLE 3. *Estimated Effect of FHA-VA Anti-Discrimination Order, Effectively Enforced, on Builder's Own Plans, by Size Category*

Estimated Effect on Own Plans	Number of Respondents Classified by Number of Housing Units Expected to be Built in 1962								
	1-10	11-25	26-50	51-100	101-250	Over 250	None	n.a.	Total
No change	718	641	330	167	98	63	28	15	2,060
Increase—Total	21	20	11	8	5	4	3	2	74
5%	3	1	1			2		1	8
10-25%	7	9	9	4	2		1		32
30-45%	2	1		2	2				7
50-75%	3	4							7
Over 75%	2	2	1			1			6
% n.a.	4	3		2	1	1	2	1	14
Decrease—Total	316	596	554	485	295	143	34	11	2,434
5%	12	17	12	9	6	3	1		60
10-25%	57	147	100	75	49	34	3	2	467
30-45%	18	27	43	40	29	18	2	1	178
50-75%	88	202	193	173	95	55	8	3	817
Over 75%	116	182	170	163	105	28	14	2	780
% n.a.	25	21	36	25	11	5	6	3	132
Not answered	406	366	209	118	66	23	66	83	1,337
Total	1,461	1,623	1,104	778	464	233	131	111	5,905

TABLE 4. *Percentage of Respondents Who Indicate a Negative Effect on Own Building Plans Under FHA-VA Anti-Discrimination Order, by Size Category*

Number of Housing Units Expected to be Built in 1962	Percentage of Respondents Expecting Decrease in Own Building Plans Under FHA-VA Anti-Discrimination Order
1-10	21.6
11-25	36.7
26-50	50.2
51-100	62.3
101-250	63.6
Over 250	61.4
Total	41.2

TABLE 5. *Number and Percentage of Housing Units Expected to be Built in 1962 by Expected Size Category of Builder in 1962*

Size Category of Builder (No. of Housing Units Expected to be Built in 1962)	Number of Housing Units		Percentage of Housing Units Expected to be Built in 1962		Builders Expecting Adverse Effect on Own Plans Under FHA-VA Order
	Built in 1961	Expected to Build in 1962	Built in 1961	All Builders	
1-10	8,478	9,887	3.4	2.8	.6
11-25	22,462	29,467	9.1	8.5	3.1
26-50	32,567	43,669	13.2	12.6	6.3
51-100	43,854	60,412	17.8	17.4	10.8
101-250	49,172	75,295	20.0	21.7	13.8
Over 250	89,992	128,925	36.5	37.0	22.7
Total	246,625	347,655	100.0	100.0	57.3

TABLE 8. *Estimated Effect of an FHA-VA Anti-Discrimination Order, Effectively Enforced, on All Builders in Respondents' Area, by Size Category*

Estimated Effect on Builder's Area	Number of Respondents Classified by Number of Units Expected to be Built in 1962								
	1-10	11-25	26-50	51-100	101-250	Over 250	None	n.a.	Total
No change	497	419	225	129	66	49	21	15	1,421
Increase—Total	27	22	14	9	7	3	4	2	88
5%	8	4	3	1	1	1		1	19
10-25%	11	11	7	4	3	1	1		38
30-45%				1	1				2
50-75%	1	4	1	1	1				8
Over 75%	2	1	1						4
% n.a.	5	2	2	2	1	1	3	1	17

Table 8. *(Continued)*

Estimated Effect on Builder's Area	Number of Respondents Classified by Number of Units Expected to be Built in 1962								
	1-10	11-25	26-50	51-100	101-250	Over 250	None	n.a.	Total
Decrease—Total	421	742	608	489	302	149	39	21	2,771
5%	13	20	18	10	3	4	2		70
10-25%	107	212	120	78	67	42	7	4	637
30-45%	37	56	60	49	30	21	2	3	258
50-75%	121	231	225	191	102	52	8	7	937
Over 75%	109	183	147	128	87	24	16	3	697
% n.a.	34	40	38	33	13	6	4	4	172
Not answered	516	440	257	151	89	32	67	73	1,625
Total	1,461	1,623	1,104	778	464	233	131	111	5,905

TABLE 9. *Estimated Effect on Own Plans and on Area Plans If Anti-Discrimination Order is Promulgated and Enforced With Respect to Conventional Financing As Well As FHA-VA*

Estimated Effect	Own Plans		Area Plans	
	Number of Respondents	% of All Respondents	Number of Respondents	% of All Respondents
No change	1,630	27.6	1,281	21.7
Increase—Total	98	1.7	110	1.9
5%	10	.2	13	.2
10-25%	46	.8	54	.9
30-45%	6	.1	5	.1
50-75%	13	.2	14	.2
Over 75%	10	.2	10	.2
% n.a.	13	.2	14	.2
Decrease—Total	3,025	51.2	3,250	55.0
5%	46	.8	61	1.0
10-25%	457	7.7	552	9.3
30-45%	191	3.2	279	4.7
50-75%	983	16.6	1,121	19.0
Over 75%	1,115	18.9	988	16.7
% n.a.	233	3.9	249	4.2
Not answered	1,152	19.5	1,264	21.4
Total	5,905	100.0	5,905	100.0

BUILDING UNDER ANTI-DISCRIMINATION ORDERS: THE LEVITTOWN EXPERIENCE

One of the largest builders of single-family suburban homes in the United States is Levitt & Sons, Inc., which builds primarily in the East. This company, in addition to numerous smaller suburban developments, has built several whole cities in the areas around New York, Philadelphia and Baltimore. The New York and Pennsylvania projects, both known as Levittown, have already been completed. Levittown, New Jersey and Bel-Air, Maryland, the two other planned communities, are still in the process of completion and sale.

The Levitt policy in New York and Pennsylvania was to sell only to white buyers.[1] This policy has been continued in Maryland.[2] During the period when the New York and Pennsylvania projects were in the process of completion, no law, state or federal, forbade this.[3] The company successfully resisted court attacks on its policy in both communities.[4]

Levitt's announced initial policy in New Jersey was the same.[5] However, New Jersey had recently enacted a law forbidding discrimination in "publicly assisted" housing.[6] Levitt's policy was soon challenged on the basis of this law,[7] and on February 9, 1960, the New Jersey State Supreme Court upheld the constitutionality of the law and ordered Levitt & Sons to sell homes in Levittown, New Jersey, to Negro buyers.[8] On June 13, 1960, the United States Supreme Court dismissed Levitt's appeal from this order,[9] and thereafter the company announced that it would comply with the order and sell homes to Negro applicants without discrimination.[10]

This article will analyze the effects of the New Jersey anti-discrimination order on Levitt & Sons' operations. Such analysis is particularly timely since this is the only large-scale builder which has been subjected to such an order. However, the President's recent executive order forbidding discrimination in federally assisted housing has caused a large number of builders to cut back their operations in the belief that their sales would suffer from integrating their projects.[11] This study will seek to determine whether these fears are justified or fanciful.

The Levittowns in Pennsylvania and New Jersey provide especially useful data for a study such as this. The two communities are in geographically similar locations, each about 15 miles from the Philadelphia-Camden area. There is no apparent factor that would make either of these communities more popular than the other, except possibly that the Pennsylvania community was constructed earlier than that in New Jersey. Levitt, however, obviously felt that there was room in the Philadelphia-Camden area for two Levittowns and the company's judgment is not likely to be wrong. The

---

1 N.Y. Times, June 7, 1958; N.Y. Times, June 29, 1958, p. 36, col. 1.

2 N.Y. Times, April 14, 1960, p. 25, col. 7.

3 The New York and Pennsylvania laws against discrimination in housing were not enacted until the projects had been completed. See N.Y. Laws 1955, C. 341, eff. July 1, 1955, N.Y. Civil Rights Law, §§ 18-b, 18-c; Pa. L. 1961, P.L. 47, eff. Feb. 28, 1961, 43 Pur. Pa. Stat. Ann. § 951 *et seq.*

4 Novick v. Levitt & Sons, Inc., 200 Misc. 694, 108 N.Y.S.2d 615 (1951), *aff'd,* 279 App. Div. 617, 107 N.Y.S.2d 1016 (1951); Johnson v. Levitt & Sons, Inc., 131 F. Supp. 114 (E.D. Pa. 1955).

5 *Supra,* n.1.

6 N.J. Laws 1957, c. 66, 18 N.J.S.A. 25-5.

7 *Supra,* n.1. See also N.Y. Times, Nov. 27, 1959, p. 31, col. 1.

8 Levitt & Sons, Inc. v. Division Against Discrimination, 31 N.J. 514, 158 A.2d 177 (1960).

9 Levitt & Sons, Inc. v. Division Against Discrimination, 363 U.S. 418 (1960).

10 N.Y. Times, March 28, 1960, p. 31, col. 5; N.Y. Times, July 13, 1960, p. 31, col. 2.

11 Wall Street Journal, Dec. 28, 1962, p. 1, col. 6.

different times during which the two projects were constructed may reasonably be disregarded.[11a]

The major distinction between the two communities is, therefore, the fact that New Jersey had a state law forbidding discrimination in "publicly assisted" housing, and Pennsylvania did not. A comparison of the two communities may be instructive in isolating the effect of the New Jersey laws (and similar laws) on housing sales.

Table I gives the figures for titles conveyed annually. While the New Jersey project is not completed, Levitt had originally planned a community of 15,000 or 16,000 homes. In the first four years of the project, Levitt sold 4,739 homes, or 31.6% of the planned 15,000. In the first four years of sales in Pennsylvania, by contrast, 13,110 homes were sold. This was 75.7% of the final total of 17,329. Such a discrepancy cannot be explained on the basis of general business conditions; each project was begun at the end of a mild recession, and continued through the subsequent upswing.

If it could be assumed that sales in New Jersey would follow a pattern roughly similar to those in Pennsylvania, Levitt's New Jersey community would eventually have only about 7,000 homes—less than half the size

[11a] Corroborating the fact that there was no overall slump in building in the Philadelphia market area are the following figures for households, compiled by Standard Rate & Data Service, Inc., in *Consumer Markets*. While these figures do not show new dwelling units as such, the formation of a new household in the area would require the addition of a dwelling unit under normal circumstances. The table below shows a steady, and sometimes a considerable rise in the number of suburban households in the three Pennsylvania suburban counties of Bucks, Delaware, and Montgomery, and the two New Jersey suburban counties of Burlington and Camden, which surround Philadelphia. Levittown, Pennsylvania, is in Bucks County; Levittown, New Jersey, is in Burlington County. This growth in number of households indicates a continued demand for dwelling units in the area housing market, during both the period when Levittown, Pennsylvania was constructed, and while Levittown, New Jersey was constructed. Levitt's ability to share in the former but not to the same extent in the latter negates the possibility that time was a decisive factor.

NUMBER OF HOUSEHOLDS IN PHILADELPHIA SUBURBAN COUNTIES
(Figures in thousands)

Date	Pennsylvania Counties			New Jersey Counties	
	Bucks	Delaware	Montgomery	Burlington	Camden
1/1/54	46.19	129.48	104.21	39.14	95.47
1/1/55	71.60	131.14	106.13	40.40	97.87
1/1/56	76.20	133.10	107.87	41.99	100.23
1/1/57	74.27	133.19	108.25	42.38	100.16
1/1/58	77.56	133.68	106.36	44.36	103.93
1/1/59	95.43	143.39	137.77	45.38	103.30
7/1/59	95.79	143.69	139.38	45.29	102.85
7/1/60	99.51	158.44	144.24	57.17	114.42
1/1/61	102.97	158.82	144.56	57.65	115.39
1/1/62	105.14	161.76	154.27	58.83	118.43

of the Pennsylvania Levittown.[12] In this connection, it is relevant to note that the New Jersey project, for the first three years, does in fact appear to be following a pattern similar to that in Pennsylvania, but on a much smaller scale. In the year ending February 28, 1962, however, sales in New Jersey continued to drop, while in the fourth year in Pennsylvania they rose. Table II, giving the figures for the first six months of the fifth year in New Jersey, indicates that sales there are continuing to decline; they are down 40% from the first half of the fourth year. This is consistent with the pattern in Pennsylvania for the entire fourth and fifth years.

The consistently smaller sales in New Jersey suggest that the factors causing that project to be less successful were operating from the beginning. This is consistent with the hypothesis that the New Jersey law was the major factor. Within 24 hours of Levitt's original announcement of the project, the National Association for the Advancement of Colored People sent a telegram to the Governor of New Jersey, claiming that the project violated the state law. If white home buyers preferred not to live in an integrated community, they would have hesitated to buy homes while the

[12] Levittown, Pennsylvania, had an estimated 70,000 people and 17,311 homes in April, 1960. Editor and Publisher, *1962 Market Guide* 409. Levittown, New York, had 65,276 inhabitants in 1960. U.S. Bureau of Census, *U.S. Census of Population: 1960; Number of Inhabitants, Final Report*. New York PC(1)-34A-17 (1961). Levittown, New Jersey had 11,861 inhabitants in 1960. *Id.*, New Jersey PC(1)-32A-13. At that same time, Levittown, New York had 15,741 housing units, of which 15,543 were occupied, 14,742 (94.8%) by owners, 14,706 by white households, 36 by non-white households; 801 were renter-occupied, 793 by white households, 8 by non-white households. U.S. Bureau of the Census: *U.S. Census of Housing: 1960. Vol. I, States and Small Areas, Final Report.* New York, HC(1)-34-21 (1962). Levittown, New Jersey had 3262 housing units, of which 2978 were occupied, 2886 (96.9%) by owners, 2874 by white households, 12 by non-white households; 92 were renter occupied, all by whites. *Id.*, New Jersey, HC(1)-32-73.

TITLES CONVEYED AND COMPLETED HOUSE INVENTORY
For Years Ended 2/28/50-2/28/62
All Figures are as at F.Y.E.

Year Ended 2/28 or 2/29	Titles Conveyed				Completed Houses Available for Sale			
	N.Y.	Pa.	N.J.	Md.	N.Y.	Pa.	N.J.	Md.
1950	4671				69			
1951	5332				94			
1952	2500				0			
1953		3086				209		
1954		4691				377		
1955		2475				956		
1956		3058				634		
1957		1553				297		
1958		1322				371		
1959		1144	896				193	
1960			1923				135	
1961			1094				258	
1962			826	988			96	62

case was pending. After the State Supreme Court's decision of February 10, 1960, and especially after the refusal of the U.S. Supreme Court to hear

TITLES CONVEYED AND COMPLETED HOUSE INVENTORY
At Month End 3/59-8/62

Month End.	Titles Conveyed		Completed Houses Available for Sale	
	New Jersey	Maryland	New Jersey	Maryland
3/31/59	108		85	
4/30/59	58		27	
5/31/59	52		62	
6/30/59	238		133	
7/31/59	281		136	
8/31/59	291		109	
9/30/59	279		88	
10/31/59	188		151	
11/30/59	133		169	
12/31/59	108		322	
1/31/60	115		207	
2/29/60	72		135	
	1923			
3/31/60	59		76	
4/30/60	26		50	
5/31/60	80		145	
6/30/60	234		143	
7/31/60	170		128	
8/31/60	110		182	
9/30/60	80		255	
10/31/60	53		319	
11/30/60	101		382	
12/31/60	77		329	
1/31/61	51		278	
2/28/61	53		258	
	1094			
3/31/61	66		213	
4/30/61	38		175	
5/31/61	54		192	
6/30/61	109		222	
7/31/61	81		275	
8/31/61	80		345	
9/30/61	79		329	
10/31/61	42	51	287	9
11/30/61	53	187	234	32
12/31/61	19	212	215	99
1/31/62	38	227	177	103
2/28/62	167	311	96	62
	826	988		
3/31/62	31	61	87	63
4/30/62	29	18	119	45
5/31/62	48	24	72	34
6/30/62	33	111	38	30
7/31/62	32	146	74	49
8/31/62	82	234	119	100
	255	594		

the appeal, on June 14, 1960, sales dropped significantly, and, except for a few scattered months, stayed well below 1959 levels. Indeed, the inventory data of Table II indicate that at times sales were so slow that new construction stopped altogether.

This reduction in sales cannot be attributed to a generally sluggish housing market in the East, as the figures for Bel Air, Levitt's Maryland project, indicate. Sales there in half of the year ending February 28, 1962, were greater than those for the whole year in Levittown, New Jersey. The monthly figures give support to the hypothesis that the New Jersey state law had a deleterious effect upon the Levitt project in that state.

It would not be reasonable, of course, to attribute all of the difference between the two Levittowns to the difference in state laws on discrimination. But there do not seem to be any other major factors which could account for a large share of that difference. Until some other factors are suggested, it appears to be a reasonable conclusion that the New Jersey law has caused a significant reduction in the sales of Levitt's houses in New Jersey.

ROBERT F. CROLL*

* B.S.B.A. 1954, Northwestern Univ.; M.B.A. 1956, Univ. of Michigan; candidate for Doctor of Business Administration in business economics and public policy, Indiana Univ. School of Business. Personal Assistant to the Speaker, Illinois House of Representatives. Appreciation is expressed to John C. Weicher, B.A. 1959, Univ. of Michigan, graduate student, Dept. of Economics (Urban Economics), Univ. of Chicago, for research on the figures used in this comment.

BOOK REVIEWS

STUDIES IN HOUSING AND MINORITY GROUPS. By Nathan Glazer and Davis McEntire. Berkeley, Calif.: University of California Press, 1960. Pp. xvii, 228, $6.00.

PRIVATELY DEVELOPED INTERRACIAL HOUSING. By Eunice and George Grier. Berkeley, Calif.: University of California Press, 1960. Pp. viii, 264, $6.00.

PROPERTY VALUES AND RACE. By Luigi Laurenti. Berkeley, Calif.: University of California Press, 1960. Pp. xix, 256, $6.00.

THE DEMAND FOR HOUSING IN RACIALLY MIXED AREAS. By Chester Rapkin and William G. Grigsby. Berkeley, Calif.: University of California Press, 1960. Pp. xx, 177, $6.00.

RESIDENCE AND RACE. By Davis McEntire. Berkeley, Calif.: University of California Press, 1960. Pp. xxii, 409, $6.00.

In 1955, the Commission on Race and Housing, a private independent citizens' group formed to combat discrimination and promote anti-discrimination legislation in housing, received a grant of $305,000 from the Ford Foundation's Fund for the Republic to study minority group housing. The foregoing five books are a product of this sponsored research. These publications have been widely acclaimed as proof of the need for anti-discrimination legislation. There is little doubt that the publications have assembled a wide variety of statistical information regarding minority housing in the United States. However, there are serious questions as to the conclusions that can properly be drawn from the assembled data.

In order to subject these studies to analysis by persons experienced in the fields involved, the symposium selected a review committee of people experienced in various aspects of the real estate field. This included management, appraisal, financial, legal, editorial (trade press), subdivision and land development, and brokerage. A majority of the committee has had experience in the brokerage of real estate. Each committee member concentrated his attention on one of the five books, while giving a more cursory look at the remaining volumes. Reviews were prepared by each member and finalized in group discussions. Hence, individual reviews represent, insofar as practicable, collective opinion. In all cases, the considerable group experience in real estate was utilized in evaluating conclusions presented in these books.

RAY O. SPECKMAN
President, Illinois Association of Real Estate Boards

STUDIES IN HOUSING AND MINORITY GROUPS

Unlike some of the other studies in the group which attempt to analyze the problem of minority housing on a national scale, this study is local in character and consists of five independent studies of Negro housing in Atlanta, Birmingham, San Antonio, Houston, New Orleans, Dade County (Miami area) and Detroit. In addition, the publication contains a study of Puerto Ricans in New York City and Japanese-American housing in San Francisco.

The study is particularly interesting in that two of the individual studies are based on a comparison of minority housing facilities between two somewhat comparable cities as well as between different minority groups within each city. Thus, in a study of San Antonio, Texas, it was found that there was considerably less prejudice against the Mexican population than against the Negro with the Mexican allowed to live virtually any place his income would allow. Despite this fact the study revealed that the Negro in San Antonio had better housing than the Mexican population which was attributed to the fact that Negroes in San Antonio had a higher average income than the general Mexican population. The author of the San Antonio study concludes: "If we were to assume that these populations [minority groups] could bid for housing under conditions of strict equality with the Anglo group, and at the same time their economic position were to remain the same, *no great improvement in their housing would result*" (emphasis added) (p. 98).

A similar conclusion must be reached as regards the comparison City of Houston, Texas. The study indicated a pattern of segregation similar to any other Texas city. Despite such pattern of segregation, the study showed a vast improvement in Negro housing both in new and existing housing in formerly all-white areas. As regards new home facilities, the study reports that the market was glutted in the $8,000 to $15,000 price bracket; that intensive sales competition developed and that at least one firm went bankrupt as a result of the failure of the development for the Negro market. The author of the study attributes the rise in housing available to the Negro to the fact that the Houston Negro is economically in a stronger position than Negroes of other Texas cities. The author also felt that "there is a distinctively strong desire for better housing among the Negroes of Houston." A comparison of population growth and total fertility between the Negro population of San Antonio and Houston suggests, according to the author, "that the Negroes of Houston may have a more stable family pattern than those of San Antonio, which would have some effect on the strength of their motivations to acquire new housing and their ability to bear the economic demands and pressures of home-ownership" (p. 103).

The report concludes that as regards San Antonio and Houston, Texas, "the chief cause of the inferior housing of minority groups in the two cities today is their poverty. It follows that *any large-scale improvement in their housing conditions involves either a rise in the level of income of the minority groups or more extensive subsidized housing*" (emphasis added) (p. 108).

The study of minority housing in Atlanta and Birmingham merits the briefest of comments. It includes a report of the problems encountered by Mrs. "Y" in the purchase of a home in an all-white area, the difficulties surmounted by an enterprising Negro builder, and a historical background of the racial zoning restrictions of Birmingham from 1915 to 1947 when declared unconstitutional. While this information provides an interesting history, there is little factual material here. The only conclusion that can be drawn is that the Negro in Atlanta is more educated, more active politically, and more interested in securing adequate housing than his Birmingham counterpart. As a result, the Atlanta Negro population has secured vastly superior housing than secured by Negroes in Birmingham despite a higher average income on the part of the latter.

The studies of Negro housing facilities in New Orleans and in Dade County, Florida are noteworthy in that they provide further evidence that the caliber and quality of available Negro housing is directly related to the income, cultural level, and family stability of the Negro himself. The study indicates that New Orleans is not a highly segregated city. In the 1950 census only 21 of a total of 142 census tracts were all white; only 33 were predominantly Negro-occupied. Thus, in well over half of the census tracts occupancy was mixed between white and non-white. Despite the freedom of New Orleans Negroes to live where they choose on a non-segregated basis, more than four-fifths of all Negro dwellings according to the 1950 census were either dilapidated or lacked essential sanitary facilities. Since the study reports that the New Orleans Negro has a lower income than Negroes in any other major southern city, it can be concluded that one of the most dynamic forces at work and causing inferior housing was economic means rather than a pattern of discrimination.

The additional effect of family stability and educational and cultural attainment is indicated by the comparison made between two large private Negro housing developments in New Orleans—Pontchartrain Park and Bunche Village. While the income of residents of the two developments was approximately the same, almost a third of the Pontchartrain family heads were professional or white-collar workers. The blue-collar group in Pontchartrain had large numbers of "upper blue-collar" workers such as postmen, skilled craftsmen and policemen. By contrast, 95% of the Bunche Village family heads were classed as blue-collar workers and included many more longshoremen, stevedores, truck drivers, porters, and laborers. The study revealed that while there was little or no payment delinquency in Pontchartrain Park, almost two-thirds of the purchasers had poor payment records in Bunche Village. While Pontchartrain Park has prospered as a desirable and good residential area, many of the homes in Bunche Village show an absence of improvement and some were reported as neglected and run-down. The author of the study reported a scattering of "For Sale" signs and expressed the opinion that new buyers would be difficult to find and that the owners would be unable to recover their equity investment.

In summary, *Studies in Housing and Minority Groups* provides valuable data as to the factors which create, maintain, and cause inferior housing facilities for various minority groups. The effect of segregation, prejudice and discrimination on housing facilities is summed up by Mr. Nathan Glazer, co-editor of the above studies, in his introduction:

> Prejudice in its pure form . . . rarely plays a decisive role in the determination of the housing of minority groups. It is in the South that the role of prejudice may be seen perhaps in its sharpest form. And yet even here every action of discrimination . . . is based on economic factors in the situation somewhat independent of prejudice . . . the decisive factors in this poor housing are Negro economic weakness and white middle-class fears of the deterioration of neighborhoods on Negro entry. (p. 4)

PRIVATELY DEVELOPED INTERRACIAL HOUSING

This book is intended as a study of private housing developments in which purchase or rental by members of two or more races have taken place. It sets forth the projects where this has taken place between 1946 and 1955, attempts to evaluate the success and problems of the developers, and seeks to appraise the effectiveness of various methods and techniques in promoting interracial developments.

The study reports that 50 such developments had come into existence, and the introduction indicates that 37 of them were studied in varying degrees of intensity. However, the introduction also states: "This study therefore is directed more to scope than to depth, more to identifying problems (and developing hypothesis) than to answering them conclusively." Because the book has this purpose, there are very few statistical tabulations and a great many subjective summations of opinions of the persons involved.

The book is a combination of factual reporting and editorializing by persons interested in proving that interracial housing can be successful. However, the bulk of the study concerns the development of a small low price project in Wisconsin, a religious development (Rolling Plain Cooperative) in Illinois, Concord Park in Philadelphia, and a 316-unit rental tract in California. Because of the relatively small number of units involved and lack of a study in depth, this survey is of little help in any over-all analysis of discrimination or anti-discrimination legislation. The principal value of the study to the student of discrimination and minority housing is in its recital of the problems and difficulties encountered in these four developments in their attempts to create interracial housing projects.

PROPERTY VALUES AND RACE

This book reports on an extremely well designed and scientifically conducted study of price trends in twenty well defined neighborhoods where non-white entry occurred in all-white areas in three cities—San Francisco, Oakland, and Philadelphia. These neighborhoods consisted primarily of single family residences occupied by owners (before and after non-white entry) and not contiguous to other areas containing non-white population. The study reviewed prices of sales in these neighborhoods during the years mid-1949 to mid-1955, a period of general housing shortage, both in all-white housing and in non-white housing.

The general conclusion, supported by factual data, is that in these areas, the sale prices tended to increase slightly more rapidly than in comparable all-white areas where there was no non-white entry. It disclosed the fact that whites did not leave the areas en masse on non-white entry, but there was almost always a decrease (sometimes sharply) in the demand by whites in the area. However, this was generally offset by a continuous demand from non-whites. In most cases, the density characteristic and the maintenance quality level of the neighborhoods remained unchanged and there was no evidence of panic selling by the whites. In the one high-priced neighborhood studied by Laurenti, it was clear that the shift from all-white to mixed occupancy led to a price decline because it appeared there were so few non-whites with the means to support a high price, combined with a drought of white purchasers in this integrated area. In an all-white area in Oakland, where the market demand had begun to sag, the shift to non-white occupancy, after first entry, was more rapid than in the others where the market had previously held more strength.

There is left unanswered, of course, the question of what future influence or changes will take place in these neighborhoods, now that the housing shortage in all-white areas has virtually changed to surplus, and the housing supply in all non-white or in mixed areas is certainly no longer considered scarce. Anthony Downs, in his review of Laurenti's work, states: "Since whites looking for homes have more alternates than they had in the period of shortage, and since most whites do not wish to live in transition neighborhoods, fewer will offer to buy homes in such neighborhoods" and "demand among whites for homes in that area will fall off much faster than it did in periods of shortage."[1]

Laurenti's study made no attempt to analyze price trends in white neighborhoods which are contiguous to mixed or all non-white areas. Thus, his work may not be said to evaluate the impact on property surrounding the huge Negro areas in Chicago, Detroit, Milwaukee and other cities. Here, non-white expansion almost always involves increased density, reduced income level of residents, and reduced maintenance standards. These conditions did not occur in Laurenti's areas.

Thus, it would seem that Laurenti has effectively challenged the stereo-

[1] Downs, *An Economic Analysis of* Property Values and Race (*Laurenti*), 36 Land Economics 181, 185-6 (1960).

type judgment that entry of non-whites in an area adversely affects property value in all cases, but conversely, he does not disprove this judgment as applied in circumstances where:

(1) Entry into high priced areas occurs.
(2) Entry produces higher density.
(3) Entry produces lower maintenance.
(4) Entry results in lower average income of residents.
(5) Entry comes at a time when a surplus of housing is in the market.
(6) Entry comes in rented multiple housing more typical of urban areas.

THE DEMAND FOR HOUSING IN RACIALLY MIXED AREAS

This study by Chester Rapkin and William G. Grigsby of the Institute for Urban Studies, University of Pennsylvania, analyzes the factors influencing white and non-white demand for housing in racially mixed areas by selected studies of the real estate market in several sections of Philadelphia. The choice of Philadelphia was a wise one. The authors indicate that the city has one of the largest Negro minorities, proportionately, of any northern metropolis, and since 1950 it has grown to 500,000 people representing 25% of the total population. (p. 5) In addition, the Philadelphia Negro has risen in economic status with home ownership rising to an estimated 44% in 1956. The authors qualify these facts, however, by noting that the cheapest homes in the Philadelphia area are in excess of $10,000 and that only 25,000 of 126,000 non-white families have incomes in excess of $5,000.

Philadelphia also was an excellent test city in that there is a wide dispersion of non-white families. While 80% of the Negro families lived fairly close to the central business district, Negroes were found in every ward in the city and in only five out of fifty-two wards were there fewer than one hundred non-whites.

The study consists of an examination of the 2,017 sales of owner-occupied dwellings taking place in 1955 in the selected test areas. The total was composed of 443 white and 1,574 Negro purchasers.

To determine the characteristics, motivations, and attitudes of white buyers, 194 of the white purchasers were personally interviewed. In addition, 100 white renters and 196 Negro purchasers were interviewed. The interviews revealed that as regards age, religion, children, etc., the characteristics of the white buyers were similar to those of the population as a whole. Over 60% of the white home purchasers had resided in the area prior to the date of purchase with 40% having resided in the area for over five years. While there existed alternate locations for the white buyers, such alternatives appeared to be greatly limited. Homes of a similar price could be found in only one-half of the city neighborhoods and approximately 50 percent of these were racially mixed. Alternatives were further limited by being beyond a reasonable commuting distance. Some 65 percent of the white purchasers gave "convenience of neighborhood" as the reason for their particular purchase. The authors of the study conclude that the most important factor influencing white purchasers was long time residence or intimate association with the general area strengthened by religious and cultural group ties.

The study contains an extremely interesting discussion of Negro proximity and proportion as it affects white demand. The discussion starts with the proposition that unless a white demand exists, areas subject to Negro entry will simply undergo a racial transition from white to Negro rather than become an integrated community. The acuteness of the problem is pointed up by the interviews conducted with white purchasers in mixed areas mentioned above. Their willingness to purchase seemed to be in direct proportion to the proximity of Negro families. Thus, while they might be willing to purchase on an all white block several blocks away from a Negro family, only a handful were willing to acquire a home adjacent to a Negro residence. Thus, if an adjacent residence can only be sold to another Negro, the inevitable result would be a transition of the entire block to all Negro residences. The study suggests that the most important qualification of this apparent inevitable result would be a lack of demand for the adjacent premises on the part of Negro buyers. Under such circumstances, the adjacent white owner would be faced with the alternative of not moving or reducing his price sufficiently so that a white buyer would overlook his objection to adjacent Negro occupancy in the interest of securing a housing "bargain."

As regards the proportion of Negro occupancy, the study notes that white demand drops drastically as the proportion of Negro occupancy increases. While one or a few Negroes in the community do not influence existing social or behavior patterns, an increase in proportion creates a situation in which existing neighborhood institutions lose support and undergo changes resulting in a real or anticipated neighborhood social change. The drop in white demand is further accentuated by a further decline based on fear of increased Negro occupancy in the future. Again, the end result— in the absence of drastic market changes—would be the complete transition of the area from all-white to non-white. The study notes that in order to generate demand by whites in racially mixed areas, *positive guarantees would have to be given that the racial composition would remain unchanged.* The study suggests such guarantees could be given, referring to the interracial Concord Park Development in which a quota system was utilized. (p. 71) The study admits that such quota guarantees would be impossible in existing neighborhoods.

The study further contains some interesting facts regarding non-white entry into the test areas. Contrary to popular belief, the study indicates that non-white purchasers paid approximately the same price as whites and secured equal or better financing. Only two out of forty-five "first families" reported any disagreeable occurrences on their entry, except that whites were moving out. As noted above, financing available was equal to or superior to that secured by whites and only a negligible number of loans were received from Negro financial sources (p. 85).

As regards housing prices in racially mixed areas, there is some conflict between this study and that conducted by Dr. Laurenti and reviewed above. The current study suggests that many of the studies of price movement, including that of Dr. Laurenti, have focused on the price shifts themselves rather than the underlying causes of the price shifts. The author further suggests that the price studies indicate that "in the face of an attrition of white demand, prices in a mixed neighborhood can be maintained only if Negroes continue to buy into the neighborhood and at the original price level. Thus, . . . white residents have a choice of declining prices or an increasing number of Negro neighbors, or both" (p. 103).

Unfortunately, the current study was able to compare price fluctuations in only one test area—that of West Philadelphia. However, the author was able to make a comparison between test zones within the area in relation to the degree of racial transition. The two test zones in which there was heavy Negro entry showed a steady increase in prices from an adjusted index of 79 in 1947 to 119 in 1955. By contrast, three zones of the West Philadelphia area which did not experience substantial Negro entry until after the other test zones showed a different pattern. While starting at a comparable base of 78 in mid-1947, the index in a strong housing market rose to 105 in mid-1948, in contrast to 98 in the heavy entry areas. With the exception of a slight dip in 1953, the heavy entry test areas showed a continuous price increase to a high of 119 by 1955. By contrast, the areas of light entry showed a steady decline in prices from the middle of 1950 until the middle of 1954. The index rose sharply in 1955, which coincides with a period of heavier Negro entry.

It would appear from the above that this study's comments regarding Dr. Laurenti's work and others studies of racial price fluctuations are valid even though the sampling was small. In substance, it indicates that prices will decline after Negro entry, unless the Negro demand equals the attrition of white demand.

The study makes the further comment that "It is unfortunate . . . that this type of analysis [price fluctuations] carries with it the implication that the justification for a social objective such as equality of access to the housing supply must be evaluated primarily in terms of the criteria of the market place" (p. 104).

RESIDENCE AND RACE

This represents the final and comprehensive report of a broad study of housing problems involving minority groups. The first part of the book concerns itself with racial residence patterns, distribution and income of occupants, age, condition, and crowding of dwellings, as compared in white and non-white areas. The second part deals with the attitudes, practices and problems, as they relate to minority groups, of those connected with the housing industry, namely, the builders, mortgage men, and real estate brokers. The third section considers the role of law and government in this problem, and the author concludes with a section which attempts to evaluate the prospects for anti-discrimination legislation in housing.

The first section of the book contains a number of statistical tables from the 1940 and 1950 censuses and various housing surveys, and draws two main conclusions from these. The first proposition is that the non-white buyer and renter gets less and pays more. This is concluded primarily from statistics on the comparison of the percentage of standard housing vs. substandard housing (without private bath, toilet, and hot running water) occupied by whites and non-whites. In this connection, it would appear that there are other factors to be considered, such as the fact that substandard housing is almost entirely located only in the older areas, which have now become segregated. More convincing would be some statistics as to rentals and prices for *similar* apartments and houses in white and in non-white areas. Indeed, in houses, the figures do show that in purchases in the higher price brackets, there is little or no difference in prices to white or non-white buyers. The second conclusion of the author is that minority residence does no harm to values, nor does it hurt market residence demands in mixed areas. This is based almost entirely on the Rapkin and the Grier studies (reviewed more fully above), which do not support this author's conclusions. In addition, almost all the figures conclude with the 1950 census. The enormous Negro housing gains between 1950 and 1960, as revealed in the 1960 census, and acceleration of gains since then, make many of the author's conclusions obsolete.

As to the position of those in the industry, in general, the book shows that the opportunity for a profitable venture is very limited in minority housing, segregated or interracial. Moreover, when this opportunity does exist, it often can be achieved only with a greater than normal effort, accompanied by peculiar and unusual problems. Since, like all other private enterprise, those in housing must find a profit in addition to meeting civic or community responsibilities, until public attitudes change, private ventures will be limited. The author's citation of a poll taken in 1956 showing that a clear majority of white northerners expressed a willingness to live in the same neighborhood with Negroes, even in the same block with those of similar income or education, is in contradiction with other facts in this study and the existing view of the majority of people. Such a broad conclusion cannot be accepted without a great deal more factual data than has been presented by the author.

In the discussion of the role of law and government, the author displays a strong belief in the use of the law to effect changes. He feels that making discrimination in housing illegal can change the social conditions which nourish attitudes of prejudice and segregation. Likewise, in the concluding section of the book, the implication of much of the material presented is that segregation in housing is a cause, rather than an effect, of the problem of discrimination resulting from prejudice. This is posited despite the author's opening statement in the conclusion that the housing problem is part of a larger problem of equal rights and full citizenship for all. A great deal of his faith seems to be based on the unwarranted assumption of a past record of the efficacy of laws and government in accomplishing and maintaining segregation.

The basic fallacy of the author's whole position is that he overlooks the fact that experience tells us that legislation resulting from minority group pressure which forces unresolved moral issues or social attitudes is not acceptable to the majority. The author's optimism that such legislation will work, based on lack of widespread or intensive opposition to it in the places where it has been enacted, rests on a foundation which cannot withstand close analysis. In those places where anti-discrimination legislation in housing has been enacted, evasion is widespread and the law itself is not respected by most of the community where it is in force. Thus, evasion seems to be the majority answer to such legislation.

ROBERT J. ANDERSON[a]
EDWARD DURSCHLAG[b]
JACK W. KLEEMAN[c]
WALTER R. KUEHNLE[d]
ARTHUR F. MOHL[e]
HERMAN O. WALTHER[f]

HOUSING (REPORT, BOOK 4). United States Commission on Civil Rights. Washington: Government Printing Office, 1961. Pp. xii, 206.

The 1961 Report of the United States Commission on Civil Rights, the second of its series of reports issued once every two years, represents a sharp decline in reliability from the 1959 Report. At that time, the Commission itself was carefully balanced to take into account almost every point of view in the race relations area, and its staff, which prepares the

[a] A.A. 1940, North Park College. Realtor.
[b] LL.B. 1937, Chicago-Kent College of Law. Realtor.
[c] B.S. 1955, Univ. of Illinois. Editor, Chicagoland Real Estate Advertiser.
[d] Realtor; Member, Appraisal Institute, American Institute of Real Estate Appraisers, National Association of Real Estate Boards (NAREB); Counselor, Real Estate, American Society of Real Estate Counselors, NAREB.
[e] Realtor; Certified Property Manager, Institute of Property Management, NAREB.
[f] M.B.A. 1926, Northwestern Univ. Realtor; Member, Appraisal Institute, American Institute of Real Estate Appraisers, NAREB; Counselor, Real Estate, American Society of Real Estate Counselors, NAREB.

reports themselves, had a degree of diversification of viewpoint. Today, most of the Commission members wholeheartedly favor integration in every aspect, and the staff is practically unanimous in this view. The result is that the report on housing is a highly partisan one and lacks the degree of objectivity or reliability one would expect to find in reports which purport to be scholarly.[1]

The opinions and facts printed in the report are largely those the Commission's staff itself wants to propagandize among the public, namely, the desirability of integration in housing. These opinions and facts were obtained in "hearings" where "witnesses" who are known in advance to support the Commission's viewpoint are called to testify. Their testimony frequently consists of fourth-hand hearsay, impressionistic judgments, and personal social viewpoints and preferences, unrestrained by the test of cross-examination or the normal rules which courts have imposed to keep out the more blatantly useless material from a factual inquiry. The report ignores published matter not consistent with its views.

Each chapter is permeated by the desirability of integration, and the report recommends that anti-discrimination measures be put into effect to accomplish this goal. It urges federal leverage in every area possible. In short, the whole report is an unvaried integrationist tract.

The 1959 report can be read by all persons of any view for its factual content. The 1961 report will be read with gusto and enthusiasm by partisans of integration. Those seeking an objective evaluation of the problems with which it deals will have to look elsewhere.

RICHARD A. NELSON*

* A.B. 1957, Ripon College; J.D. 1962, Chicago-Kent College of Law. Member of the Illinois Bar. Managing Editor, Chicago-Kent Law Review, 1961-2.

[1] Thus, the report claims that Negroes pay higher rents than whites. Yet, a recent survey of 75 "typical" apartment buildings in six areas of Chicago, undertaken by 15 real estate firms which operate them, showed that "rentals have nothing to do with color." These three-story, walk-up apartment houses, with good maintenance, private baths, original brick construction, and in which tenants pay their own gas and light bills, averaged 40 years in Englewood, Hyde Park, Woodlawn and Grand Crossing, 35 years in South Shore, and 30 years in Chatham. Some houses were occupied by whites, some by Negroes, and some were mixed. This Chicago cross-section survey showed that housing factors, not race, determined rent. Chicago Sun-Times, May 7, 1963, p. 20, col. 1. Typical rents were:

Rooms	Engle.	Hyde Pk.	Woodlawn	Gr. Cross.	S. Shore	Chatham
2	$ 75	$ 77.50	$ 75	$ 75	$ 80	$ 80
2½	80	82.50	80	80	82.50	85
3	87.50	90	87.50	87.50	92.50	95
3½	92.50	95	92.50	92.50	97.50	100
4	100	102.50	100	100	105	110
5	115	117.50	115	115	122.50	130
6	125	130	125	125	140	145

INDEX